HARVARD HISTORICAL STUDIES 132

Published under the auspices
of the Department of History
from the income of the
Paul Revere Frothingham Bequest
Robert Louis Stroock Fund
Henry Warren Torrey Fund

Ernest Gruening and the American Dissenting Tradition

ROBERT DAVID JOHNSON

HARVARD UNIVERSITY PRESS
Cambridge, Massachusetts
London, England 1998

Printed in the United States of America

Library of Congress Cataloging-in-Publication Data

Johnson, Robert David, 1967–
Ernest Gruening and the American dissenting tradition / Robert David Johnson.
p. cm.—(Harvard historical studies ; 132)
Includes bibliographical references and index.
ISBN 0-674-26060-0 (alk. paper)
1. Gruening, Ernest, 1887–1974. 2. Legislators—United States—Biography. 3. United States. Congress. Senate—Biography. 4. Dissenters—United States—Biography. 5. Opposition (Political science)—United States—Case studies. 6. Liberalism—United States—History—20th century. 7. Governors—Alaska—Biography. I. Title. II. Series: Harvard historical studies ; v. 132.
E748.G898J64 1998
328.73'092—dc21
[B] 98-16356

Acknowledgments

During the writing of this book, I benefited from an extraordinary level of assistance from Drew Erdmann and George Eliades. Both offered detailed comments on several drafts of the manuscript, guiding me from a loosely organized collection of essays revolving around Gruening's career to a more comprehensive biography and in the process teaching me invaluable lessons about how to write and think about history. In many ways the final product is as much theirs as mine, and I know that they will discern their influence as they read these pages.

LeRoy Ashby, Fred Logevall, Steve MacKinnon, and Randall Bennett Woods all read through a very early version of the manuscript; I am grateful to all of them for their comments as well as their encouragement not to scrap the project altogether. Dorothy Jones, Frank Ninkovich, and Brooks Simpson offered substantial help at a later stage in reducing the size of the book and more clearly focusing the presentation. Alan Brinkley proved generous with his time in helping me through the intracacies of twentieth-century liberalism, while an invitation from Tom Schwartz to speak on Gruening at Vanderbilt gave me an opportunity to refine my arguments at a most opportune time. I also benefited from the willingness of several of my former students, especially Jon Avina, Dave McIntosh, Dan Zuckerman, and Joel Mandelman, to share their insights about aspects of Gruening's career. As with all of my work, John Morris provided invaluable assistance throughout the research process by getting me where I needed to go.

Ernest R. May watched over this project from start to finish. The Anson Fellowship provided research assistance which helped me begin my work, and a grant from the Lyndon Baines Johnson Foundation helped me conduct research at the Johnson Library. Two research grants from the Dirksen Congressional Research Center funded the completion of the book; I am most grateful to the Center for its willingness to fund projects on congressional history. Along these lines, I owe a debt of gratitude to Don Ritchie at the U.S. Senate Historical Office, whose professionalism and editorial insight have helped me often over the past several years.

During his time in Maine, Gruening wrote Carleton Beals extolling the virtues of the Portland area for writing. I share the sentiment, and thank my parents, J. Robert Johnson and Susan McNamara Johnson, not only for providing me with a perfect environment in Scarborough for most of the writing of this book, but for all of the other sacrifices which they have made for me. As always, my sister and best friend, Kathleen, helped in a variety of intangible ways, including always finding a place for me to stay during my frequent research trips to New York City.

Finally, this book is dedicated to Akira Iriye, who, from the time when I first walked into his Chicago office during the spring of 1988, has exercised a profound influence on both my personal and my professional development. I never can repay him for all of the kindness which he has shown me, but I hope that he has a sense of my gratitude.

Contents

Illustrations

Ernest Gruening and the
American Dissenting Tradition

Prologue

On august 7, 1964, the junior senator from Alaska, Ernest Gruening, announced that he would cast his vote against the Tonkin Gulf Resolution, submitted by President Lyndon Johnson to obtain approval for retaliatory air raids against North Vietnam. The senator considered the resolution an "obvious escalation" of the U.S. military involvement in Southeast Asia. It also, he feared, provided the president with a "blank check"—indeed, a "predated declaration of war." Gruening realized that attacks on U.S. vessels by North Vietnamese forces had created "a moment when patriotic passions are aroused," but he asked his colleagues to view the incident as "the inevitable and foreseeable concomitant and consequence of U.S. unilateral military aggressive policy in southeast Asia." The Alaskan concluded by asserting that if the administration had "been waging peace with the same energy and fervor with which we have been waging war," it would have joined him in concluding that the United States should withdraw its forces from the region. The passionate nature of the dissent had little short-term effect: the resolution sailed through the Senate by a vote of 88 to 2.

Gruening's early life would not have given rise to expectations of a career culminating in such an act of defiance. Born in the late 1880s, raised in New York with extended stints in Europe, trained at the finest Manhattan preparatory schools and then Hotchkiss, privileged with an undergraduate and professional education at Harvard, Gruening possessed the credentials of what would eventually be labeled the Establishment. But despite an intense interest in international affairs, he did not become one of the "Wise Men" or the "best and the brightest." Instead of a career as a lawyer or an investment banker, Gruening chose to enter journalism. By disposition and intellect, he quickly settled into a career as a critic and dissenter, while simultaneously determining to influence policy in a way that did not require constant compromises of principle.

Gruening remained throughout his life a man of passionate convictions. He interrupted his journalistic career twice, both times quitting over the issue of editorial independence. He severed social relations with Walter Lippmann over the columnist's decision to leave his wife for another woman. This sense of principle, which often bordered on self-righteousness, led admirers to hail him as a great idealist and detractors to accuse him of treason. His ideals brought him to the Caribbean Basin, where he first attracted notice as a critic of U.S. interventionism, champion of reform, scholar of Mexican society and politics, and administrator of America's possession, Puerto Rico. Establishing his credentials as an anti-imperialist activist and interpreter of Latin American events with few peers, he pioneered the use of cross-national alliances to influence U.S. public opinion and helped to establish the link between reform sentiment on the domestic scene and anti-imperialism internationally. Most important, his crusade prompted him to move beyond Wilsonianism and tap into equally powerful but more radical elements in the American dissenting tradition. He then moved on to Alaska, where, as governor from 1939 until 1953, he revolutionized the territory's politics and played an instrumental role in its transition to statehood. Alaskans rewarded him with election to the U.S. Senate at the age of seventy-one. While in the upper chamber, Gruening emerged as a champion of causes ranging from foreign aid reform to birth control, although his tenure there remains best known for his often lonely struggle against the U.S. involvement in Vietnam.

During this varied career, Gruening intersected with the figures who defined the American century. He began his journalistic career covering the epic presidential race of 1912, which matched Woodrow Wilson, Theodore Roosevelt, William Howard Taft, and Eugene Debs. After World War I, he signed on as managing editor of *The Nation*, joining Oswald Garrison Villard, Walter Lippmann, and others in New

York City reform circles. His 1920s activism made him an intimate of progressive senators such as William Borah, Robert La Follette, and George Norris. The New Deal encouraged his move to Washington, where he mingled with Supreme Court Justices Louis Brandeis and Felix Frankfurter, worked closely alongside Frankfurter protégés such as Tommy Corcoran and Ben Cohen, came to admire Cordell Hull, formed lifelong friendships with journalists such as Drew Pearson, and tangled with figures ranging from Harold Ickes to Rex Tugwell to Sumner Welles. Gruening's years in Alaska gave him access to the next generation of American leaders and opinion makers—the likes of Harry Truman, Dwight Eisenhower, William O. Douglas, and Henry Jackson. In his return to Washington as a senator, he again distinguished himself for the friends he earned and the foes he attracted. George McGovern, Frank Church, Paul Douglas, and eventually J. William Fulbright typified the first category; into the latter would fall John Kennedy, Lyndon Johnson, and especially highly placed administration officials such as Robert McNamara and Dean Rusk.

Precisely because Gruening's career covered so many diverse contexts, ranging from the First World War through the conflict in Vietnam, his life offers unusual insight into the struggle to define the American century. Moreover, owing to the consistency of Gruening's beliefs, his story provides a panoramic view of the highs and lows of reform sentiment in the twentieth-century United States. His life represents the struggle of a progressive dissenter and a keen intellectual not just to comprehend the transformation of America and its place in the world but to act upon his beliefs. Drawing on themes deeply embedded in American history, he made the transition from critic to administrator, governor, and finally senator. In the process, Gruening confronted the dilemmas of power while facing both the limits of his ideals and the uneasy compromises needed to realize even part of them.

The successes and setbacks of this tale, moreover, challenge many common assumptions about twentieth-century U.S. history. Atypically for liberals, Gruening believed that the Senate rather than the presidency represented the most effective institution from which to realize a reformist agenda. In the 1920s he came to appreciate how the upper chamber's tolerance of dissenting positions, tradition of unfettered debate, and constitutional mandates to address international issues provided possibilities for dissenters to influence foreign policy. During his stint in Juneau, he used the Senate both as a bureaucratic ally of last resort, as in his campaign to end wartime censorship restrictions, and, through his frequent appearances as a witness at hearings, as a forum through which to frame the national discussion on issues of personal interest, such as Alaskan statehood. Gruening thus entered the Senate after a lifetime devoted to exploring the limits and possibilities of the upper chamber's role in American political life. He adapted himself well to the institution, where his success in highlighting otherwise absent policy options underscored his ability to profit from his intellectual and rhetorical skills. He also perceptively realized how Congress could use its power of the purse, through the foreign aid program, to influence overseas affairs, while his ability to exploit the proliferation of foreign policy subcommittees helped to illustrate the continued influence of the Senate on foreign policy issues during the Cold War. But, as his frustrating dissent against the conflict in Vietnam best demonstrated, Gruening underestimated how the weakening of its traditional constitutional powers—over declaring war and approving treaties—prevented the Senate from playing the more complete role on international issues that it had during the interwar years.

On the domestic front, an attachment to the ideals of the Progressive era defined Gruening's actions. He was ahead of his time in understanding the importance of the set of issues which would crystallize under the banner of rights-related liberalism following World War II. At the same time, Gruening, more so than most reformers, foresaw the political and intellectual dangers of relegating economic matters to a secondary position. His admiration for Louis Brandeis's economic theories gave Gruening his first political hero and guided his perspective on economic matters in the 1920s, from his time as publicity director for Robert La Follette's third-party presidential candidacy to his battles, as editor of the *Portland Evening News,* with utility baron Samuel Insull's Central Maine Power. Gruening's hostility to monopoly brought him into the company of New Dealers in Franklin Roosevelt's Washington, and it then provided the basis for his plans to alter Alaska's tax structure and decrease the influence of absentee economic interests. Yet, by the time Gruening returned to Washington in the late 1950s, the anti-monopoly moment in American reform had passed, replaced by a liberal agenda which focused on ensuring economic growth rather than restructuring American capitalism. In the end, Gruening's career illustrates a path not taken by postwar liberalism. His fidelity to an earlier set of principles made him a minor player on most economic issues at a time when few liberals shared his doubts about the ability of free market capitalism to generate sustained economic growth.

In the international arena, Gruening tapped into a more resilient set of beliefs. Although he began his public life as an admirer of Woodrow Wilson, he broke from Wilsonianism after World War I, convinced that the president's policies had betrayed his idealistic promise. At its most basic level, Gruening's career was defined by a quest to determine the proper nature of the relationship between the United States as a superpower with a revolutionary heritage and weaker nations bent on achieving political, economic, and social reform. He called for promoting international reform on two levels: first, by seeking alternatives to traditional power politics, and second, by assisting reformers internationally on a country-by-country basis. This framework often yielded an unclear policy agenda, which perhaps explains why Gruening seemed most confident when in opposition: he possessed a prescient ability to detect how even those policies with broad support conflicted with ideals embedded in the American heritage. His public life was framed by battles against two such U.S. interventions, in Haiti in the 1920s and in Vietnam in the 1960s, initiatives which in his mind violated the basic elements of his creed—a respect for the potency of nationalism in the underdeveloped world, an understanding of how policy decisions toward one country affected the overall international image of the United States, a suspicion of using the military to rectify political instability in weaker states, and a faith in the public's willingness to repudiate policies which contradicted traditional American ideals.

But Gruening most stands out for his efforts to develop a positive framework for the United States to assist weaker states, as in the 1920s, when he championed a cross-national reformist alliance to stabilize the Caribbean Basin; in the 1930s, when he sought to combine diplomatic, economic, political, and cultural initiatives to transform U.S.–Puerto Rican relations into an anti-imperialist model for the hemisphere; or in the 1960s, when he advocated confining foreign aid to ideologically suitable regimes. His suggestions on how the United States could function as a revolutionary force internationally suffered from a greater degree of ideological tension than did his dissents against the interventions in Haiti and Vietnam. He too often overestimated the ability of the United States to influence other societies, and too frequently underestimated the public's willingness to bear the burden of initiatives which policy makers could not justify as fulfilling short-term strategic requirements. Despite such difficulties, the connection between reform ideology and politics always fascinated Gruening, convinced as he was that ideas mattered, and that reformers could educate the public to support their viewpoint and in turn find ways to use the government to realize their agenda, both domestically and on the international stage.

~ 1

The Progressive Impulse

In 1861, at the age of nineteen, Emil Gruening fled his native East Prussia. A frustrated supporter of German republicanism, he wanted to avoid service in the army. Inspired by its reputation for ensuring individual liberty, he emigrated to the United States, and settled in Hoboken, New Jersey. The well-educated Gruening enrolled at Columbia University's College of Physicians and Surgeons, but the Civil War interrupted his time there. He enlisted in the Seventh New Jersey Volunteer Infantry, fought in the Battle of Five Forks, and was at Appomattox when Robert E. Lee surrendered his Confederate forces. Although his professional and civic careers were still before him, the Civil War made an indelible impression on young Emil. The contest matched good against evil, and the forces of virtue prevailed; the fruits of the triumph needed to be preserved. Emil interpreted political and social events in a moralistic fashion for the remainder of his life. Moreover, he never abandoned the belief that the war had redeemed the nation's honor by destroying slavery. He would retain a lifelong commitment to civil rights.[1]

After the war, Gruening resumed his studies and trained as an ear and eye specialist, paying his tuition by tutoring in German, Latin, and Greek. He received his M.D. in 1867, and then returned to Europe for work in Paris, London, and Berlin. Armed with these stellar academic credentials, he opened a practice in New York City in 1870, and was appointed assistant surgeon at the New York Ophthalmic and Aural Institute the next year. His skill as an ear and eye surgeon was confirmed in 1879, when Mt. Sinai Hospital named him an ophthalmic surgeon. Credited with the development of the mastoid operation, Emil also served as director of the New York Eye and Ear Infirmary and president of both the New York Ophthalmologic Society and the New York Otological Society.[2]

Emil's personal life was less idyllic. Shortly after the end of the Civil War, he married another German immigrant, Rose Friendenberg. But the marriage ended tragically when Rose died giving birth to their first child. Emil, who named the infant Rose, did not remain a widower for long, wedding Rose's sister Phebe. The couple had four children: Clara, May, Martha, and Ernest, born in New York City on February 6, 1887. Emil was forty-five when his only son was born.[3]

The boy arrived into a family of substantial wealth. Emil owned three three-story houses on Twenty-third Street in Manhattan; the family lived in two, with his offices in the third. The family's first language was German; Ernest did not begin speaking English until he was five years old. Emil dominated the family's outlook on the world. As a result of his own experience, the doctor believed in the importance of education, and also in exposure to life beyond the United States. Therefore, in the summer of 1894, when Ernest was seven, the family traveled to France. Rose, then attending Vassar College, and Emil returned to the United States in the fall, but Phebe and the four younger children spent the year in Paris, where Ernest enrolled in a private school. The family returned to Europe for another extended stay a few years later, spending most of their time in France but also traveling to Germany, Switzerland, Belgium, and Holland. Emil required his children to keep a detailed diary; eleven-year-old Ernest's entries often ran five or six pages, in a way providing his first experiences as a writer. But Emil did not wish his children to become Europeanized. They led a fairly cloistered life, and Ernest spent most of his leisure time swimming, dancing, or playing games with his sisters. The cosmopolitan aspect of his upbringing nonetheless laid the groundwork for an adulthood tendency to approach issues from an international as well as a national perspective.[4]

After eighteen months in Europe, the Gruenings returned to the United States, this time permanently. Emil continued to push his children to broaden their intellectual horizons. At the dinner table he discussed the editorials in the *New York Tribune*, the banner of New York reform sentiment since its days under Horace Greeley's editorship; the *Evening Post*, briefly the voice of another German immigrant known for his dissenting vision, one-time Missouri senator and anti-imperialist activist Carl Schurz; and the German-language *Neu-Yorker Staats-Zeitung*. Emil sent his son to the city's finest private institutions, beginning with the Drisler School, a private academy on Forty-ninth Street run by two sons of a Columbia University professor. After two years at Drisler, Ernest transferred to the Sachs Collegiate Institute, on Fifty-ninth Street, where a first-rate faculty instructed the children of New York City's German and Jewish elite in a rigorous curriculum including eleven hours of Greek and five of Latin each week. All of the Gruening siblings received the best available education; the four girls attended either Vassar or Smith. Still, Emil harbored particularly high ambitions for Ernest, whom he wanted to attend Harvard, enroll in medical school, and then inherit the family practice.[5]

Emil also encouraged his family to follow in his footsteps of public service. He was affiliated with a host of professional and benevolent organizations, with the exception of military and patriotic societies, which, he argued, perpetuated militarism. The father left one more important mark on his children's lives. Although born a Jew, he did not practice Judaism; his son described him as a "freethinker" who distrusted organized religion. Perhaps to make his name sound less Jewish, Emil pronounced his last name "greening" rather than "grooning," maintaining that no exact translation for the German "ue" existed in English. On religion as on all other issues, his viewpoint dominated the family's beliefs. Emil declined to affiliate his children with any religion, arguing that they could decide for themselves once they became adults. Ernest, who came to agree with his father that a god did not exist, remained a nonbeliever throughout his life.[6]

Politically, Emil Gruening considered himself a mugwump, a member of a loosely organized group within the Republican Party, centered in the Northeast and concerned with issues such as eliminating corruption. As with others who shared the designation, he voted for Grover Cleveland in the presidential elections of 1884, 1888, and 1892, attracted by the Democrat's promise of more ethical government. In New York, the mugwumps made their presence felt in the 1897 mayoral election, which matched Robert Van Wyck, nominated by the Tammany Democratic machine, against Seth Low, the president of Columbia University. Low, who as mayor of Brooklyn presided over a nonpartisan city administration which aimed to eliminate corruption and inefficiency, ran under the banner of the Citizens' Union; New York mugwumps, including Emil Gruening, dominated its membership. Ernest, who served as a volunteer in Low's 1897 campaign, brought with him from his father's activism on this issue a commitment to municipal reform.[7]

Ernest graduated from Sachs in 1902 at the age of fifteen. Unsure that his son was ready for Harvard at such a young age, Emil sent him for a year of preparation at Hotchkiss School. Given Emil's desire that his son attend Harvard, Hotchkiss represented an odd choice. Originally named Yale, Junior, the Lakeville, Connecticut, school was patterned on another Yale feeder school, Andover; twenty-six of its first thirty graduates matriculated at Yale. For Emil, however, Hotchkiss was attractive because it was close enough to New York to allow him to retain some control over his son's life. Ernest, whose small stature earned him the nickname "Mouse," did not adapt particularly well to the school, which he felt overemphasized athletics at the expense of academics. Although he easily handled its academic life, he abused the liberty associated with his first extended stint outside his parents' control, as Emil had feared. After helping to ransack one of the masters' rooms, Ernest was banished from the main dormitory and exiled to a cottage at the far end of campus known as "the Pesthouse." His disciplinary lapse, however, did not block his admission to Harvard, where he enrolled in the fall of 1903 at age sixteen.[8]

Gruening entered Harvard as the university's legendary president Charles Eliot was nearing the conclusion of his tenure. The Harvard student body increased by more than 300 percent during Eliot's forty years in Cambridge.[9] More important, Eliot changed the structure of the university by installing a free elective system, designed to encourage intellectual rebellion; philosopher William James declared that "our undisciplinables are our proudest products." John Reed, a contemporary of Gruening's in Cambridge, recalled that in his time at Harvard "there was talk of the world, daring thought, and intellectual insurgency." Outside the formal academic arena, Gruening frequented the Memorial Union addresses of national political figures such as William Jennings Bryan and Theodore Roosevelt, both of whom lectured before the Union during Gruening's time at Harvard.[10]

He devoted perhaps too much of his time to attending such extracurricular events. In an overly generous description, Gruening later termed his academic performance "mediocre." As a freshman he was placed on academic probation for an unsatisfactory midyear record, which showed him passing three courses with a D and failing his other two. He informed the dean of students that he was struggling to "concentrate his mind," but admitted that he had "not worked hard enough." The dean, acknowledging that Ernest "keenly" felt the disappointment that his academic difficulties caused his father, recommended hiring a tutor, Dr. A. E. Ahlers, to teach Ernest study skills. Two months of instruction caused Ahlers to praise Gruening's intellectual abilities but question his character. In the midst of Ernest's freshman year final exams, Ahlers accused his pupil of "some lack of straightforwardness." The tutor admitted that he could not prove the claims, however, and the matter was allowed to drop. Still, Emil grew increasingly "anxious" about his son's progress, especially since, as he complained, "Ernest himself does not write regularly, nor in detail, about his work."[11]

Ernest came off probation the next fall, only to flirt again with the status after amassing fifty-five absences over the course of his sophomore year. Alarmed at the response that he would receive from his father should he fail again, he picked up his performance somewhat as a junior. But he still did not place a particularly high priority on academics; he was forced to petition the Administrative Board when his departure date for a summer excursion to Italy, Switzerland, and France fell before the day of one of his final examinations. (He received permission to take the exam on board the ship, with a proctor, paid for by his father, present.) Gruening also continued his habit of keeping his parents in the dark about his progress. In a commentary on their ambivalent relationship, he neglected to inform Emil that he could have taken his degree after his third year in Cambridge. Ernest at the time was planning to use his fourth year to take a master's degree in philosophy, but his continuing weak academic performance put an end to the idea. He claimed afterwards that he learned more from browsing the library shelves than from his classes.[12]

Despite Gruening's academic shortcomings, his undergraduate experience affected his life in a number of ways. During his childhood, Gruening considered himself part of the upper class, summering in Europe, living in exclusive Manhattan neighborhoods, attending the best prep schools. At Harvard, however, he later recalled, he was "not included in the bluest of blue Boston circles." In addition, spending an extended period of time away from his parents allowed him to explore his own social and intellectual interests. Although it was still "taken for granted" that he would be a physician, Gruening's two best friends at Harvard, Earl Biggers, later the author of the Charlie Chan mysteries, and Richard John Walsh, later a publisher and mid-level official at the Carnegie Endowment for International Peace, were active in journalism, not medical studies. Biggers and Walsh served on the editorial boards of the *Harvard Advocate* and the *Lampoon*, and they encouraged Gruening to contribute two satirical pieces to the *Advocate*. They also joined "Ern," as some of his friends called him, in what Gruening remembered as a movement "to establish a greater measure of social democracy" in undergraduate life—weakening Harvard's social clubs. Gruening, who lived for three years in Weld Hall, one of the dingiest dorms on campus (it lacked running water and central heating), resented the special status which the clubs accorded their members. Teaming with Biggers and Walsh, he pressed the Harvard Corporation to designate Holworthy, Hollis, and Stoughton Halls in the Yard as exclusively for unpledged seniors, aiming to establish a more democratic alternative to the clubs. Gruening's emerging social democracy, however, was of a very limited variety. Certainly in the 1910s, when he won acceptance into the upper-class Boston social world, he exhibited few concerns about its restrictive nature.[13]

Though harboring some doubts about whether he wanted a career in medicine, Gruening was still not prepared to break with his father's wishes. Upon his graduation in 1907, he enrolled at Harvard Medical School, despite privately admitting that he had undertaken this course only to please Emil. Although he attempted to dedicate himself to his course work, his attraction to a variety of interests, such as contemporary fiction and current events, was simply too strong. Gruening particularly enjoyed social commentary such as George Ade's "Fables" and Finley Peter Dunne's "Mr. Dooley," and he leaped at the opportunity to move beyond the world of medicine when, during his third year of medical school, a position in journalism offered itself. Earl Biggers had signed on as drama critic for the *Boston Traveler*, and he frequently asked Gruening to cover for him. This freelance work persuaded Gruening to pursue his interest in journalism. In the spring of

1910, with a month free before starting his internship at Boston City Hospital, he secured a $15 a week job at the *Boston American*, part of the Hearst newspaper chain. Still, though attracted by "the power of the press not merely to report events but to lead public opinion," he could not bring himself to break with his father, and reluctantly returned to medical school for his fourth and final year.[14]

Gruening's time in medical school did have one lasting effect. During their third year, medical students went, in pairs, to some of the poorer sections of Boston to perform obstetrical services. Without any deep religious beliefs himself, he was stunned to discover that poor women in predominantly Irish Catholic South Boston refused to practice birth control. Religious scruples were not the only barrier; state law restricted access as well. Gruening could see no reason to prohibit the dissemination of information about the issue, and the experience shocked him to such an extent that he continued to recall it vividly sixty years later, at the end of a life committed to expanding access to birth control.[15]

Otherwise, he enjoyed the nonacademic aspects of his medical school tenure. During his third year, Emil decided to have a summer home built in Rockport, Massachusetts, and asked Ernest, as the family member closest to the scene, to oversee the project. To his father's dismay, he bombarded the architect with design revisions, such as the addition of a third floor. Once completed, the summer residence, situated on fourteen acres of oceanfront property, contained fourteen bedrooms: there was also a tennis court, another of Ernest's suggestions. Emil correctly speculated that the family would struggle to afford upkeep on the mansion after his death.[16]

Now a mature young man, Gruening was increasingly less inclined to follow his father's wishes in issues of greater import than the family's summer home. Though still "not absolutely positive" about a career in journalism, he did feel "sure" that he "did not want to do medicine." Ernest thus returned to New York City and confronted his father once and for all. He informed Emil that he had stayed the course in medical school to fulfill his father's desire to have an M.D. for a son, but hereafter he would cease living his father's dream and begin fulfilling his own. The decision deeply depressed Emil, who continued to hope that his son would change his mind until his death, from a stroke, on May 30, 1914. Upon his death, he left an estate valued at $393,972; he had bequeathed $50,000 in $1,000 bonds to each of his five children. Ironically, Emil's final contribution to his son's life was to provide Ernest with the financial means to pursue his own dreams.[17]

By the time of his father's death, Gruening had begun a meteoric rise in the world of Boston journalism which culminated in his appointment, at the age of thirty, as editor of the *Boston Journal.* He began his formal career as a journalist in 1912 covering that year's presidential campaign. With voters closely divided among the three parties, Massachusetts attracted personal visits from each of the standard-bearers. Ideologically inclined against the pro-business incumbent, William Howard Taft, Gruening had more positive things to say about Democrat Woodrow Wilson's emphasis on the evils of trusts and the need for rigorous enforcement of anti-monopoly legislation. His reading of muckraking literature, with its exposés of corrupt business practices, clearly had an impact on him. Yet, while he liked Wilson's message, he joined many Massachusetts reformers in being swept away by Theodore Roosevelt and a third party movement which he recalled as "born of resentment and inspired by righteous wrath." Although the party failed both nationally and in Massachusetts, Gruening did not think that it had "lived in vain"; if nothing else, the movement had given "an unmistakable impulse to progressive ideas" while dealing a "crippling blow to the reign of special privilege."[18]

Gruening's other significant assignment at the *Boston Herald*, covering a textile workers' strike in Lawrence organized by the Industrial Workers of the World (IWW), sharpened his emerging bias against big business. He later recalled the extent to which "the miserable conditions in the crowded, foul, mill-owned tenements and the mills themselves" made him sympathetic to the interests of the workers. Ernest was not the only Gruening sibling to hold such beliefs. Two years earlier the police had arrested Martha for picketing in front of a New York shirtwaist factory in support of striking workers, an incident which formed part of a broader pattern of progressive activism in which all the Gruening siblings engaged. Rose, for example, used her inheritance to open a settlement house in lower Manhattan, where this "calm, efficient, sympathetic, and motherly person" earned the moniker "Angel of Grand Street." She also purchased a camp in Mountainville, New York—dubbed Camp Moodna—which provided underprivileged youth a chance to escape the city during the summer. The more political

Martha, meanwhile, actively championed both women's suffrage and civil rights. At the 1911 convention of the National American Women Suffrage Association, she sponsored (on behalf of the NAACP) an unsuccessful resolution demanding that the organization express "sympathy with black men and women who are fighting the same battle." Inspired by these beliefs, she adopted an African American boy shortly after graduating from college. The experience did not work out well for either one, and the boy ran away from home in his mid-teens. Reflecting their upbringing, all four sisters were recalled by contemporaries as "brainy" but eccentric activists for various rights-related causes. The same could be said for Ernest.[19]

Unlike his sisters, though, Ernest was determined to affect change through the established system. His reporting ability attracted the eye of the editor of the *Herald*, Robert Lincoln O'Brien. Private secretary to Grover Cleveland during the Democrat's second term, he brought a wealth of national contacts as well as the fundamentally conservative point of view associated with Cleveland's policies to the *Herald*'s editorial pages. In 1913 O'Brien promoted Gruening first to rewrite editor and then assistant editor. Gruening later admitted, correctly, that he did not produce "any editorial gems," but the prestige associated with the position provided the confidence he needed to make an important change in his personal life. Meanwhile, Gruening had found Rockport attractive not merely because of the new family house. During his time on Massachusetts's North Shore, he met Dorothy Elizabeth Smith, whose family also summered in the area. The daughter of a domineering mother, Laura Huntington, and a father, George Smith, who spent his life squandering an inherited fortune, Dorothy, like her mother, graduated from Vassar. Unlike Gruening's sisters, she showed little interest in politics, concentrating instead on preserving her standing in society. Although friends of the two would later remark on how little Ernest and Dorothy seemed to have in common, they shared a passion for swimming and tennis—and, perhaps, for escaping controlling parents. Also, for Ernest, part of the attraction was clearly physical: Dorothy was a "real stunner," while "Mouse" remained slight of build and physically unattractive. After an extended courtship, the two were married at Dorothy's parents' home in November 1914; Earl Biggers served as best man. The couple then moved into an apartment on Church Street in Cambridge, near Harvard Yard.[20]

By this point, moreover, international events had produced another promotion for the young newspaperman. The outbreak of war in Europe prompted O'Brien to establish a special war news department, which he asked Gruening to head. Like many conservative Democrats, O'Brien entertained a deep suspicion of an active U.S. foreign policy, and supported Wilson's demand that American citizens remain neutral in thought as well as in deed. Gruening, however, harbored a radically different viewpoint, terming himself "violently pro-Ally," partly owing to the distrust of German monarchism espoused by his father. In September he approved a cartoon showing the Kaiser standing on the field of battle with the blood of Belgian women and children dripping from his hands. After the cartoon ran in the *Herald*'s first edition, O'Brien killed it and "severely rebuked" his deputy for his "bellicose attitude."[21]

To find another position for the competent but ideologically unsuitable Gruening, O'Brien appointed him managing editor of the *Boston Traveler*, the *Herald*'s afternoon counterpart. Gruening, then twenty-seven, compared his chief problems at the *Traveler* to "those common to many American newspapers—to try to make the management understand that a newspaper owes very definite obligations to its readers—to the public," rather than to its advertisers, based on a policy of "independence and intellectual honesty." As a result of his own experience, Gruening began by calling for honest dramatic criticism at the *Traveler* to replace the system he had inherited, which guaranteed favorable reviews to theaters placing advertisements. The policy worried the *Herald*'s advertising department, but it earned O'Brien support, since, as Gruening predicted, his tactics boosted circulation, which soared from 84,618 when he took over to 109,344 by March 1916. But tolerance of his managing editor's independence went only so far. In 1916, when Gruening penned an editorial dismissing Massachusetts's anti–birth control law as "stupid and absurd," the presses were stopped after the first printing to remove the column. O'Brien informed Gruening that if he had to stop the presses for a third time, the managing editor would be looking for other employment.[22]

Gruening's support for birth control derived from both his own medical school experience and the commitment to upholding individual rights which he inherited from his father. The latter mindset influenced all aspects of his experience with the *Traveler*, both in newspaper policy and on the editorial pages. An early member of the Boston branch of the National Association for the Advancement of Colored People

(NAACP), he considered the lack of civil rights for blacks "the worst blot" on American political history. Upon assuming the helm of the *Traveler*, Gruening ordered his reporters not to mention a subject's race in their stories, especially criminal reports, without a good reason for doing so, so as to treat "colored people . . . with approximately the same fairness that we accord other racial groups in the community." Gruening's support for civil rights also led him to question the ability of Wilson's Democratic Party, with southern politicians forming such a prominent part of its leadership structure, to enact a genuine reform program.[23]

Civil rights matters also brought Gruening into extensive contact with Boston's colorful and controversial mayor, James Michael Curley. After the virulently racist film *The Birth of a Nation* opened in Boston, Gruening appealed to Curley to use his powers as municipal censor to prohibit the film's showing. When Curley demurred, arguing that he lacked the authority to act, Gruening supported the establishment of a municipal censorship board consisting of the mayor, the chief judge of the municipal court, and Boston's chief of police, which he hoped would block other racist films. Instead, Curley used it to ban motion pictures which attacked elements of his political base, such as the Catholic Church. The experience caused Gruening to conclude that "all censorship is undesirable and has no place in a free society," thus intensifying his basic libertarian instincts. The editor grudgingly learned from his mistakes. The battle also intensified Gruening's strong distrust of Curley, which reflected the basic mugwump beliefs he had inherited from his father. The editor defended the activities of journals (such as the *Traveler*) which exposed the mayor's shortcomings, asserting that "there would have been no improvement in methods at City Hall had it not been for 'destructive criticism' and 'muckraking' by the newspapers." Gruening's campaign against Curley thus prompted him to classify himself as a muckraker for the first time.[24]

During Gruening's first two years at the *Traveler*, his belief system began to clarify. It focused on three components: a conviction in the importance of public opinion and the need to involve the people in the decisions of government, best reflected in his vision of journalism; a championing of individual rights, ranging from civil rights to a variety of women's issues such as suffrage and birth control, which flowed from both his family background and his educational experience; and a hostility to monopoly, which derived from his reading of progressive and muckraking literature. These beliefs paralleled those of progressives who were embracing Wilson's campaign for reelection, figures such as Louis Brandeis, who eventually became the most permanent of Gruening's ideological heroes. With Brandeis as his chief economic strategist, Wilson campaigned in 1912 as an exponent of the American anti-monopoly tradition, and then pushed through legislation to implement the vision, notably the Clayton Anti-Trust Act and the Federal Trade Commission Act. The president also made a significant concession to anti-monopoly activists in 1916, when he appointed first Brandeis and then John Hessin Clarke to the Supreme Court, moves Gruening warmly welcomed.[25]

Gruening evaluated the president's handling of international affairs in a less positive fashion. Unlike economic affairs, international issues allowed him to find common ground with his associates in Boston, who joined the Bay State's leading politicians—Senator Henry Cabot Lodge and Representative Augustus Gardner (Lodge's son-in-law)—in backing increased military spending. The antithesis of Wilson both personally and ideologically, Lodge championed a nationalist foreign policy, tenets of which Gruening eventually would oppose completely. In 1915, though, as Gruening supported intervention in the war on the side of the Allies, foreign policy became his newest cause. He delivered several addresses on behalf of greater preparedness measures during late 1915 and early 1916 at forums ranging from Radcliffe College to Boston's Fabian Club, where he amplified on his hostility to a regime in Berlin which had deliberately invited censure from "the humane, civilized peoples of all lands." The editor also chastised figures such as Secretary of the Navy Josephus Daniels and former Secretary of State William Jennings Bryan for their skepticism about military increases. He even joined his friend and fellow Harvard graduate Robert Benchley in a spoof mocking Daniels at a Boston navy conference. Still, he devoted little sustained attention to international affairs, and his superficial perspective on such questions correspondingly offered meager analysis.[26]

By this time, he and Dorothy were enjoying a comfortable lifestyle between their weeks in Cambridge, where he spent his leisure time at Boston-area boat and country clubs, and weekends in Rockport. The family had grown to four. Ernest, Jr., nicknamed Sonny, was born in

October 1915; a second son, Huntington, followed the next September. Outside of the family, Gruening espoused causes which did not force him to break sharply from the primarily upper-middle-class Protestant acquaintances with whom he spent his time. But the presidential election of 1916 ultimately forced him to begin to reconcile his conflicting personal and ideological agendas. Although Gruening hoped that the Republicans would nominate Theodore Roosevelt, whose domestic positions he had always supported and whose interventionist foreign policy attracted wide support in Boston, a GOP still divided from the contest of four years before instead selected Supreme Court Justice Charles Evans Hughes, a compromise choice whose progressive credentials were far weaker than Roosevelt's. The decision heightened Gruening's quandary. On the one hand, Wilson's reformist domestic agenda genuinely attracted him. On the other, he supported intervention in the European conflict much more ardently than the president, whose campaign highlighted his success at keeping the country out of war and his endorsement of a postwar league of nations. In the end, Gruening decided to place principle ahead of partisan and social concerns and endorsed Wilson. The decision also caused him to rethink his brief flirtation with the preparedness movement and entertain more sympathy for the president's overall approach to foreign policy.[27]

Moreover, Gruening's increasing admiration for Wilson coincided with a professional crisis. Throughout his tenure at the *Traveler*, his relationship with O'Brien remained correct but cool, with his immediate superior concerned about Gruening's self-righteous streak and his unwillingness to consider how his editorial viewpoints affected the financial well-being of the newspaper. This problem grew particularly acute as Gruening's battle with Curley intensified. In early 1916 the perfect opportunity to embarrass Curley appeared to emerge: despite his powers as municipal censor, Curley allowed the showing of *Where Are My Children?*, a film whose plot line involved abortion. Given the sensitive nature of the material involved, Gruening immediately publicized the mayor's decision, confident that at the very least he could cause problems for Curley's relationship with the hierarchy of the Catholic Church. He also assigned one of his best reporters, John English, to investigate the financial connections behind the film. English claimed to uncover proof that Curley had allowed the film to be shown in exchange for a payoff from Boies Penrose, the GOP boss in Pennsylvania and an investor in the movie. Convinced of Curley's moral weaknesses, Gruening immediately printed the story in the *Traveler* without confirming English's facts. He underestimated his foe. Curley immediately filed a $25,000 libel suit against both Gruening and the paper; the mayor also privately informed the *Traveler*'s owners that allowing the story to stand uncorrected could threaten their economic interests in the city. O'Brien then looked into the matter only to discover that most of English's evidence was uncorroborated. Accordingly, he authorized the retraction demanded by Curley and hoped that the issue would pass. Gruening, however, entertained other ideas. As O'Brien later recalled, the incident typified "how Gruening, when he has made up his mind to do something, is very reluctant to change it," a characteristic which gained the editor "a lot of enemies." When he refused to back down, Gruening, financially comfortable because of his inheritance, resigned his position and its weekly salary of $100.[28]

A number of job offers quickly arrived. Gruening's work on behalf of civil rights had not gone unnoticed: the NAACP organ *The Crisis* had celebrated his policy that reporters not mention the race of defendants in criminal cases, and from New York City came a request for him to join the organization's bureaucracy. His sister Martha, by this point an intimate of W. E. B. Du Bois, strongly urged him to accept, but he was too committed to journalism to leave the field. He also wanted to remain in the Boston area, where a position at the *Boston Journal* had opened. Following Roosevelt's defeat in 1912, a group of recent Harvard graduates—Matthew Hale, Warren Atwater Green, Charles Eliot Ware, and Alexander Kendall—had purchased the *Journal*, hoping to transform it into the Massachusetts voice of Bull Moose progressivism. Under Green's editorship, the paper favored much of Wilson's reformist domestic agenda but sharply criticized the president's foreign policy ventures, thus reflecting the thinking of many Bull Moose progressives. Despite these hints of tension over foreign policy matters, Gruening welcomed the opportunity to work for a newspaper which even promised him freedom to editorialize on behalf of birth control. He signed on as city editor in December 1916, and was promoted to managing editor the following February.[29]

Initially, as at the *Traveler*, Gruening's most important changes to the *Journal* were in the paper's administrative structure. He added a "Mail Bag" column, making the *Journal* the first Boston newspaper to print its readers' reactions—both positive and negative—to its editorial policy. Gruening asserted that the new feature represented one way that his editorship would place the utmost "faith in the judgment of the people." On a similar front, in a testament to his suspicion of big business, the new managing editor launched an ultimately effective campaign to free the editorial page from the influence of the newspaper's major advertisers.[30]

Gruening quickly received the authority to use this editorial independence. Unsurprisingly, given their admiration for Roosevelt, several of the *Journal*'s owners, including Green, had affiliated with the Plattsburg movement (centered in Plattsburg, New York, then a resort town on Lake Champlain), founded by Leonard Wood in 1913 to encourage universal military training. The group's agenda extended beyond military affairs. Plattsburgers tended to be wealthy, well-educated members of the eastern establishment, who hoped that military training could restore the puritan values corrupted by the modern world. (In a telling commentary on the depth of his flirtation with the movement, Gruening never summered in Plattsburg.) In international affairs, the Plattsburgers urged a stronger line against the German threat. They got their wish on January 31, 1917, after Germany renounced earlier pledges and resumed unrestricted submarine warfare. The decision presented Wilson, who still hoped to avoid war, with a diplomatic dilemma, but the Plattsburgers did not doubt that the United States would eventually enter the European conflict. Accordingly, in late February, Green was called to New York to begin training for regular military service, leaving the newly hired Gruening in full command of the *Journal*'s editorial page.[31]

Green's departure coincided with revolutionary changes in the international position of the United States. After unsuccessfully searching for an alternative, on April 4 Wilson requested a declaration of war against Germany. The president cited more than the strategic threat for entering the conflict; he also called for the United States "to vindicate the principles of peace and justice in the life of the world" by fighting "for democracy, for the right of those who submit to authority to have a voice in their own governments, for the rights and liberties of small nations, for a universal dominion of right by such a concert of free peoples as shall bring peace and safety to all nations and make the world itself at last free." This rhetoric justified U.S. participation in the war on terms which Lodge and his followers, including the editors of the *Journal*, ridiculed throughout 1915 and 1916. Green undoubtedly expected that his replacement would do the same. Yet the ambivalence in Gruening's foreign policy views in the summer of 1916 had dissipated by the following spring. He now began to see in many of the president's foreign policy positions the same commitment to progressive idealism that had attracted him to Wilson's domestic agenda. This perspective caused a shift in the editorial stance of the *Journal*, despite the risk to Gruening's continuing employment. In a pattern which by this point had become familiar, he exalted his principles above his financial interest, a course of action made possible by the security of his inheritance.[32]

Arguing that America was "marching to carry freedom and equality to the farthermost corners of the earth," the editor agreed with Wilson that the United States needed to practice a different kind of diplomacy from that usually associated with a great power. Still, although the war caused Gruening to show more interest in international affairs, as of yet he had little original thought to offer. Domestic questions, however, constituted another matter. Given his pre-1917 positions, Gruening's praise for Wilson's international initiatives contrasted with his attacks on the president's wartime domestic policies. A consistent belief in the importance of public opinion, along with his more parochial interests as the editor of a major metropolitan daily, caused Gruening to reserve his strongest criticism for the administration's support for censorship legislation. Although Wilson attempted to combine a traditional progressive pursuit of social cohesion and a desire to protect freedom of the press with his goal of clamping down on dissent and satisfying the xenophobic nationalism which accompanied the outbreak of war, the legislation he supported embodied only the latter sentiments. Gruening considered the censorship measure "dangerous," and wondered why Americans, "while fighting for democracy abroad," also needed to "fight for democracy at home." In this "war for liberty," the press more than ever served as "the people's safeguard." Once the bill passed, he promised that he and the *Journal* would continue to print the truth. The president, he regretted, did not comprehend that "public opinion in the long run is the wisest director of state policy."[33]

One important element of the Progressive movement always stressed altering the structure of government to increase the electorate's influence over public policy decisions, a motivation which appeared most prominently in reforms such as the initiative and referendum. Gruening shared this conviction in the need to respect the power of public opinion, but he went beyond many progressives in one important sense, arguing that offering the levers of power to the people would not suffice. Maintaining that, once presented with the facts, the public would select the policy option which coincided with traditional American ideals, he believed that reformers needed to concentrate on educating the public by providing access to all relevant information on issues of importance. Ensuring public participation in decision making might even compensate for reformers' weakness within the government by denying officials the secrecy they needed to adopt corrupt policies. Gruening devoted relatively little thought, however, to the differences between his definition of traditional American idealism and that of a majority of his fellow citizens. He would spend much of his career confronting the ramifications of this contradiction.

In the short term, though, the editor did not have the time to devote to such concerns, as he grew increasingly agitated about how the administration's censorship and propaganda efforts were bringing out the worst in many Americans, typified by self-styled patriotic groups such as the American Defense Society, the "pinhead organization" which deemed treasonous all dissent, support for self-determination, and suspicion of a militarist foreign policy. His father's admonition that such organizations conflicted with traditional American ideals undoubtedly reinforced his position. Gruening did his part to resist the sentiments of such groups, even at the risk of turning the nationalist fervor brought on by the war against himself. In 1916 the *Journal* hired as its military critic Anthony Arnoux, whose prewar expressions of sympathy for the German side prompted demands from Boston patriotic organizations that Gruening replace him. The editor steadfastly refused this demand, contending that Arnoux's pro-German sympathies actually enhanced his perceptiveness, at least in comparison to vehemently pro-Allied reviewers. Committed to delivering what he termed evenhanded war news, Gruening argued that magnifying Allied gains and minimizing those of the enemy did not constitute "a wise or a patriotic policy." Arnoux remained on the *Journal*'s payroll.[34]

WORLD WAR I obviously caused profound shifts in the American political landscape, and the country's political and intellectual leaders responded in different fashions. In 1912, Theodore Roosevelt, Woodrow Wilson, and Robert La Follette all had characterized themselves as progressives. Yet five years later, the views of the three men on national and international events differed radically. Roosevelt shed most of his interest in domestic reform and instead focused his energy on a nationalistic foreign policy vision. La Follette, meanwhile, grew more radical on both the domestic and international fronts, opposing U.S. entry into the war from an anti-imperialist and anti-business angle while raising an anti-monopolist, pro–civil liberties banner against Wilson's domestic policies. Wilson adopted yet a third course, joining Roosevelt in concentrating on foreign policy, but articulating a vision of progressive internationalism which called for the United States to take the lead in refashioning the ground rules governing world affairs.

For Gruening, the war forced him to deal with a host of issues he had previously avoided and in the process pushed his views to the left. Some elements of his earlier experience, such as his support for civil liberties and his suspicion of the power of monopolies over the American economy, were sharpened. Others, namely his flirtation with preparedness and his occasionally nationalistic perspective on foreign affairs, fell by the wayside. Most important, he attempted for the first time to translate many of his domestic ideals into a coherent posture on international matters. As with his initial forays into the Progressive movement, Ernest was not the only Gruening sibling to travel this road; his sisters likewise experienced the radicalizing effects of the conflict. In June, Martha was briefly jailed for distributing literature criticizing conscription; she also was charged with disorderly conduct. The next month she joined W. E. B. Du Bois in heading an NAACP inquiry into the East St. Louis race riot. Her "skillful detective work in the white community" prompted the NAACP to request her services again to investigate another racially charged massacre, this time in Houston, where black soldiers had killed sixteen whites in retribution for a series of discriminatory acts. Perhaps because they lived off their inheritances entirely, Gruening's sisters were even more inclined than he was to adopt extreme positions. But the war clearly affected all five siblings in a similar fashion, sharpening the moralistic, crusading aspects of their personalities.[35]

Although himself a supporter of the draft, Gruening had come to agree with his sisters about both the threat the federal government posed to civil liberties and the administration's horrific record on civil rights issues.[36] He also attacked Wilson's policies to finance the war effort, urging steep income taxes rather than indirect taxes or government borrowing. Arguing that "the poor have paid for all previous wars while the rich have amassed more wealth," the editor considered the issue of war taxation the "final, vital test" of Wilson's promise that idealism rather than selfish concerns would motivate the U.S. war effort. A watered-down version of the administration's measure soon encountered fierce opposition in the Senate, where Lodge led the way in denouncing it as "perfectly exorbitant." Gruening, promising to rally public opinion to ensure that "organized wealth isn't going to do all the shouting this time," continued the *Journal's* evolution away from its GOP orientation by singling out Lodge and Gardner for criticism.[37]

Gruening's anti-monopoly leanings aroused his interest in more than just the administration's war revenue measures. The alleged "rapacious plunderings of the food speculators" especially incensed him. He eventually came to believe that the traditional progressive approach of government regulation would constitute the most effective solution to the problem, a position which first attracted him to a figure who would play a key role in his political activities over the next decade and a half. Herbert Hoover, whose international reputation dated from his service as head of the Commission for the Relief of Belgium, used his post at the U.S. Food Administration to control food prices through voluntaristic and indirect means, eschewing overt regulation. Interpreting these policies broadly, Gruening contended that they showed the utility of disinterested government action on behalf of the consumer. First with Brandeis and then with Wilson, Gruening had exhibited a tendency to support uncritically political figures whose basic principles he admired. By the fall of 1917, he was well on his way to adding Hoover to this list.[38]

In normal times, Gruening conceded, questions such as civil rights, civil liberties, or economic policy could be considered solely domestic matters. But the decision to frame U.S. participation in the war as a crusade for democracy transformed such issues into international ones as well. While heralding Wilson's foreign policy as "clear and consistent in its conception," the editor worried that the administration failed to understand that "we must put our own house in order before we attempt to brand upon Europe our own mark of right and justice." But

Gruening's chief "objection to intolerance" involved a point he considered "generally overlooked": that Wilson could not sustain the political support for his foreign policies if his domestic proposals estranged him from American reformers. Indeed, Gruening argued, Wilson should encourage "peace talk" of all sorts as a way of increasing public discussion of liberal peace terms. But instead, by permitting figures such as Postmaster General Albert Burleson and Attorney General Thomas Gregory to clamp down on left-wing dissent, Wilson was playing into the hands of nationalists who never would support the type of peace that the president desired. A stress on the interconnectedness of reform in the domestic and foreign policy contexts would reappear throughout Gruening's public career.[39]

In the short run, this perceptive analysis of the contradictions embedded within Wilsonianism failed to rescue the *Journal* and, if anything, only alienated its traditional base of Bull Moose Republicans. By the summer of 1917, the *Journal* was struggling to meet its weekly payroll. Beginning a pattern which would later become more pronounced, Gruening took no salary and survived off the income from the bonds inherited from his father. He also felt "morally obligated" not to hire new personnel because he did not know "where the next week's payroll was coming from"; staff shortages left him with "more and more work," especially in the editorial section. But such moral scruples did not really guide the editor's management decisions. Gruening, who clearly enjoyed editorial work, struggled to delegate authority; having a small staff allowed him to do more of what he wanted to do without having to entrust decisions to others. The effects of the paper's downward financial spiral, however, could not long be avoided. In early October, Gruening's former employer, the *Herald*, absorbed the *Journal*'s operations. Looking to console him, one of his friends wrote, "You gave us a taste of what a real newspaper ought to be and these thousands of us who have drunk of that cup will neither forget it nor be permanently satisfied until we have more of it."[40]

Gruening wanted to stay in Boston if possible, but no opportunity presented itself. And so, when W. J. Harris, the director of the War Trade Board (WTB), asked him to work in the newly established Bureau of Imports, he accepted. But his embrace of a radicalized perspective on both national and international events continued unabated. Even though he seemed to take a step back into the political mainstream with his move to the WTB, his circle of friends in Washington testified to the profound shift in his ideological viewpoint. The Gruenings rented a house in Chevy Chase and took in two boarders—John Barry, a nationally syndicated daily columnist whose writing Gruening had carried at the *Journal*, and Irving Caesar, then beginning his career as a musician. Both had been passengers on Henry Ford's Peace Ship, an ill-fated 1915 attempt by the auto magnate to mediate an end to the European conflict. Meanwhile, after a sublet opened in the house next door, Gruening found a government position for Robert Benchley, an old Harvard chum, who, like Gruening, briefly had supported military preparedness before adopting a more radical viewpoint on international affairs. By 1917, as his son later remembered, Benchley favored "anything or anybody who was against war." The two Harvard alumni "had a great deal in common and liked to talk far into the night."[41]

Gruening's time in Washington thus sharpened his emerging dissenting vision. Then, after less than six months at the WTB, the nationalistic fervor against which he had battled during his time in Boston claimed him as a victim. In late March, accusations of Gruening's having harbored pro-German sympathies, on the grounds of his retention of Arnoux as the *Journal*'s military critic, prompted Harris to suspend him pending a full-scale investigation. "Utterly astounded" that anyone could question his loyalty, Gruening aggressively fought the "preposterous and infamous" charges and exonerated himself; after less than a month, Harris lifted the suspension. The experience, however, gave him an understandable distaste for Harris's management style, and Gruening resolved to leave the WTB at the earliest opportunity. He even considered enlisting in the army to remove any doubts about the depth of his patriotism.[42]

Instead, journalistic fate intervened. In April 1918, a few days after the lifting of his suspension, Garet Garrett, the executive editor of the *New York Tribune*, asked Gruening to take over as managing editor of that daily, long one of the country's most prestigious newspapers and a favorite of his father's. When the two met to discuss the job, Gruening told Garrett that he still admired Wilson's efforts to reconcile U.S. foreign policy with traditional American ideals of support for self-determination and reforming international relations. Garrett replied that the *Tribune* wanted him expressly because of these beliefs; the publisher wished to break with the newspaper's anti-Wilson past. Reassured, Gruening took the job, and on May 1 moved back to the New York City area for the first time in fifteen years. His mother, whom he had not seen for some time, died just before he returned; as with his father, there would be no final reunion. Dorothy, Sonny, and Hunt settled in Bay Shore, on Long Island, for the summer. Gruening spent weekdays in the city, living at his mother's old apartment, and joined his family on the weekends.[43]

Gruening quickly came to regret his decision. He had expected an atmosphere similar to that at the *Journal*, where he had enjoyed complete editorial freedom. Instead, he encountered staff resistance to his appointment (which, perhaps still smarting from his suspension, he attributed to xenophobia provoked by his German surname) and a complicated management structure in which Garrett and Neal Jones, the city editor, demanded input into all news and editorial decisions. At first his independence seemed confirmed. Less than two weeks after his arrival, Gruening killed a story brought to him by Jones, alleging that the Department of Justice would deport Morris Hillquit, formerly the Socialist nominee for mayor of New York City, on grounds of pro-German sympathies. Within a few days, Jones came to Gruening with a similarly far-fetched tale, this one alleging that the Justice Department suspected the loyalty of the German-born Hermann Hagedorn, a prominent Bull Moose Progressive and leading member of the self-styled patriotic group the Vigilantes. Gruening again vetoed Jones's contribution; he did likewise with articles praising the removal of German-language literature from the New York City Public Library and the changing of German-inspired street names. As a general rule, he forbade his reporters to use the word "Hun" in their writing, contending that doing so would only fan popular anti-German prejudice.[44]

Gruening's concern with protecting civil liberties during wartime extended beyond the use of "Hun" to describe German-Americans. He also proposed sending a team of reporters to Georgia to reopen the investigation into the case of Leo Frank, the Cornell-educated Jew lynched in 1914 on trumped-up murder charges, but on this issue he suffered his first major defeat at the *Tribune*. The editorial board overruled him, contending that publicizing past prejudice would harm the American war effort. Garrett's suspicions about Gruening's ideological viewpoint only intensified after the editor began defending peace activist Rose Pastor Stokes, who had been convicted of violating the Espionage Act after contending that Wilson's war taxation policy reflected the political influence of war "profiteers." One unfriendly associate recalled Gruening as a "bosom heaver," a man who seemed "instinctively to take the part of any individual accused of misconduct, without giving due weight to the circumstances of the charge." Garrett obviously had not expected such an editor.[45]

Despite rumblings from the staff that these policies reflected the actions of a German sympathizer determined to take "the fine, militant, American edge off the *Tribune*," Gruening, as stubborn as ever, refused to compromise. He also launched a series of administrative changes comparable to those he had implemented at the *Traveler* and the *Journal.* To oversee one such initiative—the establishment of a twelve-page Sunday photograph section—he brought in Robert Benchley, telling him that "a few months as a reporter would be essential training for almost anything he might do later." This decision precipitated the looming confrontation with management. Benchley, who shared Gruening's commitment to civil rights, opened up his first Sunday feature with an arresting image: a photograph showing the decoration for bravery of black soldiers from the 169th Infantry alongside a shot of the lynching of a black man in Georgia. As soon as Garrett saw the display, he summoned Benchley to his office, denounced the selection as pro-German, and ordered that it be replaced. Gruening defended Benchley's action without success.[46]

Against this backdrop, the rival *New York Journal* broke a story claiming that the local office of the U.S. Attorney was investigating Gruening as a possible German spy, alleging that Gruening and Edward Rumely, the former editor of the *Evening Mail,* who lived across the hall from Gruening in an apartment complex on West 103rd Street, had conspired to aid the German cause. (Rumely had been arrested for concealing the fact that German interests owned the *Evening Mail.*) At Gruening's request, Assistant U.S. Attorney Harold Harper publicly announced that there was "no evidence whatever" for the *Journal*'s charges. But, panicked, the editor also issued a press release denying the charges and claiming that he had never even spoken with his neighbor. That assertion stretched credulity. When the *Journal* produced witnesses asserting that Gruening and Rumely had in fact been acquaintances, Gruening changed his story. Garrett needed to hear no more. He dismissed Gruening on the spot.[47]

Gruening sued the *Tribune* for $32,850, charging breach of contract and slander. The suit dragged on for four years, with the *Tribune* contesting the charge on the grounds that Gruening "did not have an attitude toward the war and Germany which would normally be expected of an American at the time" and that the editor was "looked upon with suspicion and dislike" by most of the staff. While the first charge was absurd—even Garrett conceded that the contested "incidents were matters as to which a difference of opinion amongst experienced journalists might exist"—the second area of criticism contained far more merit. Kay Phelps, Garrett's private secretary, correctly guessed that Gruening was fired less because of his foreign policy views than "because he was unable to work smoothly with the other members of the staff." As his former boss, Robert O'Brien, noted—in an understatement—since Gruening was "not a very tactful person," he had "incurred the dislike of other newspaper people in Boston and New York," who in turn retaliated by "alleging that he was pro-German."[48]

Nonetheless, what the *New York Times* described as the "mysterious" circumstances surrounding his departure from the *Tribune* led Gruening to believe that he needed to prove his patriotism. Initially hoping that anti-German public statements would accomplish the goal, he issued one press release calling for the United States to prosecute the war until obtaining unconditional surrender and a commitment from Berlin for a $1 billion indemnity to France. Eventually, however, he decided that words were not enough, and enlisted in the army. Because of his education and experience, he was ordered to the Field Artillery Officers Training School at Camp Zachary Taylor in Louisville. Gruening's military career proved short-lived: less than a month after his arrival in Kentucky, on November 11, 1918, the First World War ended. A month later, he was mustered out of the service.[49]

Though brief, his time in the army planted a seed which would blossom unexpectedly in later years. While at Camp Zachary Taylor, Gruening picked up a military newspaper featuring a story on the U.S. Marine occupation of Haiti. Given the obvious contradiction between this policy and Wilson's idealistic foreign policy pronouncements, the occupation's details stunned Gruening. Before this time, the editor had never seriously questioned that the president's basic international philosophy reflected traditional American ideals of self-determination and respect for the rights of weaker states. The Haitian story, however, raised doubts as to whether the inconsistencies in Wilsonianism which he had criticized on the domestic front existed in foreign policy as well. He continued to give the president the benefit of the doubt, partly from personal stubbornness: he did not want to believe that his initial support for Wilson had been entirely misguided.[50]

Coincidentally, Gruening soon received an opportunity to probe more deeply into the nature of inter-American relations. Returning to New York upon his discharge, he lunched with a fellow Hotchkiss and Harvard graduate, José Camprubí, a naturalized businessman from Spain. Camprubí was in the market for a Spanish-language newspaper, which he hoped would promote better relations between the United States and Latin America while also improving the cultural image of New York City's Hispanics. Knowing of Gruening's background, Camprubí asked him about the plan's feasibility. Gruening recommended purchasing a struggling Spanish-language weekly, *La Prensa*, and converting it into a daily. Camprubí agreed, and asked Gruening to serve as his deputy, responsible for overseeing the day-to-day affairs of the paper. Gruening hesitated. He did not speak Spanish, and had little interest in the business aspects of the profession. Camprubí persisted, however, and, as no other attractive offers materialized, Gruening signed on.[51]

Although he had no way of knowing it at the time, the decision marked a critical turning point in his career. His knowledge of French and Latin allowed him to master Spanish quickly. Gruening's new language skills coincided with his turning his attention away from Europe and toward Latin America. His editorship at *La Prensa* brought him into contact with a number of exiles from the Caribbean Basin, such as Tulio Cestero, a former Dominican diplomat who fled his homeland after U.S. Marines occupied the country in 1916. Gruening's acquaintance with such figures caused him to contemplate inter-American relations for the first time, but the shaky financial situation of *La Prensa* prevented him from following through on Cestero's suggestion that he launch an investigation of Wilson's Caribbean ventures. Nonetheless, his doubts about the president's foreign policies continued to intensify.[52]

Camprubí had hired Gruening primarily to deal with the technical aspects of running a newspaper. The publisher gave Alfredo Callao full run of the editorial page, and asked Gruening to confine his activities to business matters such as improving the paper's circulation base of six thousand. Gruening did his best to cut costs, but his personality was not well suited to the effort, as his handling of negotiations with the Mailers' Union demonstrated. After unionizing the composing room—the only way that he could employ Spanish-speaking compositors and linotypists—he received a visit from two union representatives who told him that he would have to make the mailing room a union-only shop as well. Owing to union rules, the decision would have increased the weekly salary of mailing room employees from $18 to $108.75, and he refused the demand. When one of the representatives, who spoke with what Gruening later recalled as a "strong Irish brogue" and personified everything he had battled against in his earlier crusades for municipal reform, threatened to sabotage *La Prensa*'s newsstand deliveries, Gruening ordered the union representatives off the premises. As soon as sabotage started to occur, he de-unionized the composing room. The experience shocked him. His earlier reporting on the Lawrence strike had given him a strongly positive, perhaps naive, view of organized labor. Gruening never again would view organized labor in such an unadulterated positive light.[53]

While launching *La Prensa* absorbed Gruening's time and attention, his sisters were taking advantage of the postwar era's new intellectual currents in less mundane activities, extending the breadth of their dissenting inclinations far beyond anything Emil Gruening could have imagined. The eldest sibling, Rose, joined with the communist John Reed Club immediately after the war. Bolshevism also attracted Martha, who moved on from her prewar civil rights activism and put her inheritance to work by operating the International School of Revolution in Marlboro, New York. Finally, May, the sister with whom Ernest enjoyed the closest relationship, began "mixing with a very rough class of Bolsheviks and anarchists" in New York. Robert O'Brien, who knew May and Martha well, correctly noted that while all of the Gruenings had "always been liberal in their views," the females entertained more radical political beliefs than did Ernest. Nonetheless, their course paralleled the radicalization of Ernest's domestic and international viewpoint.[54]

In this fluid intellectual climate, Gruening's work at *La Prensa* seemed downright dull. But he remained at the paper for over a year, partly because his crisis of confidence in his own beliefs decreased the appeal of editorial journalism. Although Wilson had promised a liberal peace from the Paris Peace Conference, the resulting treaty badly compromised his idealistic vision, even though he insisted that the United States, by joining the League of Nations, could work to reform some of its more egregious clauses. This argument failed to persuade many left-wing critics at home, who denounced the treaty as a compromise with Old World imperialism. Torn between his previous naive commitment to Wilson and his more recent doubts about the president's policies in the Caribbean Basin, Gruening did not feel confident enough to enter the fray on the crucial issues which dominated American politics in late 1919 and early 1920. In fact, he never adopted a public position on U.S. membership in the League; the only hint of his true feelings came nearly a decade later, when he declined an invitation to join the League of Nations Non-Partisan Association.[55]

Attacks from former supporters such as Gruening only compounded Wilson's political difficulties. The president's right-wing critics grew immeasurably stronger after the GOP seized a congressional majority in 1918, allowing Henry Cabot Lodge to assume the chairmanship of the Foreign Relations Committee. By summer, most Senate Republicans had announced support for reservations which Wilson considered so odious that he threatened not to ratify the treaty. With the two principals in the dispute refusing to compromise, the treaty never had a chance, although the final rejection of the Treaty of Versailles in March 1920 also removed the need for Gruening to confront his doubts about Wilsonianism. Not coincidentally, he soon began to show a greater interest in national politics. The immediate occasion for this change of heart was the election of 1920, when he endorsed Herbert Hoover for president. That Gruening could move from championing Roosevelt in 1912 to Wilson in 1916 to Hoover in 1920 and call himself a progressive throughout provides a telling if unintentional commentary on the movement's eclectic nature. Roosevelt had hoped to invest the national government with the powers necessary to enact a reform program, even if his own agenda often was quite meager. Wilson had offered, at least in his first term, a strongly idealistic vision of the United States in world affairs and a domestic program that called for implementing the anti-monopoly agenda through regulation. As for Hoover, he was skeptical of increasing the power of the national government, and touted efficiency—solving political problems in a presumably nonideological, scientific fashion—as the means to reform. Indeed, much of the earlier progressive fascination with regulation had arisen from a belief that apolitical regulators could determine the proper solutions to the nation's most challenging political and economic problems. But, taking advantage of the postwar disillusionment with earlier progressive programs, Hoover elevated the concept to a new prominence.[56]

For Gruening, supporting Hoover represented another manifestation of how World War I affected his approach to politics. No longer did he automatically view the national government as a proponent of reform; rather, he worried that investing it with increased power could have harmful consequences, as Wilson's civil liberties policies had shown. Given his own performance during the war, Hoover seemed to offer a way to resolve Gruening's dilemma, since the engineer had satisfied a reform agenda without boosting government power. The endorsement also reflected Gruening's long-standing tendency to support political figures unquestioningly—as he earlier had done with Wilson—who at first glance seemed sympathetic with his overall agenda. Recalled by a leading campaign figure as "one of the staunch Hoover men in 1920," he began his crusade by hosting a meeting of "a few 'literary people'" in his New York City apartment. The group resolved to support Hoover regardless of his partisan affiliation and circulated petitions urging open endorsements of a Hoover candidacy. Dorothy even participated in the effort, serving on a committee of twelve Vassar alumnae who organized a pro-Hoover Vassar club.[57]

Gruening's renewed involvement in national affairs prompted him to send out signals that he was prepared to leave *La Prensa*. Upon hearing of his availability, Oswald Garrison Villard asked him to become managing editor of *The Nation*. Founded after the Civil War to promote racial understanding, the journal quickly adopted, in the words of I. F. Stone, editor E. L. Godkin's "moralistic approach to politics and politicians." But by the 1910s the magazine had grown rather staid, focusing more on literary and social commentary than on current events. Then Villard entered the scene. The grandson of abolitionist and pacifist William Lloyd Garrison, he championed open diplomacy and set out to transform *The Nation* into a voice for anti-imperialism and anti-militarism in postwar America. Gruening, excited about the ideological freedom the position promised, quickly accepted Villard's offer.[58]

Gruening did not end his involvement with the Hoover campaign, although events did not develop as the editor had hoped. As in most other states, Hoover's effort fell short in New York. Still, the GOP convention in Chicago opened with no Republican possessing a clear majority, and Gruening traveled to the Midwest hopeful that a Hoover boom would develop once the convention got under way. Instead, party leaders settled on a compromise choice, Ohio senator Warren Harding, who named the equally nondescript governor of Massachusetts, Calvin Coolidge, as his vice presidential nominee. Gruening had no intention of supporting the conservative Harding, while the Democratic ticket of Ohio governor James Cox and Assistant Secretary of the Navy Franklin Roosevelt, who promised to continue Wilsonian policies, likewise offered little appeal. Therefore, in a further illustration of his radicalized viewpoint on national affairs, Gruening cast his presidential ballot for the Farmer-Labor candidate, Parley Christensen.[59]

The vote for Christensen showed the degree of Gruening's alienation from the political mainstream. But, unlike his sisters, Gruening craved political effectiveness, and so supporting a protest candidacy held no appeal in the long term. To create a more favorable alternative four years hence, he searched for other ways to renew the reform sentiment eclipsed by World War I, commissioning a series of *Nation* articles on politics in the forty-eight states, Puerto Rico, Alaska, and Hawaii. Understanding that the journal's readership was not wide enough to exert the influence he wanted, Gruening secured a contract from a New York publishing house, Liveright, to compile the articles into a two-volume symposium published under the title *These United States*. Gruening intended the volumes to serve as a progressive manifesto for the 1920s. They contained fifty-one essays from prominent progressives, such as William Allen White, Zona Gale, and Sinclair Lewis, which the editor described as unified by a common "faith in the American ideal." That Gruening could only offer such a vague concept as the thesis for the work testified to its rather aimless, disconnected nature. Moreover, the book was a commercial disaster; by the 1920s, in fact, publishers had a "way of quoting the history of Ernest Gruening's 'These United States' as one of the best symposiums which didn't pay its way."[60] The failure encouraged Gruening to look elsewhere to make his mark on postwar American reform. He would satisfy this quest more quickly than he anticipated.

~ 2

The Anti-imperialist Impulse

One day in late 1920, Martha suggested to her brother that he lunch with Herbert Seligman, a former member of the NAACP's publicity bureau who had moved on to freelance journalism. That summer *Harper's* had sent Seligman to Haiti to research an article profiling the occupying Marine forces. He returned disillusioned, informing Gruening that he had uncovered evidence of Marine atrocities which contradicted the supposed idealism of Wilson's foreign policy. From what he could determine, the United States had intervened not to promote democracy but to assist U.S. financial interests that wished to exploit Haiti.[1]

Earlier, along with many progressives, Gruening had welcomed Wilson's arguments that the United States could play an active international role without functioning as a traditional imperialist power. Now, however, the editor realized that he and Wilson had tapped into different elements of the American dissenting heritage. While the president supported reforming the structure of international relations, he never envisioned that the United States would facilitate immediate self-determination for all countries, as his support for League of Nations mandates in Africa and Asia as well as the decision to intervene in Haiti itself revealed. Gruening had been blinded by his earlier uncritical admiration for Wilson; the revelation that the president not only had not lived up to Gruening's interpretation of his idealistic pronouncements but had violated them in such an egregious manner provoked a sense of personal betrayal. Throughout the 1910s, Gruening had searched for an issue to call his own, ranging from municipal reform to birth control to his World War I crusades. Now, his quest satisfied, he turned his attention to the Caribbean Basin. To begin, he used his position at *The Nation* to commission from Seligman an article comparing Haiti to victims of European imperialism such as the Congo, India, and Egypt and alleging widespread brutality by the occupying forces. A sharp retort from General John Lejeune, commandant of the Marine Corps, convinced Gruening that he was on the right track.[2]

The activities of Gruening and Seligman were part of a broader interest in the Haitian occupation among civil rights activists such as Oswald Garrison Villard and NAACP executive secretary James Weldon Johnson. In 1920 the embryonic campaign of the anti-occupation forces received an inadvertent boost when the Democratic vice presidential nominee, Franklin Roosevelt, boasted on the campaign trail that "the facts are that I wrote Haiti's constitution myself and if I do say it, I think it is a pretty good constitution." Republicans, supplied by Johnson with detailed information on the occupation, seized on the remark and made Haitian policy a campaign issue; Warren Harding promised to review matters immediately after coming to office. Both Villard and Gruening did what they could to hold Harding to his commitment. Expanding on the contacts he had made while attending the Republican convention, Gruening solicited an article on Haiti from Senator Medill McCormick (R–Illinois), the GOP's point man on the issue in the campaign. McCormick produced a surprisingly timid piece, prompting a disappointed Gruening to search for other ways to keep public attention focused on Haiti. Gruening realized that for a dissenting activist, simply placing the facts before the public would not suffice; he needed to frame information to produce public pressure on politicians such as McCormick. His first step in this effort came in early 1921, when he teamed with Johnson, Villard, and Moorfield Storey, the last president of the Anti-Imperialist League (which had been organized to oppose the U.S. colonization of the Philippines), to launch the Haiti and Santo Domingo Independence Society. He also started urging anti-imperialists in the United States to join with their Haitian counterparts in a cross-national coalition committed to ending the occupation. Haitian reformers could assist in the common cause by framing their protests to exert the maximum influence on U.S. public opinion.[3]

By this time the anti-intervention campaign was the dominant issue in Gruening's life. Working with Seligman and Johnson, he attempted to implement his theories about the utility of cross-national alliances. In March he presided at a New York City dinner for several members of the leading Haitian resistance group, the Union Patriotique, including future Haitian president Stenio Vincent and Haitian diplomat H. Pauléus Sannon. The Haitians had come to the United States to present a memorial declaration to the State Department criticizing the occupation. After Secretary of State Charles Evans Hughes refused to see them, Gruening and Seligman hastily scheduled the New York City affair, personally assuming its costs. In addition, Gruening arranged to have *The Nation* publish the Union Patriotique's statement, and began corresponding directly with Haitian resistance leaders such as Pierre Hudicourt. He then published his first article on inter-American relations, in the pacifist journal *The World Tomorrow*, urging a congressional inquiry "with the fullest publicity" and asking the "average American" to "interest himself personally" in the battle. The issue allowed him to present a broad and intellectually coherent program without tying his fortunes to any single individual, as he had done with Wilson.[4]

Meanwhile, Villard attempted to maintain the tenuous links between the anti-occupation forces and the Republicans forged during the campaign. His persistence paid off in the fall, after McCormick assumed the chairmanship of a select Senate committee charged with investigating conditions in Haiti and the Dominican Republic. The Illinois senator asked Villard to handle advance arrangements for the committee, which planned to spend only a short time in Hispaniola. Villard demurred, citing his interest in attending the Washington Conference on Naval Disarmament, scheduled for the same time. In his stead he recommended Gruening, then—ironically—busy raising money in the United States for the presentation of the Union Patriotique's case before the committee. Gruening's fluency in both French and Spanish provided the necessary linguistic qualifications, while his personal acquaintance with McCormick clinched the arrangement. At government expense, Gruening made his first visit to the Caribbean in November and December, spending three weeks in Haiti and ten days in the Dominican Republic.[5]

Gruening privately described his mission as falling "into two parts." He wished, first, to screen testimony so as to "eliminate" marginal witnesses, a function he considered especially important, given the committee's "absurdly inadequate period of time" on the island. He described his "second and more important" task as "a diplomatic function"—mediating differences among Haitian political factions. Perceptively, Gruening reasoned that unless the Haitians agreed "pretty definitely" on minimal demands and presented a united front to the committee, they would have no chance of pressuring the senators to recommend terminating the occupation. Again the role of U.S. public opinion was central to his concerns; Gruening understood that a unified local political class would undermine claims of Haitian political instability. He showed less concern with the state of the Dominican resistance movement, which, working through lobbyist Herbert Knowles, already had an effective public relations operation. In addition, with his old colleague from *La Prensa*, Tulio Cestero, among the triumvirate coordinating the nationalist resistance, Gruening was inclined to trust the Dominicans' tactical judgment.[6]

Gruening created a stir immediately upon arriving in Haiti. In a public address (in French) which earned him recognition as an honorary citizen of the capital, he denounced American racism and the existence of martial law. After spending just under two weeks in Port-au-Prince, he then set off for the rural areas, where his speaking tour continued to receive extensive coverage in the Haitian press. Conferring extensively with resistance leaders, he offered advice on handling the individual members of the committee and on determining the order and number of witnesses that should appear. Reflecting his firmly ingrained belief in the importance of appealing to U.S. public opinion, Gruening organized a Union Patriotique rally to greet the committee's arrival. He suggested several slogans, such as "Don't Make Haiti America's Congo," "Shall Haiti Be Your Ireland?" and "The American People Have Been Betrayed," which appeared (in English) at the demonstration welcoming the senators to Haiti. (Several members of the delegation commented irritably on the protest, and McCormick asked Gruening to look into its origins.) Gruening thus largely succeeded in his first task of coordinating the Haitian response to the Senate inquiry.[7]

In his second goal, however, he failed. Correctly surmising that both

McCormick and occupation officials would seize on the Haitian elite's ambivalence about the Union Patriotique's demand for an immediate U.S. withdrawal, he looked to broker a compromise local settlement. Several meetings between U.S. client President Sudre Dartiguenave and Gruening, acting in his official role, produced a conference between the Haitian leader and the resistance group to forge common demands. Both sides insisted on Gruening's presence as an honest broker. After some haggling, Dartiguenave agreed that he would not publicly oppose demands for the abolition of martial law and a withdrawal of the Marines within six months. The resistance leaders, who continued to harbor a "great deal of skepticism" about Dartiguenave's sincerity, then requested a joint communiqué on the meeting. Despite "saying that I did not think I had any business to tangle myself in Haitian affairs" (a disclaimer that no one took seriously by this stage), Gruening agreed to draft the communiqué and clear it with the president. At this point, however, Dartiguenave reversed himself, undoubtedly after discovering that Gruening was acting in a personal rather than an official capacity. The entire episode only deepened the mutual suspicions between the Haitian leader and his critics. Gruening fared better in his journey to the Dominican Republic, where Cestero introduced him to the other two principal leaders of the Dominican resistance movement, Federico Henriquez y Caraval, a former presidential candidate and Chief Justice of the Dominican Supreme Court, and Henriquez's brother Ferdinand, a doctor, lawyer, and former diplomat. The McCormick committee staffer strongly endorsed the trio's call for a U.S. withdrawal *pura y simple*, and urged them to resist Secretary Hughes's demands that the Dominicans ratify the acts of the military government as a precondition for terminating the occupation.[8]

The committee members, however, sided with Hughes on the matter, and showed even less inclination to accept Gruening's point of view on Haitian affairs. Dissatisfaction with the committee's work prompted Gruening to ask to testify publicly when McCormick convened hearings during the summer of 1922. The Illinois senator granted this rather unusual request, on the condition that the testimony focus on the state of affairs in Haiti as he had seen them. Gruening admitted that while he "naturally" had a "certain sympathy for the people" of Hispaniola, partly owing to "the instinctive feeling that one is apt to have for the underdog," the critical issue for him remained not the intervention's effect on the average Haitian but "whether the United States is going to be an Old World imperialism" and adopt the very policies that it had entered World War I to defeat. In this sense he had moved beyond Wilsonianism, which declined to define the United States as an anti-imperialist power, and embraced a more radical conception of the American past.[9]

By the time of his testimony, of course, Gruening harbored no illusions that the committee would support the principles to which he adhered. The distrust was mutual, and so, after having listened to several hours of criticism of U.S. policies, Atlee Pomerene (D–Ohio) and McCormick turned the tables. They demanded that the editor abandon his generalizations about the evils of the decision to intervene and instead address the situation at hand. Less than specific in his responses, Gruening revealed that he lacked a firm sense of what positive role the United States might play in the Caribbean. He informed McCormick of his belief that all U.S. policies should start with the premise of "restoring as effectively as possible government to the Haitian people." He recommended a constituent assembly to replace the U.S.-imposed constitution of 1917, with elections within thirty days. But he also conceded that the Marines might have to remain for several months thereafter to train a politically neutral Haitian security force. In response to fears that political instability would reappear, Gruening was even more vague and conceded that he could not offer any assurance on the country's future stability. If he was still unsure exactly what sort of policy he wanted, he nonetheless dissented strongly from the committee's report, which recommended minor bureaucratic changes in the way the United States handled Haiti but otherwise favored indefinite U.S. control.[10]

Gruening responded to these unsatisfactory findings by turning his attention to Congress as a whole. Early in 1922, Senator William King (D–Utah) had introduced an amendment to the naval appropriations bill to cut off all funds for the occupation of Haiti and the Dominican Republic. King had been a corporate lawyer before his upset victory in 1916, and little in his first term marked him as a likely foreign policy dissenter. His anti-imperialism also had clear limits: he confided to Ernest Angell, the chief clerk of the McCormick committee, that as a "strong Wilson supporter," he would not inquire into the origins of the occupation, since doing so would compel him to assume "responsibility for openly criticizing the acts" of the Wilson administration. But the

Utah senator's concern about excessive naval appropriations piqued his interest in the Haitian intervention, which drew its funds from the navy budget.[11]

Gruening privately admitted that King's gambit to end the occupation by cutting off its funds seemed radical. After his experience over the previous two years, however, of "the State Department having arrogated itself pretty near all the powers there are," he saw no alternative. "Recent Caribbean history shows clearly," warned Gruening, "that the warmaking power can be taken away from Congress provided that what we do is not called a war." Accordingly, as his *Nation* colleague Lewis Gannett reported, Gruening went off to Washington "attempting to stir up action about Haiti." Few senators, though, proved as malleable as he had expected. Arthur Capper (R–Kansas) privately remarked that while he sympathized with the aims of the King amendment, he opposed "precipitate action"; another moderate, Joseph France (R–Maryland), indicated his belief that "general legislative matters should not be passed upon in connection with appropriation bills." Many senators, similarly ambivalent, simply refrained from voting, and the amendment lost by an overwhelming vote of 43 to 9.[12]

Both the Utah senator and Gruening admitted that developments had "greatly disappointed" them. But another amendment supporter, William Borah (R–Idaho), expressed greater optimism, remarking that regardless of the final outcome, "discussion of these matters is helpful." The Idaho senator predicted that "the people of the country will not submit . . . to the program which we are carrying out in that Island when they are thoroughly informed." Gruening was therefore not alone in his focus on the occupation's effects on U.S. public opinion. Moreover, unlike King, who kept his own counsel, Borah represented a larger bloc in the Senate, the peace progressives, a coalition of around a dozen senators from midwestern and western states committed to reorienting U.S. foreign policy along anti-imperialist lines. The group criticized Wilsonian diplomacy for compromising too much with imperialist forces in Europe. The dissenters unanimously backed the King amendment, arguing that all who wished to reorient U.S. foreign policy needed to work to bring the occupation to a speedy close.[13]

The amendment's defeat prompted Gruening to broaden his activities beyond the small clique of anti-intervention activists in the United States and the Caribbean. In April 1922 he penned a report critical of the intervention, issued by the Foreign Policy Association over the signatures of twenty-four prominent lawyers, including Harvard Law School professors Felix Frankfurter and Zechariah Chafee. The next month he organized a speech by Borah at Carnegie Hall, at which the Idaho senator charged that the administration was aiming for permanent U.S. control in order to allow American financial interests to exploit Haitian resources. The *New York Times*, which rebuked the senator for forgetting "that the United States has a good record for resisting imperialism," dourly observed that literature ranging from the Union Patriotique memorial statement to Gruening's articles had been "freely distributed" to those in attendance. Gruening privately exulted that the "tremendous publicity" generated by the address had lifted "the question from the realm of obscurity where it was before." He rejoiced further two weeks later when the speech provoked a response: supporters of the occupation took out a full-page advertisement in the *New York Herald* praising the Marines for bringing civilization to backward Haitians. Reflecting a pattern of exaggeration well established by this point, Gruening predicted that with "the world's spotlight . . . turned on Haiti," the situation would so deteriorate for defenders of the intervention that withdrawal was imminent.[14]

Quite beyond its impact on policy toward Haiti, Gruening's work with anti-occupation senators prompted in him a more nuanced view of the national government. Before this time, whether in his admiration for Roosevelt or Wilson, he had seen the presidency as the chief instrument for reform. But after becoming disillusioned with Wilson, he increasingly realized the important role that Congress could play in promoting the dissenting viewpoint of U.S. foreign policy—through committee hearings and investigations, speeches aimed at mobilizing public opinion, and amendments such as King's to check the executive. At the same time, though, the defeat of the King amendment signaled the limits of congressional power, persuading Gruening that anti-imperialists needed to force ambivalent senators such as Capper and France to side with them by rallying public opinion to their cause. He was thus convinced of the need for forging a cross-national coalition to build public support for withdrawal in the United States and political and social reform in Haiti. Gruening also argued that anti-imperialists needed to frame their cause more boldly, as Wilson had done with his foreign policy proposals. Only by demonstrating the relevance of Haiti to a broader international agenda could anti-imperialists obtain enough public support to overturn interventionist policies.

By the middle of 1922, Gruening's single-minded devotion to the Haitian issue distinguished him even among those who were active in the anti-occupation campaign. James Weldon Johnson reported that the Chicago NAACP branch had opposed inviting the *Nation* editor to speak on Haiti because it was "a little timid about so-called radical stands." Johnson himself went along with Gruening's recommendations to pressure wavering senators before the King amendment vote only with great reluctance, noting that Gruening refused to recognize that the NAACP had more important domestic priorities, such as passage of the Dyer anti-lynching bill. In fact, Johnson's interest in Haiti flowed from a belief that the occupation demonstrated not just the misguided direction of U.S. foreign policy but the fundamental racism of American society. He hoped that by proving its ability to govern itself, Haiti would further the cause of civil rights in the United States. Gruening nevertheless began to look beyond Haiti to indict U.S. policy toward all of Latin America. He informed Villard that as one who had "seen enough to know that he who casts his line in the troubled waters of American imperialism invariably gets more than his bait back," he would "take a fling at Nicaragua." In an editorial dismissing Nicaragua as "the Republic of Brown Brothers," Gruening scored the State Department for "acting as private agents" of that New York investment house. As he had with Haiti, the editor had again drawn an oversimplified link between economic imperialism and U.S. policies in the region, which were actually based more on strategic concerns and an obsession with stability.[15]

ALTHOUGH HE had initially encouraged his managing editor's interest in Caribbean affairs, Villard soon feared that Gruening's all-consuming anti-imperialism was causing him to neglect *The Nation*'s pressing financial needs. Gruening, however, could not spare the time: he had never shown any interest in the business side of journalism, and redeeming the U.S. image in the Caribbean was simply more important to him than attending to circulation figures. In September 1922, faced with no choice, Villard fired him, citing budget problems. Still, the two parted amicably; Gruening had understood the weekly's financial difficulties when he first took the position, and his period with the journal had served its purpose by increasing his profile among national reformers. Once again, the financially secure Gruening's ideological crusades triumphed at the expense of his job security.[16]

Now freed from the constraints of the managing editorship, Gruening devoted himself full-time to what he privately termed his "constructive muckraking of imperialism." He soon stumbled onto an opportunity to integrate his economic self-interest with his ideological agenda, securing commitments to contribute freelance articles on Mexico to *The Nation*, *Century*, *Current History*, and *Collier's Weekly*. Although he was known for his anti-imperialist views, his writings and work with the McCormick committee had given Gruening a nonpartisan reputation as an interpreter of Latin American international politics. This reputation helped to produce a contract offer—including a comfortable advance—from Century Publishers to write what he modestly referred to as "the book" on the Mexican Revolution. He accepted with alacrity. Accompanied by Dorothy, Sonny, and Hunt, he set off for Mexico City on what he expected to be a six-month research trip.[17]

The United States and Mexico had a long and troubled history by the time Gruening first arrived in the country. The thirty-year dictatorship of Porfirio Díaz had encouraged foreign investment and stabilized Mexican politics, but the Porfiriato crumbled in 1910 when Díaz was replaced as president by Francisco Madero, who in turn was toppled by General Victoriano Huerta in late 1912. Refusing to extend diplomatic recognition to what he regarded as a "government of butchers," Wilson instead assisted the opposition Constitutionalist forces. Although the Constitutionalists eventually ousted Huerta, Wilson's interventionist tactics poisoned his relations with the Constitutionalist president, Venustiano Carranza, which only worsened after the revolutionary regime promulgated a new constitution in 1917. The document's most controversial provision, Article 27, declared all subsoil rights the property of the Mexican state, thus threatening U.S. oil concessions in the country. Two years later, Carranza himself was overthrown in a coup organized by many of his former supporters and led by Álvaro Obregón. Distracted by the debate over the Treaty of Versailles and his subsequent illness, Wilson did not extend formal diplomatic relations to the new regime.[18]

Nonrecognition continued into the 1920s. Charles Evans Hughes viewed Mexico as a test case of thc U.S. response to economic nationalism, and, despite pressure from U.S. bankers confident that recognition would allow Mexico to resume financing its foreign debt, indicated little willingness to back down. This diplomatic tension served as the backdrop to Gruening's introduction to Mexico. The family rented a home in the Colonia Roma section of Mexico City, where Gruening's social life revolved around the small but vibrant community of left-wing Americans who migrated to Mexico City in the 1920s to partake of the Mexican cultural renaissance and to experience what Gruening recalled as the "rising hum of revolutionary fervor." His friend and fellow journalist Carleton Beals was one of the more prominent of these figures; another was Frank Tannenbaum, a former IWW activist engaged in a scholarly study of Mexican agriculture. What Tannenbaum called this "regular little family," a group which resembled the literary bohemians of Greenwich Village during the pre–World War I years, also included Frances Toor, admirer of Mexican culture and publisher of the magazine *Mexican Folkways*, and the Mexican-born Anita Brenner. According to Brenner, the "social friendships" soon stimulated "a revolutionary atmosphere, almost like a workshop atmosphere." Gruening's commitment to wife and family, already evident at this stage of his career, caused him to eschew the more gregarious social activity of the group. But he did make one original contribution to the social life of the anti-imperialist activists: setting a pattern for the future, he looked to replicate his Boston and New York environment by hosting frequent dinner parties. One participant recalled the "honorable, courteous, and cultured" host both for his domination of the dinner conversation, which he steered toward "seeable, tangible, provable facts" rather than the more abstract philosophical issues preferred by other anti-imperialists, and for his ability to shake "a mean cocktail." This latter skill perhaps explained why, after the meal, dancing usually began and the atmosphere "sort of loosened up."[19]

Despite his preference for focusing on political and international events, Gruening's stay in Mexico also stimulated a lifelong interest in Mexican culture. The remainder of the family, however, lived what Hunt recalled as "pretty much of a cloistered life." Dorothy eagerly sampled a lifestyle unlike anything she had experienced in her New England upbringing, but she closely controlled the day-to-day affairs of the two children, to whom she devoted most of her time, since Gruening hired a maid to tend to domestic duties. She particularly worried about the clique's influence on the boys. When she caught one of Beals's friends, the poet Witter Byner, teaching Hunt and Sonny to smoke cigarettes, she told the boys to "try something else" for a while. (Beals himself she found even more threatening because of his well-publicized, and well-deserved, reputation as a womanizer.) These mild cases of disciplining were rare, however; one acquaintance recalled the boys as "extremely bad mannered, having been reared on the principle that nothing should be done which might hinder the free development of their personalities." Gruening himself typified this relaxed attitude toward parental control; his contact with his sons consisted of occasionally taking them horseback riding in the Mexican countryside. He had time to do little else with his family. Work assumed the highest priority, as he made clear when Dorothy discovered that she was pregnant with their third child. She wanted to return immediately to New York, but Gruening vetoed the idea. As events transpired, however, their third son, Peter, was born in the United States.[20]

Although Gruening saw little of his family, he took in much of Mexico in his research for "the book." His initial impressions of the country were mixed but largely positive. The Mexican government understood the importance of cultivating ties with Americans who were likely to present a favorable viewpoint. Within a week of Gruening's arrival in the capital, he dined alone with Obregón, discussing both U.S. nonrecognition and Obregón's domestic agenda. Obregón later reciprocated the visit, dropping by Gruening's residence to present the journalist with an autographed copy of his book *Ocho mil kilómetros en campaña.* Gruening spent several more weeks in Mexico City, speaking with revolutionary politicians, including Obregón's second-in-command, Plutarco Calles, and Finance Minister Adolfo de la Huerta. He also opened contacts with José Vasconcelos, whose Department of Education championed reviving Mexico's native culture to maintain the country's cultural freedom. In addition, he joined other anti-imperialists in admiring Diego Rivera, the muralist who was also the country's most famous communist. Gruening's close ties to the leaders of the Mexican state generated a mixture of admiration and envy from his fellow Americans, who marveled at his ability to ingratiate himself with his adopted nation's elite but who also wondered whether he had become a "fellow traveler" whose ties to the centers of power prevented him from objectively analyzing the revolution.[21]

After Gruening's time in the capital, he toured the country to get a fuller sense of the revolution's effects. At Obregón's suggestion, he capped off his journey with an extended tour of the Yucatán, accompanied by Charles Ervin, the former editor of the socialist *New York Call*. Displaying his usual pattern of translating ideological sympathy into personal admiration, he delighted in the discovery of "that most extraordinary little utopia," where, under socialist governor Felipe Carillo, "the one superlative person in all Mexico," the government was mobilizing the state's Indian majority. While in the state, he also renewed ties with a Harvard classmate, the archaeologist Sylvanus Morley. A debate over lunch with future labor leader Vicente Lombardo Toledano on whether the United States was practicing a "heartless" policy toward Latin America impressed Morley with Gruening's rhetorical skills if not his ideological perspective. Gruening, for his part, dismissed those like Morley who wrote back home describing the Mexican scene as rife with bolshevism. "Unfortunately," he noted privately, such an impression was totally "wrong." In fact, he wished "the Reds were rampant," since he believed that, as in the Yucatán, "progress in the various parts of the republic is just about directly proportional to the redness of the given section." With a newfound appreciation for the complexities of life in the Caribbean Basin, however, he conceded that "it is almost impossible to give an adequate picture of the Mexican Revolution without a lot of qualifications," since "almost every situation when you get close to it is different from the first view." The book therefore would take considerably longer to research than expected, and so he would have to delay his departure from Mexico indefinitely. That he was thoroughly enjoying himself, of course, made this decision all the easier.[22]

Gruening unsurprisingly entertained a critical attitude toward Hughes's diplomacy, which he characterized as "nothing less than a death warrant for the Obregón administration." More generally, he doubted whether U.S. civilization could "be successfully imposed on these unwilling beneficiaries," as, he argued, Wilson's Latin American policy had sought to do. While the United States should encourage reform in Latin America, he believed that it should also recognize that in many Latin American countries the ideal type of government might differ from the traditional American style of democracy. Such a sentiment, a considerable change from his touting of elections for Haiti before the McCormick committee, marked Gruening's final break with Wilsonianism and its preference for democratic elections as the proper solution to Latin American development. This more nuanced view flowed from his admiration for the social, economic, and cultural effects of the revolution. Mexico, he felt, provided an example of "the first essentially non-political revolution in this hemisphere," with the Obregón government attempting to modernize while retaining the basics of the local culture. Ridiculing "pseudo-scientific" deductions about "tinted races," Gruening challenged anyone who considered the Mexican "race" inferior to the American to witness Mexican culture firsthand. Celebrating the efforts of Vasconcelos, who oversaw the creation of Mexico's first extensive network of rural schools, was common among the anti-imperialist activists. But for Gruening, such praise involved issues closer to home: as the only foreign journalist allowed free access to Vasconcelos and his official files, Gruening developed a personal stake in the minister's success.[23]

Even so, his admiration for Mexico and Mexicans had its limits. Gruening always maintained a certain distance from the reality of the common man. Raised in a financially secure home, he enjoyed the luxury of confidently commenting on events with a sense of detachment. In this respect he was an elitist, admittedly of a peculiar sort. In Mexico, he and Dorothy always kept the door to their compound locked, and limited contact between Mexicans and their children. Also, while Gruening ingratiated himself with the political and intellectual elite, he showed no interest in bonding with lower-class Mexicans or Indians, despite his rhetorical celebration of Indian culture. One day shortly after arriving in Mexico, he and Beals tried to climb Mount Ajusco, a fourteen thousand–foot peak south of Mexico City. They got lost, however, and when night fell, had no place to sleep. "Ernest got quite panicky," Beals recalled, since "the idea of having to spend the night in an Indian hut utterly appalled him." Drawing on his medical school training, he worried about lice, typhus, bad drinking water, "and a whole set of unpleasant plagues we were sure to acquire." Eventually the hikers stumbled on an Indian who led them to the train station, where they caught a late train back to Mexico City. Gruening was so grateful that he showered silver into "the astonished Indian's palm."[24]

Gruening's ambivalence about the Mexican people did not extend to their government. The success of the Mexican experiment reinforced his theory on how transnational alliances between reformers in the United States and Latin America could end U.S. interventionism in the Caribbean Basin. A powerful Mexico could "stop our pirates physically" when U.S. anti-imperialists lacked sufficient strength to do so legislatively, as had occurred with the King amendment. In addition, he believed, since "the job of high looting always had to be done a bit clandestinely," Mexican opposition could keep the issue in the public spotlight and facilitate the public relations efforts of American anti-imperialists. Finally, if Mexico could regulate foreign interests successfully, it could serve as a model to other weak but mineral-rich countries that served as "pawns of the mighty." Ironically, Gruening contended, nonrecognition had helped to achieve this result by lessening the U.S. physical presence in Mexico's internal life. Beals later expressed the point in another way: "The salvation of Mexico, the salvation of our future with Latin America, and hence the salvation of liberal progressivism in the United States, hinges on the preservation of the present regime and tendency in Mexico more than on anything else." For Gruening and other anti-imperialists, the Mexican Revolution provided an alternative to Wilsonianism for solving the problems of Latin American development.[25]

Just as Gruening was celebrating the effects of nonrecognition, Hughes decided to normalize relations, authorizing diplomatic troubleshooter Thomas Lamont, a partner in the J. P. Morgan firm, to enter into talks with Adolfo de la Huerta, in which they worked out an agreement for Mexico to resume payment on its foreign debt. The accord paved the way for the United States to extend recognition, and the two sides to agree to a modus vivendi on other aspects of their dispute. Gruening initially attacked the change in policy, characterizing Lamont as a representative of "the most active imperialist force in the world today: the power of American money." This rather superficial analysis could not hold up, however, and eventually even he praised the resumption of relations. Just as suddenly, however, instability returned to Mexican politics. In early 1924, after Calles consolidated his position as Obregón's successor, de la Huerta joined with foes of the regime in launching a military uprising. Although Obregón quelled the unrest, he did so in large measure with military assistance from the United States, which was pleased with his regime's adherence to the repayment schedule outlined in the de la Huerta–Lamont agreement.[26]

The revolt shattered Gruening's overly positive view of Mexican politics. Although he was pleased that the pro-government forces prevailed, for Gruening personally the final outcome was more mixed, since counterrevolutionary forces had assassinated Felipe Carillo. More generally, the journalist lamented that de la Huerta's willingness to abandon his stated principles and join with military leaders had revealed the "pathetic truth" that Mexico lacked "even moderately honest, enlightened, and capable men to hold down the major posts." As with his opinion of Wilson, a sense of personal betrayal produced a violent swing in his views: before the rebellion, in a simplistic reading of Mexican politics, Gruening had extolled de la Huerta for placing principle above personal ambition. The international implications of the revolt also proved troubling. Obregón's reliance on U.S. military assistance, he feared, had reversed "one of the considerable achievements" of the regime—securing "independence from U.S. domination." The only positive result that he could perceive was the "gratifying" fact that most people in the United States seemed to sympathize with Obregón's plight. Gruening likewise derived little encouragement from the Mexican government's policies after the uprising. He strongly criticized Obregón's failure to curb the power of the military, predicting that "there can be no assurance of peace until the army is scrapped and this would have been a fine time to do it. It will be harder later on."[27]

In the aftermath of the revolt, Gruening put the writing of his book on hold. He admitted that he needed to reevaluate his interpretation of Mexican politics and society. In the spring of 1924, deeply distressed, he returned to the United States.

Caribbean Basin affairs nonetheless continued to pique his interest. Even while in Mexico, Gruening had searched for ways to integrate his anti-imperialist activism with his financial well-being, a quest which focused primarily on Haitian matters. According to Gruening, the issue provided a unique test case of the power of public opinion, since outside of a few special interests, such as the National City Bank of New York (which extended substantial loans to the puppet regime), no strong pressure existed to maintain the occupation. Confident that the truth "is so outrageous that it will not stand daylight," he predicted that a public galvanized by a "thoroughly organized campaign" for withdrawal would in turn pressure the Congress into acting. To implement the ideal, in November 1923 he had written to Roger Baldwin, head of the American Fund for Public Service, requesting a $150 weekly stipend to continue his crusade "against the newer manifestations of American imperialism" in the Caribbean. "At the risk of being held an incurable optimist and a visionary" (and the owner of a rather large ego), Gruening asserted that he could "free Haiti" with "a hundred thousand dollars." Baldwin demurred, concerned about involving the fund in contentious political events. When the plan fell through, Gruening's Senate patron, William King, sent a circular letter urging "public spirited persons" to contribute money so that a "competent investigator" (clearly Gruening) could travel to Haiti to "get the facts."[28]

Although this scheme also collapsed, Gruening, once back in the United States full-time, continued to search for ways to implement his anti-imperialist vision. His old mentor Oswald Garrison Villard provided him with the opportunity by asking for assistance in reviving the Anti-Imperialist League. On February 12, 1924, a group of illustrious anti-imperialists convened at Villard's New York City home: John Nevin Sayre, the pacifist head of the Fellowship of Reconciliation (FOR); author Scott Nearing; progressive stalwart Amos Pinchot; Roger Baldwin; Latin American specialist Adolf Berle; and peace activist Helena Hill Weed. They agreed on the need to "organize actively against the rampant new American imperialism," which flourished thanks "to a deliberate policy of censorship and distortion of news." With Villard as president of the proposed organization and Gruening its executive secretary, the new league called for withdrawing all U.S. troops from foreign territories, assuring political freedom to all countries within the sphere of U.S. economic influence, preventing the seizure of underdeveloped countries by U.S. finance, obtaining control of U.S. foreign policy by public opinion, disseminating accurate and timely information concerning U.S. government activities abroad, and promoting greater cultural exchange among the nations of the Western hemisphere.[29]

Although Gruening preferred the name "Pan-American Freedom League" for the new organization, so as to emphasize "the mutual character of the proposed enterprise," his colleagues overruled him on this point. Moorfield Storey, who consented to the transfer of the name from the old organization to the new, explained that in the United States "'Anti-imperial' has a definite meaning and people understand what that meaning is." As Storey recognized, the term captured the conception of traditional American ideals to which Gruening subscribed.[30]

As executive secretary, Gruening was charged with recruiting a prestigious membership for the organization's national board, an activity which further broadened his exposure to the foreign policy elite of the day.[31] At the same time, however, the opposition of many in the State Department to Gruening's activities limited his effectiveness. For example, Stephen Duggan, head of the Institute of International Education, confessed that membership "might act as a bar" to his maintaining influence in Washington. In addition, as in the McCormick committee hearings, the superficiality of Gruening's analysis attracted comment. Ernest Angell raised this point most directly. After his service with the McCormick committee, Angell joined Gruening in helping King to draft the language of the amendment to end the Haitian occupation. While fully willing to affiliate with the new organization, Angell was concerned about its "somewhat vague and loose" objectives. The most the new organization could do, he predicted, would be to pressure the State Department not to intervene on the side of the bankers when disputes arose. Moreover, though Angell agreed entirely that public opinion should exercise greater control over the making of Latin American policy, he doubted that "one voter in a thousand in this country cares a straw about the independence, political or economic, of the weaker Central and South American countries." He therefore cautioned that "the organization must expect the results accomplished to be slow and fragmentary."[32]

Angell's penetrating comments only heightened Gruening's newfound doubts about his anti-imperialist perspective. As would occur throughout his career when he was faced with crises of confidence in his international viewpoint, he stepped back from foreign policy and returned to activism on domestic affairs. In late April 1924 he informed Villard that despite the stimulating nature of his work with the Anti-Imperialist League, he preferred the role of a muckraker. Gruening then returned to his roots: daily journalism. Fretting over the consolidation of metropolitan newspapers, and still searching for the freedom he had enjoyed during his brief tenure at the *Journal*, Gruening lamented that few owners recognized the civic importance of an enlightened and independent editorial page; many even refused to allow investigations or editorials that challenged their own economic or political interests. He never recognized, however, the exceptional nature of the *Journal*, whose owners had purchased it for ideological rather than financial reasons. Moreover, now slightly out of step with the march of domestic reform, Gruening quickly discovered that few shared his worries about newspaper consolidation. Despite his attempt to frame his concerns as vital to ensuring an informed electorate, the issue failed to provide a particularly promising point for his reentry into American reform circles. He therefore turned his attention to national politics, especially the 1924 presidential campaign. In the process, he again demonstrated his belief, apparent in his political activities in 1916 and 1920, that progressives constituted an independent political bloc whose support depended on a candidate's principles rather than partisan affiliation.[33]

During his crusade to end the Haitian occupation, Gruening had encountered a host of senators whom he considered better qualified than Warren Harding to occupy the White House. After Harding's death in 1923, the editor urged Borah to challenge Calvin Coolidge for the Republican nomination, doubting that Robert La Follette (R–Wisconsin), the "only other acceptable possibility," could win. Although a number of progressives also urged the Idaho senator to make the race, he demurred, understanding that the party's nominating process heavily favored the GOP's conservative wing. Progressives hoping for the Democrats to provide an outlet were likewise disappointed. The party's two leading contenders, William Gibbs McAdoo and New York governor Al Smith, both sported mildly reformist credentials. Yet social questions such as prohibition and race relations dominated the convention. After over one hundred ballots, the polarized delegates turned to John Davis, a West Virginia corporate attorney who lacked any noticeable reformist sentiments but whose views on cultural issues were acceptable to both of the party's wings. Sensing an opening, La Follette launched an independent bid for the presidency, championing an increased governmental role in the economy, greater action on behalf of consumers, and a more rigorous application of the existing anti-monopoly statutes. Emphasizing its nonpartisan nature, the Progressive campaign featured a Democratic vice presidential nominee, Senator Burton Wheeler of Montana, and the endorsement of the Socialist Party.[34]

Villard, as editor of *The Nation* and one of the most powerful reformist voices in the country, served as a top adviser to La Follette, and thus gave Gruening an influential connection to the campaign. His friend recommended his "enthusiastic and energetic" former subordinate as national publicity director. In late August, Gruening decided, in his words, to "cheerfully tell the two old parties to go to the devil" and take the job. Consistent as ever on the issue, Gruening described his "only real function" as accurately disseminating "the facts about Senator La Follette's record, the principles that his career embodies, and the issues this third party campaign represents." The voters would "do the rest."[35]

Despite his title, Gruening played only a marginal role in the campaign. The senator's son, "Young Bob," coordinated his father's day-to-day activities, while La Follette himself retained the ultimate authority. Gruening turned this adversity to advantage by focusing his press releases mostly on the issues which he personally found interesting, such as the dangers of monopoly, especially the power trust, corruption in the Harding-Coolidge administration, the argument that the same principles motivated the formation of the Progressive Party of 1924 and the GOP of the 1850s, and the need to reorient U.S. foreign policy.[36]

More important, the transparently ambitious publicity director used his position to ingratiate himself further among better-known reformers who would play prominent roles at later stages of his career. In early October he received a dinner invitation from his first political hero, Louis Brandeis. Over a feast of ham, he joined John Hobson and the Supreme Court Justice, an old friend and admirer of La Follette's, at Brandeis's home; given the trio's intellectual interests, imperialism likely dominated the conversation. Brandeis's personal and ideological protégé, Felix Frankfurter, also backed La Follette in 1924. Two years earlier, Gruening had recruited the Harvard Law School professor to join the lawyers' committee protesting the occupation of Haiti; they now renewed their acquaintance. The association with Frankfurter would constitute one of the most significant long-term results of Gruening's involvement in the independent effort.[37]

Despite his lack of influence, the publicity manager pushed for investing "a considerable portion of the rather meagre contents of the war chest to reach motion picture audiences," illustrating his belief in the need to find innovative means to reach the public. Revealing a simplistic view of both the malleability and power of public opinion, he informed state campaign managers of his conviction that a general showing of the film would "carry that state, if it is doubtful, and cause an upheaval which may bring victory in a state that now seems hopeless." Gruening also worked to shift the campaign's message, joining a number of other advisers who urged the Wisconsin senator to emphasize international affairs in his stump speeches. As his national support slipped away, La Follette began to focus on foreign policy in general and imperialism in Latin America in particular, an effort that climaxed on October 30 before an enthusiastic crowd of ten thousand at Faneuil Hall in Boston. Although the remarks excited the audience, La Follette's poor showing in the election—he received the electoral votes of only his home state—confirmed Ernest Angell's earlier warning about the lack of public interest in Latin American affairs.[38]

As the Wisconsin senator's impending defeat drew near, Gruening contemplated a strategy to sustain the movement after the election. In a private letter to Young Bob, he termed it "tremendously important . . . not to let the campaign drop for a period of weeks after the election." Otherwise La Follette voters would "in large part be without news, without authoritative information, and dependent for guidance upon a hostile press which has every interest in belittling what has been accomplished." Befitting his usual tendency to mix his political and personal agendas, Gruening seemed to be angling for a permanent publicity post.[39]

But though domestic reform had served as his focus for several months, his unresolved anti-imperialist crusade continued to attract him. In the early stages of the La Follette campaign, Gruening joined Plutarco Calles, then passing through the United States on his way to a European holiday after his election as president of Mexico, in a private interview with Samuel Gompers, head of the American Federation of Labor (AFL). Gruening and the president-elect—recalled by contemporaries as "very close friends" by this point—traveled together to Atlantic City, where the AFL was preparing to endorse La Follette's candidacy. When forced to choose between his domestic and international agendas, Gruening did not hesitate. In late October he received an invitation from Calles to travel with him back to Mexico City and attend his inauguration as his guest. An excited Gruening immediately consented, even though this would mean leaving the La Follette campaign a few days before the election. The choice showed, if unintentionally, that antiimperialism remained the cause about which Gruening cared the most passionately.[40]

Renewing contact with Calles restored some of Gruening's faith in the Mexican political class. The new president went out of his way to solicit Gruening's opinions on the problems confronting his administration, even to the point of offering to pay for Gruening's hotel bill during his stay in Mexico City. Although Gruening declined the offer, noting that it could affect his reputation in the United States as an independent-minded journalist, he did receive permission from Calles to review any government documents that he needed, as well as five secretaries to aid in his research. This assistance made him the only author allowed access to the sensitive files at the Ministry of Government Archives. (As the Hearst newspaper chain's Mexico City bureau chief recalled, such actions "obviously" demonstrated Gruening's "great influence" in Mexico during the 1920s.) Calles's inauguration address, in which the new president promised to sustain Obregón's educational reforms, include the perspective of Indians in Mexican cultural activities, and implement the provisions for agrarian reform and nationalist oil legislation embedded in Article 27 of the constitution, appealed to Gruening's ideological biases. After the inauguration, Gruening remained in Mexico until early February, his desire to complete his manuscript on the revolution rekindled.[41]

This revival of interest in Caribbean affairs extended beyond Mexico. In late February 1925, just after returning to the United States, Gruening appeared before a Senate subcommittee exploring the links between commercial interests and U.S. interventionism in the Caribbean Basin. Denouncing "the connivance of the servants of American big business in the executive and legislative departments of our Government," he was challenged by administration supporter Frank Willis (R–Ohio), who observed that the Haitians had agreed to a treaty compromising their sovereignty, that the Senate had already investigated the matter, and that it "would be rather unnecessary to cover the whole thing again." Gruening retorted that the United States had negotiated the treaty, an "elaborate piece of hypocrisy," with "a pistol pointed at Haiti's head," all in an era of "open covenants, openly arrived at." This slap at one of Wilson's most famous exhortations revealed Gruening's continuing sense of betrayal at Wilson's actions.[42]

Again unsuccessful, however, in reviving public interest in the Haitian occupation, Gruening returned to his manuscript. He traveled to Mexico several times over the next two years to complete his research, although this time his family did not accompany him. Anxious to avoid depleting his inheritance further, in 1926 he formed a partnership with Harvard classmate Frank McLaughlin, the McLaughlin-Gruening Corporation, which matched (for a fee) U.S. investors interested in development projects with influential figures in Mexican politics. For access to his array of Mexican local, state, and national contacts, Gruening received $1,000 per month plus living expenses. The two men had enjoyed warm relations before entering business together. Gruening frequently dined at McLaughlin's Mexico City residence, and used his friendship with Calles to help McLaughlin obtain concessions for his oil company, El Sol. Both sides, he reasoned, profited, since the arrangement allowed the Mexican government to point to El Sol as a U.S. firm willing to comply with Calles's nationalistic oil legislation. The lawyer for anti-Calles Sinclair Oil agreed. He complained that the "machinations" of Gruening—who seemed to have "practically lived at the president's office" throughout the Calles administration—undermined the interests of established U.S. oil companies in Mexico. But McLaughlin, recalled by a contemporary as "a typical promoter," wanted assistance from Gruening in all financial ventures, not merely those that forwarded an anti-imperialist agenda. This difference of opinion dissolved the partnership after less than a year. As at *The Nation*, for Gruening, furthering his anti-imperialist agenda assumed priority, even at his own financial expense.[43]

WHILE GRUENING'S venture with McLaughlin was collapsing, Dorothy and the three boys spent a year living at the summer home in Rockport, where both Hunt and Sonny attended public school. Dissatisfied with the quality of their education, and alarmed by the fact that both had picked up a habit of cursing from their classmates, Gruening decided to imitate his father's approach and send his family to Europe for an extended stay. Both Sonny and Hunt initially enrolled in a French school in Paris. Gruening joined the family briefly in the summer of 1926, when they traveled to Italy, Germany, and the south of France. The visit allowed for a family reunion; after World War I, May had left the United States to live in Switzerland, while Martha had followed a host of disaffected U.S. intellectuals to Paris, where she was earning a living as a freelance writer. Gruening also encouraged both boys' interest in reading, especially the classics: a particular favorite was Richard Harding Davis's *In the Fog*, a tale, appropriately, about a disarmament lobbyist who failed to persuade a prominent member of Parliament to oppose the government's naval increase bill. Although Sonny took more to his father's demands than did Hunt, both boys were well versed in European culture and literature by the time they returned to the United States in 1927.[44]

Gruening looked to provide his sons with what he considered the best of his own childhood in other ways, as in the minimal role that religion played in their upbringing. Dorothy, a Unitarian, occasionally dragged the family to services on Easter or Christmas, but Gruening gave his children the opportunity of choosing not to believe if they so desired. Making sure that they knew his opinion on the question, he assured them that attending church did not make a good citizen; treating others as they would wish to be treated themselves had far more importance. If anything, Gruening's own distaste for religion had grown more pronounced. His hostility to the Mexican Catholic Church, which in 1926 openly revolted against the Calles regime, reinforced his belief in the fundamental hypocrisy of organized religion. In private he parodied the sermons of Mexican priests, whom he considered oblivious to the social and economic plight of their parishioners. Moreover, as with many agnostics, the suffering he witnessed in Haiti and Mexico left him wondering why "so much misery in the world" existed "if God is so great and all powerful."[45]

After the brief sojourn in Europe, more than the need to complete his book drew Gruening's attention back to Mexico. Relations between Washington and Mexico City had again deteriorated. As part of his campaign to implement Article 27, Calles had overseen the enactment of nationalistic land and oil laws which threatened U.S. economic interests in the country. Meanwhile, personnel changes had only worsened the situation. The new U.S. secretary of state, former Minnesota senator Frank Kellogg, was ill suited by temperament and ideology for dealing with Latin American nationalism, while the conduct of the new ambassador to Mexico, James Sheffield, a man with extensive contacts among U.S. oil interests and a deeply racist view of Mexico, only heightened tensions. By late 1926, there was widespread speculation that the United States might sever diplomatic ties with the Calles regime, perhaps paving the way for either an outright military intervention or a U.S. policy of supplying arms to Calles's domestic opponents.[46]

Although he was ostensibly wrapped up in completing his manuscript, Gruening took time to rebuke Sheffield publicly for his inability "to accomplish anything through the arts of diplomacy." Privately he worked for an alternative policy by inviting prominent Mexicans, such as Secretary of Industry Luis Morones, widely perceived as the most radical figure in the Mexican cabinet, to small meetings with friendly journalists and other anti-imperialist activists, often at the New York City Harvard Club. Such activities did not go unnoticed by those with a different perspective on the dispute between the two countries. One visit to Mexico produced a *New York Times* headline asserting that Gruening had gone off to Mexico City to "consult with the Mexican government." (He quickly issued a public denial, ridiculously comparing his ties with Calles to "the relationship of any writer or student of affairs who desires information on the political, economic, and social problems of a culture.") The State Department, meanwhile, wanted this "radical and professional propagandist . . . watched carefully" in the hopes of obtaining some "definite proof" that he was in the pay of the Mexican government; Gruening's vigilance in avoiding such support was thus well founded. Sheffield, who considered it a "moral certainty" that Gruening was the key figure in a multimillion-dollar Mexican propaganda program, needed no further encouragement. The ambassador, who forbade the embassy staff any personal contact with U.S. anti-imperialists, urged his consuls to locate damaging information on Gruening, whom he identified as one third of "a Jewish radical trinity which has been active in Mexico in recent years."[47]

The administration underestimated the adverse public reaction which its policies would produce. A broad-based effort to avert war spearheaded by the National Council for Prevention of War (NCPW), a clearinghouse committee of the 1920s peace movement, and left-wing opinion journals such as *The Nation* and the *New Republic* swung into action against Kellogg's policies. This crusade brought Gruening into contact with a man whose career frequently would intersect with Gruening's over the next four decades: Walter Lippmann. Their journeys before this meeting showed uncanny parallels. Like Gruening a product of the New York City German-Jewish elite, Lippmann attended both Sachs and Harvard, where he was three years behind

Gruening. Unlike Gruening, however, he compiled a brilliant academic record at both institutions. After briefly dabbling in socialism, he helped mold the *New Republic* into a voice of progressive reform, entered government service, and played a key role in the Inquiry, which Wilson charged with the thankless task of applying his principle of self-determination to the boundaries for postwar Europe. Wilson's wartime performance disappointed Lippmann, and he broke with the president over the Treaty of Versailles. After the war, Lippmann followed Gruening into the world of metropolitan journalism, assuming the editorship of the *New York World.* Here, however, the careers of the two men diverged. Lippmann's retreat from Wilsonianism entailed not a rededication to idealism but the articulation of a Realpolitik vision for the United States internationally and a deep distrust of the excesses of democracy at home. Nonetheless, both men similarly critiqued Kellogg's diplomacy, which Lippmann contended made the right of property "superior under international law to the right of sovereignty."[48]

The Mexican crisis also mobilized a group of religious activists who aimed at reorienting hemispheric diplomacy along cultural lines. One such figure was Samuel Guy Inman, whom Gruening had encountered during his bid to reestablish the Anti-Imperialist League in 1924. More prominent was a new organization Gruening later hailed as the decade's "most useful and vital project in promoting international relations, especially inter-American relations," the Committee on Cultural Relations with Latin America (CCRLA). Founded by Congregationalist missionary Hubert Herring, the CCRLA promoted inter-American cultural understanding through annual "seminars" in which participants selected for their ability "to exert wide influence on American public opinion" were guided through Mexico by Herring and various "lecturers" who spoke on Mexican cultural, political, and economic matters, as well as U.S.-Mexican relations.[49]

The first of Herring's missions, for which Gruening served as a lecturer, provided a clear illustration of the potential power of the cross-national alliances which Gruening had championed since early in the decade. Arriving in Mexico at the height of the oil controversy in late 1926, the group received an audience with Calles, at which he publicly agreed to arbitrate the dispute with the United States. The Mexican president obviously was looking for a favorable opportunity to indicate the acceptability of a negotiated solution, and his concession allowed administration opponents to embrace arbitration as a way out of the crisis. The effectiveness of the CCRLA was in part indicated by the fury that it aroused. Kellogg complained that the "cranks" who belonged to the group "are *never* in favor of their own country," while Sheffield barked that the "goddam goodwillers" seemed to "care more for the interests of other countries and other peoples than their own."[50]

In part as a result of this public outrage, the Senate in early 1927 passed a measure offered by Joseph Robinson (D–Arkansas) requesting that the two sides arbitrate their differences, which ended any possibility for forceful U.S. action against Mexico. The anti-imperialist coalition's victory was confirmed when the administration recalled Sheffield in the summer. Reflecting on his mission, the former ambassador complained that the State Department had ignored his recommendations for a forceful policy because of an "unholy fear" of war. He believed that the department shared his basic premises that "the carrying on of foreign affairs is distinctly the province of the Executive Branch" and that the key issue in the Mexican-American dispute was "the establishment of a rule of conduct toward property rights which should govern all cases." Yet he also painted Kellogg as a man too timid to confront a strongly anti-interventionist public. Sheffield had learned precisely the lesson that Gruening had so longed to teach: on foreign policy issues "we are governed in America by public opinion."[51]

Despite the resolution of the diplomatic dispute, Gruening's favorable opinion of the Calles government continued to involve him in controversy. In November, several newspapers in the Hearst chain published articles alleging that in February 1924, Calles had paid Gruening $10,000 to embark on a secret mission to study a strike by coal miners in England, with the hope that Mexico could team with the striking miners on behalf of a worldwide revolution. In addition, the documents claimed that several leading peace-progressive critics of Kellogg's policy had received payments from the Mexican government. A Senate committee quickly established that the documents justifying the charges were forgeries, but this result did not satisfy Gruening. Concerned that if he did not challenge the attack personally, Hearst's claims could sully his personal reputation and weaken his ability to influence the public, he filed a $500,000 libel suit. Gruening later boasted that he "made himself independently wealthy for life by suing and collecting from every Hearst newspaper." In fact, Hearst settled out of court for

$75,000, of which Gruening received only $25,000 after lawyers' fees. Despite his exaggerations, the money obtained from the lawsuit, in combination with his inheritance, kept the family afloat financially throughout the 1920s; Gruening's occasional freelance articles, for which he generally received one cent per word, brought in little cash.[52]

The Hearst charges capped off for Gruening yet another disappointing period in U.S.-Mexican relations. Elated over Sheffield's recall, he was plunged again into gloom when Kellogg selected as Sheffield's replacement Dwight Morrow, an associate of Lamont in the J. P. Morgan investment firm. Although the appointment received plaudits from Borah, Villard, and Lippmann, it "grieved" Gruening. Typically making a reflexive assessment based on superficial appearances, he fumed that "the only thing" favoring Morrow's selection "is that it is frankly 100% dollar diplomacy and that frankness is always preferable to hypocrisy." He feared that Kellogg had confirmed that "the financial aspect of our relations with Mexico is the only one Washington sees." (Many of the anti-imperialist's allies in Mexico agreed; one Mexican newspaper predicted that "after Morrow come the marines.") Gruening himself had recommended as Sheffield's replacement Governor George Hunt (D–Arizona), a man "who knows Mexicans, understands them, and has some sympathy with their problems." In the event, neither his opposition, nor that of several peace progressives, prevented Morrow's overwhelming confirmation. Discouraged, Gruening even began to neglect his freelance writing. From his self-imposed exile on Rockport's "stern and mussel-bound coast," he lamented that U.S. policy seemed hopeless, while the scrambling to succeed Calles indicated that "politics is on an even lower plane in Mexico than in the United States." Perhaps the fight had not been worth the effort after all.[53]

Burdened with this ambivalent mindset, Gruening finally completed his manuscript. *Mexico and Its Heritage* emerged as a passionate defense of the revolution, which Gruening hailed for allowing the Mexicans to redress the ills afflicting their society. Earlier, more moderate attempts could not overcome the entrenched forces of conservatism inherited from three centuries of Spanish colonial rule: the church, the military, and the unequal distribution of land. Reflecting his own biases against organized religion, Gruening described the Mexican Catholic Church as inherently reactionary, determined to frustrate all attempts to drive it from its privileged political and economic position. It received assistance in this effort, he said, from the Mexican military, an institution addicted to "treason" and desirous only of obtaining patronage for leading generals. The agrarian policies of the Díaz regime, by favoring large landowners and foreign interests, only compounded the problem by driving peasants from their land. In such a situation, Gruening considered it perfectly reasonable for these newly landless peasants to embrace revolution; indeed, "Mexico's history and present problems are of one piece."[54]

Gruening also defended the specific character of the revolution which had occurred. Despite provocations from the traditional enemies of Mexican reform, both domestic and international, revolutionary policies had remained "relatively moderate," owing to the efforts of Obregón and Calles—"men of the middle class"—to provide intellectual, military, and political leadership. Meanwhile, the educational reforms of Vasconcelos represented the "first monument to the birth of a new order." Despite these positive trends, however, the revolution remained under siege. The church's recalcitrance forced the Mexican leadership to adopt anticlerical laws. Gruening found it ironic that the Mexican clergy could complain "against the recent restrictions laid on their cult," given their earlier tendency to squelch their opponents. Yet their efforts confirmed the danger that the revolution might be undone from within. The de la Huerta rebellion provided only the most spectacular demonstration of the continued corruption of the Mexican political class. Lower-level bureaucrats remained all too willing to place personal gain over principle; corruption in the implementation of the agrarian program was particularly troublesome. These shortcomings left the administration's reform efforts incomplete and the Mexican economy in shaky condition, thus sustaining the possibility of a successful counterrevolution. Even high-level officials, such as Gruening's one-time patron Luis Morones, were not immune. By 1928, he noted, the idealism which Morones had demonstrated as a labor leader during the 1910s and early 1920s had waned. In part, Gruening admitted, "his new responsibilities had the invariably sobering effect that comes after the transition from agitator to administrator." But such an explanation alone did not account for Morones's transformation. A combination of greed and ambition had led Morones to engage in unforgivable abuses of power, such as using his influence over the relevant unions to exercise a de facto censorship power over the Mexican press.

Gruening's attack on Morones offered an insight into his view of the nature of leadership. On the one hand, Morones exemplified the danger of sacrificing principle in the name of personal or political expediency. Yet the international history of the revolution also provided examples of the opposite extreme: Wilson and Carranza. Probably no other president in U.S. history, said Gruening, had ever resisted more pressure for intervention in Mexico than Wilson; but Carranza, fearful that acknowledging assistance from the United States would compromise Mexican nationalism, had shown no gratitude. Carranza, meanwhile, deserved praise for his initiatives to lessen the influence of foreign economic interests and redefine the international relations of the Caribbean Basin; but Wilson had too frequently opposed these efforts, because the president refused to consider the merits of any foreign policy vision other than his own. In a perceptive observation, Gruening paired Wilson and Carranza as presidents who clung so much to their ideological commitments that they undermined their political effectiveness. If Morones, Wilson, and Carranza demonstrated the shortcomings of leadership, Obregón and Calles served as positive models. (Gruening praised in particular the performance of his friend and mentor Calles; he privately admitted that the book's occasional criticisms of Calles were included "in order not to have the picture unfairly favorable" and thus subject the work to attack for bias.)[55] In fact, *Mexico and Its Heritage* painted Calles as the ideal leader—committed to a sweeping reform program and yet practical enough to make the necessary concessions to translate his ideas into reality.

What, then, of the future of the revolution? As Gruening contended, "to that question any study of Mexico ultimately leads." In his view, agrarian reform remained the key, with "implications far beyond the economic." Its success would transform Mexico by giving peasants the title to land, thus laying the "foundations of a citizenry." Eventually thereafter would emerge a "democracy, not precisely like the varying imperfect democracies of the world, but one increasingly shaped by and adapted to the needs of the Mexican people." Reformers in the United States could play a role in this process, first, by preventing U.S. intervention in support of counterrevolution. In this regard, the outcome of the recent diplomatic crisis, in which a mobilized public had blocked Kellogg's "blustering" policies, offered hope. Such a negative program, however, would not suffice. To succeed, agrarian reform would take time, and the forces of reaction in Mexico remained strong. An "enlightened" American policy would aid Mexican reformers in bringing about a stable, prosperous, and enlightened neighbor. The United States and Mexico, then, should unite on a policy of building up a "progressing, flourishing, and happy Mexico—as Mexico defines progress, fluorescence, and happiness—and with only such suggestions and help from the United States as will obviously be acceptable." Though extraordinarily vague, this suggestion represented the first articulation of the ideological framework which would guide Gruening's perspective on Caribbean affairs for the next decade.

Thus stood Gruening's testament to the Mexican Revolution. In retrospect, he fundamentally misjudged Calles, who more accurately resembled Gruening's description of Morones. On the personal front, Beals's more nuanced interpretation of the Mexican leader came closer to reality, while Frank Tannenbaum correctly observed in the *New Republic* that Calles's land reform program was far more limited than rhetoric would suggest. Other parts of Gruening's analysis, however, exhibited much more sophistication, especially his understanding of how Mexico's history made a U.S.-style democracy an inappropriate vehicle for enacting meaningful reform. His efforts to establish the link between agrarian reform and the creation of a civil society not only would guide his policies over much of the next several years but also offered a sensitive interpretation of a culture with fundamentally different features from those of his own.

Much to Gruening's surprise, the book attracted widespread praise in the United States. William Richardson, vice president of the National City Bank of New York, Gruening's bête noire from the Haitian occupation, commended the book as the finest yet published on Mexican history and politics, "completely truthful and frank." Wilson's secretary of the navy, Josephus Daniels, declared that Gruening had captured the essence of Mexican history and politics "better than any other American," while George Ochs-Oakes, publisher of the *New York Times* and a supporter of Kellogg's policies in the Caribbean, admitted that *Mexico and Its Heritage* established Gruening as one of the country's leading experts on Mexico. The review in Ochs's paper contended that mastering the work would place the reader in a "position to talk and write intelligently about the Government, people, and future of the country." Understanding Gruening's motives, Carleton Beals hailed it as "a book for the student and the statesman." Frank Tannenbaum likewise commended his friend's "great achievement."[56] *Mexico and Its Heritage* thus established Gruening's credentials not only as an anti-imperialist intellectual but also as a nonpartisan expert on Caribbean Basin affairs. In his own way, then, like Calles and Obregón, Gruening had maintained his ideals while simultaneously achieving practical influence.

~ 3

The Dilemmas of Progressivism

IN THE SUMMER OF 1927, Gruening settled with his family in Rockport to complete the Mexican manuscript. After his experience at the *Tribune*, he had vowed not to return to daily journalism. But then Maine politics intervened. Phil Chapman, a law partner of Governor Ralph Brewster, asked C. Harry Tobey, a contemporary of Gruening's in Boston, to recommend a progressive editor for a newspaper to compete with Portland's three papers—the *Press-Herald*, the evening *Express*, and the *Sunday Maine Telegram*—all of which were controlled by Guy Gannett, a political foe of Brewster's. Tobey recommended Gruening. Although Chapman promised editorial freedom, Gruening still hesitated, but finally decided that after his well-publicized complaints about the state of journalism, he could not refuse a chance to translate his ideals into practice. With an exaggerated sense of self-importance, he confided to Villard that "if the tide of consolidation can be reversed in one city—of the size of Portland—it will serve as an example in scores of other cities." Accordingly, in September he was off to christen the *Portland Evening News*.[1]

The turbulent nature of politics in the Pine Tree State dated from the Roosevelt-Taft contest in 1912, which had divided Maine Republicans. At the state level, a mildly progressive faction had triumphed with the election of Governor Percival Baxter in 1920; Brewster's triumph four years later strengthened the bloc's position. At the same time, however, conservative forces associated with the state's senior senator, Frederick Hale, remained vibrant. The two sides disagreed on a host of economic issues, notably whether to repeal the Fernald Law, which prohibited the export of Maine's water power beyond state lines. Conservatives argued that repeal would improve the state's economic well-being; progressives worried that it would allow utility companies to sidestep state regulation. When Gruening arrived, the two factions were gearing up for the 1928 GOP Senate primary, with Brewster planning to challenge Hale to resolve once and for all the party's ideological direction.[2]

Gruening initially did not consider Portland, with its "deeply rooted" conservatism, particularly appealing. Prominent city residents reciprocated the feeling. A whispering campaign accompanied his arrival: because of his association with *The Nation* and the La Follette campaign, rumors abounded that he would run a socialist newspaper, an obvious problem in a city where, as he observed, "if one wishes to praise a man highly and indicate that he is a forthright and upstanding citizen, one says he is a Rotarian." Portland's prohibitionist sentiments compounded Gruening's sense of isolation. Complaining that "the hooch one gets up here is of wretched quality," he quickly discovered that maintaining his "Mexican contacts will be essential to life, liberty, and the pursuit of liquor." This perception of Portland affected his tactical approach at the *Evening News*. In a sign of his maturation as an activist, Gruening confided that he needed to "start slowly and not offend prejudices too suddenly, else they will suspect me of being a bad fellow and reject all the good advice I may proffer." Nonetheless, he promised to make the *Evening News* "the most progressive and intelligent paper in the state," even if in doing so he had to shake "up this community a bit."[3]

In fact, Gruening's combative nature immediately involved the *Evening News* in political controversy when the inaugural issue of the paper criticized a referendum sponsored by GOP conservatives to replace Maine's open primary, a key reform from the Progressive era, with a system allowing the parties to nominate their candidates through state conventions. Hale's supporters correctly reasoned that the measure would enhance the senator's chances of withstanding Brewster's challenge, but Gruening charged that its passage would make public officials responsible only to the party operatives who controlled the conventions. When the referendum fell short by an almost two-to-one margin, he privately boasted that the *Evening News* deserved "a considerable share of the credit." Chapman likewise was pleased: the outcome confirmed the wisdom of his decision to hire Gruening.[4]

The victory only whetted Gruening's desire for political influence, even at the cost of trimming his ideological agenda. Less than a month later, his *Evening News* endorsed Herbert Hoover as the "logical candidate" for the Republican presidential nomination, even though the paths of the two men had diverged sharply in the years following Harding's election: while Gruening embraced anti-imperialism abroad and a radical version of progressivism at home, Hoover had transformed the Commerce Department into a vehicle to promote American business both domestically and abroad. Touting Hoover as the "logical" choice for progressives, then, represented a far more difficult challenge in 1928 than eight years earlier. To make the effort, Gruening focused on Hoover's work during World War I, which, in contrast to that of Wilson, he wrote, "incarnated the practical idealism expressed through deeds." From New York City, Villard expressed horror when he heard about the endorsement. Gruening responded testily. He admitted his preference for the likes of Borah or George Norris (R–Nebraska), but maintained that Hoover was the most attractive possible nominee. In addition, Gruening linked the fight to the Senate primary between Brewster and Hale, contending that swinging the Maine Republican delegation, which had favored Leonard Wood in 1920, to Hoover represented a critical step in ensuring the triumph of progressives within the state GOP.[5]

But, of course, tactical reasons alone did not explain Gruening's actions. The commerce secretary exemplified his ideal of a figure committed to finding nonpolitical solutions to political problems; support for Hoover thus avoided the reformers' dilemma of whether to risk strengthening the national government. For example, the editor contended that Hoover's principles of efficiency could help end industrial joblessness; likewise they could achieve greater scientific progress, along with other aspects of his traditional agenda, such as open government. Gruening hoped that radio would allow candidates to discuss important issues rationally, thus creating campaigns which would supply the people with the facts they needed to make an intelligent political choice. (As he eventually would concede, Gruening fundamentally misread how technological advances would affect elections.) Gruening's flirtation with efficiency also brought him into contact with issues previously outside the scope of his interest, such as the campaign for a city manager form of government, which, building on biases apparent since his support for Seth Low, he touted as resolving civic problems "on a non-partisan and non-political basis, exactly as big engineering problems are worked out." This support for a "scientific" approach to local government appeared in more quixotic ventures as well, such as his campaign for Portland to absorb surrounding towns and cities, on the grounds that "size brings other benefits." Residents of the area's smaller towns, such as Scarborough, a scenic spot on the Atlantic coast just south of Portland, understandably balked at the idea, doubting that a "greater Portland" would protect their own particular interests.[6]

Gruening's pro-efficiency outlook hardly crowded out all elements of his old ideological agenda. Indeed, the controversy that defined Gruening's tenure in Portland centered on the question of regulating public utilities and sharpened his anti-monopoly outlook. The issue, which had long attracted the attention of progressives, assumed a new immediacy in the postwar era owing to the development of public utility holding companies. By 1929, sixteen holding companies controlled 92 percent of the country's private electric production, a situation which, as the historian Morton Keller has noted, reenacted "the classic morality play of antitrust." No one better played the villain in the contest than Samuel Insull, chairman of the board of at least sixty-five companies, including the dominant utility interest in Maine, Central Maine Power. But reformers struggled to come up with a coherent response to the problem. Although nearly all expressed support for increased regulation, some hoped that regulatory agencies would represent the popular will and remain subservient to progressives within the government, especially the legislative branch; others envisioned that regulation give the government greater flexibility and sophistication in dealing with industry. U.S. regulatory agencies obviously failed to live up to either ideal, and Gruening would struggle with the consequences throughout his career.[7]

In the short term, however, Gruening confronted the political ramifications of the power question, which he predicted would "supersede all other issues" and would realign the political parties along pro-consumer and pro-industry lines. Starting a reform newspaper in a hostile environment would have consumed a tremendous amount of time anyway, even for one who regularly placed his ideological crusades above his personal and financial well-being. Now, with the newspaper's fate tied up with Gruening's newest ideological crusade, the *Evening News* became his life. He insisted on writing all of the paper's editorials himself; on the rare occasions when he departed Maine, he left behind columns written in advance on generic topics such as citizenship or Portland development issues.[8]

This inability to delegate authority would haunt Gruening when he entered government service; in Maine it meant that he had even less time for his family than previously. His wife continued to carry the responsibility for rearing the three sons whom Gruening scarcely saw. Dorothy generally had the boys fed and in their pajamas by the time Gruening returned home from the office; husband and wife then dined alone. On the rare occasions when Ernest did eat with his sons, he remained absorbed in the professional world, discussing the political affairs of the day with Dorothy. He made little attempt to include Sonny and Hunt in the conversations, even though both were in their early teens. Instead, he would spend what he termed "red letter days" with the boys, parceling out a day every other month or so when he and his sons went swimming or climbed Mount Katahdin. Gruening, an avid hiker who loved the outdoors in general and swimming in particular, at least included Sonny, Hunt, and (sometimes) Peter in these activities.[9]

Meanwhile, the family's financial situation continued to deteriorate. Upon his arrival in Maine, Gruening purchased half of a three-story brick duplex on Storer Street, in the city's most exclusive neighborhood, the Western Promenade. His salary from the *Evening News* offered barely enough to get by; Gruening relied on contributions from his "financial angel," Phil Chapman, simply to keep the paper afloat. Nor did Dorothy help the situation. Perhaps as compensation for her husband's single-minded pursuit of his career and interests, she insisted on the need for live-in servants to maintain the house and to cook. Moreover, she regularly oversaw the preparation of elaborate four-course meals even when the couple did not entertain socially. The food for these meals would be delivered; Dorothy did not shop for groceries. Although Gruening occasionally complained that the family could not afford this lifestyle, he rarely pressed the issue; when he did, his wife breezily responded, "Well, Ernest, you'll just have to sell another bond."[10]

To rectify the problem, Gruening decided to act boldly. As with so many other Americans during the 1920s, the editor invested in the bull stock market, never detecting a contradiction between his personal participation in the investment frenzy and his criticism of the era's materialistic excesses. Shortly after arriving in Maine, he invested his remaining inheritance, along with the $25,000 which he retained from his successful settlement of the suit against Hearst. His broker, Hayden Stone, suggested several attractive stocks, guaranteeing that they would continue to rise. For a while they did, giving Gruening a reliable source of income for the first time since the early 1920s.[11]

Gruening fully expected his crusades in Maine to justify his personal and financial sacrifices. He achieved the first step when the state's GOP delegation committed to Hoover, although this move owed more to the decision of the well-respected Baxter to head Hoover's local organization. The editor, however, expected that the result would serve as a precursor for a successful bid by Brewster, and he threw himself into the campaign with all the effort he could muster. Gruening painted Hale as "the ideal rubber stamp for the [utility] interests," citing his votes to seat William Vare and Frank Smith in the Senate despite charges of corruption in their campaigns. He assailed the incumbent for using his chairmanship of the Naval Affairs Committee to champion increased naval spending and interventionism in the Caribbean Basin. But the question of utilities and their regulation—not corruption or foreign policy questions—dominated the campaign. Gruening privately commented that he could not recall an electoral contest "where the issues were more clearly cut between what we may roughly designate as the predatory forces and the people's interests." The "predatory forces," the state's private utility concerns, backed Hale to exact retribution against Brewster for opposing their plan to overturn the Fernald Law and allow the export of Maine power.[12]

The senior senator aggressively retaliated. He rallied support from the state's Republican leadership, garnering an endorsement from Baxter as well as from twenty-nine of the thirty-two members of the state's GOP committee, while stressing the value of his seniority for a state which received extensive naval contracts. Confident in his position, the incumbent spent the spring in Washington—attending, he said, to pressing senatorial duties—and did not return to the state until June 8, just over a week before the primary. Hale's arrival in Maine, however, did demonstrate the extent to which Gruening's charges set the agenda of the campaign. The senator denied that he had been soft on political corruption, and termed the suggestion that he was a "tool" of the Insull interests "too absurd to warrant any comment." Then, turning the tables, the Hale forces launched an attack against Gruening. Hale's campaign manager, Daniel Field, classified Brewster with the "La Follette group of radicals" in the Senate, citing "the fact that the editor of the paper generally called the Brewster mouthpiece" had worked for La Follette in 1924. Field mused that perhaps "the National group of radicals, who are now attempting to secure control of the government," sent "this radical editor, . . . this man of mystery," to confuse Maine voters into supporting Brewster. Brewster's forces responded clumsily. To ensure wider circulation of Gruening's editorials, Chapman had purchased copies of the *Evening News* in bulk and distributed them at no cost in rural parts of the state, where Brewster needed a large vote. The move backfired. Field hinted that the funds for the mass purchase came from Brewster's official state funds. Gruening's rival the *Press-Herald* described the event as Maine's equivalent of the Teapot Dome scandal. To his horror, Gruening himself had emerged as a major issue in the campaign, to Hale's benefit.[13]

The political fireworks generated a record primary turnout. But, contrary to Gruening's hopes, Hale trounced his rival by a margin of 82,874 to 46,940. The defeat for the progressives was complete: with Brewster's departure from the governorship, conservative William Tudor Gardiner captured the nomination for that office. In retrospect, the result should not have been a surprise. Maine remained a fundamentally conservative state, with reformers triumphing only when conservative forces divided among themselves or when they offered a candidate who could appeal to conservatives. Neither of these conditions applied in Brewster's challenge to Hale. Gruening, however, having anticipated victory, now lashed out at Pine Tree State voters who seemed oblivious to the importance of the contest. Disheartened "that the people themselves do not realize where their interests lie," the editor privately complained that Hale's triumph proved that "the human race loves its bondage." For Gruening, open government remained a commendable ideal only so long as the results went his way—a position that would set a pattern for the future.[14]

Gruening, nonetheless, had no intention of giving up the fight. But with Hale's election all but guaranteed, electing a national administration friendly to reform represented the only chance for Maine progressives to overturn the disastrous primary result. The editor thus looked to use his support for Hoover to alter the balance of power within the state GOP. He joined the Hoover Republican Club of Maine, but being only one of the hundred most prominent Hoover supporters in the state hardly served Gruening's interests. Accordingly, he used his contacts from the 1920 campaign to appeal to the candidate himself. In September he wrote Hoover to ask for a meeting to discuss campaign matters "in view of the obvious efforts of Democrats to capture the La Follette vote." (In fact, Al Smith, the Democratic nominee, was wooing former third party supporters by highlighting two issues with which Gruening was intimately associated—utilities regulation and U.S. interventionism in the Caribbean Basin.) The national campaign staff, acknowledging the editor's status as a "staunch" Hoover supporter, recommended that Hoover "accept his judgment" if Gruening considered it "important" that he speak with the nominee. Accordingly, on October 2, the editor traveled to Washington for a lunch meeting with the commerce secretary.[15]

Gruening's mission served a double purpose. First of all, he believed that he could offer useful advice on how to appeal to the type of voter that he personified. More important, the editor hoped that Hoover would adopt a position on power regulation that would assist progressives in Maine. On meeting Hoover, Gruening presented a plan to attract "a considerable portion of the still definitely unattached progressive voters by a vigorous pronouncement on the power question." He suggested a two-pronged statement which "would electrify [no pun, apparently, intended] millions." First, Gruening urged Hoover to announce his belief in the "clear duty of the government, federal or state, to use its regulatory powers" in the most effective way "to protect the people from the abuse of monopoly." Second, Gruening recommended issuing a direct attack on the "intolerable" attempts by private utility companies to use their financial strength to influence public opinion. He concluded by expressing his confidence that the two men shared similar sentiments on the issue of power regulation and the threat posed by monopoly to the American economy.[16]

Hoover undoubtedly listened to this scheme in a state of disbelief. Although he rhetorically favored regulating private utilities to counteract the possible "security of monopoly" and defended the superiority of state regulation to regulation by federal government, beyond these superficial similarities the agendas of Hoover and Gruening contrasted markedly. Gruening opposed increasing the power of federal regulatory bodies because he believed that the pro-business political climate of 1920s America would allow the forces of monopoly to capture them. Reformers thus stood a better chance when appealing to state regulatory agencies. Effective regulation of monopoly, not abstract constitutional concerns, formed the critical goal. For Hoover, however, the issue of federalism was vital: he feared the centralizing effects of federal regulation. On a host of other issues as well, he departed from Gruening's perspective. Hoover endorsed both increased regulation of municipally owned power plants and the free flow of power across state boundaries. He also defended the concept of holding companies, scorned government development of power as socialistic, and strongly opposed a scheme particularly dear to the hearts of progressives around the country—George Norris's plan for a government-run power facility at Muscle Shoals, Alabama. In the contest between the ideals of efficiency and anti-monopoly, the secretary of commerce had little difficulty in making a clear-cut choice.[17]

Gruening, having once again allowed his personal admiration for a figure of authority to cloud his political judgment, returned from Washington disappointed. Although he still hoped that Hoover would eventually embrace his point of view, he understood the ramifications of the meeting clearly enough to resume his outspoken support for more effective regulation during the final weeks of the campaign. In a series of perceptive editorials, he again questioned the efficacy of federal regulation. The Federal Trade Commission (FTC), Brandeis's great hope from the 1910s, and the body charged with regulating power companies, was now "packed in the interest of the great combinations of business." Congressional conservatives, as it turned out, agreed, sidetracking a bill introduced by Senator Thomas Walsh (D–Montana) urging a congressional inquiry into the prevalence of monopoly in the utility industry with a measure mandating an FTC inquiry instead. If the administrative arm of the executive branch was hostile, the political arm was even more so, a fact confirmed by the admission of Vice President Charles Dawes that he had a financial stake in several private power companies. Electing a president committed to reform on the power issue could correct these abuses, Gruening believed. In the interim, though, state public utility commissions needed to cease functioning as judicial organizations, in which the "humble citizen" had little chance, with the government being neutral and the power companies "represented by a bristling array of the ablest and highest paid legal talent in the state." Instead, he urged, the Public Utilities Commission (PUC) should act as "an investigating, searching, initiating 'people's defender' kind of body."[18]

In November, Hoover overwhelmed Al Smith, but the result hardly reversed the effects of the June primary for Maine's progressives. The editor, however, did not abandon his effort to use his national contacts for local advantage: if he could not persuade the president-elect on power regulation, then perhaps Hoover could be pressed to indicate his preference for the progressive wing of the Maine GOP in another fashion. Accordingly, Gruening dropped Hoover a note recommending that he appoint Ralph Brewster attorney general, noting that Brewster, who had always enjoyed the "unflinching support" of dry forces in Maine, was "thoroughly in sympathy" with Hoover's announced commitment to prohibition. More important (from Gruening's point of view), Brewster would bring to the office "an enthusiasm and idealism" from which any administration would profit. This effort succeeded no more than had Gruening's quixotic bid to convert America's most prominent corporatist into an anti-monopoly activist. Brewster's only letter of endorsement for any position within the new administration did not even generate an acknowledgment. In fact, the president-elect privately considered Brewster "a little 'pink.'"[19]

IRONICALLY IN LIGHT OF the prominence that domestic issues played in his decision to support Hoover, the months after the election found Gruening praising more the president-elect's positions on foreign affairs. After his victory, Hoover toured Latin America, a move widely interpreted as indicative of a desire to move beyond the tense state of inter-American relations typical of the Coolidge administration. Hoover also sided with the peace movement on two issues of critical importance, supporting the Kellogg-Briand Pact to outlaw war and opposing the so-called "time limit" provision of the pending naval bill, sponsored by Gruening's nemesis Frederick Hale and designed to limit presidential discretion to barter (unbuilt) cruisers in exchange for disarmament concessions from the world's other major naval powers, England and Japan. Gruening celebrated the moves. He hoped that Hoover's trip would signal a new era in inter-American relations, a development made all the more crucial by political changes within the nations of the Caribbean Basin. In Mexico, the standing of the groups with whom Gruening was allied throughout the 1920s weakened noticeably after a Catholic extremist assassinated Obregón in 1928. As Mexico drifted to the right, Gruening lamented that even *Mexico and Its Heritage* was under attack in Mexico City. He remained committed to the principle of cross-national alliances which he had outlined during the 1920s, when he hoped that the actions of reformers in the Caribbean Basin could assist anti-imperialist forces in the United States. Now, however, with Caribbean reformers the beleaguered party, U.S. anti-imperialists needed to marshal the forces of their government on behalf of reform in the region.[20]

The scope of this new program became apparent as an outgrowth of Gruening's pleasant surprise with the performance of Dwight Morrow in Mexico. Imitating the approach of Thomas Lamont, Morrow went out of his way to show Calles the courtesy which Sheffield had denied, and quickly worked out a modus vivendi with Calles allowing Mexico to maintain the principle of national control while not affecting those U.S. oil interests already holding concessions in the country. These initiatives, which cooled U.S.-Mexican tensions, caused Gruening to overcome his doubts about the selection of Morrow, and the two men developed a surprisingly close relationship. The ambassador commended *Mexico and Its Heritage* as the most nuanced interpretation of Mexican affairs offered in the United States, and he invited Gruening to join him at his vacation home in nearby North Haven, Maine. The editor, meanwhile, recommended a positive and "sympathetic" U.S. role to assist Mexican reform, specifically by striking out against the "menace of militarism" in Mexican politics. Gruening urged Morrow to use his ties to Calles to lobby for replacing the Mexican army, "the nation's supreme menace," with a constabulary. Anticipating one of Morrow's objections, Gruening argued that such a démarche would fall within the scope of Morrow's functions as ambassador. Since Mexico could not "lose by applying radical reform to the army," U.S. aid in achieving the goal would promote more harmonious relations between the two nations by facilitating political stability and economic development. Morrow countered that Gruening might have succeeded more in identifying the problem than in offering a realistic solution, but the editor stressed the psychological value of the move, noting that with "world peace, the abolition of war, [and] the substitution of arbitration . . . in the air," Mexico as a "signatory of the Pact of Paris could consistently abolish its Army," taking advantage of the "fluid" international and domestic situation to strike a blow at the traditional Latin American "disease" of exalting the military's role. But Morrow continued to find the proposal impractical, and let it drop.[21]

The exchange with Morrow reflected Gruening's new perspective on how the United States should handle Mexico. The de la Huerta and Cristero rebellions, in combination with the apparent ideological transformation of Calles, underscored the fragile position of Mexican reformers in their own country. Therefore, Gruening believed, the United States needed to act in a positive fashion to assist them in what he viewed as a common effort; indeed, "there was nothing fundamentally in [Mexico's] aspirations that could not be reconciled with the larger interest of the United States." Given this thesis, the United States needed to begin "bending every effort to help Mexico get on her feet" by aiding Mexican economic recovery in whatever way the Mexican regime desired. The editor hoped that Hoover would use Morrow's policies as a guide to revising inter-American relations as a whole.[22]

On a similar front, Gruening strongly defended Kellogg-Briand on the grounds that it too would terminate "private wars, such as that now going in Nicaragua." Meanwhile, he sought to organize the Portland opposition to the cruisers bill, which also provided an opportunity to strike at Hale's handiwork. Using his national contacts, he lobbied Borah to make sure that the bill—unlike other naval appropriations bills of the 1920s—did not pass on a voice vote. Peace activists then could work to defeat those senators who supported it. Revealing the ways in which his activism on inter-American issues had radicalized his overall approach to foreign policy matters, the editor called for the United States, with its geographic security and economic strength, to have "faith in diplomacy and in suasion to keep others from building too recklessly."

In the long term, Gruening recommended what he called "true defense," a doctrine which would rely on the power of transnational coalitions to ensure peace in "this new compact world of ours." In an open letter to Hoover on the matter, he added that this modern concept of defense also excluded military protection for economic interests, either those threatened by revolutionary instability in weaker states or those challenged by infringements on neutral rights during wartime.[23]

Gruening's proposal offered a mixture of interesting insights, superficial analysis of international relations, and some rather bizarre commentary. It nonetheless marked one of his first attempts to define precisely his conception of national security. The editor eschewed policies that offered short-term strategic advantages at the cost of tarnishing the traditional American ideals of supporting self-determination and seeking alternatives to the use of force in international affairs. If the United States acted accordingly, Gruening believed, in a variation on his fascination with the power of transnational alliances, reformist forces in other countries would rally to the American cause, thus ensuring the country's safety. He passed along this advice in a private letter to Hoover, but again he underestimated the gulf separating him from the president. Hoover considered the ideas so outlandish that he asked his private secretary if he had misinterpreted Gruening's argument. The president was assured that he had not.[24]

In the immediate aftermath of Hoover's election, more pressing matters hit closer to home. In early 1929, looking to consolidate their victories of the previous year, conservatives passed the Smith-Carlton bill, authorizing a fall referendum to repeal the Fernald Law and thus allow Central Maine Power (CMP) to export its product across state lines. Politically, Gruening recognized that the referendum's passage would cinch the defeat of the progressives within the Maine GOP. Economically, he feared that CMP wanted to put "the CONSUMER of Massachusetts and New Hampshire in DIRECT COMPETITION with the CONSUMER of Maine" for the limited resources of Maine's power, increasing demand enough to sustain a rate increase. In addition, he detected an ulterior motive for the power companies to back export: once the power crossed the state border, it became interstate commerce, subject only to federal regulation. Since Gruening still believed that progressives were better able to influence state regulatory agencies, he considered the Fernald Law "the only protection which the people of Maine now have in their unequal struggle against the outside interests." Repealing it would mean that "the people of Maine would lose their regulatory control for all time."[25]

The referendum produced an exceptionally bitter campaign. Still disheartened by Brewster's defeat, Gruening initially doubted whether his side could prevail. He especially feared that the Insull interests would deploy "the most gigantic slush fund ever used to influence an election in Maine." Financial concerns intensified the feeling of gloom. His political enemies increased the pressure against the *Evening News* by persuading five of Portland's six major department stores, as well as a host of other businesses, to withdraw their advertising. Gruening thus learned the hard way, contrary to his earlier theorizing, about the importance of advertising revenue to the modern newspaper. His willingness to risk the survival of the newspaper to advance his ideological agenda led one supporter to hail him as "one of the most idealistic men he had ever known." A close friend, Bowdoin professor Jim Abramson, recalled that Gruening gave the *Evening News* "its character. He was the good guy against all the bad guys, and those days they were really bad."[26]

Such moral support, combined with the national attention which his crusade received, restored Gruening's willingness to fight. In late March, Silas Bent of the *New Republic* published an article detailing the boycott, and soon Gruening's crusade against Smith-Carlton became a cause célèbre among national opponents of the utilities industry. The peace progressive senator Gerald Nye (R–North Dakota) praised the courage of "such papers as the *Portland Evening News* and its editor, Mr. Gruening," and the foremost Senate critic of the power trust, George Norris, promised Gruening his support for "the wonderful things you have been doing." Gruening responded by sending Norris a host of his editorials, and the Nebraska senator liked what he saw. He praised Gruening for presenting "the question in rather a larger and broader manner" than anything else written on the issue, and passed the editorials on to Robert Healy, the chief counsel to the FTC investigation of the utility industry. Norris urged Healy to make Portland a central case study in his inquiry by soliciting testimony from Brewster, Gruening, and "such other witnesses as Mr. Gruening might support." The Nebraskan also delivered a Senate speech attacking the "Power people" for attempting to shut down the *Evening News*, "the only means by which the people of the community could have both sides of a disputed question publicly discussed."[27]

The Smith-Carlton campaign established Gruening's national credentials on the power question in the same way that *Mexico and Its Heritage* had on Mexican history. He therefore was doubly determined not to lose the fight. Privately, he thanked Norris for the "many flattering" references in the Nebraskan's Senate remarks. Gruening predicted that the "airing of this question on the floor of the Senate will be the greatest help to us," since "power trust intrigues do not stand the daylight any too well." He mused that recent events had confirmed his earlier belief that "the Senate has in the past ten years been the bulwark not only of American liberties but of American official integrity." Perhaps only "close readers" (like himself) of the *Congressional Record*, which he characterized as "the most entertaining magazine published in America rather than the dull and lifeless chronicle it is so often asserted to be," understood this fact.[28]

The last remark confirmed Gruening's continuing fascination with the relationship between Congress and reform. He had long since abandoned his belief in the need to focus on the presidency to achieve his goals. By 1929, in addition, he had moved beyond his experience of the battle for the King amendment seven years earlier, when he called for anti-imperialists to counteract presidential policies by using the institutional powers of Congress, instead recognizing that Congress offered a broader potential. The mere airing of issues, especially in the Senate, with its tradition of unlimited and often highbrow debate, affected the political process by mobilizing public opinion. This marrying of two of his central beliefs—the importance of public opinion with the need for greater congressional input into policy formulation—previewed the conception of the office which Gruening himself would employ once he arrived in the upper chamber.

That development, of course, was well in the future. Now, recovering his faith in the public will, he launched a vigorous campaign against Smith-Carlton not only in the *Evening News* but also on a statewide speaking tour, joined by representatives from the state Grange. Even his political opponents conceded Gruening's effectiveness on the hustings. Well-educated, passionate, and articulate, the editor had been lecturing publicly since his years in Boston and was constantly improving his skills. One friend recalled him as possessed of a "blunt way of saying things." Though "not smooth," Gruening was "believable, credible, and persuasive."[29]

Gruening's lecture tour only increased his already high-profile opposition to the Smith-Carlton measure. Local conservatives looked to use this development to their advantage, as had occurred with the Brewster-Hale primary the year before. The *Press-Herald* warned voters not to be "confused by the innuendoes and suspicions fostered by certain speakers and newspapers of the state." Given the prosperity which export would bring, former governor Percival Baxter, continuing his drift to the right, denounced Gruening as a man determined to lead his "followers into the wilderness of socialism and political manipulation." In contrast to 1928, however, such attacks fell short. The referendum generated a huge turnout for a special election. By a vote of 61,999 to 54,047, Maine voters rejected the Smith-Carlton bill and prohibited power export.[30]

GRUENING INITIALLY REJOICED at the triumph. Privately, however, he conceded that owing to "the size and character of the community in which we publish," he had no choice but to "do a good many of the things that the people here want—columns on columns of purely local gossip, etc." He accepted such compromises provided that, as in the export fight, the paper could "throw light on some of the burning questions of the day" and give him influence in state politics. He told William Allen White, the Kansas newspaper editor whose national standing he envied, that the "great fight" had vindicated his "faith in democracy." Despite the power company propaganda, "the people weighed the issue carefully and voted right." It was, of course, easy to celebrate the virtues of democracy in the aftermath of favorable electoral results. In the long term, moreover, the victory proved Pyrrhic, since the boycott increased the reliance of the *Evening News* on Chapman's assistance just as Brewster's career was beginning to decline. Once again, as at the *Boston Journal* and *The Nation*, Gruening placed his ideological imperatives ahead of his publication's financial well-being. Desperate to solve his "overshadowing financial problem," he appealed to progressives nationally for financial subsidies.[31]

The fight against Smith-Carlton offered a glimpse of the strengths and limitations of Gruening's domestic vision. In moving beyond his general concern with the prevalence of monopoly to address the ramifications of the problem in a particular industry, the editor showed how progressives might achieve their goals through means other than the great hope of the 1910s, federal regulation, an important insight given the pro-business nature of the federal regulatory machinery in the 1920s. In the process, Gruening mastered the bewildering amount of technical detail associated with the utilities industry, earning a national reputation as an expert on the issue which paralleled his reputation for expertise on Latin American matters. And he made his agenda politically palatable by tapping into the broader tradition of American dissent which portrayed monopoly as a moral evil, regardless of its economic effects.

His critic's instincts thus allowed Gruening to recognize that the prosperity of the 1920s masked fundamental instability in the American economy. But his analysis of the causes of this problem—with its almost exclusive focus on the evils of monopoly—was incomplete at best. He offered little but the most general comments on economic issues which did not fit into his ideological framework, such as labor or agriculture. More surprising, given his interest in foreign policy, the editor paid little attention to the unstable international scene, such as the controversy over German reparations and war debts owed by the Allied countries to the United States. Containing the power of monopoly, so he seemed to think, would overcome all of these problems. Events in the fall of 1929 illustrated the superficiality of this analysis. That October the bubble burst at home with the stock market crash, in turn tightening international credit and sparking a worldwide economic downturn. Firms reliant on the market for steady financial returns cut their spending, causing a decline in industrial production, while imports fell by nearly 20 percent in a three-month period. By the end of the year, a prolonged period of deflation had set in, accompanied by sharp declines in the commodity markets.[32]

These developments affected Gruening personally. His portfolio surged with the market in 1928 and early 1929, but the crash wiped out him financially. For the first time in his life, he did not have his inheritance to draw upon in times of financial duress. Still, he initially gave Hoover's policies the benefit of the doubt, partly in an attempt to convince himself that the economic downturn was not as bad as it appeared and that he had not misplaced his faith in Hoover's abilities as he had earlier with Wilson's. Also, though he had failed to do so throughout the 1920s, Gruening now recognized the international ramifications of the economic downturn, and praised Hoover's quest for nonmilitary ways to contain the Great Depression's economic and political effects. One such initiative was the London Naval Conference of 1930, which secured limitations for large cruisers, submarines, and other auxiliary craft under ratios.[33]

Although he generally opposed joining any group which dealt with an issue on which he might have to comment in an editorial, Gruening chaired the Maine Committee for the Reduction of Armament, an organization demanding "nothing short of substantial reduction" at London, including an agreement to abolish all battleships.[34] The parties obviously did not reach this goal. The editor responded by criticizing the U.S. delegation for its failure to support a more advanced disarmament position, which he feared gave other powers, notably the French, an excuse for intransigence on issues such as limiting submarine forces. He continued to argue for a foreign policy centered on preserving traditional American ideals, aiming "to de-militarize [not only] physically, but mentally and spiritually" as well. Gruening commended those whom he felt could help achieve his vision, such as Borah, whom he touted as "a prophet with honor." But Hoover—"a leader who is at the same time intensely idealistic and intensely practical"—fell into this category as well. Given Gruening's desire to integrate these two characteristics himself, this compliment stood as high praise.[35]

Gruening fully expected his position to generate the same type of nonpartisan support as had his opinions on Mexican matters. Accordingly, he sent off several of his most strongly anti-French editorials to some of his associates outside Maine. The response surprised him, since those less involved in the disarmament crusade found fault. Despite their agreement on Mexican policy a few years before, for example, Walter Lippmann now chastised Gruening for this shortsighted and simplistic view of events and claimed that he had "wholly misunderstood the French mind." Lippmann maintained that Gruening's policy would increase French stubbornness, and told the editor to rethink his contention that unilateral moral actions could persuade France or any other country to alter its conception of its national interest. In addition, Lippmann argued that battleships alone were not the key issue. He correctly described the treaty's most important accomplishment as its success in bringing all war vessels under international treaty obligations. The exchange suggested that Gruening's faith in the appeal of his ideas outside the Latin American context was overly optimistic, if not entirely misguided. True to form, however, Gruening interpreted Lippmann's dismissal of his argument as a personal slight, and declined to continue their correspondence.[36]

By this point, in any case, the editor's attention was fixed again on events in the Caribbean. Just before the stock market crash, Gruening had privately admitted that he wished he could devote himself "to the ancient labor of love of trying to free Haiti." The opportunity presented itself sooner than anticipated. In late December 1929 riots broke out in Port-au-Prince, protesting the military regime's repression and the economic hardships associated with the depression. An embarrassed Hoover accelerated plans to appoint a five-man commission headed by the former governor-general of the Philippines, W. Cameron Forbes, to recommend ways to wind down the occupation.[37]

Gruening responded to the riots by running an eleven-part series titled the "Story of Haiti," making the *Evening News* undoubtedly the only newspaper in the country to devote two weeks of editorials to Haitian affairs in the midst of the depression. The editor then returned to more direct activism. In February 1930 Villard offered to fund a "flying trip to Palm Beach" to lobby members of the Forbes commission. Villard worried that without some progressive input, Forbes, who was "getting more and more fossilized" and in any case was "extremely tarred with the Leonard Wood point of view," would oversee a repetition of the McCormick committee. (Forbes reciprocated: "Oswald was born foolish and is getting more so.") Accepting Villard's offer with alacrity, Gruening went off for ten days to Palm Beach, where he worked closely with commission members James Kerney and William Allen White, urging a U.S.-sponsored election, in which he believed Union Patriotique forces would prevail. A precipitous withdrawal, however, could trigger renewed political instability, which might deny the resistance group its rightful claim to power. In the 1920s, U.S. interventionism had most threatened the success of Gruening's desired cross-national coalition. Now, with the likes of Morrow and Hoover in power and anti-reform forces on the rise in the Caribbean, anti-imperialists in the United States actually were in a stronger position than their Caribbean counterparts. Gruening therefore reversed himself on the proper policy for the U.S. government. The goal, however, remained the same.[38]

Kerney and White were amenable to Gruening's point of view. White, predicting a "long, hard job," welcomed any information on Haiti that Gruening could provide; after a few such briefings he expressed his wish that "you were in Haiti and I in Portland." The commission ultimately recommended replacing the client regime with a freely elected government before withdrawing U.S. forces, although it left vague exactly how much power the United States would retain over Haiti's finances and foreign policy after the occupation ended. The election, swept by the Union Patriotique, pleased Gruening, who remarked to his old friend Earl Biggers that "it is quite possible" that the newly elected president, Stenio Vincent, "may keep me down there as permanent advisor and power behind the throne!" Though made partly in jest, the comment reflected Gruening's conviction that changes in the region's political climate dictated positive action by U.S. anti-imperialists. On this point, however, White raised a caution. He told Gruening that he had "felt more or less out of my element in Haiti." As a journalist, he, like Gruening, was trained to work with the "weapons for making and controlling public sentiment." But effective diplomacy, he had come to understand, required "deeply different" skills.[39]

Gruening brushed off the observation and instead looked to exploit the developments in the Caribbean in every way possible. To maintain the momentum, he encouraged Villard to sponsor a public dinner to hail the commission for "restoring, to the extent that restoration is possible, America's good name in the Caribbean." Gruening added that the dinner also would represent an opportunity to celebrate *The Nation*'s ability, "throughout all these years, like the abolitionists of old," to sustain the fight, refuse to compromise, and mobilize public sentiment against the occupation. "Really tremendously cheered" after "so many defeats in the matter of foreign policy," he considered that "this complete vindication of all the things which the *Nation* voice in the wilderness contended for ten years is about too good to be true." Gruening himself profited from the turn of events in a more tangible manner: pressed for funds after the stock market crash, he hired an agent and began offering lectures around New England, especially at colleges and universities, on Haitian matters. As the Smith-Carlton campaign had demonstrated, he had a knack for public speaking, and eventually expanded both his bookings and his topics to include all Latin American affairs. The U.S. political climate on inter-American affairs indeed had changed.[40]

The recommendations of the Forbes commission also convinced Gruening of the continuing worthiness of Hoover's foreign policies, "whatever may be the defects of the Administration's policy at home." The president's rather tepid response to the nation's economic difficulties generated strong criticism from most reformers, including Gruening's congressional mentors. But the editor still placed a high priority on international concerns, crediting "friend Herbert" for "withdrawing from Haiti," even if he "has fallen down badly in many respects" on the home front. Still, he did express concern about Hoover's handling of national affairs. By late 1930, in a dramatic reversal of his earlier position, Gruening conceded that unemployment could not be resolved "without partly revising our concept of the need of 'efficiency' and without perhaps revamping our assumption that such efficiency in production can be wholly divorced from other values." Applying scientific solutions in an apolitical fashion, mostly at the state or community level, simply would not reverse the economic downturn. As a supplement Gruening recommended a "gigantic program of public works" and more rigorous regulation of business. Efficiency had provided the bond between the domestic agendas of Hoover and Gruening. With the editor abandoning the concept, intensifying his anti-monopoly outlook, and supporting increased federal spending to stimulate economic growth, this connection between the president's domestic program and Gruening's snapped.[41]

Gruening's perspective on the power issue reinforced his increasing support for a more active policy from the national government. After the rejection of the Smith-Carlton bill, Gruening championed giving the Maine PUC jurisdiction over holding companies and their political and propaganda expenditures. But he quickly realized that such issues were inherently national in nature, beyond the jurisdiction of the state PUCs. By 1931, the editor admitted that contrary to his earlier beliefs, "the allegation that the industry is adequately regulated by the state commissions is another fiction, which, above all others, the power propagandists are eager to perpetuate." Only federal action could serve the overall interests of the consumers. Other activists, such as George

Norris, likewise called for more aggressive federal action, a sentiment bolstered by the surprisingly detailed findings of the FTC inquiry. Gruening was so pleased by this support that he compiled the most relevant material, added some commentary, and published the result as *The Public Pays.* Others shared his hope that the study would have the widest possible dissemination; the material from the report constituted the basis of at least six books, although Gruening's received the most critical acclaim. His muckraking skills remained impressive.[42]

Still, Gruening had invested a good deal of intellectual capital in the 1920s touting efficiency as a way to achieve reform without bolstering the national government's power, and he remained ambivalent about jettisoning the concept entirely. Although the direction in his thought was clearly apparent, on the local level at least, he remained faithful to his pre-depression beliefs. In 1930 he staunchly opposed a referendum to return Portland to the elected mayor system, championing the retention of city management, this "pre-eminently . . . business government." He likewise encouraged a host of development projects which he viewed as civic rather than political issues, of which aid to higher education was the most significant. Revealing both his belief in the importance of his own education to his intellectual development and a more general faith in higher education common among progressives, Gruening described education as "the most important single function of a civilized state" because of its critical role in producing an intelligent electorate. He especially praised the educational philosophies of Maine's leading liberal arts colleges, Colby, Bates, and Bowdoin. He hailed Colby's president, Franklin Winslow, for not succumbing "to the tendency of some higher educational institutions of becoming trade schools," looking solely to train their graduates for careers in industry. Such attitudes drew the editor his share of admirers on the state's campuses. Outside of political activists, most of his closest friends in Maine served on the faculties of Bowdoin or Bates.[43]

In 1930 and 1931, Gruening exemplified the dilemmas of progressivism. Though inching toward more consistent support for strengthening federal power, he remained unwilling to repudiate entirely his earlier arguments that progressives stood a better chance at the state level. Increasingly frustrated with domestic developments, Gruening threw himself into foreign policy activity. An old friend provided the opportunity. After the Forbes commission issued its report, Hubert Herring told him of plans to broaden the CCRLA seminar's focus to the Caribbean. Given Gruening's expertise in the area, he was first on Herring's list of possible lecturers. The offer provided a chance to apply his newly emerging positive anti-imperialist principles. He observed that the Caribbean, with turmoil in Cuba, the winding down of the occupation of Haiti, the emergence of a dictatorship in the Dominican Republic, and an attempt at colonial reform in Puerto Rico, provided plentiful opportunities for continuing the CCRLA's work.[44]

Both Herring and Gruening expected to spend most of their time on Cuban affairs. Freed from Spanish colonial rule after the U.S. intervention in 1898, Cuba found its economy quickly falling under the dominance of U.S. sugar interests. Moreover, the Platt Amendment, which gave the United States the right to intervene to prevent political instability, limited Cuba's political freedom. In this environment insular politics degenerated, and by the end of the 1920s, Gerardo Machado was consolidating a repressive dictatorship. During the seminar's brief visit to Cuba, Gruening obtained an interview with Machado, whom he considered a "ruthless tyrant." At the same time, though, he dismissed charges made by opposition figures that the Hoover administration and Ambassador Harry Guggenheim were propping up the Cuban regime. Instead, he scored what he termed the defeatist attitude of Machado's opponents, who seemed desperate for outside support. Gruening dismissed this solution: the United States, he said, could not cure its own domestic woes, "let alone run another country." Cross-national alliances could succeed only through a joint effort of reformers in both the United States and the host nation.[45]

Gruening more than overcame his disappointment with Cuba, however, during the seminar's one-day stop in Puerto Rico. Although it was the major U.S. colony in Latin America, Puerto Rico had all but escaped the notice of the anti-imperialist movement during the 1920s. Now, however, the island's reform-minded governor, Theodore Roosevelt, Jr., son of the late president, had launched a program to relieve Puerto Rico's economic problems by diversifying the island's sugar-dominated economy. His agenda also included international elements. The governor hoped his position would allow him to become an unofficial roving diplomat in the Caribbean Basin, and he also called for making greater use of Puerto Rico to promote cultural exchange between the United States and Latin America. The partnership between Roosevelt and anti-imperialist activists was a marriage of convenience. The governor's ill-disguised ambition had alienated his superiors at the War Department, and he needed all the outside support that he could muster. Anti-imperialists such as Gruening, meanwhile, were glad to find a policy maker receptive to their ideas.[46]

Gruening had never been in Puerto Rico before 1931, but he did have some experience with the island's affairs. When editing *These United States*, he had insisted on including a chapter on Puerto Rico, and selected as its author a rising star among the island's reformers, Luis Muñoz Marín. In his contribution, Muñoz Marín advocated a program resembling Roosevelt's, calling for "a scrupulously unselfish policy" on the part of the United States directed at lessening the control of U.S. "trusts" over the island's economic life. Gruening himself came away from his visit with an admiration for Roosevelt's efforts to alleviate the "vicious circle" associated with the absentee-owned sugar industry and his "formal recognition and appreciation of the Hispanic cultural heritage and his vision of Porto [sic] Rico as a meeting ground of the two cultures, Latin-Spanish and Anglo-Saxon, which share this hemisphere." He agreed that Puerto Rico could serve as a "bridge to better understanding, a forum and laboratory for developing and extracting the best that is in each." After having spent so much time contemplating "the darker aspects of our Caribbean policy," the editor termed it "heartening to come, unexpectedly, on a picture that is happily different."[47]

Gruening and Roosevelt soon initiated a detailed correspondence on Puerto Rican matters, with the governor confident that Hoover, too, "grasped the cultural aspect" which he and Gruening had discussed. Roosevelt invited Gruening to his home at Oyster Bay, New York, to discuss matters further, and Gruening tried to arrange a second Caribbean seminar to spend more time with the governor in San Juan. In the fall of 1931, the editor also traveled to Washington, where he met with Hoover to urge full administration support for Roosevelt's agenda. When Hoover transferred Roosevelt to the Philippines, a disappointed Gruening termed the move a "tragedy." Roosevelt, whose political ambition remained strong despite his loss to Al Smith in the New York gubernatorial race of 1924, welcomed the assignment to a higher-profile post. But for Gruening, Puerto Rico was "more important than the Philippines," since he believed that the United States should focus its international efforts more on Latin America than on East Asia.[48]

In fact, Roosevelt's move from Puerto Rico to the Philippines coincided with a general shift of U.S. foreign policy away from the Caribbean Basin and toward East Asia, prompted by the conquest of Manchuria by Japan's Kwantung Army. The incident symbolized more than any other single event the passing of the spirit of the 1920s. Up until this point Gruening had rarely commented on East Asia, considering the region far removed from the nation's interests. Wondering "what earthly concern of ours is the Sino-Japanese struggle," at first he chiefly worried about the domestic effects of the Manchurian crisis, guessing that opponents of disarmament would use the event to fan public sentiment for more military spending. To counter, he accepted the arguments of the War Resisters' League, which urged young men to pledge that they would refuse induction into the army, and he predicted that "war will end when a sufficient number of individuals refuse to fight against all foes—except the common and deadliest enemy of all—war itself." Such a proposal revealed Gruening's continuing tendency to select the most extreme position when commenting on international issues outside of inter-American relations. In any case, within a matter of weeks he amended his view, having come to view the conflict as the first real test of Kellogg-Briand. In response, Gruening proposed a "spontaneous boycott" of Japanese goods.[49]

The Hoover administration likewise responded indecisively, but it eventually settled on a public statement from Secretary of State Henry Stimson refusing to recognize any territorial annexation obtained through the use of force or any diplomatic arrangement between China and Japan which violated the principles of China's territorial or administrative integrity. Gruening initially praised the nonrecognition doctrine, but thereafter again changed course, concerned that the Japanese aggression had triggered a "widespread reaction . . . that all this talk of arbitration is so much fantasy, a dream of impractical pacifists, rudely shattered by stern reality." He instead urged the adoption of a broader anti-imperialist perspective, one predictably based on an analogy to inter-American relations. Gruening compared the Japanese action in Manchuria with "the relations of the United States to the smaller, weaker, and so-called 'backward' nations in and around the Caribbean," on which the United States had repeatedly imposed its will by force.

Both imperialisms were "equally reprehensible" to him, although the fact that Japan's aggression had occurred after the signing of Kellogg-Briand "aggravates her present offense." Still, the United States needed to consider how its own policies damaged the spirit of international peace. Gruening recommended reducing military expenditures and rallying world public opinion against the Japanese action. Such an approach could succeed, however, only by first purifying U.S. foreign policy of any vestiges of imperialism. This proposal allowed Gruening to fit into a familiar framework the Japanese invasion and East Asian affairs in general, with which he was appallingly, in his own words, "unacquainted."[50]

With the foreign policy scene suddenly confusing, domestic affairs provided little encouragement. Much to Gruening's dismay, Hoover continued to resist a host of initiatives which the editor considered essential, such as Norris's Muscle Shoals bill. The administration also looked to slash appropriations for agencies such as the FTC, fresh from its inquiry into the utilities industry, as part of its "economy" program. Stunned, Gruening argued that regulatory agencies needed more, not less, funding, since their investigations exposed "many of the grave abuses which have precipitated the present depression." Their power also needed to be expanded, from "quasi-judicial bodies acting as neutral arbiters between the power companies and the consumers" to "administrative agencies intended to promote and defend the public's interests and rights." Gruening argued that the utilities issue, important in itself, also offered the perfect example of unchecked monopoly and ineffective regulation. Its ramifications thus extended "to just about everything that is in need of correction in our economic and political system."[51]

In fact, Gruening's anti-business beliefs had sharpened considerably, part of his conviction that the excesses against which he had crusaded during the previous decade explained the economic downturn. Although he continued to point to the role of international factors, he viewed as more important the link between the unchecked power of monopoly—of which the utilities industry served as the best example—and the onset of the Great Depression. In the 1920s he had believed that fortifying governmental regulatory powers would restore the U.S. capitalist system. Now, however, he was not so sure. Along with many other reformers, he questioned whether the United States would ever again experience the economic prosperity of the period before the stock market crash. The crash required bold initiatives to restructure the economy, so as to lessen the influence of the forces whose actions had triggered the downturn.

The dilemmas posed by national and international politics paled in comparison to personal events. In May 1931, Sonny, Gruening's eldest son, fell ill after going swimming during a visit home from Milton Academy. He developed an ear infection, which two operations failed to cure, and was diagnosed as septic. For two months his condition deteriorated, with Gruening frantically appealing to his contacts in the Boston medical community, seeking to reverse his son's decline. The quest failed: Sonny died on July 5. "Numb" from this "irremediable catastrophe," Gruening spent the next months "going through the motions of existence mechanically and with a forced smile to keep from being overwhelmed by the intensity" of his anguish. Yet the boy's death did not fundamentally alter Gruening's relationship with his two surviving sons. He continued to spend little time with Hunt and Peter, although he bowed to Hunt's wishes and did not enroll him at Milton, where Sonny had been quite unhappy. Instead, in the fall of 1931, and despite the family's strained financial situation, Hunt went off to Exeter Academy, with the expectation that upon graduation he would follow in his father's footsteps and attend Harvard.[52]

On the political front, after the triumph in the power export fight, Maine again turned to the right. Although Gruening had arrived in Maine filled with enthusiasm, he grew increasingly frustrated in his efforts to cultivate a reform spirit in a state where "physically and spiritually the field is extremely limited." The *Evening News* suffered financially from "the well-known Hoover prosperity" and the lingering effects of the advertising boycott dating from the Smith-Carlton bill. Gruening complained to Villard in early 1932 that since "the depression has hit Maine . . . we don't pay ten dollars for anything," including "an exclusive announcement of the second coming of Christ." A few months later, he described the paper as "a mere shell." Moreover, as he lamented to Carleton Beals, the stock market collapse had left him "broke" for the first time in his life. He therefore could find little "that offsets the otherwise disastrous experience of trying to keep a newspaper alive in these times." Financial pressures even forced him to sacrifice one of his few personal indulgences—regular train trips to New York to attend the opera or a Broadway show.[53]

Gruening turned to his "labor of love"—Haiti—to resolve these interrelated personal, ideological, professional, and political dilemmas. In early 1932, when Dana Munro announced that he would step down as U.S. minister to Haiti, the editor aggressively sought the post. He admitted that some in the State Department might prefer the selection of a foreign service officer, but realistically observed that "in itself the Haitian post is the least desirable in the diplomatic service." In a long letter to Theodore Roosevelt, Jr., Gruening also contended that his appointment would boost Hoover's support from progressives and black voters, especially as it was "becoming more and more recognized that the Democrats have nothing to offer." Playing on Theodore's jealousy of the political success of his cousin Franklin, Gruening added that the New York governor had proven the limits of his appeal to progressives with his "nauseating" policy toward Tammany Hall, and was particularly vulnerable on the Haitian matter because of his campaign boast in 1920. Furthermore, because of his tendency to "pussyfoot on every issue," Gruening judged the governor "just as likely as not" to shift on the regulation of private utilities, the "one and only aspect of Franklin's public career remaining by which he may be properly deemed 'liberal.'" As always, Gruening maintained, "the progressive following . . . is by no means committed at present to either major party." He therefore believed that a "few progressive moves on Herbert Hoover's part," such as appointing Gruening as minister to Haiti, "would be of great benefit to him in an election which is bound to be close in many states." Gruening hastened to add that his proposal was "not at all a bit of egotism but a matter of practical politics," especially since the realigning effects of the depression had left the progressive bloc "larger than ever."[54]

Gruening also secured some powerful allies to lobby on his behalf. Walter White of the NAACP informed Hoover that "the future welfare of the United States in Latin America" depended on Gruening's selection. An even stronger endorsement came from Theodore Roosevelt, Jr., who told Hoover that he was "surprised" that any one "so good" as Gruening would even "consider" the Haitian job. Gruening clearly was competent—he spoke French and was "considered by all the intelligentsia an authority in Caribbean affairs." More important, the governor-general noted, the appointment would constitute a political "ten-strike" by pacifying "an element which has been prone to criticize." These arguments, and similarly strong support from cultural anti-imperialists such as Hubert Herring and Samuel Guy Inman, made Gruening a serious contender for the slot. In mid-August, though, the State Department announced that career diplomat Norman Armour would replace Munro. Roosevelt reported that although Hoover preferred Gruening for the post, the State Department, still "very bitter" against the editor "because of the Mexican stuff," had "laid down the law" to the president.[55]

Gruening responded angrily to the decision. Once again a personal slight caused him to reverse his position on a political issue. In this instance, for the first time, he soured on Hoover's foreign policy, even expressing "a waning enthusiasm" for the president's handling of Haitian affairs. Sensing which way the political winds were blowing, Gruening suggested to Franklin Roosevelt—employing as intermediaries William King, George Norris, and Herbert Lehman, an old family friend of the Gruenings who would succeed Roosevelt as governor of New York—that he "could score a political coup" by promising to abandon the financial protectorate. The editor added that the Democratic nominee could use Haiti as an issue to challenge Hoover's overall foreign policy, since the "unfortunate and tragic" continuance of the "assault" upon Haiti's financial independence was "scarcely consistent" with Stimson's nonrecognition doctrine in Manchuria.[56]

With support for Hoover now out of the question, in November 1932, Gruening unenthusiastically cast his ballot for Roosevelt. Looking back privately on the election later in the month, he considered the result a "foregone conclusion" but also a "just verdict." Nonetheless, he rather expected "to see the Republicans back in 1936," since the Democrats faced "an almost impossible job." Unfortunately, he wrote, "we have not yet begun to liquidate the major financial crimes of the precrash years." Gruening was sure that other utilities systems would follow Insull's in collapsing, with "tragic" results "for the millions of innocent investors who usually get it in the neck." On top of all of these problems, the depression had "fundamentally" changed the outlook of the American people, producing widespread pessimism. He doubted that the new president could successfully handle these challenges. Progressives therefore needed to remain true to their traditional ideals and position themselves to take advantage of the political confusion that seemed inevitable, rather than sacrificing their political independence by affiliating with the Democratic Party.[57]

AFTER THE ELECTION, at least, an opportunity to help shape the national reform agenda emerged. In December, Gruening heard from Freda Kirchwey, his successor as managing editor of *The Nation*, who had put together a consortium to purchase the financially troubled journal from Villard. The new owners planned to have four past editors run the journal, and wanted Gruening on board. "Glad to finally shake the dust of Portland from my shoes," he immediately accepted the offer. Intellectually, the return to New York suited him well. In testimony to his growing national reputation, he was named a director of the Foreign Policy Association, and joined the Council on Foreign Relations and the American Academy of Political and Social Science. Now centrally located and freed from the day-to-day constraints of editing a newspaper, he also found more time for public speaking activities. A regular on the lecture circuit throughout the eastern seaboard in 1933 and 1934, Gruening served as a lecturer on inter-American relations at the New School for Social Research. Nevertheless, while more satisfying intellectually, the move to New York worsened Gruening's financial condition. The family moved into an exclusive apartment complex, the Turtle Bay Gardens, and Dorothy insisted on renovating the apartment, at considerable cost. When the bill came due, she offered her usual response about selling bonds to pay off their debt, but Gruening's disastrous speculation in the stock market had foreclosed this possibility. He was soon borrowing to keep afloat financially, and the economic strains began to put some pressure on the marriage for the first time.[58]

Gruening's first few months back at *The Nation* coincided with the transition period between the Hoover and Roosevelt presidencies. Rather than looking ahead, however, he confined most of his public commentary to themes familiar from the 1920s: the evils of the private utilities industry, the aftereffects of U.S. interventions in Latin America, and a celebration of the powers of Congress. The last issue allowed him to strike back at Walter Lippmann for criticizing his naïveté during the negotiations over the London Naval Treaty. Shortly after Roosevelt's election, Lippmann called for choking off "unlimited debate and obstruction" in Congress and returning to the executive branch the powers "usurped" by the legislature over the previous two decades. Gruening rebuked Lippmann for criticizing congressional power, and particularly frowned upon any move to decrease the authority of the Senate, which, as "the only debating forum left in America," remained "of inestimable value to our institutions, our liberties, to the possibility of progress along wise and sane lines." A strong defense of the upper chamber's prerogatives now formed a standard part of Gruening's ideological repertoire.[59]

Roosevelt's inauguration brought a host of figures more sympathetic to the editor's point of view into the government. Gruening responded by more frequently advancing positive policies. He greeted the new administration with a long editorial summing up his basic position on economic questions, arguing that the depression "may justly be ascribed to the assumption of control of the nation's life by the money power." Heeding the warnings of Louis Brandeis, this "great American," would have averted the collapse, and the Justice's financial theories remained just as "applicable today" as they had been in the 1910s. This viewpoint placed Gruening firmly within a wing of the emerging New Deal coalition, centered on Brandeis, Frankfurter, and their ideological followers, who championed large-scale public works, application of anti-monopoly ideals, and progressive tax legislation. Frankfurter, meanwhile, skillfully placed like-minded figures throughout the New Deal bureaucracy, while Roosevelt also named other figures of known anti-monopoly sentiments to his administration, such as the Yale law professor and future Supreme Court Justice William O. Douglas. Frankfurter introduced Gruening to Douglas during one of Gruening's visits to Washington, initiating one of Gruening's rare close lifelong friendships.[60]

Despite the influence enjoyed by Brandeis and Frankfurter, Roosevelt sent conflicting signals on the issue most critical to Gruening's economic beliefs, restraining the influence of monopoly. On the one hand, in his inaugural address he promised to vanquish the "unscrupulous money changers" and end "speculation with other people's money." On the other hand, many of the administration's early economic initiatives stressed business-government cooperation and balancing the federal budget. These ideas reflected the thinking of Roosevelt's "Brain Trust," figures such as labor attorney Donald Richberg and Columbia University professors Raymond Moley, Adolf Berle, and Rexford Tugwell. Although the members of the group disagreed on their exact policy preferences, they knew, in Moley's words, what they were rejecting: "the traditional Wilson-Brandeis philosophy that if America could once again become a nation of small proprietors, of corner grocers and smithies under spreading chestnut trees, we should have solved the problems of American life." In general, the group concluded that the prevalence of monopoly and oligopoly required a focus not on restructuring the economy but on stabilizing the industrial state as it existed. The National Recovery Administration (NRA), which sought to negotiate voluntary code arrangements with major industries to alleviate the dangers of untrammeled competition, reflected this basic agenda.[61]

Looking to coordinate editorial policy with Frankfurter's wishes, Gruening dropped a line to the law professor requesting his insights ("if it isn't trespassing too much on your time and good fortune") on the character of early administration appointments. Frankfurter responded with a detailed three-page memorandum, characteristically stressing the importance of bringing in "first-rate young lawyers." The professor's response formed the basis of Gruening's next editorial, which—in words he later would repudiate—extolled "the superb determination of Secretary [Harold] Ickes to make the Department of Interior excellent from top to bottom." Perceptively, Gruening realized that "the Roosevelt appointments reveal the conflicting interests that coalesced under his banner." Anti-monopolists, then, needed to convince the president that figures such as Treasury Secretary William Woodin, because of his previous ties to J. P. Morgan, "no longer enjoy the confidence of the people." By contrast, "no finer appointment" could be made than someone such as Frankfurter protégé James Landis, tapped by the president for a spot on the FTC. Such sentiments made the editor a welcome guest at Frankfurter's breakfast parties, which Gruening found "delightful."[62]

Unlike in the 1920s, Gruening now was attacking the system itself rather than abuses thereof. Lacking Frankfurter's confidence in behind-the-scenes activity, the editor worried that Roosevelt's unfocused and haphazard program was "not radical enough." He developed this thesis in a speech at an April rally where he joined figures ranging from Bruce Bliven of the *New Republic* to socialist Heywood Broun to Jay

Lovestone, head of the New York Communist Party. Gruening refrained from casting his lot with such adherents of more radical views. But he clearly was running out of patience waiting for Roosevelt to embrace a more comprehensive economic agenda.[63]

Meanwhile, the international outlook was more bleak than ever. In early 1933, Adolf Hitler and his Nazi Party came to power in Germany, where several of the editor's distant relatives of Jewish heritage still lived. *The Nation* featured a number of strongly anti-Hitler editorials throughout 1933, while Gruening expressed his concern about the ideological challenge of Nazism on the lecture circuit. He also joined the board of directors of the University in Exile, founded in New York and peopled by émigré scholars from Nazi-ruled countries such as Arthur Feiler, Eduard Heimann, and Max Wertheimer. The editor described the group as "the true repositories of German culture—of our common world culture," and predicted that the refugees would affect American society positively, as had the earlier generation of German immigrants (such as his father) who had come to the United States in the aftermath of the failed revolutions of 1848.[64]

For Gruening, developments in Europe and Asia only confirmed his belief in the importance of an active U.S. role in reforming inter-American relations. As he told Frankfurter, the Manchurian incident indicated that Japan would determine the fate of East Asia, with the United States at best relegated to a "passive and unimportant" role; meanwhile, the "exaggerated nationalisms of Europe" heightened the need for a "sane Pan-Americanism" as an alternative framework for international relations. He thus found it "truer than ever" that the "one field where we might actually achieve something worthwhile is Latin America." Geography and economics linked the people of the Western hemisphere, and "if to these factors can be added a true cultural interchange, it may be possible to work out . . . a great region of the world free from the strife and destruction which unhappily characterizes so many other parts." In this new order, the "most important" position in the State Department would be that of the assistant secretary of state for Latin American affairs.[65]

Intrigued by this unusual perspective, Frankfurter passed on the information to Roosevelt. The ties between the two men dated back twenty years, before Roosevelt captured the New York governorship in 1928, and their relationship grew distinctly warmer over the next four years, when Frankfurter frequently traveled to Albany to offer advice about utility regulation, public power, prison reform, and appointments to state regulatory boards. (It was no coincidence that Gruening had praised Roosevelt's gubernatorial performance on all of these issues in *Evening News* editorials.) At one meeting, two days before Christmas 1932, the subject of U.S. relations with Latin America arose. Frankfurter remarked to Roosevelt that "the fellow who I think is more wisely informed on that subject, who has written a book on that subject, whom you ought to see, is Ernest Gruening." The president-elect responded, "Ernest who?" Frankfurter then filled him in on Gruening's background, activism in Mexico and Haiti, and support from U.S. anti-imperialists. Roosevelt promised to consult the editor when the new administration began formulating its Latin American policy. Frankfurter then asked Gruening to send him a copy of the 1922 lawyers' brief on the intervention in Haiti, intending to forward it to the president.[66]

Gruening anticipated that the conversation between Frankfurter and Roosevelt would produce immediate changes in Latin American policy. Grounds for such a hope did exist: during the 1920s, Roosevelt had retreated somewhat from his identification with Wilson-era interventionism. But the new foreign policy team offered little encouragement for Gruening, who editorialized that "mediocrities" seemed to dominate the State Department. Although the president vaguely promised to orient his hemispheric policy around the principle of the "good neighbor," the new secretary of state, Cordell Hull, lacked experience in Latin American matters, allowing Sumner Welles, who had served in the Hughes State Department, to emerge as the chief architect of the administration's hemispheric policy. Roosevelt confirmed as much when he named Welles his personal representative to Cuba, with blanket authority to alleviate the unrest against the Machado regime.[67]

On his earlier visit to the island, Gruening had opposed U.S. intervention, citing the weaknesses of Cuban opposition forces. Now, however, he adopted a different view. Machado's brutality had intensified between 1931 and 1933, while Gruening had grown much more impressed with the quality of the Cuban opposition movement. Most important, however, the editor's hostility to American capitalism had become more acute. In a reversal of form, his altered domestic framework radicalized his foreign policy beliefs. Describing U.S. policy since

Cuban independence as "decidedly advantageous to American sugar producers," Gruening urged a "new deal for Cuba" to end "the infiltration of American business." In line with the evolution of his foreign policy mindset, he recommended jettisoning "the present policy of official non-interference," which, he astutely noted, though "decent in motive," failed to take into account the determination of U.S. economic forces to prop up Machado's regime. Removing Machado represented "merely the first step" in Gruening's agenda. The United States and the Cuban opposition movement then needed to work together to "control and regulate 'banksters' and financial pirates," understanding "that a solution in the interest of the Cubans would conflict with the interests of Cuba's real owners—the business and financial powers which likewise have dominated American life." As the new administration was promising to move against these forces on the domestic scene, Gruening believed, so too did it need to weaken their power internationally.[68]

Welles's appointment indicated that Roosevelt did not share this prescription for Cuba's ills. Gruening initially criticized the president's move, observing that he could "scarcely imagine a worse person for this position" than Welles, a "thorough-going imperialist and bureaucrat." Frankfurter, however, asked him to reconsider, and arranged a lunch between Gruening and the minister-designate. After their conversation, eager to remain in Frankfurter's good graces, Gruening publicly praised the appointment as a "good one." With a hint of jealousy, Gruening noted that Welles possessed "an opportunity which rarely comes to a diplomat in these modern days." The affair marked neither the first nor the last occasion when, on the basis of a personal meeting, Gruening made a snap judgment which he later regretted. In this case he quickly returned to his original opinion. Intervening blatantly in Cuban politics, Welles orchestrated Machado's ouster and his replacement by Carlos Céspedes. Gruening rejoiced, and urged Welles to move on to the second stage of his "new program" for U.S.-Cuban relations—liberating the island from domination by U.S. business interests. Welles, however, hoped that Céspedes's transitional regime would restore political and financial stability. Instead, a coup headed by army sergeants led by Fulgencio Batista toppled the regime in less than a week. Eventually, Ramón Grau San Martín, a professor at the University of Havana, emerged as head of the new government. Welles recoiled from Grau's economic and social reforms, and successfully recommended that Roosevelt deny recognition. At the same time, the president held firm to an earlier promise that Welles would return to Washington after the completion of his work in Cuba to take up the vacant post of assistant secretary of state for Latin American affairs.[69]

Gruening, for whom Grau represented "the best elements in Cuba," informed his contacts with the anti-Machado movement that he was doing his part "to shape the Cuban situation as the Cubans desire it to be shaped." His chief activity in this regard came in utilizing his politically connected friends. Able as usual to sense changes in the political climate, Gruening bypassed the contacts he had used in the 1932 campaign—William King, George Norris, and Herbert Lehman—and instead turned to Frankfurter and Colonel Edward House, whom, like Frankfurter, he knew from the campaign to end the occupation of Haiti. House no longer possessed the influence he had enjoyed as Wilson's most intimate adviser on international affairs, although during the early New Deal he functioned as something akin to the progressive conscience of the era. Gruening enjoyed several "very pleasant" conversations with the colonel, whom he described as a "thoroughly enlightened and sympathetic" figure. Frankfurter agreed with this characterization of the "charming old boy."[70]

Gruening also flooded House with letters, which the colonel dutifully passed on to Cordell Hull and Assistant Secretary of State Francis Sayre, Wilson's son-in-law. Given that "events indicate that Mr. Welles has failed to gauge the situation adequately," Gruening termed it "the height of folly" that "he should now leave Cuba on which he was supposed to be a specialist, and attempt to direct all Latin American affairs." He recommended instead the appointment of Hubert Herring, or someone else "thoroughly conversant with Latin American affairs" (clearly himself), as chief policy officer for the region. What Walter White of the NAACP termed Gruening's "plot," however, went nowhere. After House failed to smooth the way for the adoption of Gruening's scheme, the editor again turned to Frankfurter, who unhelpfully suggested that if Gruening really wanted to pursue the matter, he could write a personal letter to the White House. When Gruening pressed, Frankfurter responded sympathetically but realistically: Roosevelt had already made his decision and would bring Welles back to Washington once conditions in Cuba had stabilized. Left with no other choice, Gruening heightened his public criticism of Welles's performance, chastising him in radio remarks, addresses on the lecture circuit, and *Nation* editorials. He also obtained an appointment with Hull to make his case personally; he found the secretary attentive, but hampered by an "amazing" lack of "knowledge of what is going on in the Department." Given developments in Cuba and Haiti, where the administration retained the treaty negotiated by Dana Munro during the Hoover administration, Gruening could detect "no sign of any new deal in the one field of foreign relations where it would be possible to achieve one."[71]

Alarmed, Gruening saw the Seventh International Conference of American States, scheduled for December 1933 in Montevideo, as the final chance for the administration to define a more enlightened policy toward the region. He considered it a positive sign that Hull rather than Welles would lead the delegation. But otherwise Gruening judged the delegation "very bad," since it lacked representation from the anti-imperialist community. To redeem this oversight and, he hoped, to facilitate his transition into a policy-making role, Gruening lobbied hard for an official position. He championed a focus on replacing the Monroe Doctrine with "multilateral machinery for intervention if and when that should be necessary"; he also advocated abrogating the Platt Amendment to improve the tone of inter-American relations. Repeating a theme which he had been developing for the previous two years, he reasoned that "at a time of increasing world chaos and distrust, with international cooperation in Europe and in the Orient apparently on the decline and the use of force ascendant in international dealings," the conference afforded "an unusual opportunity to strengthen the factors that make for harmony and peace in the Western Hemisphere."[72]

Much to his surprise, his rather strong public and private criticism of the administration's Cuban and Haitian policies did not prevent Roosevelt from naming him special adviser to the delegation. Gruening conceded that the president's action indicated a "breadth of mind" in the administration that he had not thought existed. Dorothy Detzer of the Women's International League for Peace and Freedom agreed, hailing the decision as the first "convincing evidence of a new deal in United States policy toward Latin America." The appointment, however, was more reflective of the president's tactic of naming figures of widely varying viewpoints to key positions in his administration to check one another, thus ensuring that control over policy remained vested in his hands alone. The Montevideo delegation, for example, balanced Gruening's anti-imperialist outlook with that of adherents to a more traditional view of inter-American relations such as J. Reuben Clark, Morrow's successor as ambassador to Mexico, and Alexander Weddell, a career foreign service officer who had served as one of James Sheffield's consuls in Mexico.[73]

The conference started off meeting Gruening's low expectations. The instructions to the delegation, which resembled those from the 1920s, showed that the administration did not foresee a broad change in policy. Hull, whom Gruening accompanied on the boat trip to Uruguay, confirmed this point, equating a pledge against unilateral intervention with political suicide. The adviser nonetheless penned a memorandum making the case for abandoning the right to intervene just in case. Gruening also worked to defuse tensions with the delegation representing Grau's Cuba, which Hull feared would attack the United States in its address to the conference. Pleased, the secretary promised to address another of Gruening's concerns, modifying the financial protectorate over Haiti, on his return to Washington. This minor concession to his point of view was all that Gruening needed. He quickly informed the Haitian delegation to the conference (which, by coincidence, was traveling on the same ship) that Hull sympathized with their joint concerns and would support a Haitian demand to weaken the Munro treaty, now championed most earnestly by Assistant Secretary of State William Phillips, by withdrawing U.S. control of Haitian finances. Moreover, Gruening added that Hull's State Department would "lend its good offices in the matter in any way that will not involve the American Government in any further responsibility in Haiti." Phillips, caught off guard when the Haitian negotiating team presented him with an aide-mémoire summarizing the secretary's purported position, could only complain privately about being blindsided by the activities of unofficial diplomats.[74]

Then the conference itself took an unexpected turn after Hull, sensing the depth of Latin American opinion on the issue, agreed to the report of the Committee on Rights and Duties of States, which forbade intervention in the internal affairs of another Western hemisphere nation. The secretary's diplomatic flexibility impressed Gruening. He urged Freda Kirchwey to play up Hull's accomplishments, since increasing the secretary's prestige would "make it easier for him to deal with career men, who will have to be licked on both Cuba and Haiti." For his part, Hull expressed "special satisfaction" with Gruening's "highly capable and valuable cooperation" throughout the conference, where he "exhibited initiative, constructive capability, and a spirit of splendid teamwork." Given Gruening's personality, either he was on his best behavior in Montevideo or, more likely (especially in light of the Haitian affair), Hull offered the last comment tongue in cheek.[75]

THE AFTERMATH OF the Montevideo Conference produced a series of changes which dramatically altered the Good Neighbor Policy and ultimately paved the way for Gruening's entrance into government service. In late December, Roosevelt publicly commended Hull's performance in Uruguay and committed the United States to political noninterference in Latin American affairs. In line with this new policy, the administration abrogated the Platt Amendment and renegotiated the withdrawal from Haiti on favorable terms. In fact, on his return to Washington, Hull gave "every attention . . . to overhauling the San Domingan, the Haitian," and the other policies which Gruening had brought to his attention during their joint stint in Montevideo. Moreover, as the secretary assured Gruening, he knew that he could "as a last resort lay any doubtful or seriously difficult issues before the President, especially in view of his keen interest in all of these problems." Bureaucratically, these developments signaled the temporary eclipse of Welles after his controversial tenure in Cuba, allowing for new voices in the making of inter-American policy. Hull took advantage. In the secretary's interpretation of Wilsonianism, lowering trade barriers represented the surest path to world peace. In 1934 he secured a presidential commitment to the Reciprocal Trade Agreement Act, authorizing the State Department to conduct bilateral negotiations with Latin American countries to reduce tariff duties. This version of economic internationalism then joined political noninterference as the second tenet of the administration's emerging new Latin American policy.[76]

On a personal level, the return from Montevideo was distinctly unpleasant for Gruening: amebic dysentery stranded him in Lima for several weeks of convalescence. But the policy changes more than made up for the personal discomfort. Not content to rest on his laurels, Gruening urged Hull to press forward with a host of initiatives "to validate . . . by acts the faith engendered at Montevideo." Gruening's conclusion that the era of U.S. intervention in Latin America had ended also implied the passing of the era of muckraking U.S. imperialism; a return to his 1920s framework thus would serve no purpose. Meanwhile, being at *The Nation* now was less appealing than in the early 1920s. When Gruening was still establishing his national reputation, *The Nation* had given him an opening to national circles. By the 1930s, however, the small audience it reached seemed too restrictive. *Current History* and the *New York Times Magazine*, to which he contributed freelance pieces on Caribbean affairs, were more to his liking, while roundtable discussions either at the Council on Foreign Relations or after his lectures at the New School had a better chance of reaching his desired audience of politically influential figures.[77]

Gruening met privately with Hull several times in early 1934 to discuss Latin American affairs, and clearly hoped that his flattery would result in the offer of a slot at the State Department. Instead, the first attractive position that opened fell under the jurisdiction of the War Department's Bureau of Insular Affairs. Like most anti-imperialists, Gruening viewed the U.S. handling of Puerto Rico as an important element of the nation's overall policy toward Latin America, and when the island's governor, Robert Gore, resigned, the forty-six-year-old editor bid aggressively for the position. With his State Department contacts of little value, Gruening turned to Edward Moran, the onetime Democratic nominee for governor of Maine who had won election to the House of Representatives in the Democratic sweep of 1932. The *Evening News* had supported Moran's gubernatorial bids; now the congressman returned the favor, telling Roosevelt that naming Gruening would fulfill their common desire of having "the 'New Deal' extended to cover our insular possessions." Characteristically, the president praised Gruening's "splendid service" at Montevideo, but informed Moran that he had already decided to appoint Blanton Winship, a retired army officer, to succeed Gore. Summarizing the sentiment of the anti-imperialist community about the appointment, *The Nation* dismissed Winship for his "kindly contempt for 'backward' and underprivileged peoples."[78]

Given his usual reaction to personal slights, Gruening took the setback surprisingly well. Unlike in his quest for the Haitian ministership two years before, he had sought the Puerto Rican governorship only because it was the first position related to Caribbean policy that became available after the Montevideo Conference, not out of any desire for the job itself. Gruening understood from his friendship with Theodore Roosevelt, Jr., the limitations of the position: the Puerto Rican governor possessed few patronage powers, dealt with an often fractious territorial legislature, and, most important from Gruening's standpoint, reported to the secretary of war. Roosevelt's attempts to use the governorship to influence Hoover administration policy toward the rest of the Caribbean Basin therefore had excited the jealousy of a State Department eager to retain control over all aspects of inter-American affairs. Given his even more ambitious plans, Gruening undoubtedly would have generated a similar response.

Still, in early 1934, Gruening found himself in an awkward position. The transformation of U.S. policy toward Latin America seemed to have given him everything that he had wanted in the 1920s. The policies of Hughes and Kellogg were a distant memory, replaced by those of an administration committed to military noninterventionism, suspicious of the power of big business at home, and tolerant enough of divergent viewpoints to name even a confirmed critic such as Gruening delegation adviser. Yet these policy changes were no longer enough. Noninterventionism alone would not achieve Gruening's international goals, as it might have in the 1920s, when reformers enjoyed strong positions throughout the Caribbean Basin. This astute observer of Caribbean politics understood that reactionary forces in the region actually could benefit from a blanket U.S. policy of noninterventionism. In Haiti, for example, President Stenio Vincent, to the bitter disappointment of pro-Haitian activists in the United States, had abandoned his democratic promise and was governing by dictatorial decree. Gruening unsuccessfully urged Union Patriotique members to increase international pressure on the regime by resigning from the government, and then lobbied Vincent to reverse course. Vincent's private secretary knew Gruening well: he rebuked the editor for his "personal tendency, many times exhibited, to lend . . . an ear readily too complaisant only to the biased information that your political correspondents in Haiti transmit to you." (The criticism in this case was off base, although it applied in general.) Thus rebuffed, Gruening urged "outside pressure" on Vincent to end the "ghastly" situation. The NAACP agreed, suggesting another public inquiry into Haiti along the model of the Forbes commission; Walter White privately told Gruening that he refused to let those in Haiti who had betrayed the principles of the battle in the 1920s "jeopardize all that we have fought for." The administration, however, had no interest in abandoning its noninterventionist pledges to assist reformers in Haiti.[79]

Events in the neighboring Dominican Republic intensified Gruening's belief in the need for a more active U.S. role assisting the region's suddenly beleaguered reformers. He reasoned that U.S. officials should have realized that providing the politically fragile nation with an efficient, well-trained military would have disastrous consequences, as indeed it had, by paving the way for dictator Rafael Trujillo to assume power. Even "granted a policy of non-intervention," Gruening believed that the United States could still demand that "neighboring governments which seek from us loans, moratoriums, favors, and cooperation of one kind of another . . . be responsive to certain demands of elementary decency which bear on mutual welfare and joint interests." As a last resort he urged military action with other Latin American countries to oust Trujillo, though "it may well be that the mobilized public opinion of the pan-American family of nations might bring to a speedy end the existing terror and tyranny." The Dominican case, the first time in his life in which he recommended U.S. military intervention in the Caribbean Basin, showed how far he was willing to go in the name of assisting the cause of reformers overseas.[80]

With the Puerto Rican position filled, appointment to a high-level State Department post dealing with Latin American affairs unlikely, and *The Nation* still too limiting, Gruening considered an entirely different line of work: securing an academic post. The proposed career change was less startling than it appeared on the surface. His own intellectual credentials had long allowed him to move comfortably in the world of higher education, while his lecturing career and his work at the New School further expanded his contact with academics. Moreover, several other anti-imperialists, such as Samuel Guy Inman and Frank Tannenbaum, obtained positions as professors in the early 1930s. At a more basic level, Gruening's conception of politics stressed the importance of education. As a journalist he sought to educate the public as to the merit of his causes; now he looked to educate the next generation's elite. But, typically, his own sense of self-worth exceeded the view of others. He indicated that he would accept only a position as head of a department of Latin American studies, and only at a centrally located university with sufficient prestige—Columbia or Yale. When, given his lack of a Ph.D., neither school showed interest, Gruening elected to return to daily journalism, accepting an offer to become managing editor of the *New York Post*. J. David Stern, who had recently purchased the paper, was impressed enough with Gruening's credentials to grant him editorial control. Moreover, the *Post*, one of the major New York metropolitan dailies, provided an opportunity to influence a wider segment of the population than could ever be possible from the pages of *The Nation*. Gruening, "full of zest for the battle," quickly accepted the most prestigious newspaper assignment of his career.[81]

He then positioned the *Post*'s editorial pages behind the efforts of Frankfurter, Brandeis, and their protégés. Confirming a pattern evident since his closing years in Maine, he looked to Washington rather than to state governments for action. Though pleased with the overall course of administration policy—the president was showing a greater inclination to embark on anti-business initiatives, as his support for establishing a Securities and Exchange Commission indicated—Gruening was not yet willing to affiliate with the Democratic Party. Instead, he retained his conviction that progressives should act as an independent force in American politics. The editor called for Roosevelt to order his postmaster general, James Farley, to marshal his patronage behind pro–New Deal members of Congress, such as Robert La Follette, Jr. (Progressive–Wisconsin) and Bronson Cutting (R–New Mexico), regardless of their partisan affiliation. He noted that many progressives "long before the advent of Mr. Roosevelt to the Presidency foresaw the need of many of the measures and policies which he is now carrying out." Gruening clearly considered himself one of this number.[82]

Consistent with his habit over the preceding decade, even his return to daily journalism did not turn Gruening's thoughts from inter-American affairs. The editor received the opportunity to renew his interest in the matter sooner than expected. Surprised when an anti-monopoly editorial which singled out millionaire Vincent Astor for criticism never made it to press, Gruening demanded an explanation. Stern informed him that he had killed the piece. The *Post*, like so many papers for which Gruening had worked, was experiencing financial difficulties, and Stern had approached Astor for a loan. He was afraid that the funds would not be forthcoming if the editorial appeared, and asked Gruening to understand his position. Gruening refused to compromise, and, for the second time in his newspaper career, resigned over an issue of principle. He never again would work in journalism. Lamenting that the profession "isn't what it used to be," he feared that the days for innovative reporting and sharp editorial writing apparently had passed.[83]

For the first time in Gruening's life, financial difficulties made his refusal to compromise his principles a risky endeavor, especially since Hunt was set to enroll at Harvard that fall. This pressure, combined with that from high taxes, prompted him to take a step which he had resisted for years: he finally sold the Rockport summer home, for $17,500. The funds were quickly exhausted. The family's financial situation had deteriorated so much that, unbeknownst to him, Dorothy had pawned her engagement ring. Upset when he discovered his wife's action, Gruening rushed to the pawnshop, only to find that the ring had already been sold. As a substitute, he bought his wife a zircon imitation diamond, since he could afford nothing else.[84]

Luckily, Gruening was out of work for less than a week before he was contacted by an old friend, Charles Thomson, formerly the head of the Fellowship of Reconciliation's branch in Latin America. Thomson had met Gruening when the two served as the featured lecturers for Herring's CCRLA Caribbean seminar. When a shortfall of funds caused the FOR to close its Latin American office in 1932, Thomson moved on to a position as the Latin American specialist at the Foreign Policy Association, which he obtained with Gruening's assistance. In early 1934 Thomson returned the favor, asking Gruening to participate in the association's study mission to Cuba, undertaken at the invitation of Carlos Mendieta, who succeeded Grau as president (and quickly obtained U.S. recognition). The offer seemed too good to be true. Gruening would analyze the Cuban utilities industry, thus allowing him to spend time on his two most passionate intellectual pursuits—inter-American relations and utilities regulation. After several weeks in Cuba, Gruening penned a twenty-page report promoting more effective government regulation by strengthening the Cuban national public utilities commission. He rejected, however, pleas from some Cuban activists for nationalizing the Cuban utilities industry, citing cost concerns.[85]

Gruening's willingness to accept a formal State Department position at Montevideo and then work with an establishment organization such as the Foreign Policy Association reflected his conviction that anti-imperialists needed to adapt to the altered international climate by entering the political mainstream. This view, however, aroused opposition, especially from Carleton Beals. While, after late 1933, most anti-imperialists praised Roosevelt's Latin American policies, Beals, who had savagely criticized Welles's diplomacy in Cuba, developed a penetrating critique which argued that Hull's program of tariff reciprocity demanded that Latin Americans "remain dutiful little colonies under Uncle Sam's tutelage." Beals feared that the president's commitment to cease military intervention in the region had blinded anti-imperialists to the more important economic aspects of his policies. "Deeply shocked" at Beals's perspective, Gruening tartly informed his former comrade that he for one had not "succumbed to the conspiracy complex." Beals responded by dismissing Gruening as "another of our sad turncoats and boot-lickers," and exacted his revenge when the Cuban study appeared. Using *The Nation*'s pages against its former editor, Beals devoted half of a scathing review of the report to its chapter on public utilities, which he described as favoring private utility companies "under a thin veneer of academic impartiality." Since the commission concluded by recommending that Cuba hire more U.S. experts, Beals noted, he could only hope for divine assistance for "the Cubans if some of the members of this commission are a sample."[86]

In many ways, the tangle with Beals foreshadowed events to come. Beals argued that anti-imperialists could not ally with policy makers without sacrificing their basic ideals. Gruening, however, considered such an objection narrow and ultimately self-defeating. Having tasted power, he accurately sensed that the altered domestic and international climate offered a chance to translate his ideals into policy—but only by entering the policy-making fray, not by standing outside it. He remained determined not to sacrifice the opportunity when it arose.

4

The Dilemmas of Anti-imperialism

In 1933, concerned that Postmaster General James Farley was using Puerto Rican appointments to satisfy Democratic patronage needs, Gruening, then at *The Nation*, asked Hubert Herring to stop by the island on his way to the Montevideo Conference. What he discovered did not please him: Herring accused the new governor, Robert Gore, of allowing his lack of sympathy for the aims of Chancellor Carlos Chardón and his Liberal Party supporters to influence his policy toward the University of Puerto Rico. Herring left no doubt about the issue's importance. The administration, he said, needed to "take swift measures" to redress Gore's hostility to local reformers, since Puerto Rico was "a test of the reality" of Roosevelt's stated intentions to improve inter-American relations. Herring, like other anti-imperialists, had come to view U.S. policy toward Puerto Rico as part of a broader inter-American agenda, a development pioneered by Gruening in 1931.[1]

Such a perspective extended beyond the anti-imperialist community. Gore's policies prompted Hamilton Fish Armstrong, editor of *Foreign Affairs*, to solicit a long article by Theodore Roosevelt, Jr., on the subject. Echoing Gruening, Roosevelt considered ties with Latin America "the most important foreign relationships of the United States." Puerto Rico could "serve as the connecting link between the two great divisions," helping to bridge a "wide misunderstanding and antagonism between the two cultures." The protests against Gore's performance also prompted the president to establish an Inter-Departmental Committee on Puerto Rico headed by the Frankfurter bloc's ideological rival Rexford Tugwell, who hoped to structure a planned economy for the island as a model for his desired reforms in the United States. In his usual fashion, however, Roosevelt simultaneously moved in another policy direction, proposing a single colonial office, in the Department of the Interior, with responsibility for the affairs of Alaska, Hawaii, the Virgin Islands, and Puerto Rico. While administratively consolidating Alaska, Hawaii, and the Virgin Islands created little stir, the decision to remove Puerto Rico from the control of the War Department generated a good deal of criticism. George Dern, the secretary of war, opposed the move as diminishing his department's prerogatives, while Budget Director Lewis Douglas complained that thus far in the administration "nearly every transfer has been followed by a call for expansion and the expenditure of more money by the agency to whom the transfer was made."[2]

Roosevelt, dismissing these objections as "not serious," authorized the Division of Territories and Island Possessions (DTIP) on May 29, 1934. In testimony to his stature, Gruening was the only candidate considered to head the new division. Inter-American issues played the key role in both the agency's creation and Gruening's appointment. As Harold Ickes put it, the editor's familiarity "with affairs in Latin America and elsewhere outside of the continental United States" made him "particularly valuable." When offered the post, Gruening traveled to Hyde Park to express concern about the resemblance between the DTIP and the British Colonial Office, given his belief that "a democracy shouldn't have any colonies." Roosevelt, agreeing, told Gruening to "see what you can develop."[3]

Gruening's appointment received rave reviews outside the administration, as had occurred after he was named to the Montevideo delegation. Samuel Guy Inman told Gruening that the DTIP was "exactly the right place for your talents and your big heart"; *The Nation*, speaking on behalf of "liberals and anti-imperialists everywhere," termed the move "one of those acts of grace by means of which the present Administration so often redeems its political errors and disarms its critics." Herring celebrated the "grand" turn of events; Gruening responded by suggesting that Herring "at once" start CCRLA seminars for the Virgin Islands, Puerto Rico, Alaska, and Hawaii. Reformist forces in Puerto

Rico likewise celebrated. *La Democracia* noted that "liberals and anti-imperialists of all areas" were celebrating the "most important" action undertaken by Roosevelt "since he announced the New Deal." The *Washington Post* reported that liberal Puerto Ricans already were calling Gruening their "first ace in the New Deal."[4]

The most touching tribute came from Villard. The elder statesman of the anti-imperialist community and Gruening's close friend could not recall more satisfaction with any appointment in his entire life; indeed, it seemed "really too good to be true that this important position has been given to one who is ideally fitted for it." Villard predicted that Gruening's single-mindedness would serve him well at the DTIP, where his work would "have a profound effect upon our relations with the other American republics." Privately, he admitted a touch of envy for Gruening's "opportunity to translate into action the ideals that you have so long cherished and worked for." To a figure accustomed to the political wilderness, "it seems really beyond belief that one of us has received such public recognition."[5]

Gruening immediately departed from the precedents established by Tugwell during the latter's brief period of preeminence in coordinating insular affairs. Tugwell had considered Governor Blanton Winship "a fine old army man with . . . what appears to be a nice mixture of tact and firmness," and had looked for the governor's help in implementing his approach toward the island. Gruening, by contrast, had no intention of vesting authority in a governor who shared Tugwell's perspective, and overruled all plans for cooperating with the governor. Furthermore, regardless of the ideological tone of the dispute, he found Winship, previously a military aide to Coolidge, an unappealing figure personally.[6]

All concerned admitted that the task of rehabilitating Puerto Rico economically would test Gruening's capabilities as both a policy planner and an administrator. By 1930, 53 percent of the island's exports came from sugar, cultivation of which required large landholdings; 58 percent of the island's sugar production was under the control of non–Puerto Rican ownership, dominated by four U.S. corporations. Technically, a 1900 statute limiting to five hundred acres the amount of land any person or corporation could hold prevented concentrated landholding, but the law was so rarely enforced that in 1930 agricultural holdings exceeding the legal limit totaled 32 percent of the island's farm acreage. While Puerto Rico thus suffered from the effects of latifundia and the domination of U.S. capital in its production, its economic well-being revolved around regular access to the U.S. market. Before annexation, roughly two thirds of the island's exports had gone to the United States; by 1930, this figure had ballooned to more than 90 percent. These economic trends rendered Puerto Rico particularly vulnerable to the depression's effects. In 1933, with 65 percent of the half million–person work force unemployed, 42 percent of the population received some form of government relief, although by one estimate 80 percent would have qualified for assistance if more funds had been available.[7]

Shortly after his appointment, Gruening visited Roosevelt to complain that he lacked sufficient authority to address these problems. He therefore presented the president with a plan for a new organization coordinating all federal assistance to Puerto Rico. Gruening scored his first victory with ease. The executive order creating the Puerto Rican Reconstruction Administration (PRRA) was issued the next day in the precise form proposed by the new administrator. Ickes complained that he had never seen the document. Given the experimental character of this stage of the New Deal and the president's bureaucratic style, the degree to which Roosevelt endorsed Gruening's agenda remained unclear. No doubt existed, however, about the effects on Puerto Rico. After the formation of the PRRA, Gruening became the political and economic czar over Puerto Rican affairs, commanding a bureaucracy which peaked at 53,000, five times the size of the insular government.[8]

Gruening then embarked on a bold plan to fashion in Puerto Rico an alternative to the political and economic nationalism adopted by many other Latin American states during the depression. After years of frustration, he finally had the chance to illustrate how a positive U.S. policy could assist Latin American reformers. To "attack the whole problem radically and comprehensively," the PRRA administrator looked to promote land reform, encourage agricultural diversification, establish a rural cooperative movement, develop locally financed industries, and deal with the overpopulation problem as effectively as possible, given the restraints imposed by the opposition of the Catholic Church. He also termed it "imperative" to obtain assistance from the Puerto Rican legislature through local legislation to strengthen the five hundred–acre law, increase income and inheritance taxes, and create a pension program for territorial government employees. Gruening differentiated his program from agencies such as the Puerto Rican branch of the Federal Emergency Relief Administration (the PRERA), which handled insular relief before the creation of the PRRA. While the PRERA concentrated on making direct relief grants, the "whole object" of the PRRA, he said, was "to deal effectively with those social and economic trends that have led to increasing poverty, landlessness, and unemployment in Puerto Rico." Given this ambition, Gruening quickly phased out the PRERA, headed by Roosevelt's former neighbor and friend James Bourne. With Bourne's departure, the only major figure in the U.S. bureaucracy who did not share Gruening's perspective on Puerto Rican policy was Winship, whose weak institutional powers initially made his contest with Gruening appear one-sided in the PRRA head's favor.[9]

Gruening's economic program used several different elements of his ideological arsenal. First, he borrowed from what he perceived as the successes of Calles during the 1920s—especially agrarian reform. Second, his perspective on the proper relationship between government and industry remained essentially unaltered from his time in Maine, where his battles against private utilities had led him to promote policies to defend the consumer against monopoly. Finally, the evolution of Gruening's foreign policy beliefs prompted him to consider how Puerto Rico could serve as a model for inter-American relations, a framework which the United States could then apply elsewhere in the Caribbean Basin. In accomplishing this goal, he sought to create in Puerto Rico what amounted to an early version of a foreign aid program.

In line with his 1920s perspective, however, Gruening never intended for Washington to impose reconstruction on the island. But the confusing nature of Puerto Rican politics complicated his search for insular political allies. In the wake of the U.S. annexation, two major political parties emerged, the Republicans of José Celso Barbosa and the Federalists, later the Unionists, led by Luis Muñoz Rivera. Both represented the economic elite, differing on the question of political status, with the Republicans recommending statehood and the Unionists independence. The postwar era, meanwhile, featured the emergence of the Socialist Party (actually a labor party affiliated with the American Federation of Labor), which captured almost one fourth of the vote in the 1924 elections. Patronage, however, constituted the dominant theme of Puerto Rican politics throughout the 1920s, as the three major parties entered and then severed a series of political coalitions. After the Republican-Unionist alliance broke down in 1929, the paralyzed territorial legislature accomplished virtually nothing for the next three years. Another political alignment formed for the 1932 elections, as the Republicans teamed with the Socialists, though the two parties shared only a common antipathy to Antonio Barceló's Unionist forces, which reorganized as the Liberal Party. Meanwhile, a pro-independence party, the Nationalists, also appeared, led by the Harvard-educated Pedro Albizu Campos. Although the Liberals captured a plurality of the vote in the elections, a majority went to the Republican-Socialist coalition. The Nationalists, who drew only 3 percent, announced that they would bypass further participation in the political process in favor of violent pressure tactics.[10]

By the time of his arrival in Puerto Rico, Gruening confronted a complex three-track political system, with differing partisan alignments on the questions of the island's political status, patronage interests, and issues relating to economic and social reform. Given his chief interest—implementing a social and economic reform package for the island—Gruening needed to focus insular politics on the economic question while downplaying the patronage and status issues, on which the Puerto Rican reformers with whom he wanted to ally were divided. Ultimately, the success of his administration would hinge on his ability to accomplish this goal. In this task he benefited from the efforts of Muñoz Rivera's son, Luis Muñoz Marín, whom he had befriended when both were living in New York, to reconstitute the Liberals as a party explicitly committed to social and economic reform.[11] At the same time, in line with the anti-imperialist perspective both he and Gruening personified, Muñoz Marín adopted an uncompromising position on political status, demanding outright independence for the island. Luckily for Gruening, in 1934 it seemed unlikely that this question would emerge as the key issue in insular politics, given the magnitude of Puerto Rico's economic distress.[12]

During the first few months after the creation of the DTIP, Muñoz Marín, in the United States representing his party's interests, served as Gruening's principal interpreter of island politics. The two traveled together from New York to Washington just after the announcement of

Gruening's appointment, and had several joint meetings with Roosevelt to discuss Puerto Rican policy. Muñoz Marín saw as his ideological enemies not only the legislative majority of the coalition parties but also Winship, the "reactionary Archangel" whose "very strong leaning towards extending the rule of absentee capital in Puerto Rico" explained his conservative policies. Of course, such rhetoric reflected Gruening's biases as well, and he quickly allied with the reform-minded group within the Liberal Party, which also included Carlos Chardón, the chancellor of the University of Puerto Rico, and José Padín, the island's agriculture secretary. Gruening appointed important Liberals to the key local positions of the PRRA, notably the office of regional administrator (Gruening's deputy), which went to Chardón; he also stacked the PRRA executive board with Liberal members, justifying this controversial course with the argument that all board members needed to be in "thorough sympathy with the reconstruction program." The Liberals in turn supported Gruening's agenda wholeheartedly.[13]

Backing the Liberals so strongly gave Gruening a committed political base, but it also meant that he inherited enemies almost from the moment of his appointment. One such figure was Winship. Others included members of the coalition's majority party, the Republicans, whose leader, Rafael Martínez Nadal, pointed to the friendship of Gruening and Muñoz Marín, "contracted in Bohemian literary centres of New York and Washington," to explain the adoption of "wildly radical, impractical, and visionary schemes for which the people are not yet ready." He promised that the coalition would use its legislative majority to block Gruening's initiatives. The PRRA head clearly disagreed with Martínez Nadal ideologically. But, in what would set a pattern for his Puerto Rican tenure, personal dislike poisoned Gruening's relationship with the island's legislative leader, thus minimizing the possibility of compromise and compelling him to look beyond the legislature for political support. He initially hoped to use Winship's institutional powers and—implementing long-held beliefs—a public relations campaign to force his program through. The governor, however, envisioned a very different Puerto Rico from that of the PRRA administrator, and social and economic reform were not high on his agenda. Gruening later concluded that the appointment of a military man to the civilian post of governor was a mistake, and that he should have pressed harder for Winship's removal.[14]

Given the ideological and personal tensions between the two, Winship unsurprisingly reacted strongly when Gruening began giving him orders and claiming the authority to decide which candidates would fill local appointments that the governor controlled, such as the island's attorney general. When Gruening continued to press the matter, Winship ordered his legal adviser to prepare a memorandum showing how Gruening's "intervening in the internal affairs of Puerto Rico and attempting to control executive action therein" violated the island's Organic Act. Charles Fahy, the solicitor general of the Interior Department, admitted that the memorandum raised "some delicate questions," since the law clearly favored Winship. But Fahy urged looking at the spirit of the act, doubting that its authors had intended to paralyze the execution of federal policy toward the island. He therefore asked Harold Ickes to handle the matter informally by asking Winship to try to accommodate Gruening's demands.[15]

Ickes not only denied the request but also ordered Fahy to draft an opinion delineating the governor's legal authority and thus, apparently, limiting Gruening's. For the secretary, who usually defended his department's prerogatives zealously, personal considerations motivated his decision: he had come to despise Gruening, despite their agreement on most national political questions and on nearly all Puerto Rican issues. A prominent midwestern progressive Republican, Ickes revered Brandeis, and his opinion on the utilities issue had played a key role in his decision to endorse Roosevelt in 1932. This common support for the anti-monopoly tradition also led the secretary to back Gruening's economic program for Puerto Rico. Moreover, like Gruening, Ickes considered Puerto Rico a key element of U.S. policy toward Latin America. Gruening, meanwhile, initially viewed his new boss positively. While still at *The Nation*, he praised the "revolution taking place in the Department of the Interior," predicting that Ickes would oversee a "thorough" weeding out of "the agents of the monopolists, land-grabbers, and other interests who are still on the department's pay roll." The two, however, were too alike in personality to remain on friendly terms for long. Both lacked tact, tended to personalize disputes, viewed with paranoia any attempts to trespass on their bureaucratic prerogatives, and strove to extend their own power at the expense of others within the executive branch. Chatting with Tennessee Valley administrator David Lilienthal, Gruening later characterized Ickes as "the most prehensile and acquisitive man in Washington," adding that "there is no part of the Government that he doesn't want to get his hands on, and he is perfectly sure that he could run them all, and run them better than they are being run now." Ickes believed the same about Gruening. Upon Assistant Secretary Oscar Chapman, one of the few in the Interior Department to maintain cordial relations with both men, fell the thankless task of attempting to keep "things going as smoothly as possible between them."[16]

Sensing that Gruening's support in Washington might be shaky, the leaders of the coalition stepped up the pressure. Martínez Nadal acidly expressed his certainty that Roosevelt never intended to make the Puerto Rican legislature "mere decorative figures or marionettes or rubber stamps to act at the will of Mr. Gruening." In a line of argument which particularly infuriated Gruening, the coalition leader asked Puerto Ricans to compare Gruening's "words of liberty, democracy, and respect for the people" from the 1920s with his "disrespectful, unjust, abusive, partial, arbitrary, and despotic actions" at the PRRA. Illustrating the way in which all sides in the dispute interpreted Puerto Rican affairs as part of broader inter-American policy, other Republicans, such as Luis Antonio Miranda, described the island as "the laboratory where the United States must prove to measure its faithfulness to the Pan-American policies." He called on the coalition to challenge Gruening publicly, thus letting "Spanish-America know of the peril behind the friendly aims that will be offered them for the sake of Pan-Americanism." Gruening responded in kind, and by the end of 1935, the chief federal official in Puerto Rico and the leaders of the island's legislative majority were no longer on speaking terms.[17]

This local opposition, combined with Ickes's hostility, seemed to ensure that Gruening's program would never get off the ground. But the PRRA head had one more card to play. In the summer of 1935, after a frustrating ten months as chief federal policy maker toward Puerto Rico, Gruening again turned to the White House. He requested an executive order allowing the PRRA administrator to authorize spending from the administration's fund "without the approval or concurrence of any other officer of the Government." He further demanded permission for the PRRA to issue long-term loans as well as to make changes in its legal status to facilitate the development of cooperatives on the island. Finally, Gruening wanted the executive order to give him "full authority to prescribe all rules and regulations . . . necessary for the government of the Administration." In short, he sought the power to coordinate federal policy toward Puerto Rico unilaterally, with the ability to bypass the Puerto Rican legislature, Winship, and even Ickes. Bureaucratically, this strategy probably represented the only choice available in mid-1935. But structuring an entire policy around sustained support from the White House, especially given Roosevelt's tendency to abandon appointees when they became politically controversial, was a dangerous tactic. In addition, relying on executive orders contradicted Gruening's long-standing rhetorical commitment to democratic decision making.[18]

Despite the extreme nature of these requests, Gruening obtained complete support from Roosevelt. Stunned at the turn of events, Ickes asked Fahy whether he could remove Gruening for insubordination. Fahy cautioned against the move, noting that the most "peculiar" nature of the executive order creating the PRRA gave Gruening the "full power to act" without Ickes's sanction. Moreover, Roosevelt supplemented the formal grants of power to Gruening by informally boosting the position of the PRRA head. After Gruening termed it "very desirable" for Winship to hear "directly" from the president, urging him "to cooperate with the Department," Roosevelt sent out the desired letter. (A few months later Gruening reported back that Winship was "co-operating splendidly, and so is his cabinet.") The president also endorsed Gruening's request that Winship appoint a new Puerto Rican attorney general, the officer responsible for enforcing the five hundred–acre law. Roosevelt even promised Gruening the "fullest cooperation" in any Puerto Rican initiative, reaffirming that Gruening had "complete responsibility" for federal policy toward the island. Hoping that some softening in presidential backing had occurred, in May 1936 Ickes made an oral request to the White House concerning the level of support for Gruening's agenda. The Bureau of the Budget disappointed the secretary with its assurance that the PRRA program stood "in accord with the program of the President." From the State Department, Sumner Welles enjoyed no more success; the president canceled several meetings to discuss what the assistant secretary of state considered Gruening's overly prominent role in framing the administration's inter-American policy.[19]

Roosevelt adopted this course for a number of reasons. Backing the

PRRA administrator clearly firmed up support for the administration from anti-imperialists at minimal political cost. More important, Gruening and the president agreed that Puerto Rico served as the "obvious channel for establishing closer relations with Latin America" through a program of financial and technical assistance. To this agenda Gruening added a call for supporting Puerto Rican leaders of reformist and democratic inclinations. Although the United States obviously enjoyed more leverage over events in Puerto Rico than in any independent nation in the Caribbean Basin, both of these tenets, he understood, could easily form the basis of U.S. relations with other countries of the region. Finally, the PRRA administrator argued that these generous policies would provide tangible evidence of the end of U.S. imperialism. The success of his program thus not only "would mean a great deal for Puerto Rico" but also would play a key role "in improving our relations with Latin America." In its broadest sense, then, Gruening's agenda represented the third facet of the early Good Neighbor Policy, a positive complement to Hull's politically neutral reciprocal trade agreements and the politically negative policy of noninterference and nonintervention.[20]

Armed with almost unlimited power, Gruening began to implement his program. As had been the case in both Boston and Portland, his difficulties in delegating authority prompted him to coordinate all initiatives from his Washington office. (He flew to Puerto Rico at least once a month.) The most ambitious element of his economic agenda was a broad-based rural rehabilitation effort focused on strengthening the five hundred–acre law. Indicating his point of view on the question, Gruening appointed Miguel Guerra-Mondragon, the insular representative of the American Civil Liberties Union (ACLU), as his special adviser on antitrust matters, with the task of assisting in the prosecution of cases involving the five hundred–acre law. This move intensified the split with the coalition, whose leaders argued that Puerto Rico needed immediate relief more than a long-term restructuring of its land policy, and with Winship, who refused to shepherd a bill to toughen the act through the legislature. For Gruening, however, the matter's importance extended beyond the economic reform which theoretically guided the PRRA. As he argued in his writings on Mexico, agrarian reform was critical to the development of a stable citizenry on which a democracy could rest. In fact, Gruening was attempting to assemble a model for constructing a civil society which other Latin American countries could emulate with U.S. financial and moral assistance.[21]

Land reform thus represented Gruening's primary long-term aim for the Puerto Rican economy. To accomplish the short-term task of economic rehabilitation, he championed the Chardón plan, authored by Chardón, Liberal Rafael Fernández García, and Rafael Menéndez Ramos, an independent with coalitionist sympathies. Its principal feature was the creation of a government corporation to operate sugar refining mills and acquire productive sugar land, which would then be exchanged for marginal cane lands tended by *colonos*, small, independent landowners. The corporation would also create subsistence homesteads for the landless with the land acquired from the *colonos*, employ the publicly owned mill as a "yardstick" to determine a fair processing rate, thus advancing effective government regulation, and use the mill's profits (limited to no more than 8 percent) for further rehabilitation work. Chardón and the Liberals argued that the plan would simultaneously lessen the island's dependence on sugar production, increase employment, and boost land ownership.[22]

Gruening spent much of his first year unsuccessfully attempting to develop legislation either in Puerto Rico or through the U.S. Congress to establish the governmental corporation which the plan required. With time to ponder the sugar program, he concluded that the Chardón plan dealt inadequately with the problem of monopoly, since it allowed the *colonos* to receive the choice land. Drawing on his Mexican experiences, Gruening considered agricultural cooperatives a better solution. Using a "substantial grant" from Harry Hopkins and the Federal Emergency Relief Administration (FERA), he authorized the purchase of a French-owned sugar refining mill, or *central*, at Lafayette. In a "frankly experimental" plan, the PRRA sought to divide the land of the *central*, which totaled over ten thousand acres, into tracts of under five hundred acres, and then planned to organize the workers into cooperatives. The new cooperatives could serve as a means of keeping prices down, as the Chardón plan intended, but would give more people the opportunity to work their own land while also, Gruening hoped, stimulating the local cooperative movement.[23]

Gruening's scheme aroused a good deal of opposition from his usual allies in the Liberal Party. The *colonos* formed an important part of the party's electoral constituency, and some Liberals resented what they considered Gruening's shunting aside of Chardón's work. The matter raised especially difficult problems after the chief of the PRRA's rural rehabilitation division, Rafael Fernández García, resigned over the issue, charging Gruening with pitting the Puerto Rican middle class against the laborers. Gruening overcame Fernández García's opposition, but only by importing Americans to run the cooperative program through the staff of the PRRA's legal division, headed by the talented and ambitious Francis Shea. This decision would have important long-term consequences.[24]

Fernández García was correct in using the land reform program to highlight the contradictions in Gruening's approach to governing. But he overlooked the most glaring ideological tension it illustrated. From Gruening's point of view, jettisoning the Chardón plan made perfect sense once he concluded that it would perpetuate the imperfections in the island's land tenure system. Moreover, replacing the plan with the cooperative scheme satisfied his desire for Puerto Rico to function as a model for U.S. policy to the rest of Latin America. How better, Gruening mused, to achieve this purpose than for the United States to help implement an initiative most closely associated, in his mind at least, with the agrarian program of Plutarco Calles? Yet the move violated his commitment to reforming Puerto Rico through a cross-national coalition rather than simply by policies imposed from the outside. As occurred often in his career, his faith in the power of the people gave way to his adopting a guardian role, with Gruening placing his judgment over that of the masses, convinced that in the long term his choices would be vindicated.

ALTHOUGH IT DERIVED its inspiration from some unusual sources, Gruening's agricultural agenda nonetheless placed him close to the New Deal mainstream. The PRRA head also benefited from a more general transformation of the New Deal which occurred in 1935. In February, in a rare cordial conversation with Ickes, Gruening talked about his depression "over the political situation" and their shared concern that the president's domestic agenda seemed insufficiently progressive. Ickes could do little openly because of his cabinet position, but suggested that Gruening go to New York to see their mutual friend, Colonel House. Gruening took the train to New York the next day, and, in a long discussion, House suggested the possibility of a conference of progressives in Washington, an idea which Gruening took to heart. Upon his return to the capital, he met with Frankfurter, who informed him that plans for such a gathering were already in the works; its agenda foreshadowed many of the programs associated with the Second New Deal of 1935.[25]

In fact, Roosevelt was already inclined to move in the progressives' direction. Much to the PRRA administrator's delight, the National Recovery Administration (NRA) and the Brain Trust fell out of favor with the president, allowing the anti-monopoly bloc to enhance its position. This tendency manifested itself with the passage of the Revenue Act in early 1935, which boosted gift and estate taxes, raised the top income tax rates from 59 percent to 75 percent, and imposed a corporate income tax. Even more controversial was the public utility holding company bill, drafted by Frankfurter protégés Ben Cohen and Tommy Corcoran. The culmination of the progressive campaign against private utilities in which Gruening played such a prominent role, the bill authorized the SEC to break up "unnecessarily complicated" holding companies within three years, a provision which power companies denounced as a "death sentence." Roosevelt added a prohibition on all holding companies in the utility field that could not prove their need in "the operation of a geographically and economically integrated" system. The measure passed the Senate, but the House, under heavy pressure from the utilities industry, deleted the death sentence in a major defeat for the administration.[26]

Then, before the two chambers could convene a conference, Ralph Brewster threatened to derail the bill altogether. Gruening's onetime political patron had won election to the House of Representatives in 1934, but only by moving substantially to the right. Now he claimed that the chief lobbyist for the bill, Tommy Corcoran, was threatening to withhold funds for the Passamaquoddy Dam in Brewster's district unless he voted with the administration. Brewster's allegations created a major sensation, prompting the House leadership to open a formal inquiry.[27]

By this point Gruening had grown intimate with Corcoran, who was beginning to carve out a niche for himself as the leader of the "New Dealers," a network constituting, in the words of historian Alan Brinkley, "a loose and sprawling alliance of seemingly like-minded people . . . scattered inconspicuously but strategically through the bureaucracy" and known for their identification with Frankfurter. Members of the group, united by common social and intellectual interests, networked through private dinner parties at which politics formed the central topic of discussion. By 1935, Gruening had emerged as one of these New Dealers; in fact, it was he who had first introduced Brewster and Corcoran at one of the group's informal gatherings. Reluctant as ever to think that he had misjudged a onetime political ally, Gruening chose instead to believe that he and Brewster continued to share the same attitude on the power question right up until the moment when the congressman leveled his charges.[28]

As events transpired, Gruening was the only witness to the conversation in which Corcoran allegedly threatened Brewster, which occurred just before the House voted on the amendment to delete the death sentence provision. The Rules Committee called Gruening to testify on the exchange. Heightening the anticipation, both Brewster and Corcoran promised that Gruening would verify their version of events. Seeking to neutralize the fears of committee Republicans that partisanship might have clouded his recollection, Gruening opened his testimony by noting again that he considered himself an independent progressive, not a Democrat. He then denied that Corcoran had issued any threats; the lobbyist had only said that he could not trust the congressman, given that Brewster's vote had reversed a lifelong attitude on the utilities question. Gruening noted that it was he, not Corcoran, who had provided the sharpest exchange in the three-cornered conversation: he had told Brewster that his vote against the death sentence "betrayed" his former supporters. For good measure, Gruening announced that he had never, as Brewster claimed, used the phrase "death sentence," calling it "an artificial term created by the power interests similar to their tactics of putting the label 'bolshevik' on anybody they don't like."[29]

Time summed up the prevailing sentiment: Gruening's "sturdy, self-possessed" performance had transformed the Brewster charges into a "disastrous boomerang" for death sentence opponents. Frankfurter gleefully expected the incident to "stiffen F.D.'s fibre and make him realize" that on the power question, "the same old gang" was operating to block his agenda. More important, by providing evidence that the private utility interests were continuing to engage in questionable public relations tactics to maintain the status quo, the hearings strengthened public support for the measure. When the floor manager of the

Senate bill, Burton Wheeler, went to the White House to confer on the matter, Roosevelt provided written assurance favoring retention of the death penalty provision. He then assigned Frankfurter to work out wording that would satisfy the House but retain the spirit of the Senate bill. With this task successfully accomplished, the holding company bill became law.[30]

Throughout 1935 and early 1936, then, Gruening was dividing his time between Washington and San Juan, both physically and ideologically. Specific aspects of his domestic agenda appeared in a variety of Puerto Rican policy initiatives, demonstrating the fusion of his domestic and international viewpoints. He quietly encouraged "rational control of the population growth" on the island, although federal law and the political realities of fierce opposition from Catholic groups in the United States constrained what he could do officially. Gruening also continued his crusade against private utilities, demanding that Winship appoint to the Puerto Rican Public Utilities Commission officials "who cannot by any remote possibility be suspected of undue friendship with the electric light and power companies." He himself named Antonio Lucchetti, the island's former secretary of the treasury, to oversee an ambitious rural electrification program which was correctly attacked for providing the island with electrical power that it did not need while the rural poor still could not afford the power that existed. Gruening's determination to fulfill a predetermined ideological agenda manifested itself in other ways as well. Reviving his interest in the issue from his days in Maine, Gruening aimed "to make out of Puerto Rico a Caribbean tourist attraction of major importance," possibly even a "new Bermuda." This effort proved less controversial. The PRRA funded the establishment of a Puerto Rican Institute of Tourism in 1935; three years later the number of tourists traveling to Puerto Rico had tripled.[31]

Despite the parallels between his policies and those of the New Deal, Gruening nonetheless never lost sight of his primary ambition; the PRRA's program represented only a means to the broader end of showing how the United States could assist reformist forces in the Caribbean. He thus spent an inordinate amount of time on diplomatic issues which technically fell outside the scope of his responsibilities with either the DTIP or the PRRA. On his first visit to Puerto Rico after his appointment, he delivered a speech denouncing Dominican dictator Rafael Trujillo and announcing his desire to position Puerto Rico as a counterweight to the dictatorships of the region. He pressed Winship to support legislation granting Puerto Rican citizenship to the Dominican exile Miguel Pardo, contending that establishing Puerto Rico as an asylum for political refugees from neighboring Caribbean countries would maintain "our own American tradition of freedom." Gruening also argued that increasing the number of Puerto Ricans in the U.S. diplomatic service would improve the standing of the United States in Latin America while facilitating cultural exchange among the nations of the Western hemisphere. With this agenda, Gruening presaged the ideology of the Democratic Left, in which Muñoz Marín and many other Puerto Rican Liberals would play prominent roles during the 1940s and 1950s.[32]

The combination of Gruening's desire to increase Puerto Rico's prominence in the administration's inter-American policy and his longstanding support for higher education guided his policies toward the University of Puerto Rico (UPR). Recalling his stopover in Peru after the Montevideo Conference, when he was unable to visit the University of San Marcos because the Peruvian government had closed the school after political protests, he envisioned the UPR assuming the "intellectual leadership of the Island," contrary to "the plight of most Hispanic-American universities which are subject to the whims of the current dictator." The UPR could become not only "a cultural link between the two Americas" but also "the one university in a Hispanic country which under its present sovereignty will remain free, untrammeled upon." Once again, Puerto Rico would function as both an agent for improving inter-American relations and a model for future ties between the United States and its neighbors.[33]

Owing to the PRRA's limited budget, however, this program dried up funding for virtually all other educational programs on the island. PRERA educational initiatives, which concentrated on supplementing local appropriations for elementary and high schools to address the island's 47 percent illiteracy rate, were slashed, leading to frantic requests from Commissioner of Education José Padín to wind the program down gradually rather than eliminating the subsidization altogether. Gruening recognized that his educational policies would affect the average Puerto Rican adversely. In his analysis of revolutionary Mexico, he praised José Vasconcelos for having "deliberately sacrificed" higher education to channel his limited resources toward the "pressing needs of elementary schooling." In Puerto Rico, however, he confronted a different situation. Although he obviously wanted to strengthen the island's educational system, his broader international goals dictated transforming the UPR into a center for inter-American intellectual exchange and a model for other Latin American universities. On this issue as on most others, Gruening's highest priority remained Puerto Rico's place in U.S. foreign policy, not reform in Puerto Rico per se. Usually, from his point of view, the two interests coincided. But when they did not, he consistently chose the policy option that would further his agenda of establishing Puerto Rico as an anti-imperialist model for U.S. policy toward Latin America.[34]

This aspect of Gruening's program was perhaps the most controversial. Although a host of U.S. ambassadors in the region, such as Josephus Daniels in Mexico and Arthur Bliss Lane in Nicaragua, similarly championed a more active U.S. role in assisting Caribbean Basin reformers, little suggested in 1935 that Roosevelt intended to use Latin America as an arena for launching a politically positive policy centered on the principles of international reform. Indeed, the early stages of the administration featured the consolidation of a number of Caribbean Basin dictatorships with little or no protest from the United States. The strict policy of political noninterference was all the more striking when compared with U.S. economic diplomacy toward the region, in which Cordell Hull showed no hesitation in applying diplomatic pressure. Despite these trends, however, Gruening understood Roosevelt's way of operating well enough to know that administration policy could always change. So long as his program showed some signs of success, the chance remained that his ideas could form a more prominent part of the administration's inter-American agenda. Knowing the importance of unexpected developments at the Montevideo Conference, he looked to influence the makeup of the delegation to the conference in Buenos Aires scheduled for 1936. He successfully lobbied to place two of his allies, Samuel Guy Inman and Puerto Rican Liberal Jorge del Toro, as advisers to the delegation.[35]

Putting this program into place, especially given Gruening's disinclination to delegate authority to all but the most trusted of advisers (which, in this case, amounted to Francis Shea of the PRRA's legal staff), consumed an enormous amount of his time. His neglect of his family and financial situation reached new heights. Hunt, now at Harvard, struggled to find an appropriate concentration, choosing first anthropology, then economics, but received no guidance from his father. He instead found pleasure in the company of the members of the Pi Eta Club, which included his roommate Nathaniel Benchley (the son of Gruening's Harvard chum) and his next-door neighbor at Winthrop House, Joseph Kennedy, Jr. Hunt, who occasionally double-dated with Kennedy, was struck by the differences between family patriarch Joseph Kennedy, Sr., and his own father, notably Kennedy's self-conscious inclusion of his children in discussions of contemporary events. The family's shaky financial situation prompted Gruening to request his son to resign his membership in Pi Eta; eventually they worked out a compromise under which Hunt agreed to take most of his meals at Winthrop but remain in the club.[36]

The financial strains also produced a severe rift among the Gruening siblings. Gruening's eldest sister, Rose, died in July 1934. Ernest was named trustee and executor of her estate. Contending that her brother had cheated her out of her rightful share of Rose's inheritance, Martha filed a suit against Ernest, alleging misrepresentation and fraud. Her sister Clara supported her efforts, while May sided with her brother. The painful matter dragged on inconclusively until Martha's death in 1937.[37]

Dorothy, meanwhile, playing even less of a role in Gruening's life than during the 1920s, became active on the Washington social circuit. She developed her own political mentors, including Eleanor Roosevelt, whose willingness to take up causes outside the shadow of her husband Dorothy admired. As the 1930s progressed, Dorothy modeled herself on Eleanor, endorsing issues ranging from child welfare to the more controversial Washington League of Women Shoppers, an organization which united the wives of prominent administration antimonopolists such as William O. Douglas, Edward Costigan, James Landis, and Leon Henderson (peace activist Dorothy Detzer also belonged). The league urged using "consumer power for social justice" by boycotting the products of firms which did not provide their workers "decent wages, sane hours of work, and a reasonable security on the job." Dorothy also took to attending congressional hearings relating to her husband's career, prompting a complaint from Ickes that she made faces whenever the secretary received a positive mention from committee members. Gruening responded by questioning the veracity of Ickes's reports, and added that even if they were true, he could not control his wife's frowns. For Gruening himself, though, socializing remained confined to political friends such as Frankfurter, Corcoran, and other New Dealers. Though he occasionally still played tennis or bridge, politics had begun to consume all aspects of his life.[38]

Despite having to pay a personal price for his bureaucratic successes, Gruening considered the cost worthwhile. Given an extraordinary opportunity by a coincidence of bureaucratic, political, and international factors, Gruening had been able to integrate the basics of his foreign policy ideas and domestic preferences into a bold program of reconstruction for Puerto Rico. He recognized, however, that since the positive effects of his phasing out of relief, his agricultural restructuring efforts, and his improvements at the UPR would take years to materialize, he was dependent on the continued political support of his backers in both Washington and San Juan and on avoiding the emergence of any difficult issues in Puerto Rico in the interim. On every occasion when his help was requested between 1934 and mid-1936, Franklin Roosevelt intervened on Gruening's behalf, but it remained unclear how long the president would sustain Gruening's concept of a Latin American policy oriented toward the principles of anti-imperialism.

In 1936 Gruening's luck began to run out when the other two main aspects of Puerto Rican politics—patronage and the island's political status—resurfaced. The status question arose first. On February 23 two members of the Nationalist Party, Hiram Rosado and Elías Beauchamp, assassinated the chief of the insular police, Colonel Francis Riggs. The two were quickly arrested and died during what the police claimed was an attempt to escape custody. When Albizu Campos delivered an impassioned address at the funeral promising a future campaign of terrorism, Winship ordered raids on Nationalist headquarters, after which Albizu Campos and seven other Nationalists were indicted on charges of conspiring to overthrow the federal government in Puerto Rico. The first trial of Albizu Campos resulted in a hung jury, but a retrial produced convictions for him and his associates. As if the impartiality of the proceedings were not already in question, the event concluded with the presiding judge, Robert Cooper, denouncing Albizu Campos for having perverted his educational opportunities and sentencing the Nationalist leader to ten years in a federal penitentiary.[39]

The role of force in Latin American politics had troubled Gruening since his days in Mexico, and he feared that the assassinations presaged the rise in Puerto Rico of a tendency to settle political conflicts by force. Nonetheless, he privately conceded that the treason charge was "not desirable . . . simply because it glorifies Albizu Campos and raises an issue which can be disguised in terms of patriotism"; he better than most knew that "it certainly will have that appearance throughout Latin America." Having surveyed the "extremely difficult situation," however, he saw no alternative to the federal charge, since most insular juries, intimidated by Nationalist threats, would acquit Albizu Campos. One observer in the United States perceptively summarized Gruening's dilemma as that of a "lifelong liberal who is facing the possibility that too much liberty, forced on a people who apparently do not want it, may be poisonous to them."[40]

The Nationalist terrorism presented Gruening with several interrelated problems. Most important, it raised an anti-imperialist banner against the United States in the months before the conference in Buenos Aires, thus potentially destroying the entire purpose of Gruening's Puerto Rican agenda—that of creating an anti-imperialist model in the Caribbean as a way of improving relations between the United States and Latin America. In addition, the violence threatened the congressional appropriations on which Gruening's program depended. Several members of Congress openly wondered why the United States should continue to fund a massive reconstruction program if the majority of Puerto Ricans wanted independence, as the Nationalists claimed, and if a substantial minority were willing to engage in terrorism to achieve that goal. Finally, and most immediately, the increasing prominence of the Nationalists raised the issue of the island's political status, thus threatening to displace economic and social reform questions from their preeminent position on the insular political agenda.

This development, in turn, strained the relationship between Gruening and a Liberal Party which remained committed to independence despite internal divisions over how hard to push for that goal. Gruening demanded that prominent Liberals condemn Riggs's assassination and request independence supporters to refrain from violence. Muñoz Marín refused, citing the political costs associated with confronting the Nationalists and the sugar companies simultaneously. Gruening characteristically personalized the dispute, denouncing his onetime comrade for "condoning murder" and informing Muñoz Marín that he had come to consider the Liberal leader "just another politician." An angered Muñoz Marín then went public, charging that the prosecution of the Nationalists for "political offenses . . . is unnecessarily destroying in part the good will so ably and sincerely developed by the Administration in Latin America." Both sides in the dispute clearly mishandled the situation. Gruening needlessly forced the Liberals to choose between pledging him their support or publicly repudiating a party whose platform (if not its methods) mirrored their own, while Muñoz Marín later admitted that he should have condemned the assassination.[41]

On top of these difficulties, the Nationalist crisis produced the first wave of negative comments in the United States about the PRRA. Calling for some "hard thinking" about Puerto Rico, the *Washington Post* urged the administration to come up with a "coherent" policy toward the island. *Current History* ran an article charging that the PRRA had "muddled along, accompanied by waste and inefficiency, so that good results of an open-handed beneficence to a great extent have been nullified by further Puerto Rican reaction to American political methods." Meanwhile, in a series of articles syndicated by the *New York Herald Tribune*, Edward Angly used the PRRA to attack the New Deal, contending that in Puerto Rico, the United States "is carrying on an extensive experiment in government landlordism and socialization" which the government would apply to the entire United States if Roosevelt won reelection. The most extreme comment came from Representative Marion Zioncheck (D–Washington), who called for sending the Marine Corps to "clean up" the Puerto Rican "mess." With the exception of the suggestion from Zioncheck, who suffered from mental instability, the increasing criticism posed obvious problems. While some of his program did reflect the tenets of the New Deal, Gruening was far more taken with anti-monopoly and anti-imperialist initiatives than was the president. The PRRA administrator knew that Roosevelt did not attach sufficient importance to Puerto Rican matters to retain him if he became a political liability.[42]

With his hold over the Puerto Rican situation slipping, Gruening gambled. He traveled to the country residence of Senator Millard Tydings (D–Maryland) to propose their joining forces. Tydings and Gruening's friend William King of Utah, were the two members of the Senate Interior Committee most interested in Puerto Rican matters;

the Maryland senator had sponsored Riggs for the job as insular police chief. After the killing, Tydings denounced the "ingratitude" of the Puerto Ricans for the "many millions" of dollars the United States had poured into the island. Privately he considered independence "essential to stop the influx [of Puerto Ricans] into New York"; therefore, he announced his intention to introduce a resolution to allow the Puerto Ricans to vote on independence. Reassured by Gruening's visit that the two shared a similar perspective on Puerto Rico (although in fact they clearly did not), the Maryland senator agreed to allow Gruening to draft the resolution for him.[43]

Gruening rejoiced at seeming to have regained at least some control over the situation. He assured Ickes that allowing a referendum would be "consistent with the enlightened policies of this administration in relation to its neighbors." The proposal could neutralize anti-imperialist criticism directed against the United States for holding a colony, especially if, as Gruening expected, Puerto Rican voters rejected independence. Given this goal, the PRRA head pushed for a "clean" referendum, with as "generous" economic provisions as possible. After Interior Department lawyer Frederick Bernays drafted a bill which called for saddling an independent Puerto Rico with high tariffs, Gruening ordered changes "so as not to becloud the basic issue of the referendum with recriminations or objections that the question as presented did not offer a fair alternative in view of the conditions attached to the grant of independence."[44]

Bernays did as requested, but, unknown to Gruening, he already had shown his draft to Tydings, who indicated his preference for it. Unlike Gruening, the Maryland senator wanted to punish the Puerto Ricans, not work with them in a joint reform effort. The next day he introduced the measure in the Senate, announcing, in words which must have made Gruening cringe, that "the American system is not functioning properly in Puerto Rico." The Tydings bill called for a referendum to coincide with the 1936 insular elections. An affirmative vote would result in independence within four years, and immediately subject Puerto Rican products to a 25 percent annual increase in the tariff. All sides recognized the extreme nature of the bill; the Philippines, by comparison, had been granted a twenty-year hiatus before being subject to the full effects of the tariff. But Gruening was in an awkward position, since he had already persuaded Roosevelt to endorse a referendum. Privately he promised Chardón that if the referendum passed, he would work to modify the measure. Publicly, though, he praised the bill, observing that many in Latin America continued to view the U.S. possession of Puerto Rico "as a commitment of our era of expansion and an example of imperialism." As Gruening hoped, the introduction of the Tydings bill received enough praise in the Latin American press that the Puerto Rican issue no longer threatened to affect inter-American relations negatively.[45]

Gruening's concession to Chardón confirmed his knowledge that the introduction of the bill would worsen his relationship with the Liberals. Once again, as with his jettisoning of the Chardón plan, he acted unilaterally despite his rhetorical commitment to a transnational alliance. In his defense, Gruening argued that no one with democratic inclinations could oppose the idea of a referendum. He also predicted that despite the claims of Muñoz Marín, who more ardently favored independence than other prominent Liberals, the majority of Puerto Rican voters would oppose the referendum. Privately Gruening argued that the island "has everything to lose by casting itself adrift and nothing to gain," both economically and politically, given the anti-democratic trend evident elsewhere in the depression-era Caribbean Basin.[46]

He understood, however, the need for a long-term solution to the political status question. Gruening maintained in a letter to Chardón that Puerto Rico's most promising future "lay in the unique opportunity of developing a culture under the protection and with the great benefits of American citizenship." Politically and culturally, "there is more liberty in Puerto Rico today than in any other Hispanic American country," while the PRRA was "hard at work trying to rectify" the economic disadvantages associated with past U.S. rule. Gruening concluded by denying that the Tydings bill in any way affected the administration's program in Puerto Rico; it merely represented an avenue for proving that "there is no attempt, as has been alleged by critics, to keep the people of Puerto Rico 'in bondage.'" He asked Chardón, and other prominent Liberals, to withhold public comment until he arrived in Puerto Rico and could outline his position in greater detail. In effect, Gruening envisioned Puerto Rico assuming a commonwealth status, but such a concept was fifteen years ahead of its time and thus out of place in the political climate of the 1930s.[47]

Gruening arrived in Puerto Rico in early June. Muñoz Marín rejected his plea out of hand. Again insulted, Gruening bluntly announced his conclusion that Muñoz Marín was "sacrificing his people and his country to his personal ambitions and ideas." Other Liberal leaders, however, listened to what Gruening had to say. In what the PRRA head described as a "long and important discussion" with Chardón, José Padín, and Jesús Piñero, president of the Asociación de Colonos, Gruening explained that he "did not think the present situation could continue, with one group knifing and sabotaging reconstruction, the other group accepting it but saying, in effect, 'as soon as we've got your money we'll shove off' and the third group trying to force us out by violence." For Gruening, the "only hope lay in a New Deal party supporting reconstruction and permanent relationship with the U.S."[48]

Gruening thus attempted to use the Tydings bill, with its obviously unacceptable economic provisions, to complete the Liberals' transformation into a party organized around the principle of reform on economic and social issues and committed to a political relationship short of independence. This gamble represented his final attempt to firm up the deteriorating transnational, anti-imperialist alliance which he considered crucial to the long-term success of his program. Except for Muñoz Marín, the Liberals present agreed that the majority of Puerto Ricans opposed independence, but they also worried that forcing a decision could split the party. Only Padín favored Gruening's approach, terming independence a "spurious" issue and urging a continued focus on economic reform. In typical fashion, though, Gruening had convened the meeting to inform the Liberals of his plans, not to solicit opinions. He concluded the gathering by announcing that it was too late to turn back, since the relevant congressional committees were already considering the Tydings bill.[49]

Shaken by the poor reception Gruening returned to Washington to bolster his support at home. He turned to the one political figure from the Haitian campaign who remained interested in Latin American affairs, William King, who promised whatever help the PRRA head needed in the upcoming months. But Gruening had chosen a weak ally. Although the senator kept his word, writing Roosevelt directly to commend Gruening's performance, King's conservatism had alienated both the White House and other anti-imperialists. (Villard bluntly called him a "jackass.") The Utah senator's words thus carried little weight.

Moreover, even King's meager support came with a price. The senator, fixated on increasing English instruction in Puerto Rico, made it clear that he expected the PRRA to emphasize the issue more in the future. The English instruction program only increased the friction between Gruening and the Liberals. Muñoz Marín opposed it on the grounds that it "seems to assume the permanency of U.S. jurisdiction." More important, the initiative triggered a feud between Gruening and Padín, the one prominent Liberal who endorsed his gambit on the Tydings bill; Gruening accused him of using his position as insular commissioner of education to "deliberately sabotage" the program.[50]

Even though signs of a potential disaster were all too apparent, Gruening retained confidence in his scheme. Once Puerto Rican voters rejected independence, Gruening reasoned, he could solidify his base both within the administration and among those in Congress such as Tydings who contended that the nationalist agitation offered a reason to cease funding PRRA reform efforts. Laying the groundwork for what he expected to be a major post-referendum congressional effort, he called for understanding that "the most fundamental reason for the growth of dissatisfaction has been the island's economic plight." Gruening urged dropping discriminatory legislation and going "forward on all fronts" with a "careful, painstaking policy of helping the Puerto Ricans to build up as nearly as we can a self sustaining economy" complete with "political and economic autonomy." Even though such a program would "constitute for years to come a heavy financial burden" for the United States, it would eventually create a "spiritual rapprochement" between Puerto Ricans and Americans.[51]

In theory, Gruening's plan represented a clever scheme to solve a number of related problems at once. In practice, though, it only further proved his political inexperience. A negative vote on the independence referendum would be the key to his success. Therefore, even before the Tydings bill cleared Congress, Gruening started touring the island delivering speeches in opposition to independence, always carefully maintaining, in a quite specious distinction, that he spoke only in his capacity as a private citizen and not as PRRA administrator. He lost control of the matter completely, however, after the Liberal newspaper *El Mundo*, which was closely affiliated with Muñoz Marín, charged that he was purging Liberals from the PRRA because they favored independence. All major Puerto Rican newspapers as well as the *New York Times* picked up the story, and the ACLU filed an official protest with Ickes claiming abridgment of freedom of speech. Gruening angrily denied the charge, commenting with a touch of arrogance that "the PRRA does not propose to intervene in the beliefs of its employees even though those beliefs may occasionally appear to be in conflict with a minimum of common sense."[52]

Gruening obviously had not anticipated that his campaign against independence would add to his public relations difficulties. More important, he had not foreseen the realigning effect that the Tydings bill would have on insular politics. The two coalition parties seized on the bill to make the politically self-serving argument that opponents of the measure should vote for the coalition in the upcoming election. Meanwhile, Muñoz Marín led a sizable contingent of Liberals in boycotting the elections altogether, out of a belief that the party had no chance of victory given its association with the unpopular measure. For Gruening, the situation deteriorated even further when the Tydings bill failed to reach the Senate floor; his decision to paper over his ideological differences with Tydings had proved costly. As the Maryland senator later admitted, he introduced the bill only "to call to the attention of the Puerto Rican Government and people the great blessing they had in our gigantic market." With this goal accomplished to his satisfaction, Tydings lost interest in the measure and declined to use his influence to push it through the committee. Reflecting on events a decade later, an old nemesis, Rexford Tugwell, chortled about Gruening's botched attempt to "become a political manipulator."[53]

As the political status question reemerged in 1936, so too did the other traditional element of insular politics: the search for patronage. Throughout 1935, Gruening had been badgered with complaints alleging that the Liberals were using the PRRA as a political vehicle to regain power. Initially these charges came only from coalition forces, who used them as an excuse to oppose Gruening's agenda. Although Gruening did regularly order PRRA employees to maintain a "strictly neutral" attitude on political matters, the reality was less clear-cut. As he explained to Francis Shea, he wanted to "lean over backwards" to keep politics out of the organization, but given the "unrelenting, unscrupulous, and undeniable" character of the PRRA's opponents, he could not "simply allow the opposition to take advantage of our honesty of purpose." Gruening therefore demanded that all PRRA employees sympathize with the "administration," a term which he employed with deliberate vagueness to mean at times the Roosevelt administration and at other times his Puerto Rico Reconstruction Administration. Nonetheless, through early 1936 he maintained that by "the exercise of utmost care" he had succeeded in overcoming the "very difficult" problem of excluding "political influence and political pressure from the operations of the Administration."[54]

In mid-1936, however, subjected to a public attack from James Bourne on the issue, and under relentless criticism from the coalition, Gruening appointed Luis Raúl Esteves, head of the PRRA Personnel Office, to head a committee of "known political impartiality" to look into the patronage charges. He fully expected that the investigation would rebuff the coalition's claims, after which he could release the findings publicly in time for the election. Instead, Esteves uncovered evidence that Liberals had demanded between 10 and 15 percent of the salaries of PRRA employees as kickbacks. In September, in the midst of the collapse of his alliance with the Liberals over the Tydings bill, Gruening flew to Puerto Rico to assume personal charge of the inquiry, blaming the abuses on Chardón, who had authority for the local operations of the PRRA. The administrator responded by purging a number of employees and issuing an order requiring all PRRA employees to resign from any political positions they simultaneously held.[55]

The disputes over patronage and independence ended the alliance between Gruening and the Liberals. He now wondered whether some leading Liberals were more interested in playing the political "game" than in standing up for principles. In fact, Gruening deserved as much blame for the Liberal abuses as anyone else. He assumed, without any foundation, that the Liberals shared his desire to use the PRRA as part of an ideologically driven scheme to remake Puerto Rico and improve inter-American relations. He also assumed, as he had done at the *Boston Traveler* and *New York Post*, that Liberal leaders would place principle over their financial well-being. Neither of these assumptions corresponded to the reality of Puerto Rico in 1936, and Gruening should have known better. As he himself had written about Mexico in the 1920s, corruption among lower-level bureaucrats who refused to suffer "penury for a principle" had frustrated the implementation of Calles's reform program. The situation was even more acute in Puerto Rico, where the quest for patronage represented a principal element of local politics. In a society such as Mexico in the 1920s or Puerto Rico in the 1930s, without a tradition of civil service and with massive economic distress, it simply was unrealistic to expect that Gruening's calls for a Liberal-dominated PRRA would not be interpreted by some Liberals as an invitation to use the organization for patronage purposes.[56]

THE FIASCOES with the Tydings bill and the PRRA purge proved Gruening's administrative shortcomings, whatever his demonstrated bureaucratic skills in Washington. They also, however, revealed a more fundamental problem in his performance, one most perceptively recognized by his bureaucratic rival James Bourne. Bourne argued that alleviating the island's "extreme unemployment," rather than enacting a broad-based reform agenda, should be the top priority of Puerto Rican policy. Rural electrification made sense in the abstract, he acknowledged, but "the rural population is so poor that it can buy neither power nor fixtures." The university required improvement, but with the island's high illiteracy rate, elementary schools needed the money more. The education and power initiatives offered the best evidence of an administrator so attached to a preconceived program that he lost sight of the day-to-day needs of the average Puerto Ricans for whom he theoretically was responsible. In effect, according to Bourne, Gruening was guilty of the shortcoming for which he had attacked Wilson and Carranza in *Mexico and Its Heritage:* rigidly adhering to an ideological agenda regardless of the actual conditions at hand. Bourne concluded that the PRRA was "deceiving the public with glowing promises for the future which can never be realized." There was little chance that Gruening would act on any of Bourne's suggestions. As Eleanor Roosevelt, who knew them both, realized, "too much friction" existed between them for Gruening to recognize the value of Bourne's more substantive criticisms, quite apart from Gruening's usual tendency to personalize political disputes.[57]

The full effect of Gruening's political maneuverings became clear after the coalition forces successfully turned the campaign into a referendum on the provisions of the Tydings bill, displacing issues of economic and social reform from the island's political agenda. Despite the split within the party, the Liberals still managed a plurality but fell short of the combined total of the coalition parties by sixty thousand votes. This tally gave the coalition fourteen of nineteen seats in the Puerto

Rican Senate, a two-to-one majority in the lower house of the legislature, and control of sixty of the island's seventy-seven municipalities. After the result, Muñoz Marín was expelled from the party for his refusal to campaign. Both Liberal factions, however, agreed with him in attributing the party's loss to the "confusion caused by E.G.'s irresponsible action in having the Tydings Bill presented as an administration measure."[58]

By this time Gruening too had abandoned hope of creating a coalition uniting Puerto Rican and American reformers. He discussed the issue with two members of the PRRA legal staff in Washington, Harry Hall and Lester Schoene. The trio "agreed that while every conciliatory legitimate move should be made that it was impossible to yield an inch on the fundamental principle involved, namely that however far we desire to go in making this program for Puerto Ricans by Puerto Ricans, the fundamental responsibility has got to reside in Washington." Theorizing about the utility of transnational alliances was fine in the abstract. But when personal, political, and ideological tensions stood in the way, Gruening reasoned, he had better rely on his own judgment.[59]

Chardón exposed the decision-making issue shortly after the election, using the continued freedom of action of the legal division, which reported directly to Gruening, as an excuse to demand a reorganization of the "structural set-up of the organization." Gruening not only refused the request but even declined to consider the merit of Chardón's criticisms. Instead, ever more detached from the reality of his rapidly disintegrating policies, he concluded that Chardón's conduct "can be explained only on the ground of a mental break-down." Chardón promptly resigned, replaced by Miles Fairbank, who had taken over the rural rehabilitation division from Fernández García a few months earlier. The resignation triggered the departure of twenty other key members of the PRRA hierarchy, including the assistant regional administrator, the chief of the personnel division, the executive secretary of the PRRA board, the chief of the planning division, the chief of the health division, the chief engineer of the rural rehabilitation division, and the chief of the slum clearance division. In the aftermath Fairbank "purposely refrained" from convening the PRRA executive board because the large number of resignations prevented his obtaining a quorum. Although Gruening had earlier cited the board as the chief example of his desire to give the Puerto Ricans a voice in the future of their country, now, unable to find a sufficient number of Puerto Ricans of stature to fill its positions, he discontinued it altogether. No event better signaled the gap between theory and practice which characterized Gruening's Puerto Rican experience. Muñoz Marín, obviously a biased witness, nonetheless spoke for the majority of politically active Puerto Ricans when he commented that "the PRRA functions like a madhouse because Ernest, who does not know how to exercise authority, also does not know how to delegate it."[60]

In the midst of this political turbulence, Bourne's earlier warnings that Gruening's program would create massive short-term unemployment were borne out. In late fall, when the island's relief rolls increased sharply, the PRRA was unprepared to shoulder the burden. With no choice, Gruening requested a $6 million supplementary relief appropriation. The Bureau of the Budget (BOB), however, told him instead that he could allocate relief funds out of the PRRA budget. Gruening then appealed directly to Roosevelt, arguing that his entire program had been "considered, planned, and put into operation" in the belief that PRRA funds would not "be used for temporary work relief." Denying his request thus would return U.S. policy to its pre-PRRA status, "an endless pouring of relief money into the island with no prospect of . . . permanent economic adjustment." Roosevelt for the first time refused to back the PRRA head, forcing the PRRA staff, Gruening complained, "to curtail the scope of our program." With his bureaucratic lifeline to the White House cut, the chances for a successful implementation of Gruening's long-term program all but vanished.[61]

The decision signaled the end of Roosevelt's patience with Gruening's anti-imperialist experiment. Gruening's most powerful nemesis within the administration, Harold Ickes, quickly took advantage. As early as August 1936, the president mused that "there is some merit" in Ickes's suggestion that the PRRA "should be in some way under the secretary and not a wholly administrative body." Ickes responded by submitting a formal request to be placed in control of the PRRA, with Gruening remaining as administrator but compelled to report to the secretary. Roosevelt agreed. Gruening initially attempted to carry on as if nothing had changed, contending that his organization was "unaltered" by the new executive order; such "supervision and control . . . which the Secretary desires to exercise he can and will determine, doubtless after discussion with me, but it should not be exercised arbitrarily by officials of other agencies." The BOB disagreed, tartly informing Gruening "in no uncertain terms" that it would deal only with Ickes or his budget officer.[62]

Ickes then ensured that Gruening would not reverse his bureaucratic victory. In December the PRRA's Washington office reported that "a Mrs. Graham has been making an investigation" and was on her way to Puerto Rico. The inquiry, headed by Leona Graham and commissioned by Ickes, had already reached its verdict: "Dr. Gruening's lack of administrative ability," compounded by a flawed ideological agenda, explained the serious shortcomings in the PRRA program. In a forty-page attack on Gruening's tenure, Graham charged him with employing too many continentals, permitting the excessive involvement of the administration in politics, reversing his position too often on too many key issues ("seemingly the Latin American temperament is distrustful of men in authority who change their minds, whatever the reason"), spending too much time in Washington, overseeing a bloated bureaucracy, and undertaking "too ambitious a program." She concluded by recommending that Ickes demand Gruening's resignation and suggest "through the proper unofficial underground channels" that the PRRA would welcome back the prominent Liberals who had resigned in disputes with Gruening. Ickes's deputy, E. K. Burlew, gleefully observed that the report, by disclosing "a situation that is most critical," would compel departmental action against Gruening.[63]

Indeed, armed with its findings, Ickes demanded that Gruening resign as head of the PRRA, and urged Roosevelt to act "promptly" on the dismissal. Otherwise, he threatened to order a full-scale investigation of Puerto Rican affairs, something the president obviously did not want. Gruening did what he could to survive. He delayed submitting his resignation while frantically searching for allies, including Eleanor Roosevelt. (After learning of Gruening's having lunched at the White House with the First Lady, Ickes fumed that in the future he hoped "that Mrs. Roosevelt would stick to her knitting and keep out of the affairs connected with my Department.") Such lobbying held out little chance of success. The Graham report documented Gruening's administrative failings and Ickes's threat to launch a public investigation foreclosed the president's options. In July 1937, Gruening resigned as head of the PRRA.[64]

Although weakened bureaucratically, Gruening nonetheless remained head of the DTIP. But developments in Puerto Rico soon robbed him of all vestiges of his political influence. On Palm Sunday 1937, in the coastal city of Ponce, police killed nineteen Nationalists who refused to disarm before a planned demonstration. Gruening admitted the "ironic paradoxes" of his association with the side accused of killing Latin American independence agitators, but, in a comment which reflected his growing frustration with Puerto Rican events and a sense of ethnic superiority often embedded in his paternalistic policies, he observed that "unfortunately in a Latin American environment with a Latin American psychology, shooting comes far easier than it does here—and that applies to both Nationalists and police." Even Nationalist political rhetoric posed a potential danger, since "incendiary speeches in Latin American countries very definitely lead to direct acts of assassination, as they are not apt to among us on the continent." Still, he realized that the "whole business was unspeakably unnecessary and tragic."[65]

The Ponce massacre ended any hope of Gruening's turning Puerto Rico into an anti-imperialist model. Previously, even as his political base in Puerto Rico was eroding, Gruening retained the support of anti-imperialists in the United States. After Ponce, however, anti-imperialists not only distanced themselves from Gruening, but also joined the Liberals in the ranks of his strongest critics. Even in 1936, the ACLU had chastised Gruening for his handling of the Riggs assassination and the Liberal charges that he was purging the PRRA for ideological reasons. Gruening responded by asking the ACLU to "realize that a very serious situation and not a theory confronts us in Puerto Rico," oblivious to the irony that he had come to national prominence in the 1920s by criticizing policy makers who similarly defended their actions in the Caribbean Basin. Then, early in 1937, Roger Baldwin, head of the ACLU, wrote to inquire about reports from the island's Liberals, especially Muñoz Marín, alleging "subtle official pressures in violation of civil liberties and against independence." Baldwin admitted to Gruening that Muñoz Marín and his allies made "a very poor case for anything tangible," but he reminded Gruening that as a fellow anti-imperialist, he needed to adhere to a higher standard than the average government official. Gruening responded coldly, noting merely that he agreed with Baldwin's comment that the disaffected Liberals had failed to produce any tangible evidence. Baldwin then went to see Ickes, and told him that "Gruening has completely boxed the compass down there."[66]

Gruening's handling of the Tydings bill also aroused its share of controversy. A *Nation* editorial spoke for many U.S. anti-imperialists in assailing the "shabby" and "sorry" stance of its former managing editor. *The Nation* correctly realized that once the repercussions of the Puerto Rican situation on the Buenos Aires Conference had embarrassed the administration, it had confronted the people of the island with a "Hobson's choice" between voting against independence or choosing "certain economic catastrophe" because of the bill's tariff provisions. Again Gruening found being the subject rather than the author of such critiques not to his liking. He complained to Freda Kirchwey that in twenty years he knew of nothing published by *The Nation* "that equals this in unfairness and misrepresentation." He considered it inconceivable that an editorial could be "so completely false in its implications, so unjust in its slurs, and so manifest a perversion of the intent and objective of those entrusted with responsibility for Puerto Rico."[67]

Kirchwey had erred in a few specific points, opening herself up to the criticism, and the slight factual mistakes allowed Gruening to attack her editorial without addressing its main point. Such bullying tactics worked with friends: *The Nation* toned down its criticism of the PRRA following Gruening's reproach. But this nitpicking strategy more often than not exposed Gruening to ridicule. For instance, after nationally syndicated columnist George Eliot lambasted Gruening's performance, the PRRA head dashed off a letter taking Eliot to task for having written that he was a "close personal friend" of Muñoz Marín during his time at *La Prensa.* (The two did not meet until after Gruening left the newspaper.) Relishing his response, Eliot noted that he could not "deny a certain gleam of satisfaction at the reflection that in an article which contains so much critical comment on the work of your Department and of the P.R.R.A. you can find nothing more serious to complain of than a minor error with regard to the exact date when your 'acquaintance' with that gentleman commenced." Gruening elected not to continue the correspondence.[68]

Gruening's suddenly shaky support in the United States collapsed entirely after Winship's formal report exonerated the police for the Ponce massacre. Miguel Guerra-Mondragón, Gruening's antitrust specialist, let Baldwin know that the time had come "for a searching investigation of the new developments by some impartial agency." But in a revealing commentary on Gruening's obsession with personal loyalty, he begged Baldwin "to keep this and further reports most confidentially" and to address all mail to his residence. The letter convinced Baldwin that indeed something was badly wrong in Puerto Rico, perhaps even with Gruening's conduct. Once again he tried to handle the matter informally, passing on the gist of the charges and asking Gruening for additional information. When Gruening merely forwarded a copy of Winship's official report in response, Baldwin broke publicly with his former friend, nominating Arthur Garfield Hays, a onetime colleague of Gruening's from New York reform circles, to investigate the killings. After arriving in Puerto Rico, Hays quickly uncovered evidence of a cover-up by Winship and the insular police, though not by Gruening. Upon his return to the United States, he issued a scathing report condemning irregularities in Winship's version of events. At the same time, however, Hays tried to keep open his lines of communication with Gruening. He waited two weeks before releasing the report in the hope of obtaining a private meeting with the PRRA head, and confided to Gruening his "deepest regret that you have permitted yourself to be put in a position where to some extent you are colored with the same brush as the Governor."[69]

Gruening, as had become his established pattern, responded with venom, charging that the ACLU was "being used by persons who have no interest whatever in the maintenance of civil liberties." He refused to see Hays or Baldwin, despite the fact that the two had gone out of their way to keep him apprised of events and had been quite even-handed in their investigations. The PRRA head was troubled, however, that his chief editorial support came from conservative newspapers such as the *Chicago Tribune*, and he belatedly tried to rally his anti-imperialist base. Though fearful of being seen as a government official "seeking a favorable presentation of the case," he asked Freda Kirchwey to present "the other side of the picture": his contention that Hays "came down here and fell into the hands of a hand-picked committee whose interest and purpose were not to protect civil liberties but to play the game of Nationalist politics." Such pleas did not persuade even the more moderate *New Republic*, which instead used the Ponce affair as a starting point to attack the entire basis of the PRRA program. Concluding that "as things are now going, we seem in some danger of developing conditions like those in Ireland before the Free State, with increasing armed resistance directed partly against 'Yankee imperialism' and partly against the morass of poverty," the journal saw "no point in going on with the expenditure of enormous sums for relief while we also continue the economic policies that make Puerto Rico's poverty ever deeper."[70]

Oswald Garrison Villard did what he could to prevent Puerto Rican issues from shattering the remaining anti-imperialist unity. In March 1937 he announced that he too would visit the island and report back on his findings. As the mentor of many of the figures on both sides of the dispute, Villard was a man whose opinions naturally carried weight. He returned with a considerably less critical appraisal of Gruening's tenure than that offered by the Liberals or the ACLU. Villard conceded that the criticisms of Gruening "come largely from those who were formerly his personal friends and who were at first ardent supporters of the program," but added that Gruening had made a genuine effort at political, economic, and social reform: "While not denying his mistakes . . . no one could have tackled this particularly difficult problem of Puerto Rican reconstruction without antagonizing some people." Villard gave Gruening advance copies of his articles to critique, commenting that he dismissed extreme charges ranging from contentions that Gruening had sold his "soul to the sugar barons" to claims that he was "corrupted by public office." Privately he expressed his hope that Gruening would "get out of the whole mess" and promised to do what he could to ensure that Gruening left government service with his reputation intact. Villard's attempts at conciliation failed. Anti-Gruening forces in Puerto Rico criticized him for having dealt "too easily" with the PRRA head, while Gruening refused to accept even the mildest criticism from anti-imperialists. Villard then reluctantly met with Ickes to suggest an "official commission to investigate conditions in Puerto Rico." For Gruening, another long friendship had come to an end.[71]

THE DECLINE of the anti-imperialist movement predated the unraveling of Gruening's tenure coordinating Puerto Rican policy. Even before the formation of the DTIP, alterations in the international climate had robbed the anti-imperialists of much of their support in Congress and among the peace movement. Internal squabbles further weakened the movement's vibrancy as many of the key figures from the 1920s passed from the scene. But Gruening's prominent position provided one last opportunity to extend the anti-imperialist agenda to Caribbean policy as a whole. Indeed, the onetime anti-imperialist activist could not have hoped for a better opportunity to fuse his domestic and foreign policy ideologies and establish a policy model which Roosevelt could apply elsewhere in U.S. dealings with Latin America. In retrospect, though, the program suffered from too many tactical and ideological contradictions. Though committed in theory to a working partnership with Puerto Rican reformers, in practice Gruening proved reluctant to allow real authority to pass from Washington to San Juan. Personally, the skills which served him well in accumulating bureaucratic power did not translate into administrative success, while his tendency to interpret Puerto Rican matters through a preconceived ideology blinded him to the island's more pressing short-term relief needs. Even had he succeeded in overcoming all of these obstacles, however, the fact remains that Gruening never addressed the ways in which his definition of the national interest, calling for active assistance to reformers overseas, differed from FDR's Realpolitik conceptions. For the movement as a whole, the collapse of the Puerto Rican experiment came as a crushing blow. The anti-imperialists' strength derived from their unity and their single-mindedness in approaching Latin American issues, traits which allowed them to exercise political influence far out of proportion to their numerical strength. Their internal debates over Gruening's policies in Puerto Rico neutralized this political power.[72]

Once shattered, the anti-imperialist coalition would not reunify. For Gruening himself, his battle with fellow anti-imperialists over Puerto Rican policy caused him to reconsider his approach to Latin American issues as a whole. Renewed tensions between the United States and Mexico also played a role in this process. In 1938 the long dispute between the two nations finally reached a head when the government of Lázaro Cárdenas nationalized the holdings of U.S. oil companies. The Roosevelt administration was divided in its response. Ambassador Josephus Daniels, joined by Treasury Secretary Henry Morgenthau, recommended settling the dispute diplomatically, while Daniels's immediate superior, Secretary of State Cordell Hull, advocated a strong response to compel a return to the pre-1938 status quo. Gruening, still an admirer of Hull despite their disagreement over the tariff reciprocity treaties, agreed "fully" with the secretary that the Good Neighbor Policy "has got to be a two-way, a reciprocal policy." Praising Hull furthered Gruening's search for additional allies within the foreign policy bureaucracy, but it most reflected his anger with the anti-imperialists both inside the United States and in the Caribbean, who he was convinced had betrayed him. After his own disputes with the Puerto Rican Liberals, he concluded that the United States too often had appeased Latin Americans, to the detriment of both sides. Moreover, the DTIP head reasoned, Cárdenas had sacrificed a spirit of cooperation with the United States and risked the possibility of a counterrevolutionary backlash.[73]

Worried that the Mexican action might dominate the agenda of the upcoming inter-American conference at Lima, Hull asked Gruening to work up a memorandum to help him meet the situation. Again, the DTIP director looked for support in the anti-imperialist community and instead found everyone else in his "crowd" defending Cárdenas's actions. At the height of the expropriation crisis, he encountered Hubert Herring, who was in Washington seeking to build support for Cárdenas, and Stephen Raushenbush, the chief counsel of the Nye Munitions Committee. The old friends chatted for a while, then went for dinner to a Mexican restaurant in the capital. Neither the meal, however, nor a discussion about imperialism at Gruening's home which extended past midnight could restore the lost unity. Instead, Gruening accused his former ideological comrades of offering a "half-baked liberalism which sees every act of pillaging of American property or assault on American rights in Mexico [as] something noble and libertarian." By early 1939, the relationship between Gruening and the remnants of the anti-imperialist movement had deteriorated to such an extent that the DTIP head asked the FBI to investigate U.S. activists friendly to Mexico who also championed independence for Puerto Rico. This startling proposal showed how much Gruening's personal feelings had altered his perspective on inter-American affairs. Eventually he would recognize this fact, though only after overcoming his sense of betrayal against the anti-imperialist movement as a whole.[74]

In Washington throughout 1938 and 1939, and with comparatively few duties after his departure from the PRRA, Gruening worried about the response of the Western allies to Nazi aggression. He remained more consistent with his basic international perspective in his opinions on European issues, although by doing so he distanced himself from most anti-imperialists and also retreated from his own argument of the early 1930s that the United States should concentrate its diplomatic activity on the Western hemisphere. He described the German *Anschluss* of Austria as the most "disastrous week for the forces of liberty" in world history, with reverses for the Spanish Republicans in that country's civil war and the beginning of German pressure on Czechoslovakia and Lithuania accompanying Austria's loss of freedom. He considered Czechoslovakia's plight "very disturbing," and visited the Czech ambassador to express his personal support for standing firm against German pressure. When rumors of appeasement began to circulate, Gruening, with a "profound sense of helplessness and dejection," accused France of "signing its own death warrant," since war eventually would break out "under less favorable conditions than now." By late 1938, he lamented, Spain seemed the only European country willing to fight for democracy.[75]

In a much more realistic understanding of European international politics than he had exhibited in the early 1930s, Gruening saw that the menace of German fascism could be countered only by force, not by appeals to a sense of humanity that Hitler did not share. In light of these beliefs, the attitude of his onetime anti-imperialist colleagues puzzled him. A conversation with Dorothy Detzer, his comrade from a variety of anti-imperialist campaigns during the 1920s, caused him to lose respect for her "intellectual acumen," since "apparently she sees nothing more in the European situation than the clash of rival ambitions." Detzer, he lamented, was "so professional in her pacifism that she simply cannot face facts." He similarly dismissed Frederick Libby, head of the National Council for the Prevention of War and his colleague in the battles to prevent intervention in Mexico in 1927 and to block Coolidge's naval bill in 1929. European developments had made "manifest" for the DTIP head "the complete loss of the war to end war" proclaimed by Wilson two decades earlier.[76]

As Gruening soon discovered, these developments had also prompted Roosevelt to reorient his policy toward Puerto Rico. Concerned about the possibility of Nazi expansion into Latin America, the president began to look upon Puerto Rico in terms of its military rather than its cultural potential. In May 1939 he named his former naval chief of staff, William Leahy, to succeed Winship as governor. Gruening was not even consulted about the appointment, a testament to his loss of influence. He protested to Ickes against this "obvious ignoring of all the burning economic and social problems of P.R." Charging that the "Puerto Ricans have been handed a Governor much as Mussolini might hand the inhabitants of Ethiopia or Libya a new Military Governor," Gruening warned of resentment on the part of Puerto Ricans "that they should be treated like a little Gibraltar handed to a military officer as if defense were the only issue." Ickes responded by going out of his way to praise the appointment.[77]

As the summer of 1939 dawned, Gruening's world was collapsing on all levels. Personally, he was estranged from many of his former friends and associates. Ideologically, his altered framework on inter-American affairs had cast him adrift from an anti-imperialist movement which had once provided the center of his existence. Professionally, the failure of his Puerto Rican initiative had robbed him of support from the White House and threatened his position with the DTIP. Given this wide array of difficulties, many thought that Gruening's career as a reformer had passed. They were wrong.

Gruening (center) with Federico and Ferdinand Henriquez y Caraval, the two leaders of the Dominican nationalist movement, during his initial visit to the Caribbean Basin in 1921. (Courtesy of Gruening Collection. Alaska and Polar Regions Archives, Rasmuson Library, University of Alaska Fairbanks, Scrapbook, 1920s–1930s.)

Opposite, above: Gruening (at far left) as adviser to the U.S. delegation to the Montevideo Conference in 1933. In his first government post, he urged Cordell Hull to abandon the administration's brief flirtation with military intervention in Latin America. Also pictured (from left to right) were the other members of the delegation: Sophonisba Breckenridge, Alexander Weddell, Hull, J. Reuben Clark, Butler Wright, and Spruille Braden. (Courtesy of Hunt Gruening.)

Opposite, below: Gruening voting with Dorothy in Juneau, in the early 1940s. The high profile that he adopted as governor transformed the politics of the territory. (Courtesy of Hunt Gruening.)

Above: Gruening testifying before the Senate Interior Committee on behalf of Alaskan statehood. Since he championed statehood as a way for the United States to strike a blow against colonialism, the crusade played a critical role in reviving his anti-imperialist perspective. (Courtesy of Hunt Gruening.)

Opposite, above: Gruening with colleague Wayne Morse—the two no votes against the Tonkin Gulf Resolution. (Courtesy of Hunt Gruening.)

Opposite, below: Official photo of Gruening as a U.S. senator. (Courtesy of *Washington Star* collection, Martin Luther King Public Library, Washington, D.C.)

Above: Gruening sharing a moment of cordiality with Robert Kennedy. Behind the scenes, however, the two were personal as well as ideological foes. New Mexico's Joseph Montoya joined them in this photograph. (Courtesy of Gruening Collection. Alaska and Polar Regions Archives, Rasmuson Library, University of Alaska Fairbanks, Accession #76-21-612.)

Gruening with Colombian president Alberto Lleras Camargo in 1965. The senator pointed to Lleras as the type of Latin American reformer around which the United States should orient its hemispheric policy. (Courtesy of Gruening Collection. Alaska and Polar Regions Archives, Rasmuson Library, University of Alaska Fairbanks, Accession #76-21-472.)

~ 5

The Alaskan Agenda

With even Gruening conceding that Realpolitik considerations would dominate U.S. foreign policy for the foreseeable future, it was clear that his agenda represented a phase of the Good Neighbor Policy which had run its course. His bureaucratic difficulties also persisted. Villard, who found Ickes "more bitter against Gruening than ever," predicted that "there will be a change in the latter's office before too long." Gruening's friendship with the likes of Felix Frankfurter and Oscar Chapman, combined with Roosevelt's general distaste for firing his subordinates and concern that Gruening might leak damaging information to his old associates from the journalistic community, made an outright dismissal out of the question. And so Roosevelt bided his time. Then, in the fall of 1939, the governor of Alaska, John Troy, resigned. Roosevelt, undoubtedly relieved that a position had opened up that would enable him to move the DTIP head out of Washington quietly, immediately offered the job to Gruening.[1]

The proposed nominee, however, entertained other ideas. After Chapman urged him to decline the post, he informed Ickes that he preferred to remain at the DTIP, oblivious to the fact that Roosevelt intended him to have no choice in the matter. Gruening then departed Washington for a New England vacation, telling his secretary that he could not be reached by telephone because he had no planned itinerary. He avoided a last-minute phone call from Ickes demanding another meeting over the gubernatorial appointment, and left Washington convinced that he had foiled the attempt to reassign him. Such tactics proved amateurish compared to Roosevelt's. While in Massachusetts, he heard over the radio that the president had appointed him governor.[2]

Deeply shaken, Gruening hurried back to Washington. He let Chapman know that he was considering leaving government service altogether. But, understanding the implications of Roosevelt's unilateral announcement, Chapman calmed his friend down, noting that at the very least his new position promised an increased salary and financial stability. Gruening secured a meeting with the president, at which he received permission to remain as director of the DTIP until a successor could be found. He then worked frantically to frustrate the search. Although Ickes was struggling to locate a replacement for Gruening with the "required experience," he nonetheless jubilantly counted the days until he could "kiss him good-bye." Meanwhile, Gruening remained as difficult to deal with as ever, since the DTIP head chose to believe that Roosevelt had offered him the gubernatorial post "because of his outstanding abilities." In truth, as Ickes knew, the president believed that Gruening had "not done an effective job" at the DTIP. This reality eventually frustrated Gruening's machinations to avoid exile to the position described as "the Siberia of the [Interior] Department."[3]

Whereas Gruening had visited Puerto Rico on over sixty occasions during his tenure at the DTIP, he had traveled to Alaska only twice in his nearly five years running the division.[4] Consequently, he had few firm thoughts on the issues he would be confronting in a post completely unlike any he had previously experienced. In 1939 the population exceeded one thousand in only seven Alaskan cities, which were connected by less than 2,500 miles of public highway. Relations with the federal government and the fifty-two federal agencies operating in the territory were poorly coordinated. Territorial politics exhibited little more sophistication. By tradition, the governor served as the chief representative of the federal bureaucracy rather than an active participant in day-to-day political events. Meanwhile, the legislature, especially the eight-member Senate, was dominated by lobbyists representing outside economic interests, such as the canned salmon industry, which primarily aimed to maintain the territory's primitive tax structure.[5]

Federal policies had not improved conditions. Politically, Alaska was totally unorganized between 1867 and 1884. It did not have a nonvoting delegate in Congress until 1906, and only in 1912, with the Second Organic Act, did it gain an elected territorial legislature, albeit with severely restricted powers and apportionment based on the territory's four judicial divisions rather than population. On the economic front, the Jones Act of 1920 prohibited supplying Alaska from the more economical Canadian ports of Vancouver or Prince Rupert, in effect granting the Seattle shipping industry a monopoly on transporting goods to the territory. The Harding administration supplied $65 million for the Alaska Railroad, but Calvin Coolidge reversed his predecessor's policies, commenting that federal assistance to Alaska was "far out of proportion to the number of inhabitants." Finally, despite sporadic attempts in Congress to address the problem, Alaskan defenses remained meager on the eve of World War II, although, as the Japanese threat grew more menacing, the army established an Alaska Defense Command, and the navy authorized the construction of bases at Kodiak Island and Sitka.[6]

Since the territorial legislature, which met biennially, would not reconvene until January 1941, Gruening had few formal responsibilities during his first months in Juneau in late 1939. He clearly missed Washington. "Practically famished up here for news that doesn't appear in the press," he begged Chapman for "all the latest dope from the inside." Amplifying his revised framework on foreign affairs after the outbreak of a general European war with the German invasion of Poland in September 1939, he continued to distance himself from many of his allies of the 1920s. Pronouncing himself "a bit disgusted with some of our liberal Senators and Congressmen who have gone strongly isolationist," the governor failed to "see how such a position can be reconciled with liberalism or common sense." At the same time, though, he lamented the passage of the spirit of the interwar era, admitting that "for the moment and undoubtedly for some time to come, national defense will have the fullest sway."[7]

On the lookout for ways to integrate his newly emerging international realism with a pro-Alaskan agenda, Gruening further strained his relationship with Ickes. Since both men strongly favored building a highway linking Alaska to the lower forty-eight states, the governor received permission to come to Washington provided that he "work through channels." Ickes should have known better. Because it also offered the territory permanent economic benefits, Gruening touted a route connecting Alaska to Seattle, running through British Columbia, while Ickes preferred a more militarily sound interior path. When the *New Republic* later published an article praising Gruening's role in securing the authorization for the highway, the secretary fumed that the magazine's editor, Bruce Bliven, "apparently fell hard for some highly flattering opinions from Governor Gruening . . . of Governor Gruening." Ickes privately warned the governor to expect dismissal if he ever again lobbied against the stated position of the Interior Department.[8]

In any event, Gruening soon devoted himself to matters even closer to home. Both he and Roosevelt agreed that his chief task would be to "bring the New Deal to Alaska." But they defined the New Deal's basic principles in very different terms. For Gruening, the New Deal embodied more rigorous application of the nation's anti-trust statutes and heightened government spending to help the nation recover from the recession of 1937. But the anti-monopolist moment started to pass with the outbreak of war in Europe, and it waned further as the election of 1940 approached. While Roosevelt began to lose interest in domestic affairs, realizing that providing leadership in a turbulent international environment constituted his greatest political strength, profound ideological shifts in the nature of reform sentiment were also occurring. The U.S. defense buildup, which predated the country's entry into World War II, stimulated an economic upturn, restoring faith in American capitalism, while the anti-totalitarian nature of the European conflict made many liberals uncomfortable about supporting economic measures which increased the power of the state. Instead, they focused on issues such as civil rights and civil liberties, thus distinguishing the United States from the Axis powers.[9]

For Gruening, however, the goal of economic reform remained supreme. He argued that Roosevelt's first two terms had proved that political liberty—while critical—could provide "a solution to all of our problems" only if "coupled with economic opportunity." To an even greater extreme than in Puerto Rico, then, Gruening failed to confront the differences between the specifics of his agenda and the changing contours of national reform sentiment. Just before Roosevelt's successful election to a third term, the governor demonstrated his distance from the administration's political calculus, confiding to Chapman his hope that after Election Day the president would fire those cabinet officials who had "knifed" the anti-monopoly agenda. Gruening himself demonstrated his continuing fidelity to these principles when he greeted his first legislative session, in January 1941, with the longest opening address in history by an Alaska governor. He proposed a variety of social and educational legislative initiatives, but, along the lines of his fight against the Insull utility interests in Maine, focused his efforts on reforming Alaskan revenue policy by placing the tax "burden where it belongs"—on the wealthy and on absentee industries. Privately the governor conceded that the principle behind his revenue measures contained "nothing new." More than the specifics of his program distinguished Gruening from his predecessors. He also adopted an activist approach which included an aggressive lobbying campaign, inviting reporters for dinner at the gubernatorial mansion, and frequently attending legislative sessions. Dorothy, meanwhile, spent most days in the front row of the legislative gallery, occupying her time knitting when the debates got dull.[10]

Such was rarely the case, since Gruening's agenda appalled most members of the legislature. To express its disapproval in the most forceful way possible, the territorial House of Representatives urged Congress to forbid the appointment of any non-Alaskan as governor. If anything, the territorial Senate proved even more hostile, and the governor's first legislative session ended in complete failure. The totality of his defeat stunned Gruening. Unlike their counterparts in Puerto Rico's byzantine political climate, the governor's foes in Juneau showed little political sophistication. His loudest opponent, Cap Lathrop of Fairbanks, admitted that he opposed Gruening's tax program because it would increase taxation on his own business interests. He threatened to sell off his operations and trim back his work force if the revenue plan passed. Meanwhile, the lobbyists representing the canned salmon industry, headed by the more subtle and effective Judge Winton Arnold, also predicted that Gruening's program would cost Alaskans jobs.[11]

At the conclusion of the legislative session, the governor broke with precedent by delivering a public message criticizing the combination of legislators "who unabashedly and quite shamefully serve the private interest that hires them" and some among the "majority of honest legislators" who had been either "misled," "intimidated," or "tricked" into opposing his program. The governor's charges contained some merit; members of the territorial legislature privately admitted that they knew which of their colleagues the canned salmon industry had "bought off." But Gruening carried these concerns to an extreme, using his contacts in Washington to persuade J. Edgar Hoover to launch an FBI investigation of the legislative session on the grounds that "active and illegal lobbying occurred." The FBI director dispatched several agents to Juneau in the late winter of 1940–41, but they quickly concluded that "Governor Gruening did not furnish direct evidence indicating specific acts of lobbying" that violated federal law. Gruening typically had overstated his case. An angry Hoover personally forwarded a devastating forty-two-page report to the governor, which detailed the lobbying activities of both sides during the session and exonerated the industrial lobbyists of any wrongdoing.[12]

The weakness of his office clearly did not enhance Gruening's chances of passing his program. Building on long-standing beliefs, Gruening hoped to harness the power of public opinion through initiatives such as public addresses to the legislature. True to his conviction that in principle journalism remained "the most interesting and worthwhile of all callings," he also encouraged the creation of more territorial newspapers, for both altruistic and political reasons. After Lathrop's *Fairbanks Daily News-Miner* refused to print his initial gubernatorial address, he complained that too many Alaskans depended "on what we of the journalistic fraternity call the 'kept press.'" The governor still believed that "in a Democracy, public opinion is the ultimate controlling force, but unless that public opinion is informed it cannot function." Hampered by the response of Alaskans to his "pricklish" personality, Gruening enjoyed at best a mixed success in his early attempts to bolster his power. An associate recalled that, as always, the governor was "tactful as long as everything was going his way." Although Gruening maintained that he was "an easy person to get along with," later in his Alaskan tenure he candidly admitted that his "definition of a 'sound' thinker is one who agrees with me!"[13]

Alaska's sudden assumption of strategic importance caused Gruening to look beyond his early political disappointments. Throughout the autumn of 1941, tensions between the United States and Germany produced an undeclared naval war in the North Atlantic, while in East Asia, negotiations between Washington and Japan were deadlocked. Convinced of the need to strike before a crippling oil embargo neutralized its military capabilities, the Japanese government launched a surprise attack against the naval base at Pearl Harbor on December 7. The outbreak of war between the two countries, in combination with the still incomplete nature of the territory's defenses, raised the possibility that Japan might successfully attack Alaska. With his territory vulnerable to foreign invasion, Gruening reconsidered further his interwar anti-militarist sentiments. In early 1942 he returned to Washington for what he described as a "very important" conference with Roosevelt, at which he complained about the military's lack of attention to the Alaskan front. At a time when U.S. forces around the world were on the defensive, the governor urged making Alaska "impregnable" by supplying it "with the proper equipment and alertness"; he told the national press that he was even "thinking in terms of offensive warfare." In a remarkable display of strategic naïveté, he reasoned that bombing raids launched from the Aleutians against Japan could win the Pacific war. Army personnel dismissed such plans as "beyond the realm" of imagination.[14]

Gruening also had a more personal rationale for adopting an ardently pro-defense posture. He feared that the military could use any signs of recalcitrance on defense issues to justify replacing him with a retired general or admiral, and perhaps even converting the government of the territory to an outright military regime. In fact, the governor had reason to worry. Just over a month after Pearl Harbor, Roosevelt expressed concern about the possibility of a springtime Japanese attack on Alaska. After Gruening presented his bombastic war plans, the president decided to "talk with Secretary Ickes about Governor Gruening—as to whether he fills the job." In April the War Department and the Bureau of the Budget jointly drafted an executive order to place the governor under the jurisdiction of the secretary of war, who also received authorization to assume control over all civilian activities in the territory. Under orders from Roosevelt, the BOB presented Ickes with the plan before its final approval. The secretary, stunned by its scope, promised that he "would not take lying down any such proposal." When he pressed BOB representatives on why the president supported such a draconian measure, they replied that Roosevelt had lost faith in Gruening's ability to govern Alaska. This response presented Ickes with an unenviable choice. Confronting the alternatives of removing Gruening but eliminating his department's authority or preserving its power but retaining the governor, Ickes placed his department's well-being above his personal preferences. After gleefully reminding the White House "that Gruening had been the president's selection, not mine," Ickes defended the governor, and Roosevelt relented. In a move epitomizing the ironies of politics, Ickes saved Gruening.[15]

UNFAZED BY HIS NEAR-DISMISSAL, once Alaska was declared a war zone, Gruening began to feud with the armed forces after the military imposed censorship, ordered women and children out of the territory, and restricted the movement of those who remained. Given his personal history, he found the censorship in particular "unduly repressive," and pressed Ickes for permission to raise the matter directly with the relevant army officials. Ickes denied this request, but (true to form) Gruening went forward anyway. He traveled to San Francisco in September 1942 to discuss the question with the chief of the Western Defense Command, Lieutenant General John DeWitt, and the military shortly thereafter eased restrictions. To his dismay, however, Gruening discovered that the government's civilian censorship agency, the Office of War Censorship (OWC), was continuing the old policies. Using his contacts in Washington, particularly George Norris, he presented a closed session of the Senate Judiciary Committee with specific examples to prove his point that the OWC's actions amounted to the "introduction of Gestapo methods to the United States." Both Norris and Joseph O'Mahoney (D–Wyoming) then took up Gruening's cause. Privately, OWC head Byron Price conceded the damaging effects of the hearings. Ickes sympathized, admitting to Price that Gruening "gives me a great deal of trouble," since "he doesn't like to work through channels and he isn't always averse to arriving at independent conclusions respecting official matters and then going off half-cock." As Ickes anticipated, the governor continued to complain until censorship in the territory was ended.[16]

Faced with increasing difficulties in dealing with Washington, Gruening started using national security arguments to turn the tables against his bureaucratic foes. After complaining that the head of the Alaskan Defense Command, Lieutenant General S. B. Buckner, was "thoroughly uncooperative as far as the civilian interest is concerned," he launched a "revolt against military tyranny and brass-hat arbitrariness." First, in late 1942, he urged the Interior Department to support a "*positive* formula" to grant him the authority to make decisions independent of the territorial legislature and subject to a presidential veto, power of the type which he had enjoyed early in his tenure with the PRRA. He justified the suggestion in the name of getting "a psychological jump on the military," but Ickes was not persuaded. Rebuffed on this front, Gruening revived another concept from his Puerto Rican experience, proposing the Alaska War Council (AWC). Modeled on the PRRA's executive board, the council theoretically was established as a liaison between civilian and military officials in the territory. The governor actually hoped that it would function as had the PRRA to increase his own independence. At the council's initial meeting, as Gruening informed Ickes, the AWC declared that it "was no more an Interior Department agency than that of any other Department." (Gruening added in his official report that his argument in favor of maintaining Interior Department control "was much more extended than the minutes indicate," an assertion which undoubtedly amused the secretary.) All of this effort, however, produced few tangible results. When Buckner consistently bypassed the council, Gruening sought in vain an executive order "calling attention to the need of centering authority in the civil government to permit it to function."[17]

Left with no other choice, the governor began to play military politics, seeking allies within the Alaska Defense Command to prevent a united military front opposed to his wishes. He also cultivated national journalists, such as the *New Republic*'s Bruce Bliven. In this context, he renewed contact with Richard Neuberger, the Oregon journalist whom the governor had first met during his second stint at *The Nation*. Gruening praised Neuberger's flattering articles about his gubernatorial policies, although neither friendship nor exile in Juneau prevented occasional displays of arrogance. When Neuberger quoted Gruening as saying that "Alaska has the greatest potential possibilities for launching an offensive of any land under the American flag," the governor condescendingly noted that he had never "spoken of the potential possibilities of anything." Indeed, he complained to Neuberger, he trembled at facing his "former literary colleagues on the 'Nation' after they read this quotation." Even so, the two soon formed an intimate friendship, combining their love for journalism with a passion for politics. To Neuberger, Gruening confided his ultimate ambition—to cap off his career by serving in the U.S. Senate. In fact, most of his Alaskan acquaintances already assumed that he harbored such a goal, since his primary interests remained national and international issues.[18]

The passing of the immediate military threat to the territory quieted rumors of Gruening's ouster. He thus returned to his Alaskan agenda, which focused on a host of causes he had championed in various venues for fifteen years. For example, he encouraged developing the territory's "outstanding underdeveloped resource," hydroelectric power, and urged Alaskan towns to acquire public utilities. As in Puerto Rico, he saw the possibility of linking higher education with international affairs, suggesting that the university establish a chair in Slavic culture which "some of the friends of Russia" could endow or "some kind of exchange professorship" with the USSR. On the local level, the governor, still an avid swimmer, championed constructing indoor swimming pools in the territory's principal communities, an idiosyncratic crusade in which he retained a lifelong interest. More significant was Gruening's passion for civil rights. He later recalled his shock at discovering widespread discrimination against Indians and Eskimos, such as signs in stores and restaurants excluding Native Alaskans, although both voluntary and legislative efforts initially failed to rectify the problem. On a more personal level, in contrast to his ambivalent attitude toward lower-class Mexicans during the 1920s, Gruening made himself a presence in Native communities by visiting Native Alaskans in their homes, eating their food, learning about their culture, and even incidentally using his medical training on visits to isolated villages. At the same time, he remained a committed integrationist, to the point where he ignored Ickes's warnings and publicly attacked an Interior Department plan to create Indian reservations in Alaska. Having reached the end of his "patience with a man who sabotages and seems to have no sense of responsibility about following policy," the secretary promised Gruening that he would have "no hesitation" about letting him go when his term ended. Fortunately for the governor, Ickes departed his office before he could carry through on his threat.[19]

Gruening thus offered in Alaska a host of initiatives reflecting his eclectic background. Yet, as had been the case in Maine, his chief interest remained economic matters. While rights-related issues were assuming predominance in the national reformist arsenal, proposals for altering the relationship between government and business defined Gruening's tenure in Juneau. After his tax agenda again stalled in the legislature in 1943, the governor adopted a new tactic, targeting the out-of-territory defense contractors that had accompanied the military buildup. Gruening termed the national security crisis an incentive for

Alaskans to support his revenue reform proposals, noting that as long as the war continued, most of the new tax burden would fall on defense-related industries rather than on the average Alaskan taxpayer. The territory could thus achieve a financial windfall from the military buildup. (Between 1941 and 1945, the federal government spent over $3 billion in the territory on projects relating to national security.) Opponents, however, continued to argue that these schemes would ultimately cost jobs and increase the average Alaskan's tax burden.[20]

While this program earned Gruening the consistent enmity of figures such as Cap Lathrop and representatives of outside economic interests, the governor also began attracting his share of strong admirers. As he had done in both Washington and Maine, Gruening bonded with like-minded political activists, such as Robert Atwood, publisher of the *Anchorage Daily Times,* and his wife, Evangeline. Though Republicans, the Atwoods praised Gruening's efforts to prepare the territory for statehood and his willingness to confront absentee industry. Within the legislature, Gruening formed an intimate tie with Stanley McCutcheon, the scion of an old-time Alaskan political family, nicknamed "The Man" for his ability to deliver his supporters from the Anchorage area. McCutcheon came to respect Gruening "above all other men" he ever knew. Within the Juneau press corps, meanwhile, the governor grew friendly with one of the territory's most astute political and intellectual figures, George Sundborg, a columnist for the *Juneau Alaska Empire.* Gruening pressed his allies in Washington to locate funding for a position as executive assistant to the governor, to which he could appoint Sundborg. The governor's program also continued to earn commendation from those few national reformers, such as Richard Neuberger, who paid attention to Alaskan affairs.[21]

As the elections of 1944 approached, Gruening looked to translate some of this strong support into legislative victories. In the process he all but abandoned his activism on national and international matters and focused instead on weakening his enemies in the territorial legislature and their lobbyist allies, whom, borrowing a phrase from Woodrow Wilson, he dubbed "the little group of willful men." Reapportionment based on population represented one of his two chief projects. The governor termed it "absolutely necessary if the democratic process is to function in Alaska"; if it had the side effect of decreasing the power of conservatives in the legislature, then all the better. Gruening also favored enlarging the Alaska Senate from eight members to sixteen, hoping to dilute the conservative majority. The governor won approval from Washington for both schemes in time for the elections, proof, as the *New York Times* later remarked, of Gruening's "keen knowledge of the art of politics." The election results seemed to confirm this observation: candidates the governor supported won narrow majorities in both houses of the legislature. In addition, after the retirement of the territory's delegate to the House of Representatives, Anthony Dimond, territorial secretary Bob Bartlett, running with Gruening's open support, captured first a hotly contested Democratic primary and then the general election. Bartlett's triumph, described by Oscar Chapman as a "real feather" in Gruening's cap, ensured an ally in any hostile dealings with Washington.[22]

Privately (and prematurely, as events developed), Gruening contended that it was "now or never" for tax reform. He welcomed the new legislature with his longest gubernatorial message yet, a ten thousand–word diatribe against the influence of absentee interests. After telling the legislators, "Believe it or not, I do not enjoy proposing a tax program," the governor joyfully proposed a territorial income tax along with a host of revenue measures intended to have a "powerful bearing on the subject of absenteeism." When he lost command over his tenuous legislative majority, however, Gruening turned once again to public opinion to rescue his political fortunes, launching a speaking tour on behalf of his tax agenda. A combination of such public pressure, along with intensive private lobbying and political maneuvering by McCutcheon, helped to carry the House. But the Senate rejected the measure by an 8 to 8 tally, leaving the territorial budget with a deficit of over $2 million and tax reform dead. As usual Gruening blamed outside lobbyists for his failure, although again his defeat flowed more from the tactical and ideological shortcomings of his approach. Even Atwood's generally friendly *Anchorage Daily Times* wondered how Alaskans would improve themselves and the territory by curtailing the activities of enterprises solely "because they are controlled by absentee owners."[23]

Except for this significant failure, however, Gruening fared well at the hands of the 1945 legislature. His most notable achievement was the creation of an Alaskan Development Board, charged with recruiting new industries for the territory, a task the governor hoped would fortify

Alaska's economic base and thus weaken absentee economic interests. The position of executive director of the board, with its $12,000 salary, attracted two of the territory's brightest political figures, first Henry Clark and then George Sundborg, who doubled as Gruening's chief political adviser. Gruening also structured the board so that it could represent the territory in hearings before national regulatory agencies, fulfilling a proposal which he had first outlined in Maine. Indeed, it represented part of his broader attempt to "train" Alaskans to deal more effectively with the federal bureaucracy. The governor set the example, taking advantage of his legendary energy level to overwhelm federal officials who came to the territory, in the hope of impressing them with the enormity of Alaska's needs by showing them as many of the territory's problem areas as possible. Since Gruening himself generally slept only four or five hours a night—he regularly rose by 5 A.M.—this schedule presented him with few problems. The day's exhausted visitor, however, was left to straggle along as well as possible.[24]

A more sophisticated approach to governing paved the way for these legislative successes. As a political appointee, Gruening had given up his cherished independent voting status in 1939 and for the first time registered as a Democrat. In line with his new affiliation, Gruening stayed within established party lines and cooperated with the territory's Democrats in his first few years in Juneau. But the influence of the absentee economic interests on a number of Democratic senators, such as Norman Walker and Ed Coffey, ensured that the governor would have difficulty passing a reformist program by relying solely on Democratic votes. Recognizing this dilemma prompted Gruening to revive his earlier understanding of the relationship between partisanship, ideology, and political effectiveness. He had long contended that progressives served as an independent force in American politics, working within both parties to secure their ideological goals. The governor now applied this belief. He increasingly "wheeled and dealed without regard to party politics," reaching out to Republican senators such as Andrew Nerland and John Butrovich, tactics which altered the politics of the territory and made Gruening himself "the main issue in most territorial elections." The governor's Democratic opponents were left complaining that the territorial party had been replaced by a "Gruening privy council with a lot of conservative Democrats shut out." Ideology always guided Gruening's approach to politics; it came as no surprise that he returned to this perspective when the going got tough in Juneau.[25]

THE MORE FAVORABLE political environment gave Gruening an increasing fondness for life in Alaska. As the World War drew to a close, he built a "virgin forest cabin," dubbed "Eaglerock," twenty-six miles from the governor's mansion. Still, while content in Juneau, Gruening "remained a Washington D.C. man at heart." He proved the point by purchasing a sizable home on the fringe of the District of Columbia even as Eaglerock was under construction. Gruening rationalized that buying and then renting out the house would entail less expense than storing his furniture or moving it to Alaska. The purchase actually confirmed his desire to return to Washington. A friend remarked at the time that Gruening did not "have anybody to talk to in Juneau." On a different intellectual level than most in the Alaskan capital, with a substantially wider breadth of interests, he longed for the Washington environment he had enjoyed so much during the 1930s.[26]

The sojourn in Alaska, however, did soothe the friction in his marriage created by the financial hardships of the depression. Dorothy, reveling in the social status associated with her position as the governor's wife, used her "New England polish" as a frequent hostess of dinner parties—at least one per week—in the governor's mansion. She meticulously oversaw the hired help in their preparation of the meals, and her crab bisque acquired something of a local reputation. Described by Maurine Neuberger, Richard's wife and a close friend of both Gruenings, as the "type of person you would read about in an Edith Wharton novel," this "very patrician" woman "lived it up" in the "social swim." Both Neubergers speculated that the Gruenings had been living on the financial "edge" as a result of their active socializing. The entertainment budget associated with the gubernatorial position now allowed Gruening to maintain that lifestyle.[27]

Juneau was a small community throughout the 1940s, and dinner conversation at the governor's table invariably turned to politics. In the process, it became clear that despite their affection for each other, husband and wife remained on very different intellectual planes; Dorothy's tendency to offer "dense" comments earned her the nickname "Dodo." Robert Atwood, a frequent dinner guest, recalled that although Dorothy "wasn't dumb," she "often came up with some of the dumbest remarks in social conversations." Despite a desire to discuss them, she simply "didn't have a lot of depth on the current political issues of the day." Progressively less able to participate in her husband's world, she "put herself out in entertaining," focusing her life on social activities. As for the governor, the dinner parties formed "one part of the arsenal of his political advancement," allowing him to meet key figures in territorial politics in an informal setting, especially after dinner, when he fortified his reputation from Mexico and Maine as a liberal dispenser of alcohol. (Contemporaries recalled that he could down a pint of martinis, straight up, without showing any ill effects.) Since Gruening also viewed the parties as an attempt to replicate on a smaller scale the gatherings of the New Dealers on the Washington social circuit, he encouraged the high level of discussions which gave Dorothy so much trouble.[28]

Despite their differences, the governor, who never desired an ideological confidante for a mate, was more than willing to tolerate his wife's financial excesses and intellectual faux pas. By handling the bulk of the child rearing during the 1920s and 1930s and socializing during the 1940s, Dorothy proved a devoted partner who freed her husband to attend to his intellectual and political pursuits. Moreover, even now past fifty, Dorothy remained a "real stunner," while Gruening, prematurely bald and physically unattractive, wore baggy clothing that magnified the effects of his slight build and substantial girth; only after considerable pressing from Sundborg did he agree to pose for an official photograph, an unflattering shot which he used for the next quarter century. Living in his intellect and "thinking about big matters," he claimed that incidental issues such as his appearance did not concern him. The reality, however, was more complex. Gruening realistically understood the growing importance of physical appearance to political success. Only half-jokingly, he once confided to Felix Frankfurter that he would realize his dream of a seat in the upper chamber only through the passage of "an amendment which would deny a Senate seat to those elected" only because of their attractive photographs.[29]

During much of the governor's Alaskan tenure, moreover, his confidence in the "big matters" which had most defined his earlier career remained shaken: his dissenting vision for the United States in international affairs. Outside of matters directly affecting Alaska, Gruening rarely commented on foreign policy during World War II, and when he did so, he sounded quite unlike the committed anti-imperialist of the interwar era. Family concerns further distanced him from his earlier perspective, since both Hunt and Peter served in the U.S. Army Air Corps during the war. After Hunt was reported missing in action over Germany, Gruening stayed up all night listening to radio reports; to his relief, his son was located several weeks later, safe but interned in Sweden. This combination of motivations made the treatment of postwar Germany one of the few international questions in which he did show some interest. The issue renewed his contact with Francis Shea, once the coordinator of his legal division at the PRRA and now on the staff of Robert Jackson, the head of the U.S. delegation to the Nuremberg war crimes trials. In a startling repudiation of his civil libertarianism, Gruening deemed "it proper that whole categories of Germans," including all high officials of the Nazi Party, all members of the Gestapo and SS Corps, and all major industrialists and diplomats, "be considered guilty and so condemned to the death penalty."[30]

Lack of faith in his international vision provided another reason to concentrate on Alaskan issues as World War II drew to a close. The end of the conflict, however, brought with it an unfavorable partisan swing. Roosevelt's death in April 1945 elevated to the presidency Harry Truman, a figure with little national following and, at first glance, few of his predecessor's political skills. Truman's favorability ratings plunged as 1946 progressed, and in that fall's elections, the GOP seized control of both chambers of Congress for the first time since 1930. The Republican triumph extended to Alaska, where the party assumed majority status in the House for the first time since 1930 and got to organize the Senate as the result of a Democratic schism. Back in Washington after the elections, Gruening visited Frankfurter, to whom he "spoke soberly, but not hysterically, about the possibility of confusion coming from the election, not because the Republicans will be taking over Congress, but because of the lack of leadership on the part of the President." Truman, alas, was no Franklin Roosevelt. Nonetheless, the Alaskan considered it "not unfortunate that, if the Republicans were to have the House, that full responsibility for the legislative branch will be theirs." The public then could judge the GOP's record and, he hoped, reverse the 1946 results in the next election.[31]

The governor was not so sanguine about his future in Alaska. The national Republican triumph had left Gruening something of a lame duck, since Senate Republicans had deferred action on his renomination, anticipating the election of a Republican president in 1948, after which the GOP could name its own governor. On the ideological front, Republicans interpreted their victory as a mandate to trim government spending, an agenda the Alaska GOP brought to Juneau. Both personally and ideologically, Gruening embodied the Democratic Party and its commitment to increased spending. Predictably, therefore, the local GOP campaign featured a pronounced anti-Gruening bent. Republicans offered a variety of measures designed to strip the governor of most of his carefully accumulated power. They focused their effort on the Alaska Development Board, which the Senate voted to eliminate. A depressed Gruening conceded in the winter of 1947 that his "last" legislative session probably had arrived.[32]

That session was nothing short of disastrous. The territorial House ultimately declined to kill the development board, although it did terminate its funding. Gruening transformed this action into a victory, retaining Sundborg's services by appointing him to the new position of executive secretary to the governor, at his old salary of $12,000, and keeping him at his duties with the board. On other issues, however, no bureaucratic sleight of hand could save the governor. Both chambers passed measures to phase out the territorial sales tax, while the Senate rejected Gruening's proposed income tax as well. In fact, the legislature defeated seventeen consecutive revenue measures and then adjourned, leaving the territory with a $9 billion budget and only $5 billion in revenues, and prompting the governor to describe the session as "pretty close to a collapse of responsible self-government." Frustrated at the "tremendous amount of intrigue and underhanded politics being played," Gruening wondered whether his Alaskan crusade justified the effort. Even an invitation from Oscar Chapman to visit Washington failed to revive the governor's spirits; the normally energetic Gruening told his friend that he was "pretty tired" and would prefer to remain in Juneau.[33]

Gruening had reasons other than fatigue for avoiding Washington in the spring of 1947. Despite his aggressive personality, he understood from his Puerto Rican experience the need to maintain cordial relations with his one clear superior, the president. For the most part, except for a brief period in 1942, he had accomplished this task with Roosevelt, but he struggled to repeat his success with Truman, with whom he had not established a personal or political relationship during their joint period in Washington. Moreover, the new president was friendly with a number of the governor's opponents from the Seattle area. Ominously, Gruening's first meeting with Truman came in Olympia, at a dinner hosted by Truman's friend and former Senate colleague Mon Wallgren, then governor of Washington. Apart from Gruening and the president, Wallgren's only other guests were Senator Warren Magnuson, a politician Gruening considered a tool of the "fishing and timber interests," and Nick Bez, a Seattle cannery man whom the governor despised. Rumors soon surfaced that Truman was considering replacing Gruening with someone more friendly to Seattle interests.[34]

The renomination scare demonstrated the gap between Gruening's reform ideas and the dominant thinking among the national liberal community. The governor's attraction to the combination of anti-monopoly sentiment and federal public works projects, never popular with Seattle economic concerns, was also quite out of favor in Harry Truman's Washington, where most liberals were concentrating on achieving full employment while sustaining the wartime economic prosperity. These ideas formed the ideological basis behind much of Truman's domestic program, the Fair Deal, while the most powerful postwar liberal organization, the Americans for Democratic Action (ADA), likewise accorded to anti-monopoly beliefs a minor place in its economic agenda. This new mindset also guided policy in a matter close to Gruening's heart, regulatory appointments. In 1947, attempting to shift to the center for his upcoming reelection campaign, Truman moved against two of the most prominent New Dealers remaining in his administration, ousting Frankfurter protégé James Landis, the head of the Civil Aeronautics Board, and demoting Marriner Eccles from his chairmanship of the Federal Reserve Board.[35]

The rumors of Gruening's removal appeared in this context. In the end, Truman did renominate the governor, but without enthusiasm: admirers of Roosevelt had fiercely attacked the president for many of his early appointments, which seemed so out of line with the reformist principles of the New Deal. After journalist Robert S. Allen, a friend of Gruening's from his time in Washington, publicly asked whether the governor was "next on a list of New Dealers to be dropped by Truman," the president decided that an intraparty squabble over a rather minor post made no political sense.[36]

Having survived in Washington, Gruening then looked to score a political comeback in Juneau. True to form, he predicted that Democrats would fare well nationally by reclaiming the anti-monopoly legacy of the New Deal, a viewpoint which ignored the intraparty divisions caused by the independent candidacies of Henry Wallace on the left and Strom Thurmond on the right. The governor focused his attention, in any case, on the contests in Alaska. He set the ideological tone for his party's effort at the territorial convention in Ketchikan, where he contended that the sole hope for progressives lay in the Democratic Party. Gruening also guided the tactical agenda of the campaign. Pressure from constituents angered by cuts in government services after the 1947 legislative session prompted some of his foes to urge a special session to address the territory's financial woes. The governor gambled, however, that voters would blame conservatives rather than him for the crisis. He declined to call the legislature back to Juneau.[37]

In a way, Gruening was mimicking the anti-Congress approach used by Truman nationally. The tactic worked well for the president: not only did it help secure his surprise reelection, but also it set the stage for the Democrats to reclaim their majority in both houses of Congress. Likewise, in Alaska the governor's decision to run against the legislature paid dividends. The 1949 legislative session featured solid pro-Gruening majorities in both houses; *Jessen's Weekly*, a Fairbanks paper which the governor had encouraged as an alternative to Lathrop's *News-Miner*, rejoiced that at last "the people of Alaska awoke to the wisdom of Gruening's leadership." In a departure from the usual reception, Gruening's speech welcoming the legislature drew prolonged applause as the governor unveiled what he described as a "modest" budget of $17 million, easily the largest in the history of the territory. He also touted his usual agenda, although, beginning to look once again beyond Juneau, he advocated statehood much more strongly than in the past.[38]

Fittingly, the first bill introduced in the new House of Representatives was for an income tax. In addition, the legislature passed a uniform business license tax, a tobacco tax, a fish trap license tax, raw fish taxes, increased registration fees for nonresident lobbyists, and higher license taxes for fishermen, all revenue measures directed primarily against absentee business interests. The legislature, with Gruening's wholehearted support, then used the funds generated by the new taxes to appropriate $3 million for a host of educational and public works initiatives. On another front of interest to the governor, the legislature strengthened the territory's anti-discrimination statutes by passing bills prohibiting wage differentials based on the gender of employees, requiring all employers to keep and maintain wage records to facilitate employees' discrimination suits, and granting the territory the power to initiate anti-discrimination actions. Conservative forces now were left on the defensive against what the *News-Miner* described as "the mercies of predatory New Deal spenders." While favorable legislative majorities paved the way for the passage of tax reform, all involved credited the victory to Gruening's ability to sustain an "unpopular political campaign" which a less committed figure would have abandoned and then "educating" Alaskans on the necessity of tax reform.[39]

Ironically, at the time of his greatest triumph in the territory, it seemed as if Gruening's tenure in Juneau might end abruptly. With a Democratic majority in the upper chamber and Truman's assurance that he would be renamed for another four-year term, Gruening assumed that he would have little difficulty obtaining confirmation from the U.S. Senate. Instead, his Alaskan opponents promised Republicans on the Interior Committee material on the governor's "definitely destructive" behavior and policies. Sensing an opportunity to embarrass the administration, committee Republicans balked at attempts by chair Joseph O'Mahoney to move Gruening's nomination through without an open hearing, as had occurred in 1939 and 1943. This opposition compelled O'Mahoney to delay a committee vote until after holding public hearings, which he scheduled for the conclusion of the Alaskan legislative session.[40]

Clearly concerned about his future, Gruening persuaded friends to charter two planes to transport supporters from Alaska to testify on his behalf, an effort coordinated by Stanley McCutcheon. The opposition, however, took the opportunity to lead off with its witnesses, four members of the Alaska legislature, Democrats Frank Angerman and Marcus Jensen and Republicans George Miskovich and Charles Jones. The delegation leveled three primary charges. Both Angerman, a representative from Fairbanks, and Jensen, a representative from Douglas, accused the governor of exceeding his power when lobbying for individual bills. Jensen noted his "surprise" that Gruening was "the most potent single influence on the passage or rejection of legislative measures." He then detailed Gruening's "fundamental" approach: drawing up key pieces of legislation personally, shepherding them onto the floor through the cooperation of friendly representatives, and appearing "in the galleries, keeping his eye open for opposition." At recesses, he said, Gruening would buttonhole "one or the other of those who do not look favorable" and then lecture them "in the halls and in the cloak room." The second series of criticisms centered on the governor's program. Miskovich asserted that "the governor is encouraging radical elements," dating from his time in Mexico and Puerto Rico, "that are coming up from the West Coast to take over." He cautioned that Gruening's reappointment would perpetuate "a miniature dictatorship in one of the most strategic areas on earth under the American flag." Finally, all four legislators accused the governor of overarching ambition, a charge which Gruening hardly would have denied. Jensen suggested that Gruening's "striving for personal power" involved instances of graft and corruption in his appointments to various territorial boards, while Miskovich charged Gruening with using "his broad appointive power . . . to mold a following that has no relationship to established party lines."[41]

Republicans on the committee listened to this testimony in a state of disbelief. Promised evidence of widespread corruption, instead they heard four territorial legislators urge the governor's rejection on the grounds of his being overly effective, appointing too many Republicans to state boards, and harboring excessive political ambition. In a revealing commentary on what the *New York Times* later described as the "politically immature" nature of Gruening's Alaskan opposition, the hearings went downhill for the GOP once the Democratic cross-examination began. Miskovich candidly admitted that he lacked facts to back up any of his assertions, and that he really opposed Gruening because the governor was "very much against absentee ownership." When pressed, Angerman, a union activist before entering politics, confessed that he had split with the governor because Gruening favored a bill allowing the use of the territorial National Guard against strikers in a national emergency; while this position may have solidified his support among the Fairbanks labor movement, it hardly endeared him to

Interior Committee Republicans. Meanwhile, Jensen conceded that he had come to the capital to speak on behalf of four "very upset" Democratic representatives who had not received appointments to territorial boards. Since this complaint came on the heels of an argument by Miskovich that such appointments would have violated the territory's Organic Act, Jensen too lost his credibility with the committee. When Jones, the last of the four legislators to speak, noted under cross-examination that opposition to Gruening's civil rights policies had motivated his journey to Washington, the Republicans desperately sought to conclude the hearings—but not soon enough.[42]

Jones ended his prepared statement by commenting, "What I said has been written over, and it's not in the way I talk." Under questioning from Clinton Anderson (D–New Mexico), he admitted that Cap Lathrop's secretary had penned not only his remarks but those of his three colleagues as well. The Republicans then retreated from the hearings entirely, as Anderson invited Jones to criticize Gruening in his own words. The Nome senator described the governor as "a sucker, because he can talk the birds out of the trees. He tries to make you think what he wants you to think, and that is not what he is thinking, if you get my idea." Jones went on to describe Gruening's lobbying technique, commenting that he would invite legislators to the governor's mansion "and [give] them plenty of booze and lots of conversation, . . . the way he is throwing it out, you know, we have an expression, that what he peddles makes the grass grow green on the Kongarok." He conceded that Gruening was "a slick piece of goods" who knew "his stuff, when it comes to getting around." After this type of testimony from the opposition, Gruening's reconfirmation was never in doubt.[43]

Though always present in his approach, the pragmatism of which Jones spoke had emerged as one of Gruening's chief political characteristics by 1949. His desire to succeed as governor led Gruening to place Alaskan economic development ahead of dogmatic fidelity to some of his basic principles, such as his anti-monopoly agenda. In 1949, when Alcoa announced plans to invest $400 million in a plant in southeast Alaska's Taija Valley, he pressed Ickes's successor as interior secretary, Julius Krug, to help end a twelve-year-old suit against the corporation for antitrust violations. Though never "particularly a friend of monopolies," and aware "that under ideal conditions some alternatives might be preferable," he argued that "the important thing in this case is to get the development." In Alaska, he instructed Sundborg to give William King Mellon, Alcoa's advance man for the project—and the nephew of former secretary of the treasury Andrew Mellon, whose policies Gruening had excoriated during the 1920s—full use of the resources of the Alaska Development Board. In the end, opposition from Canadian authorities to Alcoa's use of water from the Yukon River killed the scheme, a defeat Gruening bitterly lamented. He believed that "one such major project should be carried on wholly by private enterprise and with private capital." Government sponsorship, he reasoned, could not fully provide for the territory's economic development, especially since "it is always a question of whether government financing will be forthcoming."[44]

More spectacular than Gruening's setting aside of his anti-monopoly sentiments was his conduct with regard to international affairs. The United States and the Soviet Union unquestionably emerged from the war as the world's two strongest powers, and in the aftermath of the conflict confronted power vacuums in the Middle East, in East Asia, and, most important, in Central Europe. Even before 1945, disputes had developed between the two nations, particularly over Soviet policies in eastern Europe. Diplomatic crises over Iran and Turkey, the deteriorating position of U.S.-backed noncommunist forces in Indochina and China, and the two sides' inability to work out international solutions concerning the future of Germany and atomic weapons only intensified these tensions. By 1947, most key figures in the Truman administration had accepted the thesis that the USSR was an expansionist state which the United States needed to contain lest its control spread throughout the Mediterranean and western Europe. That spring, when the British government announced that it no longer could afford economic or military support to the noncommunist governments in Greece and Turkey, Truman appeared before Congress to warn that this was a "fateful hour" in which the United States needed to "choose between alternate ways of life." A few months later, Secretary of State George Marshall, addressing commencement activities at Harvard, announced that the United States would provide economic assistance to help the European nations rebuild. Gruening, in attendance for his fortieth reunion, joined the crowd in applauding the proposal. At home, the passage of the National Security Act consolidated the service departments into the Department of Defense, established the Central

Intelligence Agency, and strengthened the president's bureaucratic position by creating the National Security Council (NSC). International events in the next two years—ranging from the communist coup in Czechoslovakia to the Soviet blockade of Berlin to the triumph of Mao Zedong's communist forces in the Chinese civil war—seemed to confirm the wisdom of these policies, which became popularly known as containment. Anticommunism then joined the stress on rights-related issues and support for full employment at the expense of anti-monopoly agitation as the three major tenets of what the historian Robert Dallek has called the postwar era's national liberalism.[45]

THESE CHANGES in the U.S. international position occurred against the backdrop of political turbulence in the territory in the half-decade following World War II. Gruening learned from the wild swings in Alaskan politics that he could not rely on the voters to elect legislatures to his liking. At the same time, despite all of his efforts, the only sustained federal assistance to the territory—such as the building of the Alaska Highway and the boom associated with World War II—had come when territorial developmental needs were linked with national security concerns. With the onset of the Cold War, national security issues again assumed a prominent place in American politics, and the temptation to use them to forward his Alaskan agenda proved too much to resist. Gruening recognized that stressing the Soviet military threat to Alaska offered the surest path to obtaining the desired federal aid, and thus embraced a variety of Cold War policies that he would come to oppose later on in his life. The governor used his Washington contacts to increase attention paid by the national press to the subject. Back in the capital briefly during 1949, he dined with Drew Pearson. He told Pearson that "Alaska may be the next Pearl Harbor," since the territory was defended by only 8,000 regular troops, as opposed to the 250,000 Red Army soldiers stationed, he claimed, across the Bering Strait in Siberia. Pearson then highlighted the problem in his column, assuring the governor that he was doing his best "to get Alaska fortified for you."[46]

Gruening, of course, was not the first to argue that the Cold War required boosting defense expenditures in Alaska.[47] But he stood out, in both Alaska and Washington, by expanding such calls to argue that federal assistance for the territory's economic development would serve broader national security interests. This logic appealed to the Truman administration; a confidential study commissioned by the president in 1948 concluded that "the strategic importance of Alaska to our national defense" made it "extremely unwise to wait for the ordinary processes of economic evolution" to develop the territory. The report, which Truman praised for having "a lot of meat in it," recommended "generous federal aid . . . to develop Alaskan industries, provide essential transportation, and increase the population." Sensing the public relations value of the tactic, Gruening especially utilized the Cold War argument when testifying before congressional committees, contending that the Cold War, by alerting Washington to "the fact that we have got to defend Alaska," explained the territory's need for assistance "not only militarily but economically and socially."[48]

Intimates of Gruening's from the interwar era undoubtedly were a bit surprised by the virulence of the governor's anticommunism, at least in his public statements. Oddly, for a figure long associated with reformist thought, Gruening had commented very little on communism before the late 1940s. Perhaps the relative weakness of communism in the region to which he devoted the most sustained attention—the Caribbean Basin—explained his lack of interest in the topic. Or perhaps he was secure enough in his vision of the United States as the harbinger of reform internationally and the embodiment of anti-monopoly sentiments at home that he saw no reason to look to foreign ideologies to structure an American program. In any case, the scarcity of Gruening's remarks on the issue was striking, especially given the sheer number of editorials—around five thousand—that he penned in his years as a newspaper editor. What he did write or say, furthermore, afforded no glimpse of the man who would embrace anticommunism in the years following 1945. In the 1920s, Gruening ridiculed American businessmen who described the Calles government as bolshevik; later in the decade, he wrote several *Evening News* editorials advocating diplomatic recognition of the Soviet Union. In the 1930s, his support for the Spanish Republic and a collective Western response at the time of the Munich Conference implied backing a de facto alliance with the Soviets; once that alliance was consummated, in World War II he touted postwar cultural and educational cooperation. Even after tensions between the two nations increased in the late 1940s, Gruening privately predicted that the United States would prevail in its battle over communism not by military means but by demonstrating the superiority of its ideals. Such a program, he contended, entailed adopting progressive domestic legislation so as to make the United States a suitable example of the success of democracy to the rest of the world.

In addition, the poisonous effects of the Cold War on American politics profoundly disturbed the governor. In 1950 he lamented the defeat of Senator Claude Pepper (D–Florida) after a bitter primary campaign in which the senator's opponent, George Smathers, portrayed the incumbent as soft on communism, calling him "Red Pepper." Consoling the Florida senator after his loss, Gruening expressed his hope that "the pendulum will swing back." He recognized, though, that "the international situation" had "greatly complicated" national politics by accentuating the shift toward conservatism. Indeed, surveying the national scene after the 1950 elections, he concluded that the triumphs of Herbert Lehman in New York and Thomas Hennings in Missouri constituted "the only really bright spots in what appears to be a considerable turn to the right."[49]

Despite these beliefs, Gruening embraced the emerging anticommunist framework as strongly as any prominent official in the Truman administration. Obviously, like most policy makers, he worried that the Soviets posed a military threat. But, for the most part, personal ambition explained Gruening's perspective on the related issues of anticommunism and military spending in Cold War America. Despite highlighting the need for nonmilitary solutions to the Cold War and his concern that the public's fear of the USSR would aid right-wing forces domestically, Gruening publicly employed hard-line anticommunist rhetoric and stressed the military threat from the Soviets to help fulfill his Alaskan agenda. Willing to utilize even the most circuitous logic in this effort, the governor never realized that describing, for example, increased funding for the University of Alaska as vital for the U.S. prosecution of the Cold War was ridiculous. His confidence in his public speaking and debating abilities in this sense served him poorly.[50]

Despite such exaggerations, though, the hardening and then militarization of the Cold War made Gruening's vision a reality. In June 1950, U.S. troops, under the banner of the United Nations, landed in South Korea after forces of the communist government in the North had crossed the thirty-eighth parallel dividing the country. Even before the Korean invasion, concern over the communist threat in Asia had prompted the administration to extend military aid to Thailand, then ruled by a regime which had collaborated with the Japanese in World War II, and to France for use in its colonial war against Ho Chi Minh's communist forces in Indochina. After the Korean intervention, U.S. defense spending skyrocketed, from $13.3 billion in 1950 to $60.4 billion the next year. Truman also embraced NSC 68, a document prepared by Paul Nitze, head of the State Department's Policy Planning Staff, which contended that the Soviets, guided by a "new fanatic faith, antithetical to our own," sought to impose their "absolute authority over the rest of the world." Along with the entire Pentagon budget, spending for Alaskan defenses shot up after 1950, aided by the endorsement of prominent military figures such as Curtis LeMay and Dwight Eisenhower.[51]

At the same time, however, it was indicative of the actual role that the Cold War played in his mindset that Gruening was perfectly willing to oppose those national security policies which ran counter to his Alaskan agenda. For example, he sharply criticized the military's habit of withdrawing lands from control of the territorial government for use as military reserves. The governor's opposition to the postwar foreign aid program, a vital part of U.S. Cold War policy, provided a sharper example of this pattern. Gruening believed that much foreign aid was wasted, and he consistently linked his calls for increased defense spending for Alaska with his emerging opposition to foreign assistance. In 1949, after Congress reduced spending for Alaskan defenses, the governor complained that "in the same Congress a few weeks earlier, practically everything that had been asked for aid on our eastern front in Europe had been granted." Alaskans could not help but be a little "cynical" about this apparent double standard. Gruening fumed that "every day we read of billions of dollars being shipped abroad to this country and to that country and we sometimes feel that if . . . we could hoist a foreign flag over Alaska, our needs would be taken care of." Such comments marked the origin of his crusade to reform the foreign aid program, which eventually assumed a much more creative scope intellectually. As with defense issues, Gruening reflected the overall Alaskan opinion on foreign aid matters. Indeed, throughout his tenure as governor, he rarely lost touch with his constituency on international issues.[52]

Gruening's anger about foreign aid taking away dollars that could be better spent in Alaska reflected his growing frustration with Washington policies in general. He continued to complain about the declining attention devoted to regulatory issues; when the Senate, despite its Democratic majority, rejected the nomination of Leland Olds to head the Federal Power Commission, Gruening could not help but "think we were back in the days of Sam Insull." He rebuked the Federal Maritime Commission for approving rate hikes requested by the Alaska Steamship Company; as always, the commission seemed overly "solicitous of this monopoly." He wondered whether, as a last resort, "we may have to come around to some form of Government subsidy" to bring competition to the Alaskan transportation field. Representative Henry Jackson (D–Washington), more in tune with the tenets of national liberalism, bluntly responded that neither the governor's ideological harping about the direction of national reform sentiment nor his continuing "to heap criticism on Seattle" would win the territory additional support in Congress.[53]

Rebuffed in his appeals to the legacy of New Deal liberalism, Gruening turned to national security arguments to augment his crusade against the forces of business consolidation. As early as 1945, he charged that the Civil Aeronautics Board (CAB) had decimated Alaskan air travel by tightening regulations on nonscheduled air carriers and curbing the ability of major carriers to run Alaskan routes. The CAB argued that the policy protected small local airlines; Gruening charged that it stifled competition. Truman's budget director, David Bell, dismissed the pleas as "not urgent," even after two Alaska-based carriers, Pacific Northern and Alaska Airlines, applied in mid-1950 for rights to additional routes connecting Alaska with Seattle, Portland, and Minneapolis. Then the outbreak of the Korean War gave Gruening his opportunity. Within weeks the governor was demanding "speedy action" from the administration "in view of the emergency." Undersecretary of Defense Robert Lovett agreed, urging the White House to pressure the CAB "in view of the critical international situation and the importance of building up the defenses and economy of Alaska as rapidly as possible." When the CAB refused to budge, Truman simply overruled the board.[54]

In a candid moment Gruening admitted suffering from "a local partisanship which has been described in military terms as 'theatritis'—a disease affecting military commanders who believe that not enough is being done for their theatres of operations." Nonetheless, he did not regret the fight. During his final five years as governor, military spending in the territory averaged roughly $250 million annually, and peaked at $512.9 million in 1953. The military's "heartland" policy, which called for replicating to the greatest extent possible the lifestyle of the lower forty-eight states in Alaska, continued the World War II pattern of using defense dollars to assist the development of the Alaskan civilian economy.[55]

OBTAINING INCREASED FEDERAL ASSISTANCE for Alaska was not the only aspect of Gruening's Alaskan agenda in which he attempted to benefit politically from anticommunist arguments. The tactic appeared as well in the initial stages of his pro-statehood public relations campaign, launched in 1946 after the territory's voters had narrowly endorsed the concept in a referendum. Gruening's ill-disguised ambition to serve in the Senate understandably prompted a skeptical view of his activities on this issue. In a lighter vein, Felix Frankfurter, to whom he sent copies of a number of his statehood addresses (which the Supreme Court Justice remarked "deserved to be called an 'effusion' only if length and not quality merits such a term of contumely"), teased the governor in the summer of 1950 that, before long, he might "be a colleague of Senator McCarthy's." Drew Pearson joined the banter: after the *News-Miner* canceled its subscription to his syndicated column, he asked Gruening for assistance in finding a replacement, noting that "if we are going to have statehood and if you are going to be the first Senator from Alaska, after all, we want a column or two running in Alaska." More seriously, the governor asked Richard Neuberger to tone down comments touting him as a future senator, noting that such portrayals were being used by "the opposition press which alleges that my interest is based wholly on personal ambitions." Statehood opponents in Washington, led by Senator Hugh Butler (R–Nebraska), also leveled the charge.[56]

By this time, however, Gruening had concluded that using defense and Cold War arguments on behalf of statehood would not achieve the desired result. As early as 1948 he privately admitted that despite his efforts, most people outside the territory did "not see the close relationship between statehood and military defense." Moreover, the defense expansion made it impossible to contend that territorial status ensured a defenseless Alaska. Most important, though, the tactic produced a rare personal humiliation. Confident as always in his ability to use his rhetorical skills to persuade skeptics, he assured a Senate committee that statehood would improve the U.S. position in the Cold War by hastening the development of the American way of life in the Arctic. Herbert Lehman, an old friend and a statehood supporter, privately commented that despite his general belief that Gruening's presence in Washington had helped to "galvanize support for the statehood legislation," the governor had "not made a case with regard" to this argument. Another old friend, Joseph O'Mahoney, did not even try to spare Gruening's feelings. The Wyoming senator scoffed that if a third world war erupted, it would "make very little difference whether we have two United States Senators from Alaska or not." The Cold War argument occupied a substantially diminished place in Gruening's repertoire after this exchange: the governor had no desire to be embarrassed on the national stage again.[57]

Gruening's decision to decouple anticommunism from the statehood agenda, however, came too late. Instead, the governor learned firsthand the dangers of cynically using the paranoia associated with the early stages of the Cold War to obtain political victories. In mid-1950, Senator Andrew Schoeppel (R–Kansas) charged that the "governing authorities" of the Alaska Statehood Committee—which Gruening chaired—were "Communists or Quislings" because the committee had hired Randolph Feltus, a public relations specialist who also had lobbied briefly for the government of Poland following World War II. Using information obtained from the files of the House Un-American Activities Committee, the Kansas senator also attacked Gruening for having served on the board of directors of the Garland Fund (which sponsored Roger Baldwin's American Fund for Public Service), which HUAC considered a communist-front organization. In addition, Schoeppel wildly alleged that Gruening had served as a correspondent for the Soviet news agency, Tass, during his stint in Mexico, and had exhibited "leanings toward Communism" at the *Portland Evening News.* For good measure, it also surfaced that during the 1930s Dorothy was affiliated with groups listed by HUAC as communist-front organizations, such as the Washington League for Women Shoppers.[58]

After an investigation, the Senate dismissed Schoeppel's contentions, noting that the Statehood Committee had requested Feltus's resignation after learning of his work for the Polish government. But Gruening understood that although the hearings had cleared him on the specific point initially raised, they had also revived his earlier connections to dissenting causes. Seeking to minimize the political damage, the governor increased the intensity of his anticommunism to the most extreme point of his career, contending that an "American who is a Communist or who sympathizes with Communism either has a warped mind, a perverted mind, or, if he is a man of intelligence, he is an extremely dangerous and undesirable citizen." Such public protestations, however, were not enough. Under fierce attack from congressional Republicans, Truman had authorized a government board to investigate executive branch officials accused of pro-communist sympathies. With the material from HUAC's files now in the public record, the FBI launched a loyalty investigation of the Alaska governor. Most of the over two hundred witnesses contacted by the twenty-eight special agents conducting the inquiry pointed out the absurdity of accusing a man who had spent the previous half-decade employing extreme anti-communist rhetoric to urge increased defense spending for Alaska of harboring communist sympathies. Many of Gruening's Alaskan opponents, however, found the contention all too believable; both the mayor of Fairbanks and a lobbyist representing the canned salmon industry indicated a willingness to testify to their belief that Gruening harbored communist inclinations. George Miskovich, last seen as one of the anti-Gruening witnesses at the governor's reconfirmation hearings, likewise declared his certainty that Gruening was a closet communist. For evidence, Miskovich pointed to the governor's alliance with Representative Al Owens, a colleague in the 1949 territorial legislature, whom Miskovich considered a radical because Owens pounded "on the table to emphasize his point while speaking."[59]

Despite such patently ridiculous claims, Gruening's earlier affiliations with a variety of reformist causes did look suspicious at the height of the Cold War. Recognizing the problem, the governor engaged in a bit of historical revisionism even before the airing of Schoeppel's charges. Through Richard Neuberger, he described his general position on inter-American affairs between the wars as "strictly middle-of-the-road," attacking interference by U.S. economic interests in Latin America but simultaneously warning against the influence of "extreme radicals" in the region. Now his politically savvy friends joined him in attempting to deflect the attacks before they could cause more harm.

Oscar Chapman, for example, noting that Gruening wielded "a somewhat vitriolic pen," attributed the charges to "the fact Gruening so often says the wrong thing at the wrong time." Such efforts could not prevent the investigation from weakening the governor's standing in a White House ultrasensitive to hints of communism from anyone associated with the administration. Although the final FBI report did not sustain Schoeppel's charges, Truman aide John Steelman described the findings as "inconclusive;" acknowledging that while it did not "contain evidence which would make me doubt the loyalty or efficiency of Dr. Gruening," Steelman recommended that Truman distance himself from the Alaska governor as much as possible anyway. In the end, the very anticommunist paranoia which Gruening had fostered turned against him.[60]

The governor thus understood that his tenure would end upon the expiration of his current term. Waxing philosophical, he expressed pride in his achievements during his years in Juneau. Having accepted the governorship reluctantly, Gruening initially championed an agenda which remained remarkably consistent with his earlier beliefs: civil rights, civil liberties, tax reform, and enhanced government regulation to limit the power of large-scale business concentrations. He also understood that the governorship represented the final opportunity to revive his political career. In his increased acceptance of bipartisanship and political compromise, his success at enhancing the power of the governor's office, and his ability to improvise, his political skills had noticeably improved since his days coordinating Puerto Rican affairs. Ruminating on the nature of leadership to Neuberger, Gruening claimed to have remained faithful to his beliefs while at the same time achieving political success. In general, he advised Neuberger, reformers should model themselves on figures such as California governor Earl Warren. Like Gruening's other political heroes—Brandeis, Wilson, Obregón, Calles, Norris—Warren was "a splendid liberal who is just sufficiently to the left of center to get things done." Naming "achievement" as "one of the tests of successful liberalism," he declined a historical legacy as "a voice crying in the wilderness." Instead, as he once told Herbert Lehman, he wished to be remembered for setting a "high standard of intelligence, liberalism, and sanity coupled with splendid administration."[61]

Such sentiments, however, did not come without a touch of irony for a man who, before his appointment, had prided himself on his fidelity to a basic set of ideological principles. By the final year of his tenure, a desire to achieve success in Alaska had transformed the onetime antimilitarist into a champion of military spending; at the same time, the governor had doused his reformist sentiments in international affairs so as to exploit the Cold War for Alaska's benefit. These tactics, in combination with the political incompetence of many of his foes, produced some short-term successes. For some observers, such as George Sundborg, Gruening was "at his best" during his years in Juneau. More broadly, though, his willingness to compromise many of the ideas central to his overall dissenting framework in the name of short-term political gain caused him to lose much of his relevance to national debates on economic and foreign policy matters.[62]

Perhaps sustaining this voice did not seem as important in 1952 as it once had. Statehood, and with it the prospect of a seat in the Senate, seemed as far away during Truman's final year in office as it had seven years before. Maintaining his usual perspective, he attributed Truman's plummet in the polls not to the rise of McCarthyism or the military stalemate in Korea but to the president's failure to install more progressives in his cabinet. This disappointment served as a fitting capstone for the uneven relationship between Truman and Gruening, and the governor expressed no sorrow when a surprisingly strong showing by Senator Estes Kefauver (D–Tennessee) in the New Hampshire primary forced Truman out of the 1952 race. Gruening then enthusiastically backed the Tennessee senator, who sported impeccable credentials on both decreasing the power of monopoly and supporting statehood for Alaska. He realized, however, that Kefauver's well-publicized investigations into organized crime had alienated too many party leaders. Under the circumstances, he concluded that Illinois governor Adlai Stevenson was "the best man that could have been nominated," and, in any case, he certainly preferred Stevenson to GOP nominee Dwight Eisenhower, who, though "a fine human being and a great general, . . . has no training for the presidency and is completely unfamiliar with the vast and complex domestic problems which he will have to face."[63]

The voters disagreed, not only allowing Eisenhower to sweep to victory in the November contest but also giving the Republicans control of both houses of Congress. Surveying the results from Juneau, Gruening particularly lamented "the plight of the West." During the era of the peace progressives, the region had represented "the stronghold of liberalism." After Eisenhower's election, however, the West, except for Joseph O'Mahoney's Wyoming, sent only extreme conservatives to the Senate. Realizing for the first time that even if Alaska did win statehood it might not be hospitable to a politician with his viewpoint, Gruening considered retiring from public life altogether and settling down in Juneau. He looked back nostalgically on his earlier career, recalling his "thrilling and interesting years" in Portland and the days when he was "gay, full of vim and vigor and enterprise," having deluded himself that he alone could "get rid of a Latin American dictator." He also remained conscious of his historical reputation. After the publication of Harold Ickes's *Secret Diary*, which savagely portrayed Gruening's performance at the PRRA, he recommended to all who would listen Richard Rovere's equally hostile *New Yorker* review of Ickes's tenure.[64] But, unlike that of Ickes, Gruening's career was not yet consigned to history. In fact, its high point was yet to come.

6

The Washington Agenda

DESPITE EISENHOWER'S TRIUMPH, Gruening detected at least one favorable development from the 1952 campaign season, since both parties endorsed statehood for Alaska. After the election, however, though Eisenhower continued to favor statehood for predominantly Republican Hawaii, he ceased mentioning Alaska: the *Washington Post* sensed the "murky cloud of politics" hovering over the issue. In a continuing jibe at Gruening's ill-disguised ambitions, the newly installed chair of the Senate Interior Committee, Hugh Butler, took his committee to Alaska for hearings to solicit "the reaction of the little people—not just a few aspiring politicians who want to be Senators and Representatives." (Privately, many Republican senators admitted that they opposed statehood in part because they did not want Gruening as a colleague.) Opposition to statehood, moreover, was not confined to the GOP; southern Democrats worried that senators from Alaska would contribute two more votes in support of cloture on civil rights legislation. Finally, Seattle-based economic interests, led by their chief lobbyist Winton Arnold, effectively made the case that the territory lacked the economic base to afford the costs associated with statehood.[1]

In early 1953, Eisenhower named Republican Frank Heitzelman as the new governor of Alaska. But retirement did not interest the sixty-five-year-old Gruening. Instead, out of government service for the first time in two decades, he revived his position as a policy activist, quickly falling back on familiar tactics. He stepped up his national lecture tour on behalf of statehood. He also returned to the printed word, securing a contract from Random House to write what he immodestly termed "the definitive story of Alaska," a work he promised would "stand up for a couple of generations"—or at least long enough to serve its purpose of rallying public support for statehood. His initial title—"Alaska: Four Score and Seven Years"—was intended to remind readers of Alaska's failure to achieve "the equality that Lincoln said our nation had been dedicated to." (His editor, Saxe Cummins, overruled the proposal, remarking that "too many people would wonder at first glance exactly what the application to Lincoln's Gettysburg Address there could be in a book on Alaska.") By this point the publishing house surely was entertaining second thoughts about the whole arrangement. Not only did Gruening and Cummins continue to quibble over the title, but also Gruening's two decades away from writing books had not dulled his propensity for excessive length. The two men eventually compromised on the issue (although the final version ran nearly six hundred pages), only to have the former governor complain about the price of the book, which, at $7.50, he feared would be too expensive for the average reader and thus of limited propaganda use. In any event, *The State of Alaska* finally appeared in 1954. The first part of the book traced the history of Alaska through the end of Gruening's term as governor. Its second and, from the author's standpoint, more important section concentrated on Alaska's "pending problems," and unsurprisingly concluded that only statehood could resolve what he viewed as the key issues confronting the territory: land, Indian policy, conservation, and transportation and regulatory matters. In testimony to public interest in the subject, strong sales prompted Random House to order a second printing.[2]

Gruening so enjoyed writing *The State of Alaska* that he even toyed with the idea of devoting himself to the printed word full-time. He envisioned the book as the first in a multivolume study of U.S. colonial policy, one which would utilize his experience from his "studies in Mexico and the Caribbean, 1920–1931" and his directorships of the DTIP and PRRA as well. Framing his proposal as broadly as possible, he observed that "at a time when the international relations of the United States are undergoing crucial strains, and colonialism is everywhere being re-examined and in transformation, the study will further explore the situation in regard to the territories and possessions of the United States." Perhaps, after all, he could find a way to integrate the Cold War within his traditional dissenting framework.[3]

But in the end, a retreat from the political arena did not appeal. Moreover, Gruening had a personal reason for remaining politically active: another family crisis, this one involving his youngest son, Peter. Seven years younger than Hunt, Peter matured during Gruening's tenure at the PRRA, when Gruening spent virtually no time with his family, and he grew up closer to Dorothy than to Ernest. Father pressed son to attend Harvard, but Peter declined. Instead, in the fall of 1941, he enrolled at the University of California at Berkeley. He left the school after a year to enlist in the Army Air Corps, although he did not serve overseas during World War II. After the war, again contrary to his father's wishes, Peter embarked on a career in journalism; Gruening responded by denying his son letters of introduction, commenting that otherwise Peter would never know whether he had made it on his own.[4]

Peter went on to enjoy remarkable success in his chosen profession. He received a position with the San Francisco office of the United Press, writing Dorothy of his pride in having been "offered the job by someone other than a friend of Dad's." After several promotions and an assignment covering the war in Korea, he was transferred to Singapore, where he served as UP manager for Southeast Asia, overseeing the bureaus in Malaya, Burma, Indochina, Indonesia, and the Philippines. Despite the personal distance from his father, Ernest's intellectual influence nonetheless shaped Peter's perspective on the region. He wrote several dispatches critical of the French war effort against the Vietminh, and he privately praised the efforts of newly independent Indonesia "to toddle between the armed camps of the cold war." He noted that owing to their own colonial experience, Indonesian leaders found "it difficult to believe that 'the Free World' of today is what it claims to be." From what he could witness in Southeast Asia, "colonialism as practiced by the Dutch, English, French, and yes, Americans, still strikes a far more strident note than communism." The younger Gruening believed that embarking on an anti-colonial crusade represented the "most important" contribution that the United States could make "to international understanding of this decade."[5]

If this ideological perspective mirrored that of his father, Peter's social style more revealed the beliefs of his mother. Living an upper-class lifestyle entailed a heavy financial burden; in 1949, when he was living in Honolulu, rent alone for his apartment two minutes from Waikiki Beach (which included daily maid service) consumed half his monthly salary of $150. When Peter admitted that he was "not in good shape" financially and "sure would appreciate some assistance," his father, perhaps feeling a sense of guilt as a result of his frequent absences during Peter's childhood, responded by providing cash subsidies, setting a pattern for the future. Dorothy also had impressed on her son the need to marry the proper type of woman, and Peter attempted to follow through. Something of a playboy during his first years out of college, Peter looked for a partner suitable to Dorothy's tastes when he contemplated marriage. His first wife came from an upper-class family in Hawaii; illustrative of his relationship with his parents, Peter did not inform them of his betrothal until after the wedding ceremony. The marriage ended after less than a year, when he was transferred from Hawaii and his wife declined to leave the islands.[6]

Once Peter moved to Southeast Asia, however, his personal life seemed to stabilize. Supreme Court Justice William O. Douglas, an old friend of the family, introduced him to Nancy Monktan, the daughter of an acquaintance. A native of England whose family had been active in British commercial ventures in the area, she seemed Dorothy's model of an ideal bride. With life seeming "rather heavenly" after meeting Nancy, Peter wanted to marry immediately. She was considerably less smitten, and at one point confided that although Peter was "a wonderful person," she did not love him. Eventually, though, she gave in to his pleas and consented to marriage. The union dissolved within a matter of weeks. After his second divorce, an acquaintance recalled that Peter "suffered from moods of depression, and when in that mood talked of suicide," claiming that "he was a failure and couldn't make anyone happy." On October 24, 1955, outside Sydney, Australia, his latest assignment, he took his own life.[7]

Robert Atwood, who saw news of the suicide come over the wire when he went into his office at the *Daily Times*, immediately sought out Gruening to inform him personally. The former governor had flown into Anchorage the night before, and had not arrived at his hotel until after midnight. Typically, though, by the time Atwood tracked him down, just after 5 A.M., Gruening was already dressed and in the bathroom shaving. Shocked as he was by the news, his first thought was of

Dorothy. He told Atwood that he had to reach her immediately lest she hear of Peter's death over the radio.[8]

Husband and wife responded differently to Peter's death. Dorothy refused to believe that Peter had committed suicide. At first she convinced herself that he had been murdered after stumbling onto evidence of Soviet espionage in Australia. After both Hunt and Douglas, whom she asked to investigate her theories, assured her that no evidence of foul play existed, she chose to deny that Peter was dead, basing her conviction on the fact that Hunt, who flew to Australia to attend to Peter's estate, had not identified the body (the local UP manager had done so already). For the rest of her life, she claimed to catch fleeting glimpses of her son in crowds, in magazines, or on television. The death began a process, accelerated by health problems caused by a severe arthritic condition, in which Dorothy gradually lapsed into a world of her own.[9]

Gruening, however, responded to the loss of a second son the same way he had in 1931 after Sonny's death: by throwing himself into his cause of the moment. He later admitted that the statehood campaign "was a blessing to me personally; it helped to take my mind off Peter's tragedy." Statehood thus became a personal as well as a political and ideological crusade. Convinced of the need to demonstrate how it would serve the national interest, and with his two major international arguments unpersuasive, Gruening increasingly embraced a framework derived from his arsenal of interwar dissent. In 1955 he adopted what he privately described as a "new approach," recommending that Alaskans start sending delegations to Washington to "shout about 'colonialism' at the top of their lungs." He utilized an example from the 1920s to justify increased pressure on Congress, noting that "the Irish never would have gotten their independence if they hadn't gotten really rough." If necessary, he maintained, Alaskans should bring the issue before the United Nations or consider a referendum on outright independence.[10]

Gruening publicized these suggestions in the keynote address to the Alaskan Constitutional Convention, held in Fairbanks less than three weeks after Peter's death. Privately he termed his remarks the "first time that the tag of colonialism as far as Alaska is concerned has been squarely pinned on Uncle Sam, where it belongs." In one of the most passionate speeches of his career, he noted a "peculiar timeliness" in

Alaska's bid for statehood, since "now that the United States has assumed world leadership, it has shown through the expressions of its leaders its distaste for colonialism." This "antipathy," he said, reflected "a deep-seated sentiment among Americans," making it all the more "paradoxical" that the United States would continue to hold a colony. Alaska's lack of political equality was "only a small part of the evidence of our colonialism," since the territory, Gruening contended, also suffered from the economic effects of colonialism. The "best hope" for Alaskans lay in "making the facts known widely—and especially the overshadowing fact of our colonialism—to our fellow Americans and to the rest of the candid world." Gruening thus again pinned his hopes on an informed public opinion. "Ideas are weapons," he told the delegates, and, as throughout his career, he had every intention of using them as such.[11]

In a way, Gruening's complaints about the effects of colonialism were ridiculous, given the benefits which the territory had received from the federal government during his gubernatorial tenure. More important, though, was the intellectual effect of the Fairbanks address. For the first time since his arrival in Alaska, he incorporated his traditional dissenting perspective into the contemporary international environment. With no obvious political or logical obstacles to making the claim, he expanded on his anti-imperialist charges in the years before Congress finally conferred statehood.

In this sense, then, the statehood campaign represented a turning point in Gruening's life. Rather than retire after being replaced as governor, he returned to his roots as a policy activist. The battle for statehood also helped him work through the trauma of Peter's suicide and retain his political strength after losing the perks of governorship. Gruening typically sacrificed his personal and family life in the name of advancing his ideological and political crusades. In this case his political activism provided a desperately needed center around which he could orient his existence and survive a time of personal and professional crisis. In addition, the statehood campaign prompted him to revive his anti-imperialist mindset, while at the same time he noticeably diminished the reflexive anticommunism associated with his years of gubernatorial service. Gruening had originally embraced such arguments primarily for their public relations appeal. Now that conditions had changed, he distanced himself from the bipartisan tendency among U.S. policy makers in the 1950s to interpret international events through the framework of the Cold War. He still argued that reconciling U.S. foreign policy with the country's traditional ideals represented the best way to prevail against the Soviet Union. But, of course, he had always championed a foreign policy based on fidelity to the principles of self-determination and on recognizing the link between domestic and international reform. Gruening's movement away from Cold War thinking would lay the groundwork for his wide-ranging foreign policy dissent of the 1960s.

MEANWHILE, although the statehood question remained unsettled nationally, Gruening's activity on the issue brought him into electoral politics for the first time. In 1956 Alaskan voters went to the polls to select "senators" to represent their case in Washington, a tactic originated by Tennessee in the 1790s. Given his long-standing ambition to serve in the Senate, Gruening did not hesitate to run. He drew as his opponent the legislature's senior Republican, John Butrovich, who in turn attracted substantial donations from business interests looking to strike back at Gruening for his gubernatorial policies. Unable to match this level of financial support, Gruening too sought outside funding. Felix Frankfurter, though "completely out of politics—even Alaskan politics," wished "an old and valued friend good luck." The combination of Gruening's poor financial base, his advanced age (sixty-nine), and the legacy of his controversial tenure as governor ensured a difficult race. The former governor nonetheless enjoyed the campaign, "having been rendered pachydermatous by nearly fourteen years in the governorship." He dealt with the issue of his electoral inexperience by focusing on his strengths, particularly public speaking. In this sense his basic approach to campaigning remained unchanged since his crusade against the Smith-Carlton bill nearly three decades before.[12]

In reality, though, Gruening's chief asset was neither his ideological agenda nor his oratorical abilities but the widespread perception that he would be the most effective lobbyist for statehood, the prime responsibility of the Tennessee-plan senators. This belief allowed him to squeak through—by fewer than 800 votes out of over 27,000 cast—aided by the fact that Butrovich chose simultaneously to run for reelection to his seat in the Alaskan Senate. After a life devoted to democratic government, Ernest Gruening was finally a representative of the people.[13]

Dubbed the "phantom senator" by the national press, Gruening was hardly invisible on the Washington social circuit; in fact, "vigorous and continually active," he was perfectly suited to the task at hand. Drew Pearson privately termed the Alaskan's efforts "one of the real reasons for statehood"; the former governor, renowned for his stubbornness, was "such an effective lobbyist and in some cases such a bore in buttonholing people for statehood that he finally won out." Based on that achievement alone, Pearson reasoned, Gruening deserved a seat in the Senate once Alaska finally entered the Union. Representative Stewart Udall (D–Arizona) likewise described Gruening as the "most effective" pro-statehood lobbyist, noting that his tactic of supplying members of Congress with copies of *The State of Alaska* particularly impressed them. Random House showed less enthusiasm for the strategy, but Gruening contended that he "might as well dispose" of excess copies. In any case, after a promotion agent called him Ernest "Grooning," the former governor felt little sympathy for a company whose representatives could not even pronounce his name. Gruening's efforts clearly strengthened his political position in Alaska; one contemporary noted that his detailed knowledge of the issues associated with the struggle contributed to an aura of "general respect" for him.[14]

Whereas during his time as governor Gruening had avoided commenting on international events that did not relate to Alaska, once back in Washington, he showed a broader interest in foreign policy. For example, he unsuccessfully urged Hamilton Fish Armstrong, editor of *Foreign Affairs,* to solicit an article on inter-American relations by Representative Charles Porter (D–Oregon), the most extreme congressional critic of Eisenhower's Latin American policy. The former governor termed Porter's anti-dictatorial, anti-militarist ideas "wholly sound and constructive." Articulating themes to which he often would return, Gruening reasoned that supplying military aid to right-wing Latin American regimes only helped "maintain their dictatorships, thus . . . supporting tyranny where it occurs." He recommended reserving foreign assistance "for those whose attitudes more closely approximate democratic ideals." By this time the administration's Latin American policy had drawn similar criticism from a number of Democratic senators. The issue thus allowed Gruening to manifest the revival of his personal dissenting perspective and to integrate himself into a wider opposition bloc.[15]

As the *New York Times* commented in 1958, "Where Ernest Gruening is, there is controversy. He has thrived on it most of his seventy-one years." True to form, the new senator had a falling out with his Tennessee-plan colleague, William Egan, the former mayor of Valdez. Egan, who earned his living as a fisherman, had never graduated from high school, and was recalled by one contemporary as a "salt of the earth type of guy"—all characteristics which Gruening did not share. Egan, of course, was not the only prominent Alaskan figure with whom the former governor feuded. In a fitting tribute to his gubernatorial tenure, the *Times* noted that "political party lines are meaningless when the subject of this New Deal Democrat with a sleepy look, sly smile, ready wit, and pungent speech comes up." Events had moved in Gruening's favor shortly after his arrival in Washington, when House Speaker Sam Rayburn (D–Texas) dropped his opposition to statehood; shortly thereafter, the House Interior Committee favorably reported a statehood bill to the floor. The full House approved the measure in early 1958, and a southern-led filibuster failed to prevent the Senate, on June 30, from passing the bill by a margin of 64 to 20. Gruening moved quickly to take primary credit for the bill's enactment. He scored his most spectacular victory when *Time* hailed him on its cover as the "father of Alaska statehood," a move which infuriated Bob Bartlett's supporters, who believed that the territorial delegate deserved the title. Hugh Gallagher, a member of Bartlett's staff, recalled that Gruening's behavior bordered on the "occasionally petty," as when the senator jockeyed for position at the statehood bill signing ceremony to ensure a prominent place in the photographs.[16]

Since the statehood act did not recognize the results of the Tennessee-plan elections, Gruening had to face the voters again in 1958, this time in a more difficult contest. Although Bartlett had made it clear that he had no desire to run for governor, both Egan and Gruening announced their intention to seek Senate seats. After Bartlett declared for the Senate as well, attention shifted back to the two Tennessee-plan senators. Gruening especially began to worry that his conservative opponents within the party might encourage Egan to challenge him in the primary. The feuding between the two men during their joint service in

Washington had not improved their relationship, nor did Gruening's refusal to consider how his age and numerous political enemies made him a weaker candidate for the Democrats than Egan. But Egan chose to bypass what would have been a risky primary bid, and announced that he would run for governor instead. Although the two reconciled, their relationship remained cool.[17]

Given the territorial delegate's widespread popularity, Bartlett's candidacy ensured that one of the state's two Senate seats would go Democratic, only compounding concerns of national Republicans about Alaska's Democratic tendencies. Interior Secretary Frederick Seaton therefore took it upon himself to ensure that a Republican would capture the other seat. He had already appointed Mike Stepovich as the last territorial governor with the understanding that Stepovich would use the position to launch a senatorial campaign. A World War II veteran who received his law degree from Notre Dame before becoming the first native-born governor, Stepovich stressed in his campaign his youth, his Alaskan birth, and his attractive family of nine. Gruening, armed with the motto "There is no substitute for experience," countered by concentrating on his achievements in both Alaskan and national affairs, his intimate knowledge of the Washington scene, and his pivotal role in achieving statehood. In terms of qualifications and intellectual ability, the race was a mismatch. One contemporary recalled Stepovich as a "total moron," a "non-entity" who owed his political career to Seaton's efforts. The Republican's partisans conceded as much; defending Stepovich's refusal to debate Gruening, the *Anchorage Daily News* wondered why the nominee should "debate with a man who is perhaps the best qualified public speaker in Alaska." Surely, the *News* noted, "the Golden Gloves champion" would not "accept a match with the world heavyweight" king.[18]

Gruening, however, had his share of weaknesses as well. He lacked a unified Democratic base, while Seaton's strong support for Stepovich ensured the Republican ready access to national fund-raising circles. Gruening's campaign style also left something to be desired, though the former governor considered himself effective on the hustings. Years after the event, he remained fond of recalling one incident when, soliciting votes in downtown Anchorage, he had approached a passerby, held out his hand, and said, "My name is Gruening. I'm a candidate for the United States Senate and I'd appreciate your vote." Pulling his hand away, the man retorted that he would "rather vote for the devil." Holding in check his tendency to respond to an insult with one of his own, the candidate tried humor instead: "He'd be a tough guy to beat. But if he decides not to run, do you suppose you could switch to me?" "Why, you son of a bitch," the voter chortled, "I might vote for you yet." Gruening maintained that the exchange showed his effectiveness at the personalistic campaigning which characterized Alaskan politics at the dawn of the statehood era.[19]

In reality, though, as his admirer and friend Robert Atwood conceded, the former governor lacked "the charisma that made for warm friendships." Despite his impressive ability to deliver extemporaneous speeches and a stamina on the campaign trail at which even opponents marveled, Gruening, in the words of Stanley McCutcheon's brother Steve, "didn't fly quite in the same atmosphere as the rest of us." *For* but never really *of* the people, he did not engage in small talk easily; he knew nothing, for example, of sports or popular culture. Nor was Gruening temperamentally inclined to employ a folksy campaign style. Rather, as he confided to a friend, he wanted to go to Washington to bolster "the forces of liberalism, which has so few unqualified champions to-day." Accomplishing this task required a mandate from Alaskan voters, and he therefore planned to spend the campaign addressing "national issues." From there he would "see how it goes." This strategy only compounded his apparent detachment from the day-to-day concerns of the people he wished to represent. Partly owing to these factors, Stepovich captured the open primary, in which voters could request either a Republican or a Democratic ballot, by twelve percentage points. Since neither man faced primary opposition, the outcome was considered a dry run for November.[20]

After the vote, even Gruening conceded that he faced an "uphill fight." Recognizing the shortcomings in his primary strategy, he reshuffled his campaign, appointing George Sundborg as his campaign manager. He also tied himself to the immensely popular Bartlett, to the extent of sending out his correspondence from the "Bartlett-Gruening Senatorial Headquarters," and attacked Stepovich's previously ambivalent attitude toward statehood. Finally, he unabashedly appealed to his old friends for financial assistance, over the strong objections of Dorothy, who worried that donors would expect favors if he won the election. Tom Corcoran, by this stage a well-connected Washington lobbyist, lined up contributions from his clients, telling Gruening that he remembered "what's important to me—that you told the truth for me agin [sic] your old friend Ralph Brewster." Oscar Chapman set up a bank account in Washington for Gruening's friends to deposit donations, while Herbert Lehman, who contributed $1,000 himself, asked his former administrative assistant Julius Edelstein to talk "to a few of our co-religionists in New York" and raise money "from some of the well-heeled ones." Such assistance eventually brought in $75,000, enough to mount an effective campaign, although it set a pattern for the future in which the vast majority of Gruening's contributions came from outside the state.[21]

Gruening's aggressiveness closed the gap, and Republicans responded by going negative, juxtaposing photographs of Gruening's Alaska log cabin with his Washington home to imply that he had more in common with his Washington neighbors than with Alaskans. Both sides recognized the stakes: Seaton and Vice President Richard Nixon came in to campaign for Stepovich, while Gruening attracted visits from the youthful senators Frank Church (D–Idaho) and John Kennedy (D–Massachusetts) to neutralize the GOP's quiet campaign of attacking him as too old to become a freshman senator. As events developed, the general Democratic trend in the 1958 midterm elections undermined Stepovich's rationale that Alaska needed at least one Republican in its congressional delegation. The statehood act had scheduled Alaska's elections for three weeks after those in the rest of the nation, and so by the time voters went to the polls, they were aware that the Democrats had expanded their Senate majority from two seats to twenty-eight. Gruening also received assistance from the rest of the state ticket when Alaskans finally did vote: Democrats captured the other Senate seat, the governorship, and almost 90 percent of the state legislature. Although he ran well behind the rest of the ticket, his 53 percent of the vote was enough. Old friends rejoiced at the result: William O. Douglas promised to host a luncheon at the Supreme Court "for a few of your old cronies and your own good self."[22]

GRUENING ARRIVED in an upper chamber experiencing a period of profound transition. In the early and mid-1950s, traditional power barons such as Robert Kerr (D–Oklahoma) and Richard Russell (D–Georgia) dominated the Senate, where success came from conforming to the established culture—deferring to senior senators, specializing in the issues associated with a member's committee assignments, and focusing on behind-the-scenes legislative work. Majority Leader Lyndon Johnson (D–Texas), meanwhile, used his position to orchestrate events to such an extent that one staffer described the proceedings as a "Greek tragedy," in that "nothing went on in the Senate that hadn't happened off the floor beforehand." The majority leader achieved legislative victories through lobbying skills so remarkable that *New York Times* columnist Russell Baker remembered them as "one of the rare delights of the Senate," a "form of hypnosis by movement, which seemed to leave the victim pliantly comatose." Johnson was scornful of the likes of Paul Douglas, Wayne Morse, and Herbert Lehman, figures he dismissed as "crazies" and "bomb-thrower types" mostly interested in maintaining the purity of their ideological crusades. But the institution gradually changed as the 1950s progressed. The increasing public attention to the Senate caused by such disparate developments as the Army-McCarthy hearings, southern filibusters against civil rights legislation, an increasingly formal relationship between the press and senators, and technological changes such as the proliferation of air travel, which made Washington more accessible to average voters, produced a more individualistic, staff-saturated, and publicity-hungry upper chamber. On top of these changes, the 1958 elections transformed the Senate into "a liberal institution," one in which northern Democrats outnumbered their southern counterparts by twenty, the largest disparity since the high point of the New Deal. A man like Gruening would have struggled in the Senate of the early 1950s, with its emphasis on cloakroom politics and deference to seniority. But an institution which encouraged its members to expand their activism and publicize issues through direct appeals to national audiences suited him perfectly.[23]

Gruening's election to the Senate helped to satisfy his lifelong goal of reconciling his dissenting inclinations with the desire for political effectiveness. As an administrator, he had had to compromise on matters of principle too often to suit his own tastes. As a legislator, he could influence important political developments without the associated responsibility of implementing policy. In addition, the nature of the Senate highlighted two activities at which Gruening had long excelled—bureaucratic battling and speechmaking—especially since the combination of tradition and a decentralized structure had long made the body a hospitable environment for dissenters. Gruening, of course, understood this historical legacy: peace progressives such as William Borah and George Norris, his mentors from the 1920s, had contributed to it. Moreover, his long career had given Gruening a profound respect for the Senate as an institution. This respect provided the basis for a warm friendship he formed with a fellow freshman, Robert Byrd (D–West Virginia), who, despite a differing ideological viewpoint, shared his Alaska colleague's reverence for the traditions of the upper chamber. As one contemporary recalled, Gruening "took to the Senate almost immediately." After a lifetime in politics, he finally had found an appropriate forum for his interests and abilities.[24]

Gruening's committee preferences reflected a desire to address both pragmatic and more long-standing personal and ideological interests. The new senator won positions on the Public Works and Interior committees, which he judged most "related" to Alaskan affairs and hence to his political well-being. Nonetheless, as part of his renewed interest in international affairs, he also attempted to secure a spot on the Foreign Relations Committee. In support of his request, he reminded Lyndon Johnson of his "long experience in this field in relation to Latin America," noting that he would "be helpful in this area where our relations have so sadly deteriorated under the Eisenhower Administration." He hastened to add that the appointment would help him politically, since "Alaska has a very definite interest in foreign relations," ranging from its "happy and mutually useful relationship" with Canada to its desire to further commercial ties with Japan. This final point was no more than attempted political cover. In reality, Gruening wanted again to play a role in international affairs after an absence of nearly two decades from the dissenting scene. Johnson rebuffed the request, despite his policy of naming junior senators to prestigious committee slots. He reserved such appointments for members such as Frank Church, whom he thought exhibited political promise. Gruening did not fit the bill.[25]

Disappointed, the Alaskan addressed himself to the task of assembling a staff, in the process selecting figures from the three most recent eras of his political career. In a telling commentary on his ideological perspective, he began his search by looking to the office of Herbert Lehman, who had retired from the Senate in 1956 after a career that mirrored Gruening's in its diversity: governor of New York, senator, and first U.S. representative to the United Nations Relief and Recovery Administration. Hoping to imitate Lehman's role as the voice of reform on issues which most senators ignored, Gruening selected several key staffers from the Lehman team, the most important of which was Herb Beaser, who brought a long tenure of service in Washington and extensive contacts among the federal bureaucracy to his position as Gruening's legislative assistant. A graduate of Harvard Law School, Beaser went to Washington early in the New Deal, where his work as chief counsel at the Children's Bureau brought him into contact with Eleanor Roosevelt. After her appointment as the U.S. representative to the UN Commission on Human Rights, Roosevelt named Beaser a special assistant, first stimulating the intense interest in foreign policy which he would bring to Gruening's staff. Beaser, who lived nearby in Silver Spring, Maryland, picked up the senator each weekday morning at eight to drive him to the office. The two discussed political matters on the way. An introvert who struggled to get along with the rest of the staff, Beaser was fiercely loyal to his boss, and the two developed an intimate professional relationship; ideologically, as one staffer recalled, they were like "twins." Gruening himself came to regard Beaser as a man he could "trust implicitly both as to loyalty, judgment, and knowledge of Washington."[26]

Gruening hired Beaser without the knowledge of George Sundborg, to whom the senator had promised the position of administrative assistant during the campaign. Sundborg oversaw the activities of most of the twelve-person staff, which, cramped in a basement corridor of the Old Senate Office Building, focused on handling casework and answering constituent correspondence. He also put his newspaper experience to good use by overseeing the production of Gruening's weekly newsletter, "From the Nation's Capital," to which the senator attached a good deal of importance. Throughout Gruening's tenure, Sundborg, the only staff member who called Gruening by his first name, remained the senator's closest personal confidant. As during the gubernatorial period, Sundborg also functioned as Gruening's principal political adviser.[27]

Gruening rounded out his staff by tapping into his contacts from the New Deal, appointing Antoinette (Toni) Freedman as his staff counsel. Freedman's political experience dated from the Truman era, when she served on the White House staff. Gruening himself first met Freedman through her husband, Martin Freedman, a partner of the senator's old acquaintance Oscar Chapman in a Washington legal firm. Freedman soon developed a reputation for competence on legislative concerns and quickly expanded her role. Although her title remained staff counsel, she functioned as something akin to a legislative assistant, particularly on matters outside foreign policy in which Beaser showed little interest.[28]

Small by contemporary standards, the staff was notable in at least one way for what it did not do: although he welcomed input from Beaser, Sundborg, Freedman, and Beaser's assistant Laura Olson, Gruening retained control over his Senate speeches. As always, he struggled to delegate authority, even to trusted advisers. The senator often did request drafts of speeches or statements for his frequent testimony to congressional committees. Staffers quickly learned, however, that they had to submit "clean" copy; corrections would activate Gruening's instincts as an editor, and soon the senator would be rewriting the speech in its entirety. Even the "clean" speeches, however, were subject to modification, since Gruening delivered his Senate speeches extemporaneously. Those who attempted to restore the prepared text in the published version of the *Congressional Record* would "catch hell" from their boss.[29]

Gruening clearly reveled in the life of the Senate. Drew Pearson, with whom he dined the night after his swearing in, found him "bubbling over with pride and joy—understandably so." The return from the wilderness suited him well; he had achieved, he said, the "one way" of getting "rid of the stigma" of being a governor—"election to the United States Senate." Gruening settled into his Washington home on West Beach Drive, at the tip of Rock Creek Park. The spacious residence fell within the "Neighbors, Inc." region, so named for the area group which encouraged integration in upper- and upper-middle-class Washington neighborhoods by persuading white residents not to flee to the suburbs. Gruening also made it clear that he had made his final move. He adorned the house with what one neighbor recalled as an "incredible" number of Mexican artifacts gathered during his time in that country in the 1920s; its walls were covered with paintings, usually of the Alaska landscape, or with shelves for his large collection of books. The house thus reflected its owner's style of merging his political and personal life.[30]

As Gruening adjusted again to life in Washington, he and Dorothy began to entertain actively. At least once a week, seeking to replicate the gatherings of New Dealers in the 1930s, Gruening hosted a small dinner party, with between six and twelve guests, at which black tie was often the required attire. Dorothy would spend the day overseeing the meal's preparation, hiring two additional servants for the evening. Gruening would greet his guests personally, serve a few martinis, and wait for his wife, who always made a late entrance (one friend distinguished between "standard time, daylight time, and Gruening time"). The posh four-course meals began as always with Dorothy's crab bisque. Salad followed the main course, European-style; after dessert, Gruening regularly lit a cigar and served some crème de menthe, as the conversation continued. As in Mexico, Maine, and Alaska, the host dominated the discussion, which political commentator Jack Germond, a Gruening neighbor and frequent dinner guest, recalled as "truly awe-inspiring." The quality of the guests and the scope of the Alaskan's knowledge "absolutely flabbergasted" Germond. Whenever talk veered from contemporary political events, Gruening would steer it back, even if it meant cutting off a member of the family. (On one occasion, when his son Hunt and daughter-in-law Oline joined a dinner party just after having completed a trip around the world, questions about their vacation waited until the guests' departure.) Though always present, Dorothy, increasingly infirm, rarely participated in the conversations; unlike in Alaska, she now realized that she was not in her husband's intellectual league.[31]

The dinner parties provided a panoramic view of Gruening's multifaceted life. As was the case throughout his career, his friends were those who shared his ideological point of view. Prominent Alaskans visiting Washington sometimes received invitations, as did Senate colleagues with whom he was ideologically compatible—Paul Douglas on domestic issues; George McGovern, Gaylord Nelson, and Frank Church on international matters. (Wayne Morse, a teetotaler, rarely attended.) Most enjoyable for the senator, however, was the opportunity to reestablish ties with old friends from the interwar era, such as Tommy Corcoran, Drew Pearson, William O. Douglas, Ben Cohen, and Maury Maverick, the former Texas congressman. Gruening admired each for remaining faithful to what he considered the true New Deal vision in domestic affairs—the partnership between government spending to stimulate economic development and the more traditional anti-monopoly heritage of American reform. David Lilienthal, also a frequent dinner guest, rejoiced at the return of Gruening, "one of the Tennessee Valley people," to Washington.[32]

The dinner parties exemplified a process in which the senator, as his son later recalled, "became so engrossed in politics that it came to dominate him." Gruening gave up tennis and bridge during his last decades, leaving hiking and swimming as his only leisure activities. In reality, the gatherings themselves provided his most pleasurable moments. He clearly enjoyed the dialogues the evenings produced, and took a "mischievous delight" in needling close friends, such as Douglas, to stimulate even more interesting exchanges. Several guests recalled with amazement the intellectual breadth and depth which he exhibited in the "high-brow" and "hot" debates over the pressing political issues of the day.[33]

TRANSLATING THE BELIEFS expressed at these evenings into concrete policy initiatives was another matter. Despite his initial hopes, the only mandate which Gruening received from his tight victory in 1958 was to concentrate on Alaskan issues. He promised Sundborg that he would avoid the "temptation" to involve himself with broader fare, believing that Alaskan development required his fullest efforts and that such an approach represented the most politically astute path for him to take. The senator even indicated his willingness to trim his domestic ideology in order to attend to the state's concerns. One day in early 1959, he encountered Robert Kerr in the Senate cloakroom. The Oklahoma senator ticked off the Alaska projects in which Gruening had expressed an interest, and made it clear that Gruening's voting his way on a measure to weaken the cloture rule by allowing a simple majority rather than a two-thirds vote to invoke cloture (thus making it easier to cut off southern filibusters on civil rights votes) was the price of his support. The longtime member of the NAACP sided with Kerr.[34]

His willingness to make this type of compromise, coupled with his continued championing of increased federal assistance for Alaska, led some of his colleagues to dismiss Gruening as parochial, a perception fueled by his habit of introducing himself to each new senator and representative, handing them a copy of *The State of Alaska*, and then requesting an appointment to discuss his state's "peculiar needs." In fact, a desire to avoid being written off as someone who lacked interests broader than local patronage, combined with a resurgence of his dissenting viewpoint, led the senator to violate his promise to Sundborg almost immediately. Although he did focus on Alaskan issues during his first few years back in Washington, he also resumed his natural position as a dissenter with a wide range of concerns.[35]

International affairs unsurprisingly provided the first glimpse of this pattern. Throughout most of Eisenhower's tenure in office, Senate Democrats offered what Hubert Humphrey (D–Minnesota) described as a "limited" dissent, criticizing the administration chiefly for not prosecuting the Cold War vigorously enough. Although Gruening hardly objected to increasing the Pentagon budget—so long as Alaska received more than its fair share of the appropriations—he had more trouble with his colleagues' disinclination to question both the rigid anticommunism of the early Cold War and the deference to executive authority which characterized the era. He illustrated the point in his first major foreign policy proposal in the Senate, an amendment requiring foreign aid agencies to submit detailed budgets for at least 90 percent of their funds. Testifying before the Foreign Relations Committee, Gruening reasoned that since foreign aid was "a radical departure from the historically established conduct of our foreign relations," the Senate had a special responsibility for oversight, given its traditionally prominent "role in the conduct of foreign affairs." Confident that his amendment would win approval easily, he dropped a note to Foreign Relations Committee chair J. William Fulbright (D–Arkansas) a few days later to outline his next step—striking at the "nonsensical" and "wholly wrong" classification policy (using national security concerns to label foreign aid information "classified"). Fulbright bluntly responded that he considered the amendment's premise "mistaken." Even conceding Gruening's constitutional argument, Fulbright termed the Alaskan's remedy "extreme." Administration officials agreed, noting privately that the amendment would deprive the president of the "flexibility" needed to operate the foreign aid program effectively.[36]

The exchange provided Gruening with his first indication that, unlike in Alaska, the foreign aid program enjoyed wide support among national Democrats. He nonetheless introduced his amendment on the Senate floor when the committee failed to report it. (His boldness alone marked him as a figure to watch; in the previous session only 25 percent of the freshmen had sponsored floor amendments.) The Alaskan made it clear that behind his constitutional objections to the structure of foreign aid lay fundamental policy questions. Programs focusing on cultural and intellectual exchange, such as the Fulbright Scholarships—which he considered an example of "sound internationalism" promoting understanding and goodwill—achieved the kind of results that Gruening wanted. By contrast, little more than a fear "that if we don't do this, the Russians will rush in" motivated military aid and economic assistance to many countries. Such policies reminded him of the discredited "Dollar Diplomacy" of the interwar era.[37]

These arguments did not prevent Gruening's amendment from failing by a voice vote. But his contention that the foreign aid program represented the best way for the Senate to preserve its foreign policy powers offered an intriguing intellectual and political insight. He understood that the general nature of Cold War foreign policy, by expanding the power associated with the commander in chief clause, had vastly enhanced the president's independence in foreign affairs, while the Senate's role in the approval of treaties and the confirmation of ambassadors had become "perfunctory and routine." To succeed in the altered postwar environment, congressional dissenters needed first to prove that Congress had a right to comment on the issue at hand, and then to persuade their colleagues of the merits of their case—an all but impossible task. Because Congress retained the power of the purse, however, foreign aid provided an exception to the new constitutional calculus. Gruening hoped to exploit this opening and use the program as a vehicle to influence the overall course of U.S. foreign policy.[38]

A few colleagues joined Gruening in challenging the rationale behind the foreign aid program. One was Frank Church, who urged targeting aid to "those regimes which have broad backing and are genuinely concerned" with improving conditions for their citizens. Although thirty-seven years younger than his Alaskan colleague, the Idaho senator possessed a remarkably similar international viewpoint that formed the basis for a cordial relationship. Born and raised in Idaho, Church had interrupted his undergraduate education at Stanford to enlist in the army during World War II. He served with distinction in China and Southeast Asia, where this self-described "champion . . . of the down-trodden" witnessed the passing of the era of European imperialism. In his view, "the same things that motivated George

Washington and the American rebels" inspired Asian nationalists. After the war, Church married the daughter of a former Idaho governor, worked his way into a position of influence within the state Democratic Party, and, in 1956, narrowly won election to the Senate. As part of Lyndon Johnson's campaign to reward junior Democrats with prominent committee positions, he received a slot on the Foreign Relations Committee, the same committee on which his political idol, William Borah, had distinguished himself. Like Gruening, Church reconciled himself to the anticommunism of the early Cold War period, but anti-imperial sentiments always remained prominent in his outlook.[39]

The other key player in the emerging Democratic critique of the foreign aid program was Wayne Morse (D–Oregon), a figure whose historical reputation would become intertwined with Gruening's. After growing up in Wisconsin as an admirer of Robert La Follette, Morse emigrated west first to teach at and then to become dean of the University of Oregon Law School. Befitting this training, a strict interpretation of the executive's constitutional powers, a fidelity to international law, and support for strengthening international organizations formed the central elements of his foreign policy ideology. Though first elected as a Republican, Morse grew increasingly estranged from the party, and, in 1952, angered by Eisenhower's selection of Richard Nixon as his running mate, he renounced his GOP affiliation. After spending the next two years as the Senate's only independent, he joined the Democrats in a deal brokered by Lyndon Johnson in which he received a long-coveted slot on the Foreign Relations Committee. A well-deserved reputation as an egomaniac, compounded by his frequent use of personal invective, did not prevent Morse from establishing himself as a formidable member of the upper chamber. Colleagues marveled at his keen intellectual skills, which served him well; journalist David Halberstam hailed the senator for his "compelling sense of international law and an almost faultless sense of where the weak spot in an issue resided." Much as with Gruening, the combination of a considerable ego and a well-developed belief system gave the Oregon senator the confidence to dissent, even on controversial international issues.[40]

In addition to his activism on foreign aid, Morse used his position as chair of the American Republics Affairs Subcommittee to lead the Democratic attacks on Eisenhower's Latin American policies. True to his background and his belief in the "tragic" deterioration of inter-

American relations during the 1950s, Gruening joined in the criticism. The Alaska senator focused on one of his earlier interests: U.S.-Mexican relations. He described Mexico as of "prime importance in our international relations," since, "as we improve our relations with Mexico, we improve them thereby with all the other Latin American countries." More broadly, as he had in the interwar era, he called for focusing U.S. foreign policy on the Western hemisphere. Gruening's opinions on Mexico thus had come full circle, with his hostility toward the Cárdenas regime dissolving into a position similar to that of the 1920s. In a sense, Mexican policy served as a barometer of the strength of Gruening's dissenting vision in international affairs.[41]

At the same time, Latin America provided the best example of the limits on the dissent even of Democrats who, like Gruening, denounced Eisenhower for allowing the "crypto-Communist" regime of Fidel Castro to come to power in Cuba. In fact, Cuban policy served as only the most prominent example of how anticommunist and partisan issues unified Senate Democrats in the 1950s. For Gruening, personal concerns further constrained his dissenting inclinations. Despite his predictions to the contrary, military spending in Alaska continued to fall even after the achievement of statehood, largely because the development of intercontinental ballistic missiles made Alaskan bases less important. Gruening bitterly complained, reviving arguments from his gubernatorial tenure. Although the senator admitted that "we Alaskans might possibly be charged with a certain amount of localism" on the matter, he claimed that "our interest is the national interest." Humphrey's characterization of Democratic opposition to Eisenhower's foreign policy as one of "limited" dissent thus applied to Gruening's performance later in the decade as well.[42]

The anticommunism which played such a prominent role in the 1950s Democratic perspective on foreign policy issues constituted only one element of the postwar era's national liberalism. On the domestic front, reform sentiment had changed since the Progressive era or even the 1930s, when the combination of public pressure, bureaucratic alignments, and economic distress made a comprehensive bid to restructure the economy possible. The prosperity of the postwar years and the increasing economic complexity challenged the arguments of Brandeis and his followers to such an extent as to make the traditional anti-monopoly agenda passé. True believers such as Gruening, however, had always been more concerned about the corrupting influence of big business on the American political process than about the economic costs associated with monopoly. Since he viewed the issue through this moral prism, the Alaskan retained the traditional anti-monopoly agenda essentially unchanged from its earlier form, even though the conditions from which it derived had long since passed from the scene.

Gruening still tried to make the case that the power of monopoly damaged the economic well-being of his constituents. He carried to the Senate his "perennial war" against the "monopolistic shipping practices" of the Alaska Steamship Company. To constituents who questioned the merits of his confrontational tactics, the senator responded bluntly, "I know that I am right." What Gruening most wanted, however, was to revive "the principle of having the regulatory agencies protect the public interest" as part of a broader reform agenda. In anticipation of the 1960 presidential campaign, Gruening approached Chester Bowles, chair of the Democratic platform committee, about the role an anti-monopoly agenda would play in the year's effort. He recommended making a major issue out of Eisenhower's allowing private companies to patent discoveries generated from federally funded research. A handful of his colleagues shared these concerns, if with a somewhat narrower accompanying agenda. Most prominent in this group were two-time presidential candidate Estes Kefauver and Illinois senator Paul Douglas, an acquaintance of Gruening's from the campaigns against the U.S. occupation of Haiti and the Insull utilities empire in the 1920s. As always, Gruening's friendships mirrored his ideological agenda; he enjoyed no closer relationship with a colleague than his friendship with Douglas.[43]

Like the anti-monopolist liberals of the New Deal era (and, of course, many postwar Democrats less wedded to the reform tenets of an earlier generation), Gruening retained a faith in the positive benefits of federal spending. But, as his experience coordinating Puerto Rican affairs best demonstrated, his effectiveness at framing issues ideologically far exceeded his skills at the kind of horse-trading needed to pass legislation. When he introduced a bill to authorize the payment to Alaska of a so-called equalization grant of $20 million annually from the national road program, his demands, quite appropriately, struck most others as extreme, and his argument that the measure constituted "a matter of simple equity and justice" rather than an attempt "to secure special and more favored treatment" for Alaska persuaded no one. Bob Bartlett's more politic requests for assistance provided the behind-the-scenes lobbying necessary for the appropriations to clear the Senate. On another front, Gruening urged increased federal aid for local education, noting that inadequate tax bases were preventing most Alaskan communities from funding their educational budgets sufficiently. Once again, however, he only alienated his colleagues. After he tweaked Senate Minority Leader Everett Dirksen (R–Illinois) for minor inconsistencies in his position on the issue, Dirksen responded that he was too busy trying to make policy to find "the leisure time to spend half the night and most of the day running down the *Congressional Record* and picking out the little divergences and variations the Senator has brought up." Gruening's reputation preceded him to the Senate: as had been the case since his years in Maine, he remained an avid reader of the *Record.* The previous day's tearsheets were delivered to his home, and the senator often would point out interesting sections to Beaser during their drive to the office.[44]

Gruening's boldest attempt to obtain federal assistance for the state came in a cause which also reflected a long-standing personal interest: public power. The senator championed the development of the Snettisham Dam for southeastern Alaska, the Rampart Dam in the interior of the state, and the Eklutna project for suburban Anchorage. The most controversial of these initiatives was the Rampart Dam, a $1.3 billion proposal which aimed to generate 5 million kilowatts of power, but at the cost of submerging the Yukon Flats, one of North America's largest wildfowl breeding grounds. This aspect of the project drew the ire of environmentalists, while Indian activists worried that construction of the dam would require the relocation of between one thousand and ten thousand Indians. Meanwhile, the Eisenhower administration, which frowned on new dams for the West, expressed concern with Rampart's projected costs. This powerful opposition frustrated Gruening's hope of winning quick approval for the project.[45]

The issue consumed more of Gruening's time than any other domestic matter during his first two years in the Senate. In 1960, unaware that the trip was actually designed as a junket for the six-member delegation to visit Paris, the Alaskan participated in a Public Works Committee study mission to Norway and Sweden. Gruening's enthusiasm for his task prompted one of the mission members, Stephen Young (D–Ohio), a fellow member of the class of 1958, to complain that the senators' arrival in Paris was being delayed because "Ernest Gruening has just smelled another fertilizer plant." The year before, Gruening had joined Edmund Muskie (D–Maine) and Frank Moss (D–Utah) in a monthlong inspection of hydroelectric power facilities in the USSR. After Moss discovered that the seventy-two-year-old Gruening had twisted his knee a few days before the delegation's scheduled departure and was on crutches, the Utah senator expressed his regrets that Gruening would be unable to make the trip. The Alaskan responded that he had no intention of passing up the opportunity to visit Siberia at last. Though hobbling throughout, he was the party's most active member; one member of the delegation, which included a number of public power activists, recalled him as "literally indefatigable."[46]

One member of the excursion speculated that Siberia fascinated Gruening because "he saw so many parallels with Alaska." After attacking Soviet development in the region for years, Gruening returned home with an altered perspective, convinced of the importance of detaching economic development issues from power politics. Reflecting beliefs he had first outlined during the U.S.-Mexican crisis of the mid-1920s, he expressed his "firm conviction" that greater personal and cultural interchange between the United States and the Soviet Union would create "a new atmosphere of friendliness and understanding." To facilitate this development, he asked the State Department to press the Soviets to allow regular commercial flights (via Alaska Airlines) between Anchorage and the Siberian cities of Vladivostok, Magadan, and Khabarovsk. Gruening's changing approach to Siberian issues offered yet another example of how his jettisoning of Cold War principles prompted him to abandon positions he had assumed while governor.[47]

SUCH HISTORICAL REVISIONISM was hardly shared by most Democrats nationally, as the 1960 campaign demonstrated. In contrast to 1952 and 1956, when he had aggressively championed the presidential bid of Estes Kefauver, Gruening took a rather low profile in the contest for the Democratic nomination. Most prominent Alaska politicians, including Egan, Bartlett, and the state's lone congressman, Ralph Rivers, endorsed Lyndon Johnson. Gruening declined to do so, though he remained grateful for the majority leader's assistance in securing statehood and his "helpfulness" during Gruening's first two years in the Senate. But like other well-educated northern liberals, Gruening had come to regard Johnson as a crude and unprincipled political operator, from whom he increasingly distanced himself personally as well as politically. Johnson's characteristic flattery only heightened the Alaskan's scorn. One day the Texan took Sundborg aside to comment on his great expectations for Gruening, whom he called a "brilliant and perceptive statesman." For the senator, such transparent flattery confirmed his view of his colleague as a "fraud." Privately the majority leader reciprocated the scorn, complaining of Senate "intellectuals, who can never imagine me, a graduate from poor little San Marcos, engaged in an actual debate." At the same time, Gruening opposed the choice of many liberals, Adlai Stevenson, for more personal reasons: he refused to forgive Stevenson for abandoning his commitment to Alaskan statehood in 1956 under pressure from southern Democrats. With Stevenson and Johnson unacceptable, he endorsed John Kennedy, convinced that the youthful, telegenic Massachusetts Democrat would make the party's strongest candidate against Vice President Richard Nixon. Gruening praised Kennedy's promise to reverse Eisenhower's policy of "no new starts" on federal dams in the West; on a less parochial note, the Alaskan championed the Democratic ticket as the best hope for ending an awkward and unnatural period of divided government. When Kennedy narrowly prevaled in November, Gruening rejoiced at the "thrilling victory."[48]

Kennedy's major appointments, however, offered little indication that the new administration would embody the kind of reformism which Gruening personified. For secretary of the treasury, Kennedy nominated C. Douglas Dillon, a Republican investment banker known for his doubts about large-scale government spending and his support for a balanced budget. To offset Dillon, the president named as chair of his Council of Economic Advisors MIT economist Walter Heller, a Keynsian who advocated reducing taxes to stimulate economic growth. Meanwhile, Kennedy's appointments to key international positions reflected the tenets of the Cold War liberalism which he had espoused in the Senate. Both Robert McNamara, the former president of Ford Motors, and Kennedy's personal adviser on military affairs, retired general Maxwell Taylor, advocated sharp increases in spending on conventional arms. The new national security adviser, former dean of the

Harvard faculty McGeorge Bundy, brought to Washington impeccable establishment credentials, as did Dean Rusk, the new secretary of state. Though successful in attracting "the best and the brightest"—both in background and in intellect—to government service, Kennedy also placed clear limits on the types of men he considered for high posts. Those, like Gruening, who harbored anti-monopoly views on domestic matters or doubts about the Cold War internationally rarely appeared on the president's short lists.[49]

But Alaskan affairs initially inclined Gruening to overlook the matter, as his approach to defense policy revealed. Shortly after coming to office, Kennedy and McNamara proclaimed a new strategic doctrine, flexible response, which called for improving conventional forces to respond to international crises in which the threat of using nuclear weapons would have little effect. These policies generally drew strong support from Congress, and Gruening was no exception, since he continued to view military spending as a good way to funnel federal assistance to Alaska. George McGovern (D–South Dakota) came away from one private discussion with the senator feeling that he was "sympathetic" in the abstract to efforts to reduce defense appropriations, but since "there were a number of important defense installations in Alaska," the matter "concerned him politically." The Alaskan criticized Kennedy only for not soliciting congressional opinion on military questions more formally; the base cuts of the late 1950s had made him skeptical of allowing military professionals to handle such issues alone. Gruening was hardly the only reformer in the upper chamber to approach defense spending with patronage concerns uppermost in his mind. Stephen Young, for example, while privately supportive of a reduced Pentagon budget, confided that his "main concern is in seeing to it that Ohio is not discriminated against when economic measures are put into effect."[50]

Defense spending was only one of a number of initiatives to boost federal largesse for his state which consumed Gruening's immediate attention in early 1961. The senator also proposed a $375,000 appropriation to field an Office of Indian Affairs vessel to compete with Alaska Steamship, a plan which Republicans such as Karl Mundt (R–South Dakota) denounced as reminiscent of "the special considerations provided a territory." Without, as one contemporary recalled, "any concept of the limits of what he ought to do," Gruening chose to continue the debate rather than retreat to the cloakroom and lobby for votes. He responded to Mundt with a ridiculous resurrection of the national security theme, maintaining that the federal government had a special obligation to assist the Eskimos because of their "vital role in the national defense" as sentries on the Alaskan frontier. Mundt sarcastically commended his colleague's "intriguing" argument. Then, as often occurred on Alaskan matters, the more politically astute Bob Bartlett saved the day, persuading all but seven of the Senate's Democrats to vote for the amendment, which passed by a five-vote margin.[51]

Gruening's persistence on Alaskan issues likewise irritated Democrats. John Carver, an Interior Department official with whom he regularly feuded, nonetheless could not help but admire "the old goat still carrying on in his independent fashion." Others were less charitable. Kennedy's deputy congressional liaison, Mike Manatos, regularly complained that the Alaskan "pestered" his office, but his boss, Lawrence O'Brien, realized that it was "impossible to totally block off Gruening" on minor issues. As the senator himself later noted, "Never say it doesn't pay to fight till last ditch." The congressional liaison office was not alone in facing the Alaskan's persistent lobbying efforts, as when Gruening demanded that Kennedy implement his pledge to move forward on the Rampart Dam. The request was not unanticipated. The day after the election, one aide lamented to Kennedy that as part of his western sweep Nixon had even carried traditionally Democratic Alaska. The president-elect laughingly responded, "Thank God"; he hoped that the failure of Alaska's Democrats to deliver their state would lessen their push for patronage. Gruening had no intention of letting the administration off so easily. The senator began by traveling to Tucson for a "very cordial conversation" with Stewart Udall, the incoming secretary of the interior. But the relationship between the two quickly cooled once the Arizonan's hostility to building new dams in environmentally sensitive areas became apparent. Gruening then resorted to familiar tactics, launching a vigorous public relations campaign which kept the issue alive but failed to prevent Udall from referring the matter for further study to the Army Corps of Engineers.[52]

Disputes on Alaskan matters, however, soon seemed minor in comparison with the emerging rift between the new administration and Gruening on economic philosophy. For Gruening, as always, the relationship between government and business was the domestic question about which he cared the most, and he dreamed of a "renaissance of the enthusiasm for public service and Government dedicated to the public interest which was evident in the regulatory agencies in the years preceding World War I." Although Gruening had not enjoyed the warmest of relationships with federal regulatory agencies while governor, he remained strongly committed to the principle of federal regulation. In classic progressive rhetoric, he maintained that "the test of an administration can be found in the character of its appointees to regulatory agencies." If so, Kennedy, who believed that regulatory agencies should both preserve a "balanced competitive economy" and "further the expansion of certain facets of the economy," failed the test. Gruening correctly maintained that the independent commissions could either regulate monopolies or promote industrial expansion. Performing both tasks, however, would represent a conflict of interest in which the desire to regulate would always be subordinated to the shorter-term needs of economic progress.[53]

As Gruening thus quickly discovered, the administration did not place a particularly high priority on using the power of the government to break down business concentrations. This fact was clear by 1962, when Gruening and roughly a dozen other senators, referred to by the senator as "our little group," made their presence felt against a wide array of administration policies which they criticized for promoting monopolies. The most passionate such fight came after the president introduced a bill to create the Commercial Satellite Corporation, or Comsat, a partnership between the government and AT&T to develop space communications. Kennedy hailed the measure as a "step of historic importance" to safeguard the public interest while also advancing national security. To its critics, however, the proposal represented a government sellout to the interests of a monopoly, and they launched a filibuster in the hopes of killing the bill. In the event, Gruening reveled in the opportunity to make long public speeches and display again his remarkable energy level. In a series of extemporaneous addresses, the seventy-five-year-old senator returned to familiar themes: the danger that the proposed corporation "might operate as a monopoly against the public interest" and the need to strengthen the regulatory machinery of the government. Despite the spirited opposition, the Senate ended the so-called "liberal filibuster" by enacting a cloture resolution for the first time in thirty-five years.[54]

Throughout his tenure in the Senate, the anti-monopoly perspective remained as vibrant for Gruening as when he had first embraced it in the 1910s. As William O. Douglas recalled, the senator frequently spoke "movingly" about Brandeis's contributions to American reform ideology. But, as the debates over Comsat and Kennedy's regulatory policies demonstrated, even a limited anti-monopoly agenda enjoyed little support by the 1960s. The Alaskan was left to wonder how he could penetrate the "mists which surround the economic thinking in this administration." Gruening initially harbored a more positive view of the administration's international initiatives, largely because Kennedy came to office promising reforms in inter-American relations and foreign aid. But the senator quickly realized that the president brought a fundamentally different ideological orientation to these issues as well. By the end of 1962, Gruening and Kennedy were articulating fundamentally different visions of the American role in world affairs. In the process, the Alaskan emerged as among the most vociferous and effective Senate critics of the administration's foreign policy.[55]

Like his predecessor, Kennedy accorded to foreign assistance a prominent role in the nation's prosecution of the Cold War. The president was especially influenced by the theories of "action intellectuals" from Harvard and MIT such as Walt W. Rostow, who called for tailoring aid to allow underdeveloped countries to achieve self-sustaining economic growth, thus minimizing the period of poverty on which communism supposedly fed. The new president launched a host of programs, such as the Peace Corps and Food for Peace, to demonstrate that "economic growth and political democracy can develop hand in hand." He also departed from his predecessor on military aid policy, though not in the way that many of the critics of the program hoped. Whereas Eisenhower had generally justified such assistance on the grounds that it would improve the U.S. strategic position in the event of a military confrontation with the USSR, Kennedy rationalized that military aid would help emerging governments stabilize internal political conditions while enacting the social and economic reforms necessary for modernization. To implement this agenda more effectively, he created a single bureau responsible for the program, the Agency for International Development (AID).[56]

This framework reflected a quite different vision of foreign aid from that entertained by Gruening. Still, the senator recognized that so long as reform of the program was on the table, Congress would have some input into the matter. In 1961, looking to increase his influence, the Alaskan cast a vote for the final version of a foreign aid bill, for the first and only time in his Senate career. Nonetheless, he fought for a variety of amendments, though these battles brought him into conflict more with Fulbright, who served as floor manager for the bill, than with the administration. In addition to his strong commitment to foreign aid, the Arkansas senator had a substantially more limited vision of the congressional role in foreign affairs than did Gruening. In 1961, Fulbright theorized that the "primary obligation of the Senate" was to contribute "to the establishment of a national consensus" by explaining the principles of American foreign policy to the people. Nevertheless, he reasoned, the upper chamber ought not to "initiate or force large events, or substitute its judgment of them for that of the Executive." The "disastrous and reckless Senatorial excursions into foreign policy" in the 1920s (Fulbright and Gruening obviously interpreted congressional activism during that decade differently) exemplified for him the dangers of an overactive legislative body.[57]

These different conceptions of senatorial power prompted Fulbright to urge his colleague to stop trying to "act as secretary of state." The patronizing comment reflected the dismissive attitude which the Foreign Relations chair assumed toward Gruening, whom he initially viewed as one in a long line of Senate demagogues who attacked foreign aid as an easy political target but devoted little real thought to the issue. During a quorum call after one of the Alaskan's tirades, the Arkansas senator, speaking to staffer Pat Holt, compared Gruening—short, bald, slightly overweight, with "those baggy pants and suit that's too big"—to a burlesque comedian.[58]

Profound differences of opinion over the nature of the foreign aid program intensified the personal antipathy. A revealing exchange came in August over a Gruening amendment to limit the interest rates charged by the national banks of countries which received U.S. economic assistance. The Alaska senator worried that without such limits, the "utterly fantastic" rates of inflation, especially in Latin America, would nullify the effects of foreign aid. Fulbright, exasperated, told Gruening that anyone who knew "how we can legislate on this floor to change the interest rate in Chile or Brazil . . . would be a genius." The Alaskan, better at recognizing problems than at proposing realistic solutions to them, blandly responded that the Senate needed to address such matters. Otherwise, U.S. aid would only cause the rich to get richer and the poor to get poorer. Fulbright retired from the Senate floor, leaving John Sparkman (D–Alabama) to fend off Gruening. Like Fulbright, Sparkman doubted the wisdom of compelling reform in another country by legislation. Faced with this strong opposition, the amendment failed.[59]

Reflecting on his defeat a few months later in a long letter to his fellow anti-imperialist from the interwar era, Samuel Guy Inman, Gruening noted that in attempting to use the leverage obtained from economic aid, he was still looking for ways to facilitate the creation of cross-national reformist alliances. He confessed that when first approaching the issue, he had harbored some squeamishness about urging interference in another country's internal affairs. After pondering the question, though, Gruening "increasingly felt that the [assistance] money should be granted to countries that were performing in accordance" with democratic principles and withheld from nations that declined to uphold these values. For instance, continuing assistance to the regime of Spanish dictator Francisco Franco, despite its strategic importance, "nauseated" the Alaska senator, who considered such support "particularly disgraceful at a time when we are trying to present an image of friendship to democracies." For Gruening, then, foreign aid provided not only a way to increase Congress's power over foreign affairs but also a new means of implementing his long-standing goal of strengthening reformers overseas.[60]

FROM HIS POSITION on the Government Operations Committee, Gruening sought to exploit what he perceived as Congress's special power over the foreign aid program to address his concerns with the overall nature of Kennedy's foreign policy. Though strengthened by the Legislative Reorganization Act of 1946, Government Operations was one of the least attractive committee assignments. The Alaskan agreed to serve on it only after receiving a strong request from Lyndon Johnson's confidant, Secretary of the Senate Bobby Baker; he clearly hoped that by doing so he would improve his chances for moving onto the Foreign Relations Committee at a later date. Best known for its Permanent Investigations Subcommittee, from which Joseph McCarthy launched his anticommunist inquiries in the early 1950s, the committee in fact possessed potential power over a wide array of government activities, including relations between the United States and international organizations to which it belonged. It was on this portion of the committee's charter, which gave Government Operations an entry point into international relations, that Gruening based his foreign policy inquiries.[61]

In 1962, Gruening used the committee to target the administration's policies in the Middle East. Personally, he remained so squeamish about his Jewish heritage that he instructed George Sundborg to contact any publication that characterized him as Jewish to correct the mistake. Nonetheless, Gruening admired Israel's ability to maintain a democratic government in a region dominated by dictatorships, an interest Beaser, whose support for closer U.S.-Israeli ties dated from his service on Lehman's staff, encouraged. Kennedy, however, came to office determined to pursue an evenhanded policy in the Middle East, maintaining the traditional U.S. support for Israel while simultaneously reaching out to the nationalist Nasser regime in Egypt. "Perturbed" that Kennedy was continuing Eisenhower's policy of "generous loans" to the Arab states "without exacting any quid pro quo" in terms of their policy toward Israel, Gruening toured the region in 1962, ostensibly to investigate U.S. foreign aid expenditures in ten Middle Eastern and North African countries. But, as one State Department official noted, the senator "confined himself to broader issues" of U.S. foreign policy rather than the specifics of AID programs. In fact, Gruening had scheduled the visit in order to gather firsthand information for his critique of administration policy.[62]

Gruening returned to the United States and issued a characteristically lengthy report of four hundred–plus pages which he claimed contained recommendations "obviously applicable to our foreign aid program throughout the world." The senator noted "far too great a tendency" by foreign aid administrators to assume "that any nation in the Free World not only should, but is entitled to, receive U.S. foreign assistance," a misperception that tarnished the U.S. image by identifying the country with right-wing dictatorships. As an alternative, he recommended nine criteria for determining a country's eligibility for assistance, ranging from a "reasonably efficient system of government" to an assurance that the country would not engage in an "unprovoked" military attack or arms buildup. One observer described Gruening's findings as "scathing," but also full of "constructive proposals for reform." The report, issued in April 1963, served as an early sign of an impending congressional revolt against Kennedy's policy in the Middle East.[63]

By this stage, however, the full range of Gruening's dissent from the administration's foreign aid policies had manifested itself on a matter of more personal and professional concern, inter-American relations. A member of the Morse subcommittee while in the Senate, Kennedy used the deteriorating image of the United States in Latin America to his political advantage in 1960. After his election, he established a task force, headed by the veteran U.S. diplomat and former New Deal Brain Truster Adolf Berle, to look into Latin American policy. To dissociate social revolution "from Communism and its power politics," the task force urged generous economic aid to the region combined with support for social democrats such as Venezuelan president Romulo Betancourt. Berle's vision was implemented in 1961 at the first Punta del Este Conference, where Douglas Dillon pledged $20 billion in private and public U.S. aid to Latin America within the decade. Dubbing this program the Alliance for Progress, Kennedy hoped that the increased assistance would stimulate Latin American economic development and undercut the appeal of Fidel Castro's communist regime. This same anticommunist stance led the president to increase military assistance to the region (totaling some $77 million by fiscal year 1963) for internal security purposes.[64]

Speaking, he said, as "both an idealist and a realist," Gruening entertained doubts about the practicality of the Alliance from its inception. For Kennedy, the goal of U.S. aid was to weaken communism in Latin America. For Gruening, the Alliance would fail or succeed based not on the amount of assistance supplied by the United States or the recipient regime's anticommunist credentials but on the willingness of recipient countries to enact social and economic reforms. Recalling his experience in Puerto Rico, he understood the difficulty of imposing reform from outside. He therefore pressed the administration to allow Latin American reformers to set the agenda. Pointing to the fact that leaders ranging from Luis Muñoz Marín in Puerto Rico to José Figueres in Costa Rica put much less emphasis on combating communism than did administration officials, the Alaskan feared that the anticommunist rationale for the Alliance could cause the undertaking to backfire. A preoccupation with communism might prevent the administration from acting against strongly anticommunist forces in Latin America, such as the military or the upper classes, thus strengthening "the impression, which already exists, that we are in favor of the oligarchical and feudal setup which exists down there."[65]

This framework initially prompted Gruening to concentrate on issues that barely attracted the attention of the administration, which focused its hemispheric diplomacy first on Cuba and then on nations which it perceived as vulnerable to communist expansion, such as the Dominican Republic, Venezuela, and Brazil. Gruening, by contrast, directed his efforts toward Mexican and Puerto Rican affairs. He played the most active role of any senator in the U.S.-Mexican Inter-Parliamentary Conference, which originated in 1961. Patterned on a similar arrangement between the United States and Canada, the conferences lasted three or four days, with the delegations breaking up into small groups to discuss political, economic, and border issues of concern to the two countries. Gruening, who rarely missed a chance to visit Mexico, volunteered to serve on the U.S. delegation, where he distinguished himself for his intense interest and solid preparation. At one conference, a fellow member of the delegation, Frank Moss, remembered Gruening—still fluent in Spanish—as constantly in the middle of conversations with his hosts; indeed, the Utah senator noted, it seemed as if the Alaskan were "known to the Mexicans almost as well as the Americans." Gruening's pro-Mexican viewpoint prompted another colleague, Thomas Kuchel (R–California), to nickname him "Ernesto."[66]

On another front of long-standing concern, Gruening hailed U.S. policies toward Puerto Rico for demonstrating "one less bit of colonialism." He assured Muñoz Marín, by this time the island's governor, of his intention to "support Puerto Rico's needs" whenever called upon to do so. In 1949 the two had set aside their personal differences during a visit by Gruening to Puerto Rico. Upon reflection, Gruening had seen the merit in the critique of the Puerto Rican Liberals that they needed more freedom in setting the insular reform agenda; ironically, this very point now formed one of his central complaints about the Alliance for Progress. Meanwhile, Muñoz Marín had adopted Gruening's point of view on the political status question, abandoning his call for independence and instead championing commonwealth status. Once again comfortable with his old friend, the Alaska senator responded by urging, as he had while at the PRRA, generous U.S. assistance for the island; he also renewed his earlier pleas that Puerto Rico play a greater role in the making of U.S. policy toward Latin America and revived his idea of transforming the University of Puerto Rico into a pan-American university. His position on the Interior Committee enhanced his influence over such issues.[67]

As long as Gruening concentrated on Mexico and Puerto Rico, he refrained from broad-based attacks on the administration's overall approach to Latin America. But such reserve could not last forever, especially given the senator's (basically correct) belief that his experience gave him a more nuanced understanding of Latin American affairs than that of most key administration officials. Gruening began 1962 committed to focusing on Mexican issues, since the United States was now host of the U.S.-Mexico Inter-Parliamentary Conference. It was "damn hard," staffers planning the event acknowledged, to find anyone else willing to serve on the U.S. delegation. Once the conference began, Gruening, unlike his delegation colleagues, diligently attended and participated in the sessions. Moreover, to stress the importance which he attached to the gathering, he hosted a private dinner at his home for the Mexican delegation. The senator's interest in Latin American affairs soon broadened beyond Mexico, in large part because of a July 1962 coup which toppled the government of Manuel Prado in Peru. On the surface, the coup confirmed the warnings of critics of military aid that the program threatened Latin American democracy: the Peruvian military used a U.S.-supplied tank to penetrate the presidential palace. The administration instantly suspended relations with the junta, but this decision was more show than substance. As special assistant Arthur Schlesinger, Jr., explained to Kennedy, "Obviously we will have to resume relations in due course; but the important thing now . . . is to do so in a way which will not cancel out the great gains we have made." What Schlesinger found obvious Gruening did not. Though "gratified" at the suspension of aid, the senator asserted that "decisive action" at an earlier stage might have prevented the coup altogether. Two options existed: conditioning aid on the adoption of democratic reforms or continuing the present policy of "being dragooned by crisis after crisis into making huge grants of funds on vague promises." Gruening feared that backing down in Peru would invite more military coups in the future, thereby condemning the Alliance's reform agenda to failure. As an alternative, he recommended withholding all aid from Latin American military regimes and eliminating military aid to Latin America altogether. The senator cited Costa Rica, which had abolished its army in 1948, as the model for the United States to encourage.[68]

In the process, Gruening offered two broad criticisms of the president's handling of inter-American relations. First of all, the Alaskan chastised the administration for not sufficiently supporting Latin American reformers in their internal political battles against the armed forces and representatives of the oligarchy. He specifically accused Kennedy of taking too lax a stance on the issue of military coups, charging that the administration's obsession with the communist threat was leading it to support only the most timid of reforms, out of a fear that a more dynamic policy could cause reform to spin out of control and facilitate communist triumphs in the region. Second, the senator worried that Kennedy's preoccupation with military aid was neutralizing the positive effects of even this limited U.S. economic assistance, since the arms strengthened the very forces in Latin American society—the military and its allies in the oligarchy—that the United States should seek to weaken. In retrospect, as Ralph Dungan, who coordinated Latin American policy on Kennedy's National Security Council, conceded, Gruening "hit a lot of right chords" in his dissent. At the time, however, administration operatives dismissed him as the "old curmudgeon type." The Alaskan thus understood that he would have to mobilize the institutional power of the Senate to make Kennedy pay attention to his point of view.[69]

This recognition caused Gruening to assume an increasingly outspoken posture which culminated in his emergence as the most aggressive Senate critic of Kennedy's Latin American policy. The senator was interviewed on NBC's *Today* show to discuss his proposal to bar military aid to Latin America. He also drew enthusiastic support from several of his colleagues, notably Stephen Young. Cold War liberals, however, subjected him to both public and private criticism. Despite their friendship, Paul Douglas confessed that he found it "impossible" to agree with what Gruening had said about Peru: the need to support stable, anticommunist regimes in the region made the Alaskan's suggestions too risky. More important, Gruening's position came under attack in his bid for reelection. His GOP opponent, former Interior Department solicitor and future Alaska senator Ted Stevens, challenged him to explain his opposition to "sending arms to South America just as the Russians were beginning the buildup in their arms to Cuba."[70]

Since his arrival in the Senate, Gruening had feared that his activism on foreign policy issues would impair his chances of reelection. In fact, however, the senator successfully balanced his dissenting inclinations with attending to the state's patronage concerns. Bob Bartlett, surveying the Alaskan scene in early 1962, reported back that his colleague was "as strong as tiger's piss." Stevens tried to make an issue of the senator's age, asking Alaskans to "imagine a junior senator being 81 years old"—as Gruening would be at the end of a new six-year term. To appeal to Kennedy supporters as well as Republicans, the GOP challenger contended that "the nation has turned to young people for leadership," and reasoned that Alaska, "as the youngest state in the Union, with the youngest voters in the nation," needed "at least one aggressive young man in the United States Senate." At every stage of the campaign, however, the challenger found himself outmaneuvered. When Stevens attacked Gruening's anti-business rhetoric, the incumbent responded with a public endorsement from the executive vice president of Alcoa, who recalled his having done "everything humanly possible" to assist the company in its unsuccessful attempt to establish an Alaskan operation. Stevens's charge that the absence of campaign appearances from cabinet officials proved that Gruening's dissenting posture had "alienated every single department of the federal government" proved a bit tougher to deflect. The senator retorted that whatever the nature of his personal relations with top administration officials, he had brought back federal assistance for the state. This tactic fulfilled his first maxim of Alaskan politics: "Speak to their self-interest." When combined with the goodwill remaining from his role in the statehood campaign, it garnered Gruening a comfortable 57 percent victory. In a complete reversal from 1958, moreover, the senator topped the Democratic ticket, outpolling Egan and Rivers in their successful reelection efforts.[71]

The senator chose to view the triumph as an indication that he had become "sufficiently entrenched politically" to take even more political risks. In fact, Gruening won because he had successfully exploited the advantages of incumbency, while Stevens suffered from poor name recognition, especially in the Anchorage area, which hampered his fund-raising ability. Despite the attacks on issues such as the incumbent's opposition to military aid, the challenger was simply too weak politically to exploit the growing perception in Alaska of Gruening as an "internationalist," a figure too busy "flying in the international atmosphere," as one observer noted, to concentrate on Alaskan matters.[72] But, in retrospect, Gruening knowingly misinterpreted the election results. All along, service in the Senate had appealed to him because of the opportunity it presented to discuss national and international issues of importance. With six years to go before he would again have to face the Alaskan voters, he was determined to exploit the opportunity.

7

The Dilemmas of Dissent

With his victory over Stevens fortifying his sense of political security, Gruening abandoned any pretense of concentrating on Alaskan issues. Looking to be "a liberal yet an effective politician," he increasingly emerged as a wild card in Senate politics. Maurine Neuberger, who joined him as a colleague following her husband's death in 1960, recalled that the Alaskan's growing reluctance to "kowtow" to the powerful, mostly southern, Senate leaders lessened his political clout: there would be no more deals with the likes of Robert Kerr. For an alternative path to influence, Gruening fell back on his oratorical, bureaucratic, and intellectual skills. Neuberger described the Alaskan as "intellectually above his colleagues," a judgment shared by figures ranging from friends, such as Jack Germond, to rivals, such as Stewart Udall. This approach also suited the senator temperamentally. Recalled by Germond as one of the two or three people he had ever encountered who seemed "entirely secure" in himself and his position in life, Gruening had attained his ultimate ambition—service in the Senate—and this sense of fulfillment and self-confidence "affected the way he dealt with everybody"; the Alaskan remained a man who "intellectually didn't suffer fools gladly."[1]

One casualty of this tendency, however, was the relationship between Gruening and Bob Bartlett. For their first few years in the Senate, they generally cooperated on Alaskan matters, but they were too different to remain on close terms for long. On a personal level, as one observer noted, Bartlett was "one of the common men," in contrast to the "more aloof" Gruening, the "intellect who ivory towered." These personality differences guided their approaches as legislators. Within the Senate, as Stewart Udall recalled, Gruening was not "notoriously collegial," while Bartlett was "more inclined to see two sides to a question." He used his smoother personality to cultivate a "wider circle of influence," in the process becoming far more effective than Gruening at getting bills passed. On the other hand, Gruening's intellectual abilities and self-confidence fueled a streak of jealousy in Bartlett. Endowed with what some viewed as "unbelievable arrogance," Gruening regularly insulted his more personally insecure colleague without seeming to realize it. The first such insult—Gruening's maneuvering to take credit as the key player in securing statehood—set the stage. The perception then developed in Bartlett's office that the junior senator was "stealing" his colleague's ideas on Alaskan issues in a search for publicity. When Bartlett complained about the matter, Gruening tartly told him to be "civilized." In response, Bartlett began referring to Gruening as "His Honor," "His Worship," or "His Nibs." But even Bartlett, unwilling to confront Gruening publicly, kept the attacks private.[2]

In the long term, Gruening's failure to remain on good terms with his colleague would prove costly. In the short term, however, he was concerned with a different agenda. Once the new congressional session opened in January 1963, the Alaskan resumed his frustrating attempts to return the Democratic party to anti-monopoly principles. One avenue for this effort was provided by a series of subcommittee hearings probing shortcomings in federal regulation of the drug industry. Gruening also maintained his opposition to Comsat, emerging as a strong backer of a Kefauver amendment to delete Comsat's $50 million funding. During debate over the measure, the Tennessee senator turned white, broke out in perspiration, and retired from the Senate chamber, claiming indigestion. He actually had suffered a heart attack. Not knowing the seriousness of his colleague's condition, Gruening took over as floor manager of the amendment. When, two days later, Kefauver died in Bethesda Naval Hospital, the Alaska senator melodramatically eulogized his colleague as a "battle casualty" in the "fight against monopoly, intrenched privilege and the covert alliance of big business and its representatives in government." In high praise, Gruening ranked Kefauver the second most accomplished member of the Senate in the twentieth century, ahead of Borah and behind only George Norris.[3]

By this point Gruening was regularly criticizing the administration's handling of economic issues. In May 1963 the senator privately wrote Kennedy to urge a shakeup of the Federal Maritime Commission. When the president failed to act, Gruening campaigned to deny reconfirmation to the commission's vice chair, Ashton Barrett, named by Kennedy on the advice of James Eastland (D–Mississippi). The Alaska senator attacked Barrett, who described himself as a "sound conservative American businessman" but was dismissed by many familiar with his work as "Ashcan" Barrett, for operating under the "odd concept" that his agency should enhance the position of the U.S. shipping industry rather than protect the public interest. If Barrett represented the "hopes for a New Frontier in maritime regulation," Gruening sarcastically noted, then perhaps a return to the neglect characteristic of the Eisenhower years might be preferable. In challenging Barrett, who listed as his chief qualifications his experience "in the essential services of building construction, laundering, and dry cleaning," Gruening had selected an inviting target. Nonetheless, the senator not only failed to prevent the confirmation, but could not even force a roll call vote on the question.[4]

The battle revealed the fundamentally different conception of his office that the Alaskan brought to the upper chamber; unlike colleagues reluctant to challenge the tradition of senatorial courtesy by opposing Eastland's choice, he chiefly aimed to fulfill his ideological agenda. Ironically, though, this intellectual in politics, and others like him, failed to lay out a convincing and consistent rationale for the scope and function of regulation. Did Gruening, for example, want to appoint nonpartisan experts who would implement presidential initiatives to break down or regulate unhealthy concentrations of economic power? Or did he envision regulatory agencies representing the will of congressional reformers within the bureaucracy? Or did he dream of a fourth branch of government, immune from public, congressional, and presidential pressure? Obviously regulation—even if it had attracted the political and ideological support for which Gruening called—could not have fulfilled these often contradictory objectives. In the end, the Alaskan settled for the much vaguer notion that the character of its appointments to regulatory agencies offered the best indication of the economic principles of the administration in power. This agenda allowed him to apply a litmus test to the policies of the presidents under which he served, but it provided little positive policy guidance. Still, as Mike Manatos noted, Gruening did have "a field day . . . raking the entire Maritime Commission over the coals during the confirmation hearings," and presidential counselor Theodore Sorensen conceded that in the future the administration would have to pacify Gruening somewhat if it hoped to remain on friendly terms with him on other matters.[5]

Such perceptions, however, offered little comfort to a man determined to revive the Progressive era goal of strengthening the federal regulatory structure. Indeed, Gruening's failure to prevent Barrett's confirmation kept alive an uninterrupted streak of defeats in confrontations with the Kennedy administration on domestic issues. Gruening suffered neither a lack of broader interest nor a string of losses on Latin American policy, however, where the senator enjoyed a disproportionate amount of influence. He got his opportunity to offer an alternative to the Alliance for Progress in late September 1963, when a military coup in the Dominican Republic toppled the democratically elected government of Juan Bosch. Immediately thereafter the Foreign Relations Committee met in executive session and testily debated the event's lessons. In the view of Albert Gore (D–Tennessee), the coup illustrated the "enormous gamble" of using military aid to put "big guns into the hands of irresponsible militaries." The committee's ranking minority member, Bourke Hickenlooper (R–Iowa), noting that Bosch had "let all the Commies come back into the Dominican Republic," countered that "we have a responsibility to . . . not get so deluded by this intriguing term 'democracy' that we lose perspective."[6]

Gruening, concerned that senators on both sides had acquiesced too quickly to the coup, considered the tone of this debate troubling. In fact, the Alaska senator maintained, Bosch's overthrow, if handled properly, could allow the United States to aid reform in Latin America in a spectacular fashion. On September 30 he revealed his plan. Asserting that the Dominican military "must not be permitted to reap the advantages of their ill-considered actions," he called for withdrawing diplomatic recognition and terminating all economic and military assistance. Even then, he reasoned, such a purely negative policy would not suffice. Once before, in 1934, Gruening had considered military action to assist reformers in the Dominican Republic. Now, nearly three decades later, he returned to the option, calling on the administration to show some "courage" and "take whatever steps are necessary" to return Bosch to power. The Alaskan conceded that there was "no precedent exactly" for his recommendation, but he denied proposing gunboat diplomacy, reminding his critics that he, better than any other senator, knew what that concept entailed. Instead, he maintained, the proposal represented a creative response to a difficult diplomatic situation.[7]

From outside the Senate, Drew Pearson, who highlighted Gruening's activism in his syndicated column, hailed the "terrific speech." In the upper chamber itself, the most positive reaction came from Stephen Young, who expressed "complete agreement" on the "clear" duty of the United States to prevent the Dominican military from consolidating its power. Frank Church questioned the plan's practicality, but he nonetheless termed it "audacious and provocative," as well as "characteristic" of Gruening's tendency to "seize the initiative" and offer "refreshingly bold" positions. For Gruening, though, such praise was offset by the response from Wayne Morse. Knowing the importance of obtaining the endorsement of the chair of the American Republics Affairs subcommittee, the Alaskan wrote his colleague before making his proposal. Anticipating Morse's likely objections, Gruening argued that the United States needed to act quickly and unilaterally. A multilateral intervention sanctioned by the Organization of American States (OAS), although preferable in theory, could not succeed, since "too many countries are dominated by dictators who won't be sympathetic." The plea failed to move the Oregon senator. Despite "heartily" endorsing Gruening's goals, Morse privately dismissed his colleague's reasoning as "not persuasive." More problematic, Morse denounced the plan on the Senate floor, asserting that it would make "us an aggressor nation," in "clear violation" of international law and treaty obligations.[8]

Although Gruening and Morse later emerged as the Senate's most outspoken critics of the Vietnam War, their visions of the proper American role in international affairs differed quite sharply, as their disagreement over the Dominican coup illustrated. For Morse, upholding the tenets of the law—on both the domestic and international fronts—reigned supreme. For Gruening, fulfilling the country's revolutionary heritage as a champion of international reform remained the central purpose of U.S. foreign relations. This task generally meant refraining from military intervention—but not always. Washington could respect international law and the noninterventionist principles of the OAS at the cost of permitting the Dominican military to remain in power. Or the administration could act resolutely, using military might if necessary, to assist the beleaguered forces of Dominican reform. A stronger stance against Latin American coups, particularly a year earlier in Peru, might have avoided these unpalatable choices. But with only two options available, Gruening had no hesitation in accepting even a potential breach with Morse.

Even though it failed to draw substantial Senate support, Gruening's proposal made the senator a player in the upper chamber's response to the Dominican crisis, with the effect of encouraging his colleagues to take more outspoken positions against the administration's course. In this sense, it provided a good example of how Gruening used his abilities to influence—if in a somewhat unconventional fashion—those issues about which he cared passionately. When the Foreign Relations Committee next considered the matter, in closed session on October 3, Gruening was present, marking the only occasion in his Senate career when he participated in a Foreign Relations Committee hearing as anything other than a witness. The Alaskan quickly asserted himself. As one "very familiar" with the Dominican situation—the only man in the chambers who had been "down there before Trujillo"—the senator felt secure in describing the coup as "a terrible blow to our foreign policy." Looking to reestablish "our purpose and image throughout the Americas," Gruening concluded that "we hold all the cards and spades, if we want to use them," since "if we threaten them with no aid, and withdrawal of the sugar quota, and no recognition, they would cave in tonight." The suggestion did not persuade Edwin Martin, Kennedy's assistant secretary of state for inter-American affairs, who, like most in the administration, attributed Bosch's downfall to his incapacity for leadership and argued that "democracy cannot be created from outside." Other Democrats, however, sided with Gruening. Morse pronounced himself "completely in disagreement" with Kennedy's inter-American policy, while Church, addressing the crisis "within the context of the larger policies and objectives of the United States," demanded as a minimum an amendment triggering an automatic cutoff of all assistance to governments which came to power through a military coup.[9]

Three days later, Martin, prompted by Kennedy's concern that "certain quarters" in the Senate were contending that the coup "reflected a collapse of the Alliance for Progress" and "were using this as a springboard to attack the Alliance appropriations," released a hastily prepared memorandum on the issue. The assistant secretary ripped into the "impatient idealists" who measured administration policy not against historical reality "but against somewhat theoretical notions of the manner in which men should and do operate in a complex world." He conceded that more military coups had occurred in Latin America over the previous three years than the administration wished. But he blamed this development on the fact that in those countries an "insufficient body of opinion, civil or military," was willing to defend democracy, and suggested that the United States should respond by working more closely with Latin American militaries, attempting to reform them from within. The alternative policy, that of imposing democracy from without, offered little prospect for success, as the U.S. experiences in Haiti, the Dominican Republic, and Nicaragua in the earlier part of the century had shown. The next day a "shocked" Gruening claimed that the missive would encourage "military coups throughout Latin America" and thus constituted a "grave betrayal" of the Alliance.[10]

In the end, the Dominican crisis exhibited Gruening's ability, as Jack Germond perceptively noted, to "define the limits of issues." By expanding the range of debate, as he did on Latin American matters throughout the Kennedy administration, Gruening forced the consideration of points of view which might otherwise have remained off the table. In this task the Senate provided a perfect forum for this natural dissenter and critic. As Martin later conceded, the fierce attacks by Gruening and a few like-minded colleagues prevented the administration from embracing even those military governments which it believed more capable of resisting local communists than their constitutionally elected predecessors. Instead, as in the Dominican Republic, Kennedy was forced to go through the motions of a public protest, including severing U.S. aid to the new regime, even as the president privately admitted that "if it were not for the Congress, I'm sure that we ought to recognize now."[11]

Personally and ideologically, Gruening preferred, as he did throughout the Dominican crisis, to focus his efforts on Senate speeches, where he could use his rhetorical and intellectual skills to the maximum advantage. At the same time, however, despite a general lack of interest in the specifics of legislation, he was perfectly willing to use the institutional powers of the Senate to further his foreign policy agenda, as in his efforts on foreign aid policy. In 1963, Gruening played a key role in the consummation of an unusual political and ideological alliance that revolutionized how Congress handled foreign aid issues. By the time that the authorization for the year's foreign aid bill was finally completed, Congress had placed more restrictions on the implementation of the program and had reduced the administration's funding request more than in any other year since the inception of the U.S. foreign aid program. *U.S. News & World Report* spoke for the consensus of Washington opinion when it labeled Gruening and Morse the two "spark plugs of the foreign aid revolt."[12]

Before 1963, the chief congressional challenge to foreign aid came from the House of Representatives, where Otto Passman (D–Louisiana) regularly used his position as chair of the Foreign Operations Subcommittee to slash the executive's authorization requests. In the Senate, a bipartisan coalition of conservative Republicans and southern Democrats occasionally succeeded in reducing funding and placing some restrictions on the program's operations, but in most cases, northern Democrats, joined by liberal and moderate Republicans, prevailed in the final vote. This outcome neutralized the effect of the House cuts, since in conference the two bodies usually split the difference between their authorizations. Since both Eisenhower and Kennedy inflated their foreign aid requests knowing that the lower chamber would make some reductions, the conference authorizations generally gave the executive branch what it wanted.[13]

With the exception of the challenges from Gruening and Morse, liberal Democrats had rarely questioned the concept behind economic aid; most of them viewed it as a preferable alternative to more hard-line Cold War policies. In 1963, however, with the conservatives still hostile to most economic assistance, the emergence of Democratic critics such as Gruening, Gore, Church, Young, and Morse altered the political balance in the Senate. In part to meet this new threat, Kennedy appointed a prestigious committee headed by retired general Lucius Clay, former U.S. high commander in Germany, to suggest reforms. After the Clay committee recommended applying "stricter standards of selectivity," the administration reduced its request from $4.9 billion to $4.5

billion. The president also named David Bell as the new administrator of AID. (Bell found the job "totally unappealing," since he knew that it "required above all else the development of effective relations with Congress.") As events turned out, neither of these moves proved sufficient to stem the tide of congressional opposition.[14]

THE NEW BALANCE OF POWER in the Senate revealed itself when, for the first time since his arrival in the upper chamber, several of the amendments offered by Gruening passed. In fact, the Alaskan enjoyed some remarkably easy successes, as in the approval of his previously blocked amendment to sever military aid to Latin American regimes which came to power through military coups. Timing (the Dominican coup occurred as the Senate was considering the amendment) and tactics (the amendment permitted the president to offer military assistance if he deemed it in the national interest) allowed the amendment to pass on a voice vote. Praising the initiative, Young observed that while the Alaskan had confined his offering to Latin America, "the principles behind it have more than regional significance." This outcome was just what administration forces feared. Lawrence O'Brien complained that day after day the Senate was accomplishing "nothing whatever" because of the general "antipathy to AID and frustration over Vietnam, military coups in Latin America, etc."[15]

Gruening had to fight harder to achieve other victories. In 1962 he introduced an amendment to eliminate all foreign assistance to states that waged aggressive warfare, citing Egypt and Indonesia (which was then threatening to invade Malaysia) as his first targets. Nasser's decision to send seventy thousand troops to intervene in Yemen's civil war, undermining administration claims that U.S. aid had moderated Egyptian foreign policy, notably improved chances for the amendment's passage. Touting his measure as "based on a perfectly simple principle," the senator somewhat simplistically reasoned that conditioning U.S. aid on their international conduct would force leaders such as Nasser and Indonesian president Sukarno to choose between a belligerent foreign policy and their countries' domestic well-being. The Senate leadership strongly disagreed, but, unlike in the case of the Latin American military aid amendment, Gruening had the votes, and therefore refused to compromise. The Senate upheld him by a vote of 46 to 32, leaving Fulbright to complain privately of "the Zionists" overriding "those of us who oppose the use of the aid bill for this purpose." AID, meanwhile, termed the amendment "dangerously restrictive," and, as with the military aid proposal, worried about its "potentially broad application." Kennedy officials understood that Gruening never intended to confine his anti-aggressor precepts to Egypt and Indonesia alone; indeed, as Dean Rusk privately noted, his colleagues viewed the measure "in context of strong Congressional opposition" to the administration's foreign policy as a whole.[16]

As Gruening hoped, the anti-aggressor amendment had an immediate and deleterious effect on U.S. relations with Egypt. The Egyptian ambassador, terming the amendment a "particular shock" to his government, denounced Congress for "playing the role of God" through an initiative which demanded "searching consciences . . . to determine aggressive intent before the fact." Reports from the U.S. embassy in Cairo blamed the Gruening amendment for inflaming Egyptian nationalist sentiments, but conceded its "strong impact." Kennedy, meanwhile, singled out the measure for criticism, declaring that, whatever the Alaska senator preferred to believe, "it's a very dangerous, untidy world, but . . . we're going to have to live within it." Defending his colleague, Morse rebuked the president for speaking "more in wrath than with logic."[17]

The passage of his anti-aggressor and military aid amendments confirmed Gruening's prominent position in the 1963 foreign aid revolt; the administration complained that despite his party label, it could not "depend on him at all." His strong antipathy "to U.S. policy generally" combined with his aim to increase congressional supervision to produce a dangerous foe. Behind the specifics of his amendments, moreover, lay a more fundamental challenge in which several other Democrats joined. These dissenters hoped to revolutionize the program by making the ideological character of the recipient regime rather than its strategic importance the key factor in determining its worthiness for assistance. Gruening summed up the group's position: "The acid test of U.S. common sense, determination, and backbone is whether we are going to continue to be blackmailed by foreign governments which are allegedly anti-Communist." Along these lines, all left-wing critics called for greater selectivity in the program, assuming that ideologically distasteful regimes would be the first ones eliminated from the list of foreign aid recipients. In addition, the group challenged the notion that the program would increase the likelihood of a recipient nation's allying with the United States. Gruening complained about the "mistaken belief which exists in headquarters here that you can buy friendship and reform age-old conditions by the expenditure of American dollars." More generally, Morse feared that, much like British practitioners of balance-of-power politics in the nineteenth century, "we have deluded ourselves with the fanciful notion that through large enough amounts of foreign aid we can control these nations to advance our own interests." Bourke Hickenlooper, stunned at the course of events, correctly observed that "the major part of the caustic criticism [of administration policy] this year seems to be coming from the Democrats and it takes a variety of directions."[18]

These intellectual developments not only resulted in the Senate's placing new restrictions on the foreign aid program, but also produced severe cuts in the administration's authorization request. In early November, AID accurately predicted "that the 'dissident liberals' will continue to harass and obstruct," while the *Washington Post* blasted the "Democratic know-nothings" for precipitating a session in which, "in a wild melee worthy of the Keystone Cops, the bill has been carved and recarved on the Senate floor in a string of amendments so confusing that Senators were voting on dollar figures tossed in the air, often with only the most vagrant notion of what was at stake." Of course, Gruening and Morse delighted in this kind of disarray. Since they had devoted more attention to the issue than most other senators, they could take advantage of the confusion by slipping in desired changes; in 1963 they introduced ten of the sixteen amendments considered most substantial by the administration. Public attacks, private patronage offers, or even concessions on policy questions did not quell the revolt. As David Bell perceptively observed, "the basic causes of Congressional requests for a revamping of aid are rooted in the objections to some elements of our foreign policy and in Congressional frustration with the world as it is . . . conditions which could not be relieved by reorganizing the aid program." The administration ultimately pushed its authorization through the Senate, but only after its original request was cut by 34 percent, or more than $1 billion. The politics of foreign aid would never be the same.[19]

Gruening had little time to savor his victory, however. One apparently minor element of the foreign aid revolt was a Church amendment, which Gruening co-sponsored, to sever aid to the dictatorial regime of Ngo Dinh Diem in South Vietnam. U.S. assistance to Vietnam, in fact, represented a major commitment by this time. Although the 1954 Geneva Conference had called for national elections to reunite the two Vietnamese states, the Eisenhower administration had instead encouraged the creation of Diem's separate noncommunist regime. To improve South Vietnam's strategic position, the United States established the Southeast Asia Treaty Organization (SEATO), to which South Vietnam adhered as a protocol state. The new government also received lavish U.S. financial and military assistance. But Diem's repressive political style spawned armed opposition to his regime, which coalesced in 1960 as the National Liberation Front (NLF). For the Kennedy administration, Southeast Asia loomed as a testing ground for the new doctrine of flexible response, and though the president declined to place U.S. combat troops in the region, he did increase assistance to the Saigon regime by $42 million in 1961. When this aid failed to stem the insurgency, U.S. military involvement in Southeast Asia gradually escalated. By the end of 1962, the United States had nine thousand "advisers" stationed in Vietnam (the Geneva accords permitted just over seven hundred) and had assumed much of the responsibility for training the South Vietnamese military.[20]

Although some Senate Democrats, notably Gore and Morse, privately questioned this policy, a fear of the role played by the People's Republic of China (PRC) in Southeast Asian affairs tempered most congressional dissent.[21] Kennedy officials pointed to the traditional Chinese interest in Southeast Asia to suggest that if Diem's regime collapsed, the resulting power vacuum would benefit the PRC. On few aspects of U.S. foreign policy did such a solid consensus exist in the early 1960s: even Gruening supported efforts to contain the PRC.[22] Torn between conflicting desires, the Alaskan and most of his colleagues undoubtedly would have preferred to let the executive quietly resolve the Vietnam problem. The deteriorating political and military situation in South Vietnam, however, foreclosed this option. In May 1963, over ten thousand people protested after police in Hue killed nine Buddhists. The next month, after the government repudiated an arrangement to end laws discriminating on the basis of religion, a Buddhist monk set himself on fire; Kennedy remarked that "no news picture in history has generated as much emotion around the world." The president nonetheless ruled out withdrawal, though his new ambassador, Henry Cabot Lodge, made it clear that the United States expected a more conciliatory policy to neutralize the political instability. Instead, on August 21, Diem declared martial law.[23]

Despite the crisis, George McGovern later doubted that Vietnam was of interest to more than five members of the Senate as late as the fall of 1963. Among the handful, however, was Gruening, though not because of any particular interest in Southeast Asian policy per se. Instead, press reports of the first U.S. casualties raised his suspicions that the involvement represented another example of the misguided nature of Kennedy's overall approach to international affairs. In the midst of his battles with the administration over Latin American and foreign aid policies, Gruening asserted that if a son of his died in Vietnam, "I would not feel that he was dying for the defense of my country." Although he admitted that an NLF triumph might eventually produce a communist triumph in all of Southeast Asia, the Alaskan nonetheless said that he "would be perfectly satisfied if we pulled out." In theory, of course, Gruening was willing, as in the wake of the Bosch coup, to support military intervention to aid beleaguered reformers; but since Diem lacked Bosch's reformist credentials, there was no justification for any substantial U.S. commitment. Contrary to the Alaskan's hopes, the administration's plunge into the Vietnamese morass deepened in early November. Encouraged by Lodge, a group of dissident military officers replaced Diem's regime with a government headed by General Duong Van Minh. The next day, Diem and his brother, Ngo Dinh Nhu, were assassinated.[24]

Diem's overthrow represented John Kennedy's final initiative in Vietnam. Three weeks later, on November 22, Kennedy's assassination elevated Lyndon Johnson to the presidency. The Texan yearned to complete the unfulfilled domestic agenda of Roosevelt and Truman by expanding the welfare state and enacting meaningful civil rights legislation. Much less interested in international affairs than Kennedy, Johnson also had far less confidence in his ability to handle foreign policy and was obsessed with unfavorable comparisons to his predecessor. He therefore retained all of Kennedy's chief foreign policy advisers (with the exception of those responsible for Latin American affairs), and sought consensus among the upper levels of his administration before undertaking major international initiatives. This tactic only resulted in a more pronounced Cold War mindset coming from the executive branch than in 1961 through 1963. Like most in Washington, Gruening was shocked by the assassination. His initial reaction, however, was pragmatic, not emotional. Immediately upon hearing of the events in Dallas, he expressed his dismay at the timing of Kennedy's death, noting that Johnson would be able to run for reelection in 1964 and again in 1968. That Gruening would have such a reaction at a time of national grief testified to his poor opinion of the new president. Gruening had disagreed fundamentally with Kennedy on a wide array of issues, but through it all he had retained a sense of personal respect for the president. The same did not apply to Johnson.[25]

Ironically, given events to come, Gruening welcomed Johnson's first initiatives in international affairs, particularly the decision to replace Edwin Martin with Thomas Mann, Kennedy's ambassador to Mexico and a longtime friend of the new president. The Alaska senator believed that Mann "certainly understands the Latin-American psychology and will make a success of his job if anyone can." Mann, for his part, went out of his way to pacify Gruening, meeting with him on several occasions in early 1964 to solicit his advice on Mexican, Haitian, and Dominican issues. Gruening reciprocated, adding Mann to the regular guest list at his dinner parties; he came away from one "nice talk" convinced that Mann would support his perspective fully. In fact, as frequently occurred during his career, personal considerations clouded Gruening's better judgment. Flattered that key policy makers suddenly seemed interested in his insights, Gruening overlooked Johnson's intention to stress stability and anticommunist principles over the promotion of democracy and social reform in the region.[26]

While the administration was preparing to apply anticommunist principles to Latin American policy even more rigorously, Gruening was confirming the degree to which he had moved beyond the Cold War framework. The senator articulated this perspective most clearly in a long letter to Romulo Betancourt, the former president of Venezuela. Outlining his long-standing belief "that a number of countries need a revolution" in Latin America, he pointed to Mexico to illustrate his point. A "purely indigenous" revolt, "responding to the experience of the Mexicans and their appraisal of what their country needed," had produced a "continuing revolution." But "unfortunately," Gruening observed, most post–World War II revolutions were "infiltrated by the Communists," who then merely changed the type of oppression suffered by the common people. Still, he believed, the United States needed to encourage a Mexico-like solution elsewhere in Latin America instead of supporting dictatorships, as Kennedy had done, out of a fear that reform could spiral out of control. The success of leaders such as Betancourt, he said, demonstrated that "a Latin American country can have both social and economic progress under democratic procedures." This view explained the greater importance Gruening attached to promoting democracy in the 1960s than he had in the 1920s. Still, despite the changed international climate, Gruening's fundamental vision for Latin America had remained unaltered.[27]

Seeking an outlet to apply these beliefs (and to sustain his reputation as among the "travelingest" members of the upper chamber), the Alaskan launched an investigation of the Alliance for Progress in early 1964, traveling to Haiti, Colombia, Ecuador, Peru, Venezuela, and Chile, joined by Dorothy and Herb Beaser. The senator's days generally started between 7:00 and 7:30 A.M. and continued through late-evening dinners, with study missions, conversations with "people of all social strata," and informal meetings with the likes of Betancourt and Peru's Victor Haya de la Torre sprinkled in between. Embassy officials found him to be "energetic, tireless, eager to participate in any event, and sincerely desirous of increasing his knowledge" of the region. (Dorothy, by contrast, "found it difficult at times to keep up with the Senator's pace.") The Alaskan had a "clear idea" of his needs: visits to educational facilities and discussions about Latin American social and economic conditions were high on the agenda; meetings with local military officers, briefings from representatives of U.S. military aid programs, and packaged tours of U.S.-funded projects were not. One official recalled the senator as "a friendly, gentle man, with a dry-as-dust wit, devoted to swimming, to the fierce excitement of politics, to good conversation, and to the welfare of people everywhere." Gruening's fluency in Spanish generated a "remarkable" reception from Latin American officials, despite the senator's bluntness with his hosts, as in Colombia, where he "dented the oligarchs with comments on social consciousness," chatted with medical school faculty about the latest developments in birth control, and offered "shrewd arguments" about the course of hemispheric relations during a roundtable discussion with newspaper editors. The tour, the most extended of his Senate tenure, improved Gruening's sense of Latin American reform sentiment, thus sustaining his self-confidence for the battles to come.[28]

GIVEN THAT GRUENING and the new administration subscribed to fundamentally different points of view on the American role in international affairs, the threat that violent change in the underdeveloped world posed to the United States, the role that force and military issues in general should play in U.S. foreign policy, and the degree to which Washington should champion reform in areas plagued by political and economic inequality, a clash of major proportions between the Alaska senator and Johnson was inevitable. But the split would not first manifest itself in Latin America, the region of the world in which both Gruening and Johnson had exhibited the most interest throughout their careers. Instead, it appeared in Southeast Asia, an area to which both had so far devoted relatively little attention.

The initial sign of this divergence came on March 10, 1964. Before a nearly empty chamber, the Alaskan delivered the first full-length Senate speech demanding that the United States withdraw its armed forces from Vietnam. Gruening started by raising the question of how the new administration could move beyond "the dead hand of past mistakes." He called for Johnson to recognize the "basic truth" that foreign troops could not win the war. Indeed, there were "serious drawbacks" to a policy of military escalation. Unconsciously harking back to his own activities in the Caribbean Basin during the 1920s, Gruening urged the administration to give more credence to the critical portrayals of events in Vietnam offered by correspondents on the scene, such as Sam Castan, senior editor of *Look*, Jerry Rose of the *New Republic*, and Bernard Fall, considered by Gruening the most astute foreign observer of Southeast Asian affairs. Pointing to the trio's work, the Alaskan described events in South Vietnam as a civil conflict matching a broad-based coalition of Vietnamese reformers, including indigenous communists, against supporters of Diem's corruption. Given this perspective, the senator asserted, saving the South Vietnamese regime was not worth the life of a single American soldier.

Having challenged the basis of the U.S. commitment to South Vietnam, the speech then turned more passionate. The administration, Gruening argued, needed to realize that already its policy had resulted in the deaths of twenty U.S. soldiers "to shore up self-serving corrupt dynasts or their self-imposed successors." He urged his colleagues to ask themselves what they would think if their sons had been among the twenty; as for him, he would feel "very definitely he had not died for our country, but had been mistakenly sacrificed in behalf of an inherited folly." The time had come for "a little hard rethinking." The war was not winnable. The commitment had already tarnished the U.S. image. The United States could not "jump into every fracas all over the world . . . and stay in blindly and stubbornly." Consequently, U.S. troops should return home "with the knowledge that the game was not worth the candle."[29]

The *New York Times* commented that the "normally mild-spoken" senator "surprised colleagues by his choice of strong words" in the address. If, however, Gruening believed that his charged rhetoric would trigger a reappraisal in the administration's policy, he misjudged badly. His arguments did not strike policy makers as particularly innovative, and, unlike colleagues such as Mike Mansfield (D–Montana), Gruening lacked the background in Southeast Asian history (as opposed to inter-American or foreign aid initiatives) to compel attention to his opinions. His age compounded the problem. Seventy-six years old, with his slight build and baggy clothes, he looked "doddery"; on the Senate floor he "sort of shuffled along," in the words of one observer. The gallery sometimes wondered if he would make it up the aisle. Although Gruening was actually quite spry and in remarkably good health, his idiosyncrasies provided an excuse to dismiss him as a sort of "curiosity" rather than a serious player on national security issues, and thus permitted his opponents the luxury of not addressing his often perceptive criticisms. To the contrary, hard-liners in both the Senate and the administration used his remarks to rally the White House behind their point of view. As with Dominican affairs, Gruening succeeded in broadening the range of Senate debate on Vietnam policy. But the final outcome was not exactly what he had anticipated.[30]

Quickly, moreover, more than the Alaskan's policies sustained attack. Gruening's opposition to foreign aid and Latin American policies had poisoned his relations with most of Kennedy's foreign policy team, and in particular had alienated him from Dean Rusk. Rusk's vehement anticommunist viewpoint had distinguished him even in Truman's State Department, where he served as assistant secretary of state for Far Eastern affairs. As secretary of state, Rusk was the target of frequent barbs from Gruening. The two had publicly clashed in 1963, when, after the Senate passed the anti-aggressor amendment, the secretary criticized "the tendency in the Congress to legislate foreign policy." On March 19, nine days after Gruening's Senate speech, Rusk fired back in an address in Salt Lake City designed to start "a quiet campaign to answer those who said, 'South Vietnam is not worth the life of one American boy.'" Rusk's basic thesis—that prevailing in the "central struggle between international communism and the free world" guided his approach to foreign policy—offered nothing new. The conclusion of the speech, however, raised eyebrows. The secretary attacked "those who would quit the struggle by letting down our own defenses, by gutting our foreign aid programs," actions which amounted to abandoning "the field to our adversaries." He then pointedly added that "insofar as anybody here or abroad pays attention to the quitters, they are lending aid and comfort to our enemies." When questioned about these comments a few days later, Rusk disingenuously denied that he was accusing any senator of treasonous activity, and refused to offer an apology.[31]

For Gruening, Rusk's thinly disguised attack on his patriotism personalized Vietnam policy, with two immediate effects. First, he abandoned the hope, well before any of his colleagues, that quiet persuasion would encourage the administration to modify its course. Second, he decided to deliver a series of Senate speeches on Vietnam, again well before other dissenters regularly addressed the issue in public. Before March 19, Vietnam represented one of many foreign policy questions on which Gruening assumed a dissenting position. After March 19, the conflict received his total attention. He argued that it perfectly illustrated the faults of U.S. foreign policy: a tendency to address political problems through military means; a pattern of supporting dictatorial regimes in the name of anticommunism; a lack of sufficient congressional input into the formation of policy; and a failure to maintain the image of the United States as a power committed to reform on all levels of international politics. The personal and ideological motivations behind the senator's dissent would transform Vietnam into Gruening's passion during his final years in the Senate.

He began his crusade by attacking Rusk for attempting to stifle Senate dissent. In much stronger language than he employed in his March 10 address, which blamed the Vietnam quagmire on Eisenhower and Kennedy, the senator denounced the Johnson administration for perpetrating a "hypocrisy and a fraud" by covertly escalating the U.S. commitment. Gruening did not know what Rusk thought of the events of the previous ten years, but to him it seemed a decade of "tragic futility," in which the United States had poured "billions of dollars into the bottomless pit for a people exploited by corrupt dictators." Given that experience, withdrawal remained the preferable option. Taking up Rusk's challenge, he remarked that if adopting his suggestions "makes us quitters, then I say we should indeed quit this bloody and costly folly." His son Hunt recalled that his father, who always "thrived on controversy" anyway, said to him around this time, "Show me a man who's controversial, and I'll show you someone who stands for something."[32]

Over the next couple of months, Gruening regularly spoke out against the administration's policy, and in the process spelled out the basics of his dissenting viewpoint. The Alaskan described the involvement in Vietnam as a classic example of policy makers blindly applying the principles of containment, a doctrine he once had embraced but now considered "disastrous" and irrelevant to many aspects of contemporary international relations. The stakes in Southeast Asia were high, Gruening maintained, but for a different reason than the Johnson administration believed. Continuing to apply the framework of containment despite its being outdated had resulted in the United States' supporting "puppet governments, dictatorships that elicit little or no enthusiasm from the people they rule." Intervening to prevent one such regime from falling, as in Vietnam, could establish a precedent for the future. Sensing that the administration's approach in Vietnam violated the basic tenets of his foreign policy vision—indeed, the policy seemed destined to make "the United States reverse its traditional principles"—the senator "reveled" in his dissent. For the first time in his career, Gruening had found an international issue to call his own outside of his traditional specialty in inter-American affairs.[33]

After the March 10 fiasco, though, Gruening understood that controversial Senate speeches would not force the administration to reverse course. He therefore spent the spring of 1964 seeking to replicate the tactics which had yielded victory in his Latin American and foreign aid initiatives the year before: combining his own tenacity and willingness to use his position to publicize previously ignored issues with an ability to take advantage of unusual legislative splits in the makeup of the Senate. Fresh from his 1963 successes, however, he underestimated the difficulty of this new quest.

Ironically, given their opposite positions in the foreign aid fight, Gruening began his crusade by targeting Fulbright. In mid-March he privately urged the Arkansan to convene a public hearing of his committee to determine what Robert McNamara had meant by describing the U.S. commitment to South Vietnam as unlimited and total. Fulbright considered Gruening's complaint worth enough merit to schedule a closed session on the issue on March 26. The day before, meanwhile, Fulbright delivered a major speech noting a "divergence between the realities of foreign policy and our ideas about it," a result, the Arkansas senator claimed, of U.S. policy makers' clinging to anticommunist principles that were no longer valid. To Gruening this rhetoric sounded very much like his own repudiation of containment, and he praised his colleague for realizing that "our foreign policies are rigidified by habit, timidity, and fear." He hoped that the address suggested Fulbright's willingness to break with the administration on Vietnam policy. But the Arkansan, who argued that withdrawal could not be "realistically considered," offered either Johnson's policy or substantial military escalation as the only alternatives. Disappointed, Gruening went on the attack, describing Fulbright as the epitome of those policy makers who proposed "to continue to give the patient more of the same medicine which has failed to cure him." Gruening called not for dismissing unconditional withdrawal without explanation, but for ascertaining public sentiment on the question. In more than a slight exaggeration, he said that he expected to discover "virtually unanimous" support for his position.[34]

Unable to convert Fulbright, Gruening turned to the comrades from his battles against Kennedy's Latin American and foreign aid policies. Again, as with Fulbright, he had reason for optimism in this quest. As the *New York Times* noted in late March, Vietnam dissents were "stirring unusually harsh controversy among Democrats." The next month, NSC staffer James Thomson cautiously reported that "although Morse and Gruening appear to have made no admitted converts during this period, they have encountered little rebuttal from their colleagues." At the same time, the congressional liaison office commented that "a growing number of Senators are privately sympathetic with the Morse-

Gruening position," an observation confirmed by the senators' private correspondence. In June, for instance, a "very troubled" Church worried that in Vietnam "our close connection as a White Western nation with this government in Saigon might very well be a powerful stimulus to Communist propaganda." Gore likewise admitted that the administration's policy "mystifies me a bit," while Gaylord Nelson (D–Wisconsin) called for confronting "the question right now of whether it would be wise to disengage and extricate ourselves."[35]

At the same time, though, none of these senators joined Gruening in recommending immediate withdrawal. Bartlett had considered the option in a Senate speech the previous autumn, as had George McGovern. But Bartlett's close ties with Johnson prompted him to cease his public attacks, while McGovern, agreeing with Fulbright that the United States could not "simply withdraw," looked for a "more reasonable way" to disengage, such as entertaining suggestions by French president Charles de Gaulle for neutralizing the area. A combination of a disinclination to challenge a president of their own party in an election year and fear of benefiting the PRC further tempered any consideration of withdrawal. McGovern summed up for the group, concluding privately that while "we ought to find a way to disengage ourselves before events overtake us," it was "unfortunately . . . much easier to raise questions than to find the answers."[36]

Although Gruening could do little to resolve the senators' partisan concerns, he directly challenged their contention that withdrawal would aid the PRC. Building on his view of the conflict in South Vietnam as a civil war, he contended that policy toward expansionist communist states such as the PRC or Cuba involved "factors other than those to be considered in the Vietnam situation." The PRC proved the point with its intervention in the Korean War, its invasion of Tibet, and its border war with India, just as the Castro regime had done with its subversive activities throughout Latin America, especially against Betancourt in Venezuela. Countries that repressed their citizens deserved the opprobrium of the United States. Those that subsequently chose to export their dictatorships—whether of the right or the left—were worthy adversaries for a country which remained the "cradle of revolution." Neither of these conditions, Gruening maintained, applied to the forces opposing the United States in Southeast Asia.[37]

With no other alternative in the Senate, Gruening turned to his most reliable ally, Wayne Morse, though cognizant of the personal and tactical reasons that dictated distinguishing his dissent from that of his colleague, since Morse's vanity and prickly personality had alienated a large portion of the Senate. Moreover, reflecting the differences in their ideological agendas, apparent in their divergent responses to the Dominican coup the year before, Gruening and Morse offered quite different arguments against U.S. policy in Southeast Asia. While both strongly criticized the tactics of the military, considered the conflict in South Vietnam a civil war, and were critical of the reactionary nature of the Saigon regime, Morse assigned a higher priority than did Gruening to upholding international law, pointing out the dubious constitutionality of Johnson's policies, and resolving the issue through the UN. Finally, Morse was concerned that Johnson's policy violated the "ideals and morality" of Christianity. (For obvious reasons, Gruening never referred to God or religion in his speeches.) Still, Morse remained a passionate battler: when, in the spring of 1964, CIA director John McCone started "telling everybody" that Johnson could "easily" get a resolution sanctioning his Vietnam policy through Congress, McGeorge Bundy told him to "convert Morse first."[38]

Gruening understood, however, that an alliance with Morse would not produce enough Senate pressure to compel the administration to change its course, at least in the short term. He needed to go back no farther than the duo's joint crusade against foreign aid to confirm the point: only in 1963, by which time opposition to the program had spread to the bloc of "dissident liberals," did the political calculus on the issue change. To achieve a similar result on Vietnam policy, Gruening, as he had throughout his public career, turned to the power of public opinion, seeking to use his position to educate the public about the shortcomings of Johnson's policy. In this process he appealed to another prominent figure simultaneously emerging as an administration critic—Walter Lippmann. The paths of the two men had diverged sharply since the early 1930s. While Gruening had entered government service, become Alaska's governor, and then won election to the Senate, Lippmann had established a reputation as the nation's most influential foreign policy commentator. The foreign policy viewpoints of Gruening and Lippmann derived from quite different intellectual traditions, but once before, in their opposition to Coolidge's Mexican policies, they had joined forces. Now, nearly forty years later, they again agreed on an international matter of consequence. In late May, Gruening extended his "heartiest congratulations" on a Lippmann article which contended that "there has never been a time when a military victory, or anything like a military victory, has been possible" in Vietnam, and recommended convening an international conference modeled on Geneva. Gruening admitted that "there may be some difficulties in achieving" their shared position, "but they aren't comparable to the incredible disasters that will befall us if we attempt to fight this war."[39]

Upon reflection, however, the senator drew back. He had never particularly liked Lippmann, even in the 1920s, and that dislike had grown much stronger in the intervening years, intensified by a moralistic streak never far beneath the surface of Gruening's personality. The senator, who harbored what George McGovern described as an "old-fashioned sense about marriage and morality," expected his associates to respect the bonds of marriage, as he himself had for four decades. Those who did not were not suitable allies. For instance, Stanley McCutcheon, his most important political ally during the gubernatorial period and the man whom Gruening once anointed his preferred successor in the Senate, fell out of favor after he divorced his first wife and married a younger woman. Lippmann was guilty of an even higher-profile indiscretion, having (in the 1930s) become involved in a scandal after an affair with Helen Armstrong, the wife of *Foreign Affairs* editor Hamilton Fish Armstrong. He then divorced his first wife, Faye, to marry Helen. Three decades after the event, Gruening still "couldn't swallow" Lippmann's actions. Although the Alaskan considered Lippmann "very bright," agreed with the columnist on Vietnam, and privately dismissed Armstrong's *Foreign Affairs* as a "dull quarterly which represents the conventional views on our foreign relations," the senator shied away from embarking on a major foreign policy crusade with a man he "couldn't stand."[40]

He thus decided to act unilaterally, using the prestige associated with his position as a U.S. senator to return to his most familiar position—that of a muckraker against imperialism. As with Haiti forty years before, the Alaskan believed that the people would understand that escalation violated traditional U.S. ideals; Vietnam, no less than any other foreign policy matter, was thus an issue which would "largely be settled by public opinion." He continued to maintain that his position already enjoyed strong public support, regularly informing his (undoubtedly skeptical) colleagues that 99 percent of his mail favored his views. Unlike his successful Latin American and foreign aid initiatives, however, Gruening's outspoken opposition to the administration's Vietnam policy only reinforced his isolation. With U.S. troops already on the ground in Southeast Asia and the specter of PRC expansionism looming over policy miscalculations, the Alaska senator's positions seemed dangerously extreme. Bryce Nelson, then an aide to Church, recalled that his boss and like-minded senators, worried about the "strident" nature of Gruening's rhetoric, "did not want to be lumped in" with such a person, "at least initially." His tactics, moreover, reinforced this impression. After a particularly exaggerated claim—that his mail indicated opposition to the administration's course by a margin of at least 300 to 1—one of his sharpest Senate critics, Gale McGee (D–Wyoming), ridiculed the figure. In any event, McGee added, the stakes in Vietnam were too high for the United States "to project its foreign policy with a five-cent postage stamp."[41]

MEANWHILE, Alaskan events intervened to remind Gruening of the importance of maintaining favor with the administration. On March 27 an earthquake measuring 8.4 on the Richter scale struck southern Alaska, devastating Anchorage and causing nearly $500 million in damage. Expecting that his position on the Public Works Committee would ensure favorable treatment from Washington, Gruening privately served "notice that this Senator would not be excluded" from events of importance to his state. As frequently occurred on Alaskan matters, he overstated his case and had to be rescued by Bartlett. Although the administration proposed extending nearly $200 million in federal assistance to the state, Gruening did not consider these funds sufficient. He therefore abandoned his private "needling" and offered a series of amendments providing for even more aid, complaining that with the United States spending so much on foreign assistance, Alaska deserved a generous settlement. The tone of his comments alarmed Democratic leaders: with the administration's measure under consideration, Mike Mansfield bluntly told Bartlett "to get him off the floor or we're not going to get this through." Bartlett did as instructed and the bill passed; the episode did nothing to improve relations between the two colleagues. Bartlett, grateful to Johnson for acting as quickly as he had, was also concerned that Gruening's outspoken opposition to the administration's Vietnam policy would further alienate the president.[42]

Also in the balance at this time was the fate of the Rampart Dam, challenged by Interior Secretary Udall's delaying tactics and a well-organized coalition of environmental groups and Indian organizations. Complaining that "the campaigners against Rampart have no scruples" (a comment which many involved in the issue contended more accurately applied to him), Gruening concentrated his fire on "extremist" conservationists who exhibited more concern "for a nesting duck and an anadromous salmon than for the economic welfare of a multitude of people." True to his general tendency, he attributed the basest of personal motives to his opponents. After one environmental activist complained that Rampart would devastate duck breeding grounds, the senator privately asserted that "the only reason some of these people want to preserve the duck breeding grounds is so that they can shoot the ducks as they fly over the other states." Again failing to recognize that extreme and unsubstantiated claims could backfire, Gruening, without foundation, recalled his battle against the Smith-Carlton bill in the 1920s and alleged that "one new ingenious method for sabotaging public power projects is for private utility employees to infiltrate conservation groups, and, as fervent conservationists, to oppose construction of a given dam—if Federal—by viewing with alarm the possible peril to fish and wildlife."[43]

Forced to resort to such desperate claims, the senator unsurprisingly continued to lose ground. In June, the Fish and Wildlife Service delivered what he admitted was a "devastating blast" against Rampart, contending that "nowhere in the history of water development in North America have the fish and wildlife losses anticipated from a single project been so overwhelming." Unsuccessful in his search for a "competent biologist or group of scientists" to counter the report's criticisms, the senator made the case himself, announcing that "experience with other great river development projects has shown an improvement of wildlife habitat and of recreational values as a result of these programs." Privately, however, he revealed his true beliefs: even if the conservationists were correct that the construction of Rampart would result in the extinction of a variety of species of salmon, ducks, and beavers, "it would not be a major loss." Gruening fared better with more conventional tactics. The Bureau of the Budget, conceding that the senator "obviously has been very active," noted that the Army Corps of Engineers, to which Udall referred the matter, "is under maximum pressure by the congressional delegation, headed by Senator Gruening, to produce a favorable report." The project thus remained alive, though just barely. As one contemporary recalled, Gruening "never stopped," pressing forward in "whatever ways were available to him." This persistence, combined with his knowledge of the locations of "lots of skeletons" at the Interior Department, made him a formidable advocate. But with Udall enjoying consistent support from the White House, the odds were stacked against the senator.[44]

Neither Vietnam nor Alaska, however, was the focus of attention in the nation's capital during the summer of 1964. Instead, the talk of the Washington political class centered on the president's civil rights initiatives and the political maneuvering in advance of the two parties' national conventions. Fulfilling a long-standing goal to offer himself as a national politician, Johnson introduced a bill to strengthen the enforcement procedures of previously enacted school desegregation and voting rights measures. The most ambitious such offering since Reconstruction, it unsurprisingly triggered determined resistance from southern senators. Gruening warmly backed the legislation, and the seventy-seven-year-old actively participated in the successful attempt by northern and western senators to break the southern filibuster. (Dorothy commented that the "civil rights bill matter makes planning so difficult for Ernest" in scheduling their dinner parties.)[45]

Fittingly, however, the senator passed his time during the eleven weeks of debate poring over the most recently published works on the history of the conflict in Vietnam, such as Bernard Fall's *Two Vietnams*, which Gruening considered "invaluable to anyone who wants to understand the present mess there." He spent summer days when the Senate was not in session sunning himself on his back porch in khaki shorts, reading everything he could find concerning Vietnam, discussing the war over drinks with visitors. Although by this stage he had been an outspoken critic of administration policy for several months, Rusk's attack had prompted Gruening to devote his full attention to Vietnam prematurely. He recognized that he lacked the detailed knowledge that he could draw on when commenting on Latin American matters. Ultimately, Gruening never did establish an expertise in Southeast Asian affairs; like his foes in the administration, he interpreted events in Vietnam in terms of a preconceived ideological agenda rather than a nuanced understanding of the region's political and social realities.[46]

On the political front, with no major elections in Alaska, Gruening focused on the scramble for the Democratic vice presidential nomination. In the early summer, he joined Gaylord Nelson, George McGovern, and Daniel Inouye (D–Hawaii) in promoting Hubert Humphrey's vice presidential candidacy, looking to counter what the Alaskan privately termed Robert Kennedy's "tremendous campaign" for the position. In a reflection of his unease with the legacy of John Kennedy's administration, Gruening continued to criticize Robert Kennedy after he decided to run for the Senate from New York, charging him with using the campaign as a stepping stone to the presidency. "If successful," Gruening feared (revealing not only his personal dislike for Kennedy but also his more long-standing concern about the political effects of his own less-than-handsome appearance), "it will mean that any glamorous figure with plenty of money can run from any state." Privately he rooted for the reelection of the GOP incumbent, Kenneth Keating, with whom he had developed a warm personal relationship because of their support for liberalizing access to birth control.[47]

In the midst of this political maneuvering, in early August a confused naval skirmish on seas scarcely any American had ever heard of—the Gulf of Tonkin—brought the nation's attention back to Vietnam, setting into motion a series of events which would transform the nation's history and Ernest Gruening's place in it forever. On August 2, North Vietnamese patrol vessels fired on the destroyer *U.S.S. Maddox* after South Vietnamese patrol vessels had bombarded two islands off the North Vietnamese shore. Two nights later the *Maddox* reported another attack, although the ship's commander, Captain John Herrick, conceded that "freak weather conditions and an over-eager sonar man" might have accounted for the supposed sightings of North Vietnamese vessels. Two hours after the event, however, such doubts were not apparent in deliberations in Washington. Johnson had been anticipating such a contingency in any event. Earlier efforts to persuade the president to introduce a resolution authorizing the use of force in Southeast Asia had failed to come to fruition owing to Johnson's fear, in the words of one administration official, that "Morse and Gruening would have fought it, and stirred up a big debate about the war." Now, however, with the North Vietnamese themselves having initiated hostilities, the president was free to act; he sent to Congress a bill allowing him to "take all necessary measures to repel any armed attack against the forces of the United States and to prevent further aggression." The House unanimously passed the measure, while its fate in the Senate, with Fulbright and Richard Russell serving as its floor managers, never was in doubt.[48]

Unlike the overwhelming majority of his colleagues, Gruening considered the Tonkin Gulf Resolution a dangerous expansion of executive authority. He also feared that the measure could lay the groundwork for increasing the level of U.S. involvement in Vietnam. He therefore resolved to oppose the bill as strongly as he could. He admitted the difficulty in opposing a presidential request, "especially one which is couched in terms of high principle and national interest." But the Alaskan pleaded with his colleagues to defend the ability of senators to express views embodying "doubts or dissent." For Gruening, the resolution's supporters overlooked a series of important facts: that the United States, without assistance from its allies, was continuing a colonial war initiated by the French; that peace could not be established by military means; and that given the policies of Diem and his successors, the "allegation that we are supporting freedom in South Vietnam has a hollow sound." He returned to the central themes of his earlier dissents: that the resolution represented "an inevitable development of the U.S. steady escalation of our own military activities"; that the public was "overwhelmingly committed to a different policy"; and that "all Vietnam is not worth the life of a single American boy." The Alaska senator worried that by voting for the resolution, dissenters might lead the public to conclude that a consensus existed among top policy makers about the wisdom of Johnson's policies. The vote therefore represented a critical test: Senate skeptics needed to have faith that the public would rally to defend traditional American ideals. As had been the case over the previous five months, however, this stance only confirmed the ideological and political gap separating Gruening from the rest of his Senate colleagues. The resolution sailed through the upper chamber by a vote of 88 to 2.[49]

In the end, only Morse stood alongside Gruening. Later admitting the difficulty of the choice in an atmosphere of patriotic fervor, the Oregon senator presciently characterized the resolution as an affront to constitutional propriety, indeed a "predated declaration of war." Other Democrats, however, were swayed by the two arguments presented privately by both the administration and Fulbright—that the requirements of the Cold War dictated congressional unity and that an overwhelming endorsement would help the president politically in his fall campaign against Barry Goldwater. Gruening tried to counter this logic with pragmatic political arguments, contending that Johnson could lose in November only by escalating U.S. involvement. Polling figures, however, contradicted such claims: Johnson's approval rating jumped thirty points, from 42 percent to 72 percent, after the retaliatory raids. As McGovern later recalled, other Senate Democrats considered Gruening's interpretation of the national political climate "just wrong"; Consequently, no one "really sympathized" with the Alaskan's approach to the issue. Johnson himself was especially unwilling to forgive. Shortly after learning of the Senate vote he exploded. "He's no good," the president said of Gruening. "He's worse than Morse. He's just no good. I've spent millions on him up in Alaska," Johnson complained, but could not count on the senator to vote with the administration on a matter of pressing national security. No comment better captured the different conceptions of politics held by Johnson and Gruening.[50]

In the months immediately following the August vote, few senators reconsidered their decisions. While Barry Goldwater, the Republican presidential candidate, recommended a massive bombing effort against North Vietnam, Johnson expressed his opposition to supplying "American boys to do the job that Asian boys should do." Typifying views among Senate Democrats, McGovern concluded that "Johnson was clearly preferable to Goldwater not only on the Vietnam issue, but on everything else" and decided to cease public criticism of the administration's Vietnam policies altogether. Under the pressure of the campaign, some senators generally sympathetic to Gruening's point of view in international affairs even retreated from previously expressed positions. Stephen Young, for example, engaged in a tough reelection fight against Robert Taft, Jr., praised the administration's determination to "prevent the Communists from sweeping down and taking all of Southeast Asia and the Philippine Republic and other parts of the free world."[51]

IN NOVEMBER, Johnson trounced Goldwater to win election in his own right, carrying forty-four states and capturing 61 percent of the popular vote. The passing of the election and the inescapable signs of a continuing U.S. escalation finally prompted a wider Senate debate on Vietnam policy. In early 1965, Church, McGovern, and Nelson all publicly questioned Johnson's policy.[52] But there were limits to their dissent: all three opposed an immediate withdrawal and supported retaliatory bombing raids against North Vietnam. Gruening accordingly judged that they had framed their dissent "so moderately that it means little." Ideological and tactical concerns continued to separate the Alaskan from other Senate critics of the conflict.[53]

These differences, however, paled in comparison with the ideological gap separating the Alaska senator from the White House. In early February 1965, after NLF forces attacked a U.S. helicopter base in Pleiku, Johnson authorized Operation Rolling Thunder, which by the end of April had resulted in 3,600 bombing sorties over North Vietnam. This further escalation strengthened Gruening's conviction of the need to mobilize the public against the war. From 1965 onwards he embraced an activist conception of his role as a senator, turning his attention to public speaking appearances against the war, even at the cost of scanting his formal duties in the Senate. His 1965 attendance record, a weak 79 percent, was the lowest of his career to date; in 1966 it plunged further, to 60 percent, the third lowest of any member of the Senate. He especially targeted college youth, reasoning that if he could not persuade policy makers, he would attempt to reach the next generation's elite. In the first few months of 1965 alone, Gruening bypassed roll call votes to appear at teach-ins or lectures at the University of Alabama, Hofstra, UCLA, Berkeley, the University of Miami, Albion College, and the University of Puerto Rico, in public protests in Washington, Chicago, and several times in New York City, and in debates from Des Moines to Laurinburg, North Carolina.[54] When challenged by some constituents for being "so busy running around the country speaking to college and university students" that he was neglecting his formal responsibilities, he described shaping public opinion as an equally important part of his job. Moreover, Gruening had always enjoyed public lecturing. Nonetheless, he was not at his most effective in his crusade against the Vietnam War. As McGovern later noted, Gruening "hated [the conflict] with such a passion" that he "couldn't contain himself," and offered instead increasingly extreme statements about U.S. policy. In many ways, the South Dakotan concluded, the "war became an obsession with Ernest Gruening."[55]

Some of his efforts to mobilize public opinion demonstrated remarkable connections to Gruening's dissenting past. April, for example, featured what the *New York Herald Tribune* termed an "unprecedented debate" between the senator and William Bundy, the recently appointed assistant secretary of state for East Asian affairs. Tension existed even before the proceedings began. When, during the sound check before the debate, the senator intoned, "Now is the time for all good men," Bundy finished the sentence: "to come to the aid of their party." The assistant secretary then turned to Gruening, smiled, and added, "and that means Democrats." Gruening, described by one observer as "a small man behind a forest of microphones, with an old, strong, and amiable voice," was not amused. During the debate he stressed his usual points; as Bundy later recalled, the two men essentially talked past each other. Gruening had long since given up hope of winning over the administration, while the administration considered the Alaskan so "unreachable" on Vietnam that it made no attempt to convert him on the issue.[56]

Even though his own conduct during the early stages of the Cold War and his skittishness while in the Senate over supporting reductions in the Pentagon budget illustrated how severely the Cold War had weakened foreign policy dissent, Cold War ideology never coopted Gruening's central foreign policy principles, as his opposition to Vietnam demonstrated. While policy makers employed Wilsonian rhetoric to justify their Southeast Asian initiatives, Gruening used more traditional dissenting principles to challenge mainstream policy in the region. In a way, though, this development impaired his effectiveness by preventing him from recognizing that many policy makers considered the ideology of the Cold War a reflection of the country's cardinal international principles. Because he essentially could not understand his opponents' agenda, he failed to address their central arguments coherently. Bundy in this sense correctly realized that he and Gruening were operating on different levels at the debate.

The New York reform activists in the audience had no doubt which side prevailed in the exchange; Gruening at one point had to ask them to refrain from applause so he could finish his presentation. Murray Kempton of the *New York World Telegram* spoke for the majority in praising Gruening's articulation of a "conception of the national honor which he has the strength so matter of factly to express at a moment very like a time of war." In attendance, Freda Kirchwey, a former associate from *The Nation*, "was suddenly jerked back to those early twenties when Gruening was denouncing in the pages of *The Nation* the same—exactly the same—acts; only then it was Haiti and Santo Domingo." Likewise, upon hearing of the debate, Hubert Herring, a colleague in the campaign to prevent U.S. intervention in Mexico in 1926 and 1927, detected links between the principles of Gruening's Vietnam dissent and the pair's earlier crusades in the Caribbean Basin. The senator himself shared the sentiment, noting privately that he believed his international viewpoint had not "modified except by being intensified with the passage of time."[57]

These principles prompted Gruening to depart from most other prominent politicians in his opinion of public protests against the war. Pro-war forces obviously had little good to say about such demonstrations; Robert Byrd termed them "senseless, diabolical, abominable, disgraceful, and hurtful," while Dwight Eisenhower lamented the "moral deterioration" of America's youth. More striking, however, was Morse's opinion that the anti-war rallies failed to "help the cause of peace," or that of Nelson, who described them as "absolutely disgraceful." Gruening, by contrast, praised the protesters, contending that "there is no higher form of patriotism than to try to guide their country with appeals to each individual's conscience." At the same time, though, the senator failed to consider the extent to which the tactics and agenda of the more radical protesters were creating a public backlash against the anti-war position.[58]

Gruening, however, did attempt to persuade the conflict's more extreme opponents of the merits of his approach to international affairs. In April 1965 he was the sole member of Congress to address a Washington rally of sixteen thousand sponsored by the Students for a Democratic Society (SDS), the most controversial of the major anti-war organizations. On the eve of the march, a host of moderate peace activists repudiated the event, concerned that the SDS's inclusion of communist and NLF sympathizers would allow conservatives to portray all anti-war activists as pro-communist. But Gruening went forward with his appearance, rationalizing it as another element in his campaign to influence the younger generation. Before an enthusiastic audience, the senator called for an immediate "cessation of our bombings in North Vietnam" and an international peace conference. Most speakers at the rally agreed with these proposals. Gruening then asserted his belief that the United States "threw away" an opportunity to make Southeast Asia a "showcase" for translating its anti-imperialist heritage into practice when it supported a reimposition of French colonialism following World War II.[59]

Despite his favorable reception, Gruening's hope that opposition to the war would bring the United States around to his own ideals failed to carry the day. The highlight of the rally was not Gruening's speech but rather that of the organization's twenty-five-year-old president, Paul Potter, who claimed that the war "has provided the razor, the terrifying sharp cutting edge that has finally severed the last vestige of illusion that morality and democracy are the guiding principles of American foreign policy." To strong applause, he implied that the United States, as a capitalist country, could not pursue a moral or idealistic course in international affairs. While with the protesters, therefore, Gruening was not among them. They were united in their view of the war in Vietnam as immoral. But they offered fundamentally different analyses of the role that the United States might play in world affairs. At the most basic level, the radicals repudiated American traditions, seeing the United States as decadent, exploitative, destructive, and hegemonic. Gruening instead viewed the American past as a struggle to realize the country's finest ideals, and thus embraced the tradition of American dissent that sought to fashion community—both domestically and internationally—based on principles of liberty, self-determination, and anti-imperialism. An intellectual alliance between the senator and the radical anti-war activists was doomed from the start.[60]

At the same time, Gruening's passion overrode his usually keen ability to frame his dissent in such a way as to make it politically appealing to those of more moderate views. The liberal *New York Post*, for instance, denounced him for helping to turn "the march into a one-sided anti-American sideshow." Pro-war Democrats, McGovern recalled, considered him a "gentle, likable old man who was a little out of touch with the realities of international politics." As always, citing his age allowed opponents to dismiss the senator without addressing his arguments; as his Utah colleague Frank Moss noted, Gruening's frenzied pace and keen intellectual abilities allowed him to handle the issue "very well." The Alaskan also succeeded in distinguishing himself from the egotistical Morse, being "regarded as a more sober and thoughtful man." Still, even senators who questioned Johnson's policies believed, in McGovern's words, that "it was a more practical course to show one's disagreement with the war by not hammering the administration so hard personally." They instead urged a negotiated settlement that would not require the United States to admit defeat. Gruening considered this outcome insufficient, contending that only through such a concession could the United States redeem its honor and restore its international image.[61]

The senator also did not share his colleagues' ability to decouple their ideological agendas from their personal relationships. Fitting a long-established pattern, then, his Vietnam dissent shattered the already tenuous ties between Gruening and Johnson. By this stage, most administration figures were ignoring Gruening. Johnson, however, took the senator's criticisms personally. The president shared Gruening's belief that the adverse "reaction on the Hill" suggested a lack of public support for his Vietnam policy. Moreover, fretful that his "Congressional support was very uncertain and wobbly" and liable to disintegrate rapidly under the pressure of "speeches by Morse [and] Gruening" and hostile statements by other skeptical senators, he launched an "intense personal campaign with sympathetic senators [to] get them on their feet." As part of this effort, the president called the Alaskan aside at a White House function in early 1965 to say that Morse's behavior did not surprise him, given the Oregon senator's loose party ties. But he could not understand how Gruening could engage in such fierce attacks against a Democratic administration. Johnson obviously did not know of Gruening's self-conception as an independent progressive, and in any case the Alaskan was in no mood to compromise. The president then turned confrontational, telling Bartlett that he "would be damned if he appointed" any Gruening supporter to a prominent administration post. He implemented this threat by blocking a bid by Bartlett and Gruening to move George Sundborg into an open assistant secretaryship in the Interior Department. By mid-1965, the White House was also bypassing Gruening's office when announcing federal projects for Alaska.[62]

Gruening, however, did not respond to the pressure as the president had anticipated. The same combination of age, independence, and supreme self-confidence that cast him as an outsider in the Senate also made him all but impervious to attempts to silence him on Vietnam.

Indeed, as he told one friend, the confrontation caused him to enjoy his Vietnam dissent all the more because he now knew that "it drove Lyndon Johnson crazy." Sundborg recalled that his boss and the president quickly became "personally bitter" toward each other as a result of the war. Given Gruening's tendency to personalize policy disputes (a habit which Johnson shared), the split between the two men was all but inevitable.[63]

In part to avoid this fate, other Senate critics of Johnson's policies continued to reject Gruening's tactics. As Church privately noted, "Morse and Gruening may be right, but they have been written off, and so exercise no influence on a future course of events." The Idaho senator confided to McGovern that what guided his strategic approach was a hope "that we can and will continue to make our influence felt." He was "convinced that it will avail nothing to shoot against the wind," since "the game depends entirely on how the president may be induced to move." Church even speculated that "once freed of Vietnam, it is possible that Lyndon Johnson will be much less inclined to follow the counsel of those who call for American troops every time a civil war in some remote little country seems not to be going our way."[64]

INDEED, it still seemed possible that Church might be right. On April 7, hoping to quiet the growing criticism, Johnson delivered a major address at Johns Hopkins University in which he declared his willingness to enter into "unconditional discussions" to achieve peace. (He then qualified the statement by conditioning any settlement on "an independent South Vietnam.") To "replace despair with hope and terror with progress," Johnson also offered to fund a $1 billion development of the Mekong River delta if the North Vietnamese ended the war. For five days in early May, the president took a step toward implementing the ideals outlined in the address by halting the bombing of North Vietnam. Most Senate dissenters warmly welcomed these developments. Church, Gore, Young, McGovern, Joseph Clark (D–Pennsylvania), and Eugene McCarthy (D–Minnesota) all publicly praised the address, which Church maintained vindicated the strategy of "those of us who have tried to influence policy by tempering our criticism with restraint." McGovern later admitted, however, that while Johnson's gambit "effectively throttled . . . the questioning type of dissent," it did not persuade Morse and Gruening.[65]

Gruening, indeed, had nothing but scorn for what he termed Johnson's "very phony performance." In retrospect, it appears that the Alaskan interpreted the president's remarks in a much more sophisticated fashion than had his colleagues. He correctly noted that Johnson's insistence on "a free and independent South Vietnam . . . tragically and unwarrantedly" disregarded the terms of the Geneva accords. With this point as a basic U.S. demand, no chance existed for successful negotiations. The senator also dismissed the Mekong Delta development proposal as nothing but a "bribe": however much the administration wanted to cloak its aggressive actions with talk of massive economic aid, "the disguise is too thin."[66]

The only tangible effect of the address on Gruening's foreign policy perspective came in his reevaluation of his perspective on foreign aid. Through early 1965, despite his often intense criticism of the program, he continued to entertain, as he had in the 1930s, the possibility of positive U.S. action to assist the cause of reform overseas. During his 1964 visit to South America, for instance, embassy staffers with whom he came into contact regularly expressed surprise about his abstract commitment to the program's principle. But after the president's transparent attempt to salvage the administration's Vietnam policy by promising economic assistance, Gruening returned to his 1920s framework, in which the U.S. government itself stood as the chief barrier to international reform. Given such a position, abandoning the foreign aid program entirely represented an alternative worthy of consideration.

Gruening's dismissal of what seemed like a genuine peace overture attracted its share of criticism. Columnist William S. White lambasted the "largely Democratic left-wing that recoils from the use of force anywhere, for any reason, however honorable," while the president himself privately dismissed Gruening and Morse as senators who would "duck their tails and run." In the increasingly charged atmosphere of the nation's capital, other critics of the war, such as McGovern, also came under attack. (Since the Alaskan characterized McGovern's dissent as "always minor," he offered little sympathy, and instead expressed frustration with "those who cry 'peace, peace,' and support the escalation of the undeclared war.") Gruening also became the target of personal barbs on the Senate floor. Gale McGee responded to the Alaskan's constitutional theories by expressing his doubt that "the times afford us the luxury of a semantic debate over the meaning of 'war.'" The Wyoming senator, a history professor before entering the upper chamber, contended that history, not specific decisions by individual policy makers, best explained the administration's policies. This comment provided too much of an opening for someone with Gruening's debating skills to resist. The Alaskan mockingly replied that such reasoning constituted the first time he "ever knew that history had that kind of motive power." Furious, McGee retorted that "history creates events that even Republicans and Democrats, or the Senator from Alaska, sometimes cannot control."[67]

Confident that he held the upper hand in any debate with the Wyoming senator, Gruening enjoyed give-and-take with the likes of McGee. He knew from his own newspaper experience that such exchanges stood a good chance of getting press coverage. By the late spring of 1965, however, more ominous opposition to the senator had developed, in Alaska. Accurately sensing that his position would offer no political benefits in a state where 66 percent of the population had some tie to the military, Gruening steered clear of the issue when back at home, stressing instead his success at obtaining federal patronage projects for the state. His prominent position, however, inevitably drew local attention, and in late April, Gruening privately noted that "things are warming up." First, the *Anchorage Daily Times* and the *Fairbanks Daily News-Miner* ran editorials critical of his opposition to the war. Then William Egan joined the fray. The governor termed it "regrettable" that "there are those who believe that our United States of America should stand idly by and permit the North Vietnamese to insidiously pursue their terroristic acts." The next day Ted Stevens, comparing Gruening to the appeasers of the 1930s, asserted that no man had more harmed U.S. security and international prestige than Gruening, with "his incessant attacks upon our foreign policy." Gruening sensed "an organized campaign" which was "no doubt White House inspired," a sentiment shared by the less emotionally involved Bob Bartlett.[68]

Gruening's estrangement from Bartlett, still the state's most popular politician, compounded his local difficulties. Disagreement over Gruening's Vietnam tactics noticeably heightened the existing tension between the two. Bartlett, who remained close to Johnson politically and personally, did not consider harsh public condemnation of the president proper, especially after Johnson's assistance following the Alaskan earthquake. Others in Alaska shared this sentiment. Despite widespread respect for Gruening's intellectual abilities and his role in the statehood campaign, more and more Alaskans, especially those new to the state, began to worry that his ideological crusades were interfering with his ability to protect the state's interests. Gruening's Vietnam dissent thus compounded a problem which predated 1965. Robert Atwood noted that most Alaskans had wanted a senator who would concentrate on fighting the state's battles against the federal bureaucracy, as Gruening had done during his stint as governor. Instead, they got a senator with "world problems always in his mind," even, apparently, at the expense of Alaska's needs.[69]

As the attacks from Alaska grew more pronounced, developments in Washington once again illustrated the senator's extreme position on the war. In early May 1965, Johnson submitted a $700 million supplemental appropriation measure for materiel for troops already on the ground. Lest anyone miss his point, the president asserted that an affirmative vote would endorse "our effort to halt Communist aggression in South Vietnam." Faced with the choice of voting for the appropriation or opening themselves up to the charge of denying equipment to troops in the field, all but three senators supported the president. Gruening unsurprisingly was among the three, alongside Morse and Gaylord Nelson. But he justified his course of action in an unusually defensive forty-minute address designed mostly to neutralize expected attacks on his vote. He took special care to note that he yielded "to no one" in the intensity of his "opposition to the international Communist conspiracy." Such comments had been standard fare during his years as governor, but by 1965 they were very much out of character.[70]

The Alaskan also looked to exploit an almost simultaneous international development to provide political cover. In the process, he took the most contradictory action of his Senate service, compromising principle for political advantage in the area of his greatest expertise, the Caribbean Basin. As Gruening started coming under criticism at home, the Dominican Republic returned to the headlines after a pro-Bosch revolt broke out within the Dominican military. On April 27, when U.S. ambassador Tarpley Bennett reported that the instability threatened American citizens in Santo Domingo, the president sent in 22,000 Marines to restore order. Although Johnson offered the need to protect American lives as the justification for his action, privately Dean Rusk stated that "our primary objectives are retention of law and order, prevention of a possible Communist takeover, and protection of American lives," in that order.[71]

The Dominican intervention posed a severe dilemma for Gruening. On the one hand, the senator disagreed in private with the administration's actions. On the other, eager to prove his anticommunist credentials, he decided that supporting the intervention might pacify some of his attackers in Alaska. Despite a history of opposing such policies, Gruening gambled on the truth of the administration's claim that an impending communist revolution threatened the lives of Americans in the Dominican Republic. He announced his support of the intervention on May 6, during his remarks opposing the supplemental appropriation for Vietnam. Based on "his longstanding familiarity with Caribbean affairs," he described the intervention as the only alternative to a communist-directed takeover. He publicly reiterated this position the next week. Again asserting that he could "speak with some authority" on the matter, he contended that "the Cold War greatly complicated the operation of the inter-American system" by making Latin America a target for communist infiltration. Privately, however, he continued to condemn the administration for "piling up troops." Such "clumsy, inept" tactical decisions cost Gruening the support of admirers from the gubernatorial era, including Robert Atwood. The two often spoke frankly off the record; Gruening's admission that he had compromised on issues such as the intervention to maintain his political base led the Anchorage newspaperman to view him as a "much smaller man" in the Senate than during his time as governor.[72]

Backing the Dominican intervention represented one facet of a two-pronged approach to shore up his deteriorating political base. The senator also went on the offensive, targeting his most outspoken Alaskan critic, William Egan. Gruening challenged the governor to a public debate on Vietnam, an option for which Egan had little stomach, given Gruening's widely recognized rhetorical skills. The *News-Miner*, attempting to deflect the issue, recommended that "instead of needling Alaska's governor, Alaska's world-junketing junior senator should get to work" on state problems; Egan for his part proposed dates which avoided weekends when the senator planned to return home. Gruening called the governor's bluff, though, and made a special trip back to Alaska to debate on June 5. He also agreed to Egan's demand that the debate occur in a television studio rather than before a live audience.

On the day of debate, the senator began to wonder about the wisdom of his decision. To prepare himself, he scheduled his first Alaskan speech against the war, at West Anchorage High School. The address attracted only 120, filling the auditorium to less than 5 percent of capacity.[73]

The poor reception provided a portent of things to come. The governor—opening with what his foe considered "a violent personal attack"—argued that Gruening's antiwar addresses "comforted" U.S. "enemies." He further scored Gruening for ignoring "the facts as they exist in Vietnam" and demoralizing U.S. troops with his fierce dissent. In contrast to Egan's self-confident approach, Gruening appeared surprisingly low-key. He posited as his central thesis not the immorality of the conflict, the uselessness of the containment doctrine, or the need to preserve traditional U.S. ideals, but the essentially pragmatic argument that "the plain fact is that the policy isn't working—and it won't work." This contention did not move the audience. Later that night the senator privately admitted, "I did not do nearly as well as I should have, . . . partly because I was tired and also disconcerted by the personal nature of the attack." Stunned at having been bested in an arena where he was so accustomed to victory, even Gruening admitted that "Bill won" what the *News-Miner* termed an "unusually bitter verbal conflict." Obsessed by his fear that the debate represented the beginning of an effort that would culminate in Egan's challenging his renomination in 1968, Gruening began trying to demonstrate how his opposition to the war benefited his state, generally by contending that spending for the war reduced funding for Alaskan development projects. Such arguments, however, were too little, too late.[74]

Just as the decision to debate Egan backfired, so too did Gruening's public support for the Dominican intervention. Back in Washington, pro-intervention forces took note of the senator's surprising position. Syndicated columnist Robert Allen noted that the White House was "missing a big bet in not making forceful use of Senator Ernest Gruening to espouse the President's handling of the Dominican problem," since the Alaskan "could be of utmost value throughout Latin America and here at home." The personal enmity between Johnson and Gruening blocked consideration of Allen's scheme, and in any case adopting a higher profile on the issue was the last thing the senator wanted to do, especially as it became clear that Johnson had intervened not to protect American lives but to prevent a restoration of Bosch. Gruening ceased public comment on the Dominican matter altogether after mid-May. Although he denied claims from critics such as I. F. Stone that he had backed the intervention "perhaps to balance off his opposition to Johnson on Vietnam," he implicitly admitted the truth of the charges by not personalizing the controversy, his usual approach when attacked.[75]

The constantly changing administration rationale for the Dominican intervention (by June, Johnson was claiming that before the troops landed, "some fifteen hundred innocent people were murdered and shot and their heads cut off") made Gruening's hasty support even more embarrassing. By September, he had retreated completely, denouncing the administration position as "highly specious," criticizing the failure to work through the OAS, and charging Johnson with secretly wanting to install a military dictatorship. The intervention only confirmed what the senator had remarked to Betancourt about the U.S. response to revolutionary change: "If we oppose any revolutionary movement on the grounds that it is supported by the Communists, we will inevitably find ourselves supporting oligarchies, the military, and reactionaries." The entire experience was "most depressing," especially for one generally so self-confident when addressing foreign policy issues.[76]

As the summer of 1965 drew to a close, Gruening's failure seemed all but complete: the escalation in Vietnam continued unabated; his support for the Dominican intervention had left him personally embarrassed and ideologically compromised; and the erosion of his political base in Alaska persisted. The foreign policy victories of 1963 must have seemed a distant memory. But the senator had no intention of giving up the fight.

~ 8

The Limits of Dissent

THE EGAN DEBATE and the Dominican intervention affected Gruening deeply enough that he abandoned (briefly) his concentration on international affairs. As he had throughout his career when confronted by similar crises of confidence, he threw himself into activism on domestic matters. This move only further exposed the senator's differences with the tenets of postwar liberalism guiding the Johnson administration. As the president spent the early months of 1965 pushing through Congress his domestic program—expanding the welfare state, establishing Medicare and Medicaid, and strengthening the nation's civil rights laws—Gruening's anti-monopoly agenda was out of place. On non-economic issues, the senator more comfortably joined other liberals in according a greater emphasis to individual rights, although even here he focused on unusual topics, such as federal assistance to higher education and the arts and improving public access to information on population control. His passion for the latter issue, of interest since his days as a medical intern, prompted *Life* to hail him as "Mr. Birth Control."[1]

In 1963, Gruening introduced the first congressional bill to promote birth control in American history. It called for increased research in reproductive biology by the National Institutes of Health and the establishment of a presidential commission on population control. Although the resolution never emerged from the Labor Committee, the Alaskan returned to the issue in early 1965 with what he considered a "really quite innocuous" measure to establish an Office of Population Problems in both the State Department and the Department of Health, Education and Welfare (HEW) and to authorize a special conference on the population crisis. The time seemed particularly propitious for such an initiative. With Planned Parenthood already firmly established, 1965 also saw the launching of a more mainstream pro–birth control group, the Population Crisis Committee, under the leadership of retired general William Draper. In addition, the legal barrier against which Gruening had struggled since his days as a journalist crumbled in June, when the Supreme Court, in *Griswold v. Connecticut*, recognized the right of privacy by declaring unconstitutional a law prohibiting the use of contraceptive devices. By the time Gruening's bill reached the Senate floor, it had attracted twelve co-sponsors, including Philip Hart (D–Michigan), a Catholic. Six identical measures were introduced in the House of Representatives.[2]

Despite these positive developments, Gruening never deceived himself that such politically explosive legislation would actually pass the Senate. In 1965, though, he knew that the bill would at least receive a hearing. Ironically, the opportunity flowed from his activism on foreign aid. Since arriving in the Senate, he had remained on the lookout for a slot dealing with international affairs. After forty years of bureaucratic fighting of one sort or another, he recognized openings when they appeared. In late 1964 a shakeup in subcommittee chairs on the Government Operations Committee occurred when Hubert Humphrey resigned from the Senate to assume the vice presidency. Gruening had served on Humphrey's Reorganization and International Organizations Subcommittee, which, although it dealt primarily with domestic matters, authorized his foreign aid investigation in 1962. Even though the subcommittee was set to expire with its chair's departure, Gruening saw an opportunity: if he could not secure a position on an established foreign policy committee, he would simply create one on his own.

In early 1965 he met with Julius Cahn, the subcommittee counsel, to discuss the prospects for the subcommittee's survival. Gruening told Cahn that "to me the foreign aid investigations seem important," though he would "have to do a lot of persuading with John McClellan [chair of the full committee] to keep the subcommittee alive." The Alaska senator also had to tangle with his old nemesis Henry Jackson, chair of the National Security and International Operations Subcommittee, who wanted to consolidate control over all Government Operations subcommittees addressing international affairs. Gruening responded by striking a bargain with Abraham Ribicoff (D–Connecticut), another member of Humphrey's subcommittee, who in only his third year of Senate service did not stand to inherit a subcommittee chair. The Alaskan proposed dividing Humphrey's subcommittee in two, with Ribicoff taking over a new subcommittee to concentrate on domestic matters and Gruening inheriting the Humphrey subcommittee's powers over foreign policy. Ribicoff in turn agreed to pacify Jackson, and in February McClellan approved the request on behalf of the full committee. The Subcommittee on Foreign Aid Expenditures (SFAE), established "to examine, investigate, and make a complete study of any and all matters pertaining to the operation of foreign assistance activities by the Federal Government," thus came into existence under the chairmanship of a senator described by one White House staffer as the leader of the "anti-aid fanatics."[3]

Profiting from the postwar Senate's decentralized structure, Gruening controlled the subcommittee's agenda. But since his subcommittee was created at the very moment when he was experiencing doubts about his international vision, he defied expectations that he would use the SFAE to continue his "vendetta" against the foreign aid program. Instead, Gruening convened hearings on his birth control legislation, despite the bill's scant connection to foreign aid. The Alaska senator offered several broad reasons in support of his measure. As he explained to J. Edgar Hoover, in a vain attempt to obtain the FBI director's support, a "definite correlation" existed "between intelligence and education and family limitation." Gruening added that "large families tend to aggravate the very conditions of the Negro community" which Johnson's anti-poverty campaign was attempting to rectify. If the middle class did not awaken to the political ramifications of the issue, the senator feared, "overpopulation can engulf us all." Such comments mirrored the essentially defensive arguments offered by birth control advocates since Margaret Sanger, while also reflecting a more general concern, which would manifest itself in the Moynihan Report a few years later, about the threat posed by demographic trends to domestic welfare programs. If population control could satisfy a traditional progressive desire to preserve the status of the middle class, it could also prevent the United States from becoming "one vast urban sprawl, . . . an increasingly suburban community from coast to coast," a prospect which made Gruening "shudder." Population control was thus a quality of life issue, since "man needs a little space around him where he can have privacy and release, think and get away from the pressures of life today, at least for a little while." Given the senator's lifelong love of the outdoors, the issue assumed both personal and ideological importance. In its most basic form, Gruening's plea reflected a desire to recapture a lost past embedded in American dissenting ideologies dating from Jeffersonianism.[4]

Gruening's activism on population control offered a glimpse of his domestic framework on issues not associated with the relationship between government and business. The senator focused not on passing legislation but on placing information about population control before the public. Indeed, the opportunity to hold hearings was Gruening's principal reason for introducing the bill. As always, the senator wanted to provide the public with the facts needed to make an informed choice, and, as always, he remained confident about what that choice would be. To "stimulate the public's awareness," he played to the media in all ways possible. Drawing on his own journalistic experience, he instructed his staff to feed information to press contacts, especially from the *New York Times* and the *Washington Post*, understanding that overworked reporters likely would reproduce the supplied information. Less helpfully, at one hearing Gruening explained the virtues of the IUD by waving one before the audience; at another, in hyperbolic fashion, he compared the prestige of the subcommittee's witnesses with that of the signers of the Declaration of Independence, those who ratified the Constitution, and "others whose names were appended to and made possible some of the great turning points in history." These witnesses appeared in thirty-two public hearings in what the *Washington Post* described as "the longest running show on Capitol Hill."[5]

Although the hearings did not produce favorable action on the bill, the senator did achieve his basic goals. The *Boston Globe* commented that "Gruening's hearings have produced probably the world's most extensive collection of information on the population crisis." The *Christian Science Monitor* agreed that "the Gruening hearings fulfilled a much-needed educational function"; it credited "any stepped-up interest by the executive" in the issue to the Alaskan's work. A Philadelphia newspaper columnist perceptively described the hearings as characteristic of this "quietly controversial" senator.[6]

Other initiatives in the summer of 1965 also reflected domestic issues of long-standing interest. Thinking about his father one evening after debating Egan, Gruening admitted that he owed "everything I have achieved to him and his solicitude for our education." As he surveyed the national scene, he worried that the deteriorating quality of the educational system would deny future generations the opportunity for an immersion in the liberal arts. In part, he contended, this problem was part of a broader national neglect of the arts and humanities sparked by the Cold War era's emphasis on mathematics and science. To address the dilemma, the senator introduced a bill to create a National Humanities Foundation, thus permitting the government to aid not only science and technology but also "the other great branches of man's activity such as scholarship, literature, and culture." Claiborne Pell (D–Rhode Island) was thinking along similar lines, and introduced a bill shortly thereafter which ultimately authorized the creation of the National Foundation for the Arts and Humanities. The Alaska senator joined Pell as a co-sponsor, and considered the matter of far more importance than most of his colleagues: without an educated public, his entire theory of politics, reliant on an informed and reform-minded citizenry applying pressure on elected officials, would become inoperative.[7]

Despite his efforts on issues relating to education and birth control, Gruening never strayed far from his preeminent domestic interest: government policy toward big business. The issue appeared in a number of forms during the summer of 1965, most notably in a resolution introduced by Russell Long (D–Louisiana) to preserve public access to patents derived from federally funded research. Disappointed to see so "many Democrats vote against what is clearly in the public interest," Gruening bitterly remarked that the measure's 55 to 36 defeat made it "increasingly difficult to distinguish between Democrats and Republicans." The continuing strength of the Alaskan's sentiments surfaced in his decision to reissue *The Public Pays.* Convinced that "the private utilities are up to the same old game," the senator left the text unchanged from the original depression-era edition, and added only a new preface detailing the attempts of "private utilities and other reactionary groups" to influence public opinion after the 1930s. With his "deep and abiding interest in matters affecting the public interest in the regulation of basic utilities," Gruening continued to urge liberals to devote more attention to the issue. Instead, Democratic divisions blocked consideration of utilities reform legislation throughout the decade. Unlike the Alaskan, most of his colleagues recognized that the economy's transformation rendered policies from the interwar era inappropriate.[8]

On a related matter closer to home, the senator still refused to concede defeat on the Rampart Dam, even though by now his activism on this issue bordered on the obsessive. In 1965, when the Public Lands Subcommittee (which dealt with conservation issues) split in two, Gruening demanded a spot on each of the new subcommittees. When Interior Committee chair Henry Jackson refused, Gruening went ahead and attended meetings of both new subcommittees; so as not to violate a committee rule that limited service to two subcommittees, he dropped out of the Indian Affairs Subcommittee, which he claimed did not deal with issues affecting Alaskan Indians anyway. Jackson eventually caved in. Even the Washington senator realized the futility of battling Gruening on minor bureaucratic issues; as one contemporary noted, "Gruening could get away with murder sometimes, simply because people didn't want to take him on." By this stage, however, Interior Secretary Udall's tactic of delaying a decision on Rampart had essentially killed any chance of its being built. The secretary believed that the project progressed as far as it did only because of Gruening's intense efforts.[9]

DURING THE SUMMER and fall of 1965, the Alaskan's ventures into foreign affairs occurred only in arenas where he was personally and professionally comfortable, such as policy toward Mexico. The previous November he had interrupted a hectic schedule to attend the inauguration of President Gustavo Díaz Ordaz of Mexico, an "important event" which recalled for him his first Mexican presidential inauguration, that of Plutarco Calles forty years before. Still calling for the foreign aid program to assist Latin American reform, he lamented that because Mexico was not threatened by communism, it was not "a high priority for our A.I.D. dollars." The senator, as always, volunteered for service on the U.S. delegation to the Inter-Parliamentary Conference, held in 1965 in Mazatlán. At the gathering, Gruening's background and his fluency in Spanish made him, in the words of Pat Holt, the chief staffer for the U.S. delegation, a "real p.r. asset with the Mexicans." Indeed, he provided the highlight of the event. The "designated hitter" for the U.S. side during the opening speeches, the senator "enthralled" the Mexicans with a lengthy address in "flawless" Spanish about his experiences in the country during the 1920s and his continuing support for Mexican reform. Nevertheless, his idealized version of the Mexican past and present prevented him from realizing the distance between the policies of leaders such as Díaz Ordaz and the revolutionary heritage they claimed to embody.[10]

Few other senators registered any concern with such matters during 1965; Vietnam, not Mexico, was the year's key foreign policy issue. In early summer the administration made its final decision to Americanize the conflict when Johnson authorized increasing U.S. combat forces from 75,000 to 175,000 by year's end, with the possibility of another 100,000 troops in 1966. At the same time, the president deliberately downplayed the policy change in public, concerned that congressional conservatives would use the war as an excuse to block funding for his domestic agenda. Those Senate dissenters who had hoped that quiet pressure would persuade the administration to change its policy nonetheless realized the futility of their effort. Albert Gore found "discouraging" his inability "to halt the constant widening of the war," while Frank Church began to consider abandoning his strategy of "trying to work within the context of the situation." If the situation really became intolerable, the Idaho senator noted, he might even wash his "hands of the whole affair, as Wayne Morse has done, and enter the 'never-never-land' of radically ineffectual dissent." In an even more important change on the Senate foreign policy scene, relations between J. William Fulbright and President Johnson cooled after Fulbright authorized a Foreign Relations Committee inquiry into Dominican policy and publicly questioned Johnson's handling of the crisis. The Arkansas senator then began to alter his views about the wisdom of executive conduct of the nation's foreign policy, to the point of considering the open committee hearings on Vietnam recommended by Gruening eighteen months before.[11]

Encouraged by the heightened Senate opposition to the administration's policies yet fearful of the outcome of those initiatives, Gruening signaled his return to antiwar activism with a series of addresses in

December exploring the roots of the involvement in Southeast Asia. He stressed, however, that his chief concern remained the broader lessons that the war raised, namely, the need to avoid "the role of self-appointed 'citizen fixit,' of world policeman," throwing "our young men into every cockpit in the world where Communist totalitarianism rears its ugly head." Meanwhile, in early 1966, Fulbright's decision to convene public hearings set the stage for the strongest Senate questioning of administration policy to date. The hearings, which attracted a national television audience, featured George Kennan and retired general James Gavin, who both expressed skepticism about Johnson's justification for intervening. But as they also opposed withdrawal, the main ideological challenge to the administration came not from their testimony but from the hostile questioning pursued by committee members Fulbright, Morse, Church, Clark, and Gore. Demonstrating the administration's increasing concern with congressional dissent, Mike Manatos began to suggest ways to "take away completely from the Foreign Relations Committee the spotlight it has managed to focus on Vietnam" while also counteracting the appeal of "the 16 Senators like [Vance] Hartke, McGovern, Gruening, etc. who have no standing as Foreign Relations experts but who are endeavoring to call attention to themselves at the price of aid and comfort to the Viet Cong."[12]

Throughout early 1966, this band of senators frequently met to discuss common strategy. A self-conscious policy of conciliation by Fulbright, who admitted that he found the function of "trying to enlarge and improve" the opposition bloc "a new role, . . . and not a very easy one under our system," facilitated this process: the Arkansas senator frequently apologized for his failure to act more forcefully at an earlier stage. In addition, those senators who were beginning to assume more outspoken antiwar positions showed increased appreciation for Gruening's efforts. McGovern, for example, told the Alaskan of his admiration for "your great moral courage on Vietnam and other issues." Encouraged, Gruening showed more willingness to compromise in the name of group unity than in the past; he wondered whether he might have given up too quickly on using the institutional powers of the Senate to challenge the administration on Vietnam policy. Joined at a February strategy meeting by Senators McGovern, Church, Clark, Young, Nelson, McCarthy, Fulbright, Morse, Lee Metcalf (D–Montana), Quentin Burdick (D–North Dakota), and Vance Hartke (D–Indiana), Gruening offered to withhold an amendment he was considering to prohibit the sending of draftees to Vietnam (on the grounds that a vote on it would show the shallowness of the extreme antiwar opposition), provided that Morse withdraw his amendment to repeal the Tonkin Gulf Resolution. But the Oregon senator, who believed that every member of Congress who had voted for the resolution had "violated his oath of office," refused to budge. The decision illustrated the weakness of the Senate dissenting movement, which McGovern later described as a "general informal arrangement to encourage a continued onslaught on the war." There never was a tightly woven caucus with agreement from its members on ideological positions, tactical questions, or key votes, as had been the case with Gruening's allies, the peace progressives, in the 1920s.[13]

Faced with Morse's decision, Gruening pressed forward with his own amendment, fully aware that it had no chance of approval. He hoped, however, to "provoke the widest possible debate on our entire Vietnam policy." It therefore disappointed him when his initial speech on the matter, a rather dry set of remarks which called for sending to Vietnam troops stationed in Europe rather than draftees, received "negligible" press coverage. Gruening responded with a series of more passionate addresses charging the government with "reaching into every American home, taking our young men as draftees, and sending them to the slaughter in southeast Asia." He claimed that Vietnam exemplified a pattern of U.S. support for "dictators, crooks, and scoundrels of the worst stripe merely because they . . . were anti-Communist." As intended, these comments triggered a response: Russell Long charged that Gruening wanted "what could properly be described as a surrender."[14]

The Louisiana senator additionally observed that his colleague seemed to deliver antiwar speeches "once a day," capturing a growing perception that Gruening had lost all sense of proportion on the issue. Indeed, his hopes dashed by the collapse of unity among his antiwar colleagues, the increasingly frustrated senator spent 1966 pursuing a variety of often extreme initiatives. Some of these attempts, such as his crusade to loosen classification policy, simply fell flat, prompting the senator to complain about how few of his remarks had "been picked up by the daily press or the periodicals, except occasionally in a derisive way." Most often his efforts backfired by making him seem out of touch with the realities of both international politics and mainstream Senate opinion. The amendment to prohibit the sending of draftees to Southeast Asia represented one such issue; his use of the SFAE to attack the military for its handling of Vietnam was another. In March, Gruening opened hearings alleging that the army was disposing of excess materiel which the troops could use in Vietnam. This finding, he claimed, at best raised "considerable" doubts about the Defense Department's management effectiveness and at worst indicated a "systematic fraud and deception" perpetrated by the Pentagon to use an alleged lack of supplies for the troops as a way of increasing its appropriations. Using his prerogative as chair, the senator permitted subcommittee investigators to present their "shocking story" on the first day of hearings, a Friday, and prohibited Pentagon witnesses from appearing until the next Monday in the hopes that the charges would receive sustained press coverage throughout the weekend. Instead, the Defense Department issued what the *New York Times* termed an "unusually sharp rejoinder" accusing Gruening of wanting "the American soldiers in Vietnam to fight with junk"; even the antiwar *Times* chastised the senator for "some exceptionally exaggerated charges." Sensing that he had overplayed his hand, Gruening toned down the level of inquiry thereafter.[15]

These tactics reinforced Gruening's image of having little pragmatic advice to offer on how to end the conflict. The senator tried to dismiss these concerns by arguing that "recommendations for extrication . . . are not the responsibility of those who for years have dissented from United States policy in Vietnam." In fact, however, he consistently offered suggestions, such as permitting conscientious objection for individual wars, with little political appeal. Privately, he even hinted at supporting draft resistance, recalling his interwar flirtation with the ideas of the War Resisters' League. When asked by a parent of a sixteen-year-old who opposed the war what the boy should do if drafted, Gruening responded, "If he feels strongly that this war was immoral and indefensible—a view which I completely share—I would suggest he follow his conscience." The senator instructed his staff to counsel antiwar activists who requested assistance in avoiding the draft, describing such aid as "part of the service that we should render."[16]

Gruening's intense opposition to the conflict in Vietnam also radicalized his overall foreign policy viewpoint. In August the seventy-nine-year-old led a protest of two thousand in Los Angeles criticizing the

United States for both its Vietnam policy and the use of the atomic bomb on Hiroshima. Joined by folksinger Joan Baez, and speaking from behind a platform bearing the sign "Shame America" showing red, white, and blue bombs falling on a cowering nude woman clutching two infants, the senator shouted to the audience, mostly in their twenties, "My friends—keep up the fight—keep on! keep on!" Such actions polarized opinions of Gruening; he was hanged in effigy before an appearance at Ohio State. One headless dummy bore the caption "Senator Gruening Seems to Have Lost His Head," while the other (which retained its head) equated him with Benedict Arnold. Gruening proceeded with his Columbus speech anyway, announcing his "painful" conclusion that the United States was the aggressor in the war.[17]

DESPITE HIS INTENSE COMMITMENT to the antiwar cause, Gruening remained an active participant in debates on European, inter-American, and foreign aid policies. In sharp contrast to his generally rigid and extreme views on Southeast Asia, he offered nuanced and often insightful commentary on these other foreign policy issues. In turn, he preserved his influence, both in terms of framing Senate opinion and through helping to assemble coalitions favorable to his point of view on specific votes.

The SFAE proved especially valuable in this regard. Apart from the fiasco of the Defense Department excess materiel investigation, Gruening effectively used the subcommittee, benefiting from changes within the culture of the Senate in the process. In January 1966, Frank Church commented that by aggravating divisions within the Foreign Relations Committee, the emergence of Vietnam and related foreign policy issues, had left "the role of dissent as well as the advocacy of alternative courses to individual senators," even those not on the committee. Gruening responded by enhancing the position of the SFAE, obtaining both an increased budget and more staff. The senator also persuaded the General Accounting Office to lend the SFAE twenty additional staffers, whom he used for various overseas investigations.[18]

The bureaucratic implications of these moves aroused some concern. Claiborne Pell wondered about the need for the SFAE, given that Gruening's interests and those of the Foreign Relations Committee seemed to center "on the same subject." Carl Marcy of the committee staff agreed, singling out the SFAE and Henry Jackson's National Security Subcommittee for trespassing on the committee's prerogatives in "the field of policy." He argued for strengthening the power of the Foreign Relations subcommittees in response. His deputy, Pat Holt, predicted that failing to check Gruening's power would "likely cause the committee trouble" in the long term. Fulbright, however, allowed the SFAE to mushroom without challenge, a sharp contrast to the Arkansas senator's handling of the Jackson subcommittee. While Jackson, who supported the war in Vietnam and favored maintaining the traditional precepts of the NATO alliance, clashed ideologically with Fulbright, the Foreign Relations chair had come to agree with Gruening on most foreign policy issues, even foreign aid. He privately informed his Alaska colleague that "as I look back on my part in the aid business, I am quite sure that I was mistaken and you were correct on many counts, but I confess that this Administration has departed from what I thought was its policies." Controlling the bureaucratic jealousies of Marcy and Pell formed part of the Arkansas senator's process of atonement.[19]

Having preserved the power of the subcommittee, Gruening used it to delve into topics quite far from foreign aid. The Alaskan had believed all along that the program represented the clearest avenue for Congress to engage in broader commentary on U.S. foreign relations. Political turbulence between the United States and France gave him a chance to prove the thesis. Relations between the two countries had been frosty throughout the 1960s, largely because of de Gaulle's attempts to play a more independent role internationally. Recognizing that this recurring tension could produce a reevaluation of policy toward Europe, Gruening looked to influence developments by quietly expanding the investigation into Defense Department disposal of overseas property into a reconsideration of the future of the Atlantic Alliance. Three study missions to Europe convinced him that it was "clear that an enormous amount of surplus is going to foreign aid," and also, more significant, that the Pentagon had "overdone" its military preparations in Europe. He discovered not just "a vast potential of overkill but of oversupply," the result of a "military binge" which had all but escaped the attention of most in the United States—"including the Congress." After a military briefing in Italy, the senator noted with astonishment that "the assumption is still as it was ten years ago that Russia will attack." He returned home convinced of the need to decrease U.S. military spending in Europe. In fact, Gruening was reconsidering the wisdom of Cold War defense policy as a whole, to the point of reviving the tactic (which he had championed while at the *Evening News*) employed by the peace progressives in the interwar era—protesting the national security policies of the administration in power by voting against the defense budget.[20]

Gruening's second mission to Europe coincided with de Gaulle's announcement that France would withdraw from NATO and his demand that all U.S. troops leave French soil by April 1, 1967. Gruening realized that while the turn of events posed "some very difficult problems," it also gave him a clear opening, since de Gaulle's order transformed the U.S. military equipment in France into surplus supplies, thus undeniably subject to SFAE jurisdiction. The senator argued that the whole affair demonstrated that "NATO is obsolete." The organization had been founded at a peculiar time in international relations, when the USSR seemed poised to invade western Europe and when the Europeans seemed incapable of resisting. Neither condition any longer remained. Moreover, Gruening contended that NATO was actually hindering the U.S. international position since its existence blocked consideration of issues that might allow international relations to move beyond the Cold War framework, such as the political unification of Europe. In addition, the need to fulfill its military requirements provided an excuse to keep U.S. military spending needlessly high. Although several other senators joined the Alaskan in reconsidering the basis of the European alliance, only Stephen Young called for such a thorough abandonment of one of the fundamental policy assumptions deriving from the containment doctrine.[21]

Undaunted, Gruening urged his colleagues to derive broader lessons from the French episode. At the very least, Congress needed to intensify oversight of U.S. bases abroad. It was "evident" that the executive branch had "thoroughly neglected the question of what would happen to our bases in France when the time came for us to leave that country," perhaps owing to "the tendency of our military people to interpret the worldwide responsibilities of the United States as requiring the establishment of permanent bases abroad from which we would not depart in the foreseeable future." The senator predicted that the "forced withdrawal" from France "is likely to be followed by withdrawal from other NATO countries as the changing nature of the Soviet threat . . . no longer requires the maintenance of large forces in Europe."[22]

Gruening's inquiry into European surplus property offered a glimpse of the opportunities which the SFAE provided him. But it came as little surprise that the most ambitious undertaking of the new subcommittee dealt with his area of greatest personal concern: inter-American relations. Since his arrival in the Senate, the Alaskan had urged AID to conduct a single country case study of U.S. foreign aid to determine how the United States could best assist reformers overseas. With the creation of the SFAE, Gruening could implement his ideas unilaterally, building on the information he obtained during his 1964 South American tour. Learning from his experience with the Middle Eastern report, which received little attention because of its breadth and length, he framed the Latin American inquiry as a case study, focused on Chile, which had been touted as the best example of the Alliance for Progress's success.[23]

The resulting report leveled three broad criticisms against U.S. policy toward Latin America. First of all, Gruening claimed that AID, excessively influenced by the postwar experience with Europe, had failed to recognize the differences between Europe and Latin America, notably Latin America's lack of an industrial infrastructure which could be revived simply by channeling funds "in Chile's direction with assurance that they would contribute to that country's long-range growth." Second, the senator attacked the agency for not thinking through the long-term implications of its program. Since the whole concept of foreign aid to the underdeveloped world was relatively new, AID knew "very little as yet about inducing innovations in alien cultures." From his days with the PRRA, however, Gruening had more familiarity with the topic, and he doubted that AID's preference for U.S.-conceived initiatives would succeed. Finally, as he had after the Johns Hopkins address, the senator fretted about the consequences of linking foreign aid with Cold War aims. Knowledge that the United States likely would continue aid out of a fear of communism encouraged recipient nations to "postpone harsh decisions on fiscal discipline and reform."[24]

The senator boasted that the report provided "perhaps the most comprehensive, objective, and factual analysis of the foreign aid program yet undertaken," an analysis seconded by some impartial observers. More important, for Gruening it represented the culmination of three decades of thought, beginning with the PRRA experience, on how the United States could influence affairs in countries with political and cultural backgrounds different from its own. Gruening initially believed that transnational alliances represented the surest path to success. His failure in Puerto Rico, however, underscored the difficulties that could arise when both sides of the alliance were not equally committed to the same program. After his initial backlash against Muñoz Marín, he concluded that Puerto Rico had been best served by developing a reform agenda on its own, thus creating the domestic political base necessary to sustain fundamental change. The United States still could assist in this process, largely by ensuring that its policies did not weaken the position of Latin American reformers. With his dissent over Vietnam intensifying, Gruening returned to a framework more associated with the 1920s. As had occurred in Haiti, Mexico, and Nicaragua during the 1920s, and as was the case with Vietnam, the Dominican Republic, and Europe during the 1960s, he believed that the U.S. government was threatening rather than facilitating international change. Reformers from the United States, then, needed to focus on events at home, fulfilling an essentially negative agenda of blocking harmful policies, such as the military aid program, which Gruening viewed as the postwar equivalent of the Marine interventions of the interwar era.[25]

Gruening thus delivered an unusually perceptive critique of the Alliance for Progress. As often occurred, however, the senator expressed deep disappointment that the report "was much slighted by the daily press, most of which . . . feels that any criticism, no matter how constructive, is an assault" on foreign aid. One impartial observer agreed, commenting on the State Department's relief "that the Gruening Report failed to command any serious attention in the press." In fact, for once Gruening may have underestimated his influence. For instance, while the pro-administration *Washington Post* argued that "some of the broad conclusions of the report seem misleading," it also conceded that "the amount of serious inquiry and research that has gone into this report sets it apart from many blanket criticisms of AID." With even critics offering some praise of the report, it came as little surprise that those closer to his point of view welcomed the Alaskan's findings. The study solidified Gruening's credentials as the most innovative thinker among the Senate dissenters on the issue of aid to Latin America.

Morse cited it to prove his claim that the Alliance was in "disarray." The work likewise was celebrated by Fulbright, Gore, and Church.[26]

GRUENING'S REPORT appeared just as the foreign aid revolt was beginning to gather momentum once again, fueled by criticism of Johnson's Vietnam and inter-American initiatives. The congressional rebels especially targeted the military aid program, succeeding to such an extent that one White House staffer observed, "It is becoming increasingly difficult to equate Military Assistance to the mutual security of the United States, the argument being that this kind of assistance to Latin America and Africa, for example, does no such thing, or does very little." Gruening, of course, continued to attack economic assistance as well, which he characterized as providing billions of dollars to "unscrupulous dictators whose only claim to the taxpayers' dollar is a questionable anti-Communism." Morse, his longtime ally on the issue, agreed, but, unlike in the early 1960s, their rejection of the program's rationale now spread to other Democratic senators. Gore described foreign aid as a combination of "a subsidizing of our own business enterprises in foreign investment" and an attempt to bolster unsavory but friendly local regimes. Even Fulbright, conceding "a change in my views," lamented that "our policies seem to have changed recently," directed more "toward total intervening with force" in other nations' affairs; such policies amounted to a kind of "welfare imperialism."[27]

Views such as these resulted in the foreign aid revolt of 1966 becoming much more polarized along ideological lines than its counterpart earlier in the decade. Under the new circumstances, AID director David Bell realized that "the Senate was liable to do something that was nearly as hostile as what the House had done," making "the legislative process much more difficult than it had been previously." Gruening soon discovered, however, that the new politics of foreign aid also subjected the SFAE to attack from conservatives who had once encouraged the Alaskan's own attacks. Gruening in any case had long attracted resentment from colleagues concerned that he was too active on foreign policy matters for a senator who did not serve on either the Foreign Relations or Armed Services Committee. Conservative senators looked to tap into that sentiment in February 1967, when they rallied around an effort by Frank Lausche (D–Ohio), considered by the White House its most effective ally on the Foreign Relations Committee, to slash the SFAE's funding. But Gruening again prevailed. Although the Ohio senator's efforts resulted in a $15,000 cut, the SFAE retained a $100,000 authorization, more than adequate for the Alaskan's purposes and nearly 50 percent of the Foreign Relations Committee's allotment. Within that committee, another former ally on foreign aid, Bourke Hickenlooper, looked to weaken the SFAE's power by proposing the creation of a foreign aid subcommittee equipped with its own staff. Lack of interest, however, derailed the proposal, leaving the SFAE the only Senate subcommittee devoted exclusively to the issue.[28]

Having survived the latest challenges to its existence, the subcommittee remained at the center of the intellectual and legislative revolt against foreign aid into 1967. The key event of the year was the second Punta del Este conference, designed to update the Alliance for Progress at its midway point. In March, the Johnson administration, acting through Senator John Sparkman, introduced a resolution to obtain congressional approval for any economic aid that the U.S. delegation might promise at the conference. Fulbright, however, was worried about the resolution's open-ended nature. "Increasingly convinced" that Congress was more qualified than the executive branch to set the country's foreign policy agenda, the Foreign Relations Committee chair decided to hold in-depth hearings on the resolution. He invited Gruening to appear as the chief witness.[29]

The Alaska senator did not disappoint his onetime rival. He raised a number of specific objections to Johnson's "inconceivable" proposal during the lengthiest appearance as a committee witness of his life—over three and a half hours. He cited the Chilean investigation for evidence that "large-scale assistance weakens the host country's initiative to attack basic problems"; instead, he feared, "after a time the recipient nation comes to depend on outside aid and to regard it as its right." The Alaskan reasoned that with "disquieting signs of a burgeoning arms race in Latin America," economic assistance only freed up funds for military spending that otherwise would have gone to pressing domestic matters. (This argument appealed to many who usually supported foreign aid, such as McGovern.) Long and friendly discussions followed between Gruening, Fulbright, Gore, and Morse concerning what Gore termed the "fallacious" nature of the "whole concept" of economic aid to Latin America. Fulbright noted that the success of the Mexican Revolution had shown that U.S. "aid is not necessarily the solution to all the problems in Latin America," a point which Gruening heartily endorsed. The Alaska senator added that "an important factor in the excellence of our relations with Mexico is the firm stand that the Mexicans have taken in behalf of their principles," which had forced the United States to "come to respect these principles." After listening to the tenor of the conversation, John Sherman Cooper (R–Kentucky) remarked that "if the President to going to get any support, it is more likely to come from this side of the aisle."[30]

Church then entered the fray. The Idaho senator, long interested in the question of nationalism in the undeveloped world, asked his Alaska colleague to discuss this issue. As he had three years earlier in his letter to Betancourt, Gruening asserted that "most of these countries need a revolution," and doubted that the Alliance's emphasis on peaceful evolutionary change would meet Latin America's needs. This assertion left Church to wonder whether violent upheaval might represent the region's best hope. Gruening concurred, observing that "our colonial forefathers practiced a little violence in our revolution." Again citing the Mexican example, he contended that the United States should not necessarily fear political turmoil in the underdeveloped world. Given the anti-revolutionary climate of the Cold War, this point of view attracted few adherents; the scope of the discussion nonetheless continued to expand. Gruening discussed the findings of the SFAE European investigation, which, anticipating historian Paul Kennedy's imperial overstretch thesis, showed that "we are needlessly overextended" in Europe. Fearing that "we are following the example of ancient Rome," since "our legions are everywhere," he predicted that "this attempt to act as would-be policemen could lead to a similar downfall if not restrained." Gruening lamented that the policy had also caused neglect of the nation's domestic well-being. He for one never considered giving priority to domestic needs "a narrow, selfish program," since "part of the strength of the Nation is . . . in the example that we set to the world." Church, commending the "belief of our Founding Fathers that the great force of this country would be the force of example," seconded the analysis; the Idaho senator did not know "of a single empire that based its influence upon missiles or great fleets of airplanes or vast sums of money poured out on the fringes of its empire that ever lasted." Remarking that the "eloquent" nature of the colloquy would force him to reconsider even his support for multilateral aid, Fulbright praised his colleague for having "inspired one of the most interesting hearings we have had this year." In the short term it helped pave the way for the adoption of a watered-down resolution which one administration official considered "worse than useless." In the aftermath, Walt Rostow proposed using cross-national alliances in a way Gruening never envisioned, recommending that the administration seek the cooperation of governments such as Peru, Chile, Colombia, and Brazil to help "us cope with Congressional pressures on the AID bill."[31]

As the discussion during his testimony against the Punta del Este resolution showed, Gruening was no longer the only senator addressing foreign policy issues from a traditional dissenting viewpoint. Church had anticipated this development a few years earlier in his musings on one of Gruening's first political idols, William Borah. Although the Idaho senator admitted that some of his predecessor's ideas had lost their relevance, Church remained attracted to those premises Borah had "held so strongly which still remain applicable to our life and times," notably "his reluctance to use force as a method of international diplomacy and his refusal to accept any form of imperialism." The dissenters particularly sought to revive what they pictured as the traditionally friendly attitude of the United States toward overseas revolutionary movements. It was no coincidence that McGovern called his opponents "neo-imperialists, who somehow imagine that the United States has a mandate to impose an American solution the world around"; to address these concerns, the South Dakota senator championed returning to the "original American ideal," that is, the "Jeffersonian concept of revolutionary change."[32]

Gruening, of course, had been expressing such sentiments for most of his career. The Alaskan believed that viewing international relations through the prism of a contest between the United States and the USSR had prevented policy makers from recognizing that the United States lacked the power to uphold the status quo through military means. Moreover, he consistently maintained, adjustments to the status quo, even those that employed violence, did not necessarily threaten U.S. interests. More important, Gruening reasoned, this policy weakened the standing of the United States as a symbol to the world. He urged a heightened focus on domestic reform, while recognizing that a U.S.-developed approach toward economic and political issues might not be appropriate for other countries. Indeed, the revolutionary, reformist heritage of the United States made any other foreign policy framework irreconcilable with the country's traditional ideals. In its most elemental form, Gruening's dissent represented an alternative conception of how the United States could wield power internationally.

As was the case throughout his career, though, articulating these ideals was not enough. To translate them into policy, the senator continued to champion cross-national alliances with reformers in other countries. One chance to utilize this framework came in June, at the U.S.-Mexico Inter-Parliamentary Conference. Gruening had long been the senator most passionate about the conferences. In 1967, however, Fulbright, Morse, and Church joined him in the Mexican capital, where the senators, in the words of an administration source, "sharply attacked the Administration in executive committee sessions on Vietnam, the Dominican Republic, Military Assistance in Latin America, and our inability throughout the world to deal with 'revolutionary situations.'"[33]

SHORTLY AFTER THE CONFERENCE, Gruening returned to the legislative battlefront in an attempt to see his vision of inter-American policy triumph once and for all at the expense of the principal Democratic alternative, the Alliance for Progress. It was Robert Kennedy who set the stage. The New York senator, who visited Chile shortly before Gruening issued his hostile report, returned with a different lesson than did his Alaskan colleague: he called for the United States to rededicate itself to his brother's legacy by increasing funding for the Alliance. In August 1967 he introduced an amendment to increase U.S. economic assistance to Latin America from the total recommended by the Foreign Relations Committee, $578 million, to $650 million. Jacob Javits (R–New York) described the stakes: the vote on the amendment stood "as a vote of confidence or no confidence in the future of the Alliance for Progress." Kennedy framed his proposal in terms which sharply contrasted with the anticommunist rationale most frequently used by his brother. He contended that most of the funds would benefit the children of Latin America. Ultimately, he suggested (in words Gruening could have spoken earlier in the decade) that the fight against overpopulation and poverty—not against communism—was the key "battle of the hemisphere." First Fulbright and Morse responded skeptically, then Gruening took the floor. Turning to Kennedy, the Alaskan announced that he did not yield to any colleague in his "longtime demonstrated interest and sympathy for Latin America," a region where his experience "antedates that of any Member of this body." Having reminded his listeners of his credentials, he then faulted Kennedy's reasoning, contending that the amendment assumed an increased U.S. presence in the hemisphere, an outcome he viewed as poisonous to the long-term fate of reform. As an alternative, he pointed again to the Mexican Revolution—"the outstanding example of self-help and progress among the Latin American countries." Sensing a shift in the momentum of the debate, Kennedy returned to the fray to describe his amendment's rationale in very different terms, warning that "almost all of the Latin countries have the potential of becoming so unstable that they would accept a Communist government." Employing a very different set of lessons from the past than had Gruening, Kennedy asked his colleagues to recall the Cuban missile crisis to understand the security risks to the United States that such a development could pose.[34]

Kennedy's resort to such outlandish Cold War rhetoric indicated his desperation. Having helped transform the nature of the discussion on yet another Latin American issue, Gruening watched with satisfaction as the Senate voted down the amendment 53 to 38. Conservative Republicans and most southern Democrats predictably voted no, but a bloc of eight Democrats and one liberal Republican provided the swing votes which sent the amendment to its defeat. Gruening, Church, Fulbright, Gore, Morse, Young, Bartlett, Burdick, and Mark Hatfield (R–Oregon) had all begun the decade supporting more generous U.S. economic assistance to Latin America. In 1967, though, all voted against the Kennedy amendment, sharing Gruening's doubts that the U.S. government could act as a reformist force in hemispheric affairs. In the aftermath, administration sources lamented the "serious psychological effects throughout the Hemisphere" of the vote. For all practical purposes, chances of expanding the Alliance had vanished.[35]

The defeat of the Kennedy amendment showed Gruening's continuing influence on international issues outside of Southeast Asia. But by this stage, as George Sundborg recalled, the senator's "real priority was opposing the war in Vietnam," the ramifications of which affected all aspects of his Senate service. The tension between Gruening and Johnson over the war also manifested itself in the barely concealed hostility between the senator and administration officials in his birth control hearings. Pointing to the lessons of Vietnam, the Alaskan argued that "the Executive Branch must be given direction if it is to progress," while the administration dismissed Gruening's proposals as "mostly window-dressing symbolism." In fact, the intensely personal nature of the dispute made the senator less likely to support the president on any measure. By 1966, Gruening was backing Johnson on only 37 percent of Senate roll call votes, one of the lowest scores in the Democratic caucus.[36]

Foreign policy matters, combined with long-standing personal biases, likewise separated Gruening from the administration on another important domestic issue—policy toward organized labor. While unions remained a key element of Johnson's domestic coalition, the Alaska senator continued to view organized labor suspiciously. Gruening certainly was no friend of big business: the U.S. Chamber of Commerce gave his voting record a zero rating throughout the Johnson administration. But, for a northern Democrat, he also earned poor marks from the major labor lobbying organization, the Committee on Political Education (COPE), which in 1964 gave him a 70 percent score, the lowest tally among northern Democrats; two years later his 75 percent rating ranked third lowest among Democratic senators from north of the Mason-Dixon line. A 1966 machinists' union strike, which resulted in the folding of one of his former employers, the *New York Herald Tribune*, intensified his anger. In strong language, he termed the strike "an American tragedy" caused by "the stupid mechanical departments who are really unconcerned with the real values of a newspaper and a free press." Reflecting a conception of journalism that was growing passé, Gruening denied that radio and television could substitute "for the printed word, which obviously can be read and reread, filed and retained for permanence." The "American people are the losers," he lamented, as "the heyday of the newspaper . . . is coming to an end." Disagreement with the unions' mostly supportive posture toward the Vietnam War only strengthened his dissatisfaction with organized labor. Having "become painfully aware that the labor movement had lost the idealism and wider range of concern that had once characterized it," the senator added "labor" to Eisenhower's "military-industrial complex."[37]

This tendency to interpret domestic events through a foreign policy lens provided another illustration of how all-encompassing Gruening's interest in international affairs had become. George McGovern, one of his closest friends in the Senate, could not recall ever having had a conversation with the Alaskan on a domestic matter. With the exception of a period during his time as governor of Alaska and a few months in 1965, Gruening had always shown more interest in international affairs than in domestic matters. But the difference in the amount of time that he devoted to the two was greater in the late 1960s than at any other point in his life. The combination of the war in Vietnam, the opportunities the SFAE provided to explore a seemingly unlimited range of international issues, and the frustration caused by his domestic defeats led him to concentrate almost exclusively on foreign policy concerns.[38]

On the most important of these issues, the conflict in Vietnam, the Alaskan only grew more isolated as increasing opposition to administration policy from senators outside the antiwar movement appeared, even from Senate Republicans, a development which especially angered the president. In September, after Clifford Case (R–New Jersey) attacked the administration's "misuse" and "perversion" of the Tonkin Gulf Resolution, Johnson instructed aide Joseph Califano to tell Case that "if I want advice like that I'll get it from Morse and Gruening." The growing skepticism presented senators on record against the war with both an opportunity and a dilemma. On the one hand, by mid-1967 perhaps a third of the upper chamber opposed Johnson's policy, making dissent a much less lonely activity than had been the case for Gruening in 1964. On the other hand, the new critics, Republican or Democrat, entertained moderate visions of both international affairs and policy toward Vietnam. Most antiwar senators responded by narrowing the range of options they considered to end the war, with an eye toward attracting the broadest possible Senate support.[39]

Political considerations also dictated a policy of caution, since a number of dissenters, including Gruening, faced reelection contests in 1968. The issue did not affect the Alaskan, who pledged in 1967 that he would oppose the war "whatever may be the political consequences," confident in any case that in the end, public opinion would rally to his cause. None of his colleagues shared this optimism, however. In May, Church penned a public letter encouraging greater flexibility by the North Vietnamese in peace negotiations. He warned Hanoi that "it would be tragic indeed if there were any misconception," but even Senate critics of the war remained "steadfastly opposed to any unilateral withdrawal of American troops from South Vietnam." The statement, which carried the signatures of McGovern, Fulbright, Nelson, Clark, Young, and Morse, attracted widespread editorial praise. As one Church aide put it, the manifesto allowed the dissenters to take a "cheap hawk position."[40]

Gruening declined the opportunity. Privately, the Alaskan acknowledged that the motivation for the letter "seemed to be to get Frank off the hook at home," but his concerns extended far beyond its motivations: he feared that Church's wording "completely endorsed the administration line that Hanoi was the villain and that failure to come to the conference table was Hanoi's." Gruening therefore lambasted the signers for having "abjured unilateral withdrawal," which remained his preferred policy. The whole event confirmed the danger of playing politics with the war. By adopting contradictory positions, critics only allowed pro-war forces to confuse the issue and weaken the ability of the dissenters to appeal to public opinion. Armed with this belief, Gruening took to the Senate floor to correct the "mistaken impression" left when the *Washington Star* listed him as a signatory. He announced that he did not "share the view expressed in that letter that the responsibility for not coming to the conference table is Hanoi's," nor did he believe that it was aggression from the North that had caused the conflict. For good measure, he also denounced White House peace overtures as unrealistic because they denied that "this is a civil war" and likewise offered "incompatible and contradictory solutions."[41]

As Church's gambit showed, most Senate dissenters believed that their opposition to the war would harm them politically. Whenever possible, then, they downplayed perceptions that they had adopted extremist positions. Morse, despite representing a state with an active peace movement, continued—"on moral grounds"—to retreat from his earlier support of unilateral withdrawal, predicting that it "would leave behind us one of history's most ghastly bloodbaths." His denial of ever having supported this option prompted NSC staffers to joke about his suddenly "faulty" memory. McGovern, meanwhile, publicly reiterated his support for military authorizations for the war while expressing his "contempt for those who advocate that young Americans avoid their military obligations." Confidentially, though, he wrote to Gruening that he had "not supported you 100 percent on all your efforts because of the extremely conservative nature of my state and my forthcoming campaign, but my heart is always with you even when I have not been able to vote with you." He also conceded the logic in Gruening's position on the Church statement, but hoped that its issuance at least would give "the lie to those who are charging that it is the critics who are prolonging the war."[42]

Convinced of the importance of consistency, and correctly understanding that minor compromises would not appease pro-war forces by this stage, Gruening departed from his colleagues' approach, adopting instead confrontational tactics when dealing with war-related issues. As 1967 progressed, the administration increasingly responded in kind. In August, Undersecretary of State Nicholas Katzenbach told the Foreign Relations Committee that the combination of the Cold War and the development of nuclear weapons had rendered the congressional right to declare war outdated. After maintaining that the administration would not consider itself bound even by a congressional resolution demanding the withdrawal of U.S. troops, he then taunted the committee by noting that if Congress really wanted to express its displeasure with the war, it could vote against the defense appropriation bill.[43]

The Alaska senator embraced the challenge, reminding his colleagues that Katzenbach had been "kind enough . . . to point out the one means available to Congress to make its opposition to our involvement in Southeast Asia effective." Keeping in mind the findings from his European inquiry of the year before, Gruening then voted against the defense appropriations measure. Although Morse and Young joined him in opposition, other Senate opponents of the war violently disagreed with his move. Fulbright spoke for this group in his refusal to oppose providing "the materiel and the equipment needed by our gallant men who are doing the fighting and dying thousands of miles from home." Gruening's vote obviously ended his pro-military posture from his period as governor. As he had in the 1920s, the senator again considered it tactically and ideologically acceptable to vote against the defense budget as a whole.[44]

This decision, however, clearly weakened his standing in Alaska, the state with the highest proportion of voters serving in the military. Moreover, local politics showed signs of drifting even further from his point of view in 1966, when the GOP captured the governorship, the state's lone congressional seat, and both chambers of the legislature. By

1967, Alaska had three times as many residents as when Gruening first arrived in Juneau; and since the harsh climate and high cost of living discouraged older residents from remaining in the state after retirement, Gruening's patronage efforts from the territorial days were now a distant memory. In addition, the discovery of large oil deposits had attracted emigrants unsympathetic to the senator's faith in government activism against forces of business consolidation, as a 1968 poll, in which three times as many Alaskans described themselves as conservatives than as liberals, made clear. In short, Alaska was becoming an increasingly inhospitable climate for a figure such as Gruening, regardless of how his positions on Vietnam and military spending were alienating him from the state's military voters. Cracks were also appearing in Gruening's political base, notably in the Alaskan Native community. The senator's support for the Rampart Dam and his opposition to what he perceived as the separatist platform of Native leaders caused one activist to accuse him of treating the Native community like "the faithful dog . . . who having been given a few pats and kind words remains wagging his tail, while his master swings a few well aimed kicks at his head."[45]

Despite these ominous trends, the junior senator fully expected to win reelection in 1968, at age eighty-one, by using the same tactics which earlier had brought him success. In Washington, a vain attempt to obtain administration support for his patronage needs prompted Gruening to back the White House on domestic matters about which he cared little, such as Johnson's proposal for public funding of presidential elections. In Alaska, he looked to finesse the Vietnam issue by stressing his ability to bring federal assistance to the state. In addition, the senator continued to frame his dissent differently in Alaska than elsewhere, even while claiming that "the people of Alaska who voted for me expected me to vote and speak in accordance with the dictates of my conscience." He even occasionally—and unsuccessfully—attempted to use his oratorical skills to convert his opponents. His most spectacular failure came at the 1966 convention of the Alaska American Legion, when he spoke against the war for ninety minutes, during which he himself admitted that he "was listened to attentively but silently." Scoffing that "protest has become a way of life for some people," Egan followed with another blistering attack, after which the Legion passed a resolution condemning Gruening's position.[46]

Those on the senator's staff expressed far more alarm than did Gruening himself about how the combination of the state's political changes and his foreign policy record would affect his reelection bid. In 1967, Don Greeley, a former top aide to Congressman Ralph Rivers who joined Gruening's staff following Rivers's defeat in 1966, looked to squelch rumors of a study of the "effect of disarmament on Alaska's economy at this time," fearful of inciting fears that Gruening's antiwar stance would cause the state to lose another of its military bases. Sundborg and Laura Olson, Herb Beaser's chief deputy, joined Greeley in attempting to persuade the senator to tone down his Vietnam dissent in the name of political expediency, as other Democratic colleagues had done. Gruening listened to such pleas politely, and then quietly chuckled. He maintained that Alaskan voters would indulge his foreign policy positions so long as he could prove his ability to deliver patronage for the state. This strategy obviously had worked in the past. It now was left for Gruening to see if his outspoken opposition to the conflict in Vietnam, in combination with his renewed dissenting perspective on a host of other foreign policy issues, would cost him the Senate seat to which he had aspired for most of his adult life.[47]

9

The Frustrations of Dissent

In November 1965, Gruening ended all speculation about his political future by assuring the *Anchorage Daily Times* that only death would prevent him from running for reelection in 1968. In fact, despite occasional private comments to the contrary, he never doubted that he would stand for a third term. Serving in the Senate fulfilled his lifelong ambition, and he was, as one staff member recalled, entirely "absorbed with the job." Retirement did not appeal to a man who believed that "participation from the side-lines" could not provide "a satisfactory substitute" for service in the upper chamber. Moreover, his father "used to reiterate that retirement was the one end of life he wanted to avoid." Emil always said that he wanted to "die in harness." And so he had. His son desired no less.[1]

Gruening's quest for reelection involved occasionally swallowing his pride, as when he asked Bartlett for permission to announce all new federal projects for the state, hoping to gain some good publicity and in the process overcome the White House's tactic of working through Bartlett's office alone. As usual, he showed no hesitation in calling on old friends for assistance. Tom Corcoran sent along a "generous contribution," while William Douglas, even though on the Supreme Court, appeared at a Gruening fund-raising dinner to hail the senator as the "conscience of America." The "only thing" that the former Yale Law School professor could "think of to say *against* Ernest Gruening is that he went to Harvard." For the first time, the senator authorized a campaign biography, while he transferred the politically astute Sundborg to Anchorage to coordinate the reelection effort on the scene. Gruening hoped "to stress domestic and Alaskan issues primarily," with his foreign policy positions appearing only "if and when raised by the opposition."[2]

But no doubt existed that the issue would arise in a state where one poll indicated that 83 percent favored escalating U.S. military activity in Vietnam. In addition, Gruening's outspoken opposition to the war had already triggered substantial negative constituent feedback. A navy sailor wrote the *Anchorage Daily Times* of his embarrassment when his commander denounced Alaska as the most disloyal state in the union because it sent Gruening to the Senate. (Typically, Gruening demanded that the Pentagon investigate the incident and discipline the commander upon confirmation of his remarks.) Nonetheless, the partisan implications of such attacks could not be avoided. Terming Vietnam "a 'gut' issue," one party activist informed the senator that although he had never voted Republican, he could not support Gruening's reelection; a Sitka Democrat likewise accused Gruening of "following the Communist line," and promised to vote Republican for the first time in her life if he were renominated. Although some of this criticism had quieted by early 1968, the senator himself recognized that the silence indicated that his opponents had given up trying to influence him rather than that he had succeeded in changing their minds.[3]

At the same time, however, most in Washington as well as many within the Alaska Democratic Party considered Gruening the clear favorite to retain his seat. As the campaign season got under way, there were no signs of primary opposition, while his strongest potential opponent, Representative Howard Pollock, who had ousted Ralph Rivers in 1966, declined to enter the race. In Pollock's stead, two Republicans maneuvered for the opportunity to challenge the senator—Ted Stevens, the 1962 nominee, and Elmer Rasmuson, the wealthiest man in the state and the former mayor of Anchorage. Gruening correctly guessed that Rasmuson would hold the edge in such a pairing, and did not appear particularly intimidated by the GOP front-runner. Indeed, he privately quipped, he would prefer "a banker for an opponent every time."[4]

Gruening also benefited from the advantages of incumbency. The

SFAE, for example, allowed him to revive his gubernatorial tactic of linking his foreign policy proposals with an Alaskan agenda. In early 1968 the subcommittee launched an inquiry into how foreign aid subsidies to the fishing industries of countries in Northeast Asia were "seriously and adversely" affecting Alaskan fishermen. Though not directly related to foreign aid, the announced plans of Japanese firms to fish for tanner crab in the eastern Bering Sea and off the Pribiloff Islands were also investigated by the SFAE. Gruening urged "aggressive action" from the State Department to protect this "unique resource of the state of Alaska." In contrast to most of his foreign policy crusades, he ensured that his opposition "to any action that will result in increased foreign competition for our fishermen" received the widest coverage at home.[5]

These initiatives did little to dissipate the perception in Alaska that Gruening's foreign policy activism had made him a less effective senator. His refusal to tone down his rhetoric on Vietnam compounded this belief. In early 1968, Gruening returned to his traditional tactic of appealing to public opinion through the printed word. Written to "counter the official propaganda which has so long kept the American people in ignorance of our military involvement," *Vietnam Folly* repeated familiar themes, including the senator's demand for a unilateral U.S. withdrawal. The volume also illustrated the deleterious effects of age on Gruening's muckraking skills. Pressed for time, the senator dictated large sections of the book to his secretaries, an approach which yielded nearly four hundred pages of the most minute detail on the path to the U.S. escalation and two hundred pages of appendixes of widely available documents. The *Library Journal* indicted the book as a "filing cabinet of dates and quotations"; Joseph Buttinger, writing in the *New York Times Book Review*, more accurately described it as "really a gigantic political pamphlet." Given these shortcomings, the senator failed, despite persistent efforts, to have *Vietnam Folly* published in a paperback edition. He did what he could to disseminate his position informally by providing copies to fellow Senate dissenters and by asking friends such as Drew Pearson to plug the book in their columns.[6]

Gruening sustained his criticism of the war in other ways as well. Despite the condemnation he had received on the issue in 1966, the SFAE continued to explore the foreign aid and surplus property programs in Vietnam. His decision not to terminate the investigation paid off in early 1968, after what he described as "intensive investigations" by SFAE staffers uncovered allegations that the CIA knew of smuggling involving high-level South Vietnamese officials. The incident, which Gruening termed indicative of "wholesale corruption on every level" in South Vietnam, proved that "no chance whatsoever" existed that the Saigon regime would reform itself, thus vindicating his calls for withdrawal. The Defense Department issued angry denials, but, unlike in 1966, Gruening did not come under attack for overstating his case. The senator even attracted some rare public praise from his colleagues, as when Frank Church heralded the Alaskan's battle to preserve the moral image of the United States. The Idaho senator maintained that on this point, as on so many others concerning international affairs, Gruening had stated "a proposition so simple that most of the country is blind to its truth."[7]

Church's comment, made in late February, indicated how national and international events suddenly seemed to be moving in Gruening's direction. On January 30 the NLF launched a major offensive against the urban areas of South Vietnam, and for a brief time penetrated the U.S. embassy compound in Saigon. Although the Tet offensive ultimately yielded a U.S. military victory, its political effects were the reverse. Early press reports stressed the attack on the embassy, and the heavy fighting challenged optimistic progress reports on the war. Unable to repair the administration's position, Johnson ordered his new secretary of defense, Clark Clifford, to reevaluate U.S. policies in Southeast Asia. At the same time, the president's political fortunes suffered a severe setback when he barely edged Eugene McCarthy in the New Hampshire presidential primary. McCarthy's showing prompted the more politically formidable Robert Kennedy to enter the race for the nomination. Then, on March 31, Johnson stunned the political community by withdrawing from the race. After the announcement, a jubilant Gruening joined George McGovern and McCarthy's wife, Abigail, in being among the first five people to call the White House to offer congratulations. The president grumbled that he "knew something was wrong when all of them approved." In April, 49 percent of those polled termed the involvement in Vietnam a mistake, a figure which ballooned to 58 percent later in the year.[8]

Developments in Alaska, however, threatened to neutralize the positive political effects of these national and international events. After

Egan's failure to win reelection in 1966 eliminated him as a viable opponent, it was widely assumed that, as in 1958 and 1962, Gruening would receive the Democratic nomination uncontested. Then, only days before the filing deadline, the former speaker of the state House of Representatives, Mike Gravel, announced his candidacy. The relationship between Gravel and Gruening had deteriorated substantially in the decade since their first meeting. Born in Springfield, Massachusetts, Gravel emigrated to Alaska in the mid-1950s. After serving as a volunteer in Gruening's 1958 campaign, Gravel initiated a successful political career in his own right which culminated in his election as speaker during Egan's second term. Sharing with Gruening a transparent ambition, Gravel had no intention of patiently waiting his turn to make the move to Washington. Instead, in 1966 he challenged incumbent Ralph Rivers for nomination to the state's lone House seat. Because of Rivers's support for the war, Gravel hoped for Gruening's endorsement. But, concerned about setting a precedent which could be used against him two years later, the senator privately rebuked Gravel "unmercifully" and worked behind the scenes to secure Rivers's renomination. Rivers narrowly prevailed in the primary, but, weakened, lost badly in the fall election. Meanwhile, word of the senator's maneuvering soon got back to Gravel. Embittered by what he considered Gruening's duplicity, Gravel resolved to challenge Gruening, but kept word of his decision quiet until the last moment so as to lull the senator into a false sense of security. Expecting to win "hands down" on the age issue alone, he opened his campaign by quoting ninety-three-year-old Carl Hayden (D–Arizona), who had announced his retirement from the Senate, remarking that "contemporary times require contemporary men." Thirty-eight years old, handsome, and charismatic, Gravel seemed to personify the description.[9]

Gruening had faced the age issue throughout his political career, and generally handled it quite well. His energy amazed even longtime associates; after spending two days with him, one commentator described him as perpetually "in motion, charged with a life force packed into a small package." Gruening slept only three or four hours per night, supplemented by an occasional brief nap in the afternoon. Such physical attributes were reinforced by a psychological one: since he did not believe in the existence of an afterlife, Gruening aimed to live life to the fullest. Still, the effects of age inevitably surfaced. His appearance became more frail, he grew less patient, and his tremendous pace began to work against him. Don Greeley, who took over as the senator's chief scheduler in 1967 after Sundborg's transfer to Anchorage, tried to set Gruening's key appointments in the morning, when the senator was most fresh. But Gruening loved to talk politics, and, perhaps overly confident that his rhetorical abilities remained on the same high level as in years past, rarely refused an invitation to speak in public, either in Washington or in Alaska. Now past eighty, though, he tired more easily than he once had, and appeared noticeably fatigued at evening gatherings, only compounding the perception that he had passed his prime.[10]

As with Mike Stepovich and Ted Stevens before him, though, Gravel soon discovered that the age issue alone would not defeat Gruening. Gravel's own "maverick" reputation among Alaska Democrats also worked against him. To exploit Gruening's other principal weakness—the perception that the senator did not devote enough time to local matters—Gravel increasingly focused on this issue. Although he once had privately praised Gruening's vote against the Tonkin Gulf Resolution, Gravel later admitted that in the campaign he had "tried to waffle" on Vietnam, "deliberately" seeking the "middle ground" on the issue. As the *New York Times* noted, the challenger paired Gruening's ideological and sartorial idiosyncrasies by portraying the senator as a "senile, cantankerous, doddering dabbler with baggy pants," preoccupied by a "concern with world affairs." In one advertisement, Gravel promised to work for Alaska first, inviting those who preferred to elect a senator for Laos or Thailand to cast ballots for Gruening. Gruening meanwhile overruled the advice of his campaign consultants and instead relied on his traditional campaign style. In doing so he underestimated the changes in Alaskan politics since his previous campaign. Politically, Gruening remained strongest with Alaskans who had been active during the territorial days. By 1968, however, many of his most faithful supporters had died, retired from politics, or left the state, while the vast expansion in Alaska's population meant that the senator's committed band of loyalists no longer formed anything close to a majority, even among the state's Democrats.[11]

Still, as the campaign began to pick up momentum, it became clear that Gravel might have underestimated the value conferred by Gruening's incumbency. A late April poll gave Gruening a comfortable lead, with 42 percent to Gravel's 20 percent. Gruening hoped to maintain the momentum by using his office to stress the issues on which his opinions still reflected mainstream thinking in the state. For example, after the assassinations of Martin Luther King, Jr., and Robert Kennedy, the senator vehemently opposed all gun control legislation, on the grounds that it would cause "an unbearable hardship" for Native Americans who depended on hunting for their food. That Gruening needed to fortify his frayed ties with the group obviously encouraged his activism: he would not compromise on Vietnam for electoral advantage, but domestic issues were another matter. When he returned to Alaska to campaign full-time in August, it appeared as if his tactics, combined with an energy level which, in the words of the *Anchorage Daily Times*, continued to leave "men half his age standing in awe," would suffice. With his own polling showing him trailing by double digits, Gravel gambled. In the ten days before the primary, the challenger saturated the state's airwaves with a thirty-minute documentary titled "A Man for Alaska." The blanket advertising campaign, a novel tactic for Alaska, confused Gruening, whose own media effort was ineffective. Campaigning through the bush country, with its predominantly Native vote, Gruening sensed a shift in momentum, and even a dip into the Arctic to prove his continued vitality could not halt his slippage in the polls. Upon his return to Juneau, he confided to Sundborg that for the first time he thought that he might lose.[12]

Nonetheless, on primary night the incumbent remained cautiously optimistic. When early returns favored Gravel, however, the mood at Gruening's headquarters became gloomy. It turned to shock as the tallies from southeast Alaska arrived. The senator, with his official residence in Juneau, had been so confident about his strength in the region that he had spent virtually no time campaigning there. Gravel profited from this neglect, and carried the area by a nearly two-to-one margin, enough to offset Gruening's favorable showings in Anchorage and Fairbanks. Down by nearly two thousand votes as the canvassing concluded, Gruening initially refused to concede defeat. Even though Gravel's film provided the turning point in the campaign, the combination of his age and his foreign policy dissent laid the foundation for Gruening's loss. As the upset winner remarked the day after the primary, "by taking an extreme position on Vietnam and sticking with it," Gruening had "placed himself out of the mainstream of American and Alaskan life." By contrast, senators such as McGovern and Church, who had worried constantly that their opposition to the war might harm them politically, found their positions on Vietnam of electoral benefit; both enjoyed the easiest reelection campaigns of their careers.[13]

DEFEAT ALWAYS brought out the worst in Ernest Gruening. He blamed the collapse of his Puerto Rican program on others—the dictatorial ambitions of Muñoz Marín, the mental instability of Chardón, the refusal of anti-imperialists to understand his need to compromise. After his agenda stalled in his first legislative session in Juneau, he pressed for an FBI investigation of his political opponents. This electoral setback, magnified as it was by its very personal nature and by his age, only intensified these habitual reactions. A private unity meeting with Gravel found the senator "shocked" and "sullen," shuffling papers in front of him as his primary foe attempted in vain to engage in "cordial" conversation. With, as his son recalled, his ego "knocked for a loop," Gruening was in no mood to compromise. He even continued his habit of deliberately mispronouncing his opponent's name, stressing the first rather than the second syllable. When Gravel asked for an endorsement, Gruening pointedly refused.[14]

The senator instead returned to Washington, where his defeat drew expressions of sadness from his lifelong admirers. William O. Douglas hailed Gruening's career as "a great battle," characterized by the Alaskan's standing "firm on principle"; *The Nation* praised him for a lifetime of having "served the public, people not institutions, and people not only in America but everywhere in the world and most particularly in the world of Latin America." With time running out to complete his historical legacy, Gruening looked to settle old personal scores and more fully explore the range of his dissenting vision. On the former front, he campaigned against Johnson's effort to replace Earl Warren as Chief Justice with Abe Fortas, whom he had disliked since Fortas's tenure as Ickes's deputy in the wartime Interior Department. When Republicans attacked Justice Fortas for having accepted a $15,000 fee, funded by his former business partners, to conduct a nine-week seminar on law, the senator privately coined the adjective "Fortasian" to describe excessive greed. Surveying the outlook on confirmation, one White House staffer observed that "we will be lucky if we can get Gruening to go salmon fishing instead of voting." The administration was not that fortunate. In September, when Democrats introduced an unsuccessful cloture motion against a GOP filibuster, Gruening was one of three northern Democrats to side with the Republicans on the question, even though he knew that doing so might ensure Warren's succession by a Republican appointee. The Alaskan then tweaked Johnson by urging the president to abandon Fortas and nominate Wayne Morse, an obviously unacceptable choice.[15]

The Senate shortly thereafter considered a measure to fund the Department of Defense for the next fiscal year, which, at $71.9 billion, was the largest spending bill to that point in American history. Befitting the changing conception of his role as a senator, the Alaskan understood that his decision to vote against the bill would not affect the upper chamber's action on the military budget—owing to his colleagues' "feeling that military budgets have about them an aura of sanctity"—but he hoped that his tactic would have some public relations value. Fittingly, the vote was the last one that he cast in the Senate. The next day, he left for Alaska.[16]

Still unreconciled to his defeat, Gruening did not go home to plan his retirement. Instead, he launched a quixotic effort to retain his seat by running a write-in campaign against Gravel and Elmer Rasmuson, who had edged Stevens for the Republican nomination. Many of his associates in Washington—Herb Beaser came in to manage the effort—convinced him that the campaign could succeed. Even some veteran Alaska observers agreed. Privately, Gruening predicted that the write-in campaign would confirm the "widespread feeling in Alaska that the electorate erred." (To the end, his faith in the people's judgment lasted only so long as the public's choice mirrored his point of view.) Such sentiments represented wishful thinking. His closest political confidant, George Sundborg, told him bluntly that the write-in campaign had no chance. Still, the effort seemed a no-lose proposition to the embittered senator, for even if he failed to retain his seat, mobilizing his committed political base figured to deny the election to Gravel.[17]

Armed with strong support from students at the University of Alaska and Alaska Methodist University, Gruening touted his effort as a "bridge between generations." His college-age supporters reciprocated the admiration, modifying the antiwar cry to "Never trust anybody over thirty unless he's also over eighty." Though filled with enthusiasm, the campaign was hardly a professional effort. Instead of focusing on the formidable task of tutoring Alaskans, especially in rural areas, on the mechanics of supporting a write-in sticker candidacy, it relied on gimmicks such as the slogan "Stick with Gruening" and green buttons inscribed with "ing" to symbolize the pronunciation of the senator's name. Meager fund raising, which fell well short of the $100,000 goal, also hampered the effort. Convinced that duplicating Gravel's tactics would reverse the primary result, Gruening funneled what limited funds he did raise into producing a promotional film modeled on "A Man for Alaska." The campaign ran out of money, though, and the film was never completed.[18]

Gravel, meanwhile, successfully rallied the state and national party apparatus behind his effort. Traveling to Washington after the primary, he discovered that Bob Bartlett was "incensed" at Gruening's candidacy. The senior senator believed that the only reason Gruening "was ever elected to anything" was that before 1968 he had not "met every Alaskan"; personal contact, Bartlett joked, only gave his colleague "the opportunity to berate and insult." He observed that Gruening had "lost and he should take it gracefully." Since, however, "it seems impossible for him to do so," Bartlett consented to appear in a television advertisement on Gravel's behalf. So too did one other senator—Edward Kennedy (D–Massachusetts). Gruening's personal and ideological dissents came back to haunt him. While Gravel and Gruening scoured the state for Democratic votes, Rasmuson was finding that his substantial war chest could not overcome the effects of a stiff personality in a state still accustomed to personal campaigning. With both Rasmuson and Gruening spending most of the campaign attacking him, Gravel positioned himself as a centrist between two extremes. Ironically, then, Gruening's deteriorating political skills produced one final miscalculation: the write-in campaign actually aided Gravel. Gruening's most passionate and committed supporters, like the senator himself, viewed Gravel's primary challenge as a betrayal; few would have wound up in his column in the November election. By amassing 14,118 votes (17.4 percent of the total), however, Gruening split the anti-Gravel vote, allowing the underfunded Democrat to slip through with a plurality.[19]

For Gruening, his own loss to Gravel, combined with the narrow victory of the youthful Bob Packwood over Wayne Morse in Oregon, suggested that "the accent for success is certainly on youth and good looks" rather than on qualifications; both results, along with the victory of Richard Nixon in the presidential election, confirmed for him "the unwisdom of our electorate." In the end, the senator concluded, "the people get the kind of government they deserve." These obviously were the words of a man embittered by defeat. But they also reflected a tendency which had manifested itself throughout Gruening's career. The senator had always maintained that he desired only that government policies reflect the people's will. But he also always believed that this will and his own ideological viewpoint were one and the same. When he was confronted with evidence to the contrary, whether forty years earlier when Maine voters selected Frederick Hale over Ralph Brewster or in 1968 when Alaskans chose Mike Gravel as their new senator, Gruening's only recourse was to belittle the electorate's judgment.[20]

In his last official act as a senator, he represented the Interior Committee on a tour of U.S. possessions in the Caribbean. Deeply depressed, Gruening drank heavily during the trip, downing as much as a bottle of rum in an evening's sitting. He recovered his equilibrium enough to attend the inauguration of the newly elected governor of Puerto Rico, Luis Ferré, at which he "got a very good round of applause." Further soothing his ego, many Puerto Rican reformers greeted him "warmly" and praised his work with the PRRA. With the inauguration, he bid "good riddance to 1968, . . . a terrible year for the nation and for me."[21]

Though defeated, Gruening found that his status as a former senator entitled him to access to the Senate floor; he considered it "a queer, almost eerie sensation to be back in the Senate and yet not of it." After over three decades in government service of one sort or another, Gruening struggled to make the transition to private life. Able to retain his SFAE office for three weeks after leaving the Senate (the subcommittee itself passed out of existence with his defeat), he could barely "resist the impulse to rush over and vote" when the bell rang for quorum and vote calls. His disinclination to leave his office and his ubiquitous presence on the floor raised comments among both his former colleagues and Senate staffers that Gruening was desperate to hang on, at whatever cost.[22]

Eventually, of course, Gruening had to depart the Senate chambers. Oriented as always toward the nation's capital, however, he decided that he would remain in Washington rather than retire to

Alaska. He spent late 1968 seeking foundation support to conduct a research project on the Alliance for Progress. Unsuccessful in this effort, Gruening started a "new phase" of his life the next February, joining Beaser at the Population Crisis Committee, where he concentrated on lobbying Congress to increase spending on birth control efforts. To supplement his income, he joined the board of directors of Alaska Airlines (although he refused to lobby Congress on the airline's behalf), and also was named president of the Alaska North American Development Corporation.[23]

But the major effort of Gruening's retirement years came in writing his autobiography. He began combing through his personal papers almost immediately after leaving the Senate. In the process of reviewing the experiences of his life, he initiated personal contact with figures from his dissenting past, such as the former peace progressive senators Gerald Nye and Burton Wheeler, two leading critics of U.S. interventionism in the Caribbean Basin during the 1920s. He joined them at peace activist Jeanette Rankin's ninetieth birthday celebration; Wheeler later commented that he had followed Gruening's "remarkable career" and had "agreed with him on almost every position he has taken." Gruening even revised his opinion of the paths followed by the peace progressives and much of the peace movement during the 1930s, praising the "gallant attempt" to keep the United States out of World War II. Looking back on events twenty-five years later, Gruening reasoned that the conflict had "paved the way for an unprecedented militarism which has led our once peace-loving and treaty-abiding Nation into unfathomable depths of deception, violence, disruption, and betrayal of its previously accepted ideals and standards." Although he still believed that the United States had had no choice but to enter the war, he nonetheless praised the "courageous" fight as "a story that should inspire others to pick up the torch that circumstances wrenched from their hands."[24]

The war in Vietnam obviously accounted for Gruening's historical revisionism. At an April dinner held in his honor in Washington, he declared, "There is no hope of peace or progress in America unless we cease giving top priority to the killing business." With hundreds of military bases all over the world, he continued, "we are now witnessing a repetition of history: 'The Decline and Fall of the American Empire.'" With little hope that Nixon would reverse the consolidation of "the military–industrial–labor union–Congress complex," Gruening urged reformers in Congress to employ the body's institutional powers to assume control of U.S. foreign policy. After ending the "monstrosity and inequity" of conscription, rescinding the Tonkin Gulf Resolution, and forcing withdrawal from Vietnam by "unflinchingly" blocking all military appropriations, the legislature ought to examine all postwar executive agreements, such as "our commitments to Dictator Francisco Franco." After full hearings, the Senate could transform "those that are clearly vital to our country into treaties" and scrap the rest. "To recall a phrase from the Wilsonian era," he noted, the time once again had come for "open covenants openly arrived at." Traditional American ideals had atrophied in the twenty-five years since the end of World War II; only a thorough cleansing could restore them.[25]

To implement these ideas himself, Gruening sustained his opposition to the selective service system. Having concluded that the Thirteenth Amendment, which outlawed slavery, forbade conscription as well, he termed it "nothing less than criminal to keep sending our draftees to fight in violation of their consciences." Gruening thus hailed those who refused to serve as "the real patriots." Throughout 1969 the former senator predicted that the conflict would end through a mass refusal of draftees to serve, an idea which recalled his interwar flirtation with the War Resisters' League. In May, hoping to offer "the draftees a community backing," he appeared at a Philadelphia meeting on behalf of resisters, which resulted in about fifty men turning in their draft cards. Later that month he heard from Albert Gore that his son, Albert, Jr., about to graduate from Harvard, wanted to go into teaching to avoid the draft; Gore said that he would not try to stop him, although he feared it might cost him reelection in 1970. Gruening, taking a more positive approach, "told him his son was doing the right thing and that he should encourage him and meet the issue boldly."[26]

Still looking for a venue to reach the public, the former senator accepted an offer to return to *The Nation* as a contributing editor, marking his third time on the masthead. The decision, made in haste, only confirmed that his sense of his own worth exceeded that of editor Carey McWilliams. When McWilliams understandably rejected several of his contributions as unoriginal, Gruening severed his formal association with the journal once and for all. The entire experience planted doubts in his mind as to whether his era in American history had ended: if *The*

Nation no longer found what he had to say compelling or intellectually stimulating, then would the public show any interest? Privately, Gruening showed signs of recognizing that his time had passed. As early as 1967, he recalled his sixtieth anniversary gathering at Harvard as "a warm and nostalgic affair," since "we all knew it would be 'the last round-up.'" The deaths in 1969 of a number of close friends, such as Drew Pearson and Frank Tannenbaum, did nothing to diminish this sensation.[27]

Still, Gruening battled on as effectively as he could, although American politics in the early stages of the Nixon presidency showed few signs of moving in his direction. The Republican had claimed during the 1968 campaign to have a "secret plan" to end the war, but Nixon unveiled no major policy initiative until the following November, when he announced that he would continue the "Vietnamization" policy inherited from Johnson by withdrawing U.S. forces gradually and turning over their responsibility to the South Vietnamese army. Then, speaking on behalf of the "silent majority," he denounced peace activists as an irresponsible minority intent on sabotaging his efforts to negotiate an honorable end to the war. When polls indicated support for the policy, Nixon rejoiced, declaring, "We've got those liberal bastards on the run." Gruening, meanwhile, dismissed Vietnamization as "a plan to prolong and even to perpetuate" the war. He feared that the "continuing credibility gap" caused by the difference between the government's stated policies and its actual initiatives in Southeast Asia was causing "the alienation of our young, the impairment and even destruction of their faith and confidence in our system." As always, his basic priority remained "an America that will live up to its promise."[28]

Nixon's domestic policies struck Gruening as equally cynical. The Supreme Court nominations of Clement Haynsworth and G. Harrold Carswell, whom the president praised as "strict constructionists" of the Constitution, especially triggered his fury. The former senator, who denounced the nominations as "typically slimy," considered Haynsworth a racist, thought Carswell "the worst nomination in our history," and lobbied almost twenty undecided senators against both men. He was pleasantly surprised that principle seemed to prevail when the Senate declined to confirm either nominee. The next year, Gruening expressed horror when Justice Hugo Black retired, allowing Nixon to select yet another "terrible" nominee, William Rehnquist. This time adherents of

Gruening's point of view were not so lucky, and Rehnquist won confirmation after a bruising battle. Alarmed that "every additional Nixon appointment pulls the nation down that much further," the former senator begged William O. Douglas not to follow Black's course. If his health deteriorated to the point where he had "to be carried to the Court on a litter," Gruening hoped that the Justice would "insist on that form of transportation."[29]

Gruening continued to try to influence debate on the issues about which he cared most, such as reforming inter-American relations. In April 1970 he renewed contact with Carleton Beals. The two ancient anti-imperialists spent an evening together at Beals's home in Connecticut, an evening which persuaded Gruening to do a little muckraking of his own. That January, Arthur Schlesinger, Jr., had penned an article for the *Atlantic* defending the Alliance for Progress. Gruening responded with a long letter to the editor ridiculing Schlesinger's overly "generalized" recommendations. He argued that the solution to the downturn in inter-American relations remained "*not* to reduce the amount of aid, but to channel it differently, derive it from different authorities, and place the responsibility where it belongs—on the recipient country." The former senator also urged eliminating "our bloated and needless military missions," a legacy of military aid, which had "been misused repeatedly to overturn democratically elected and public-spirited regimes." In an issue of new concern, Gruening encouraged Latin American economic integration, which, though he realized it might challenge U.S. economic superiority in the region, the United States needed to accept "in the interest of improved hemispheric relations." To the end, his general framework for inter-American relations remained unchanged.[30]

DESPITE HIS BITTERNESS following his own defeat, Gruening had not lost all faith in the political process. As the 1970 campaign season got under way, he helped raise funds for Representative George Brown (D–California), who ran for the U.S. Senate on a peace platform. (John Tunney edged Brown in the primary, and then went on to capture the fall election.) Gruening also appeared on behalf of fellow dissenting Democrats Albert Gore, who lost, and Vance Hartke, who won. His intense antiwar activism, however, shook his moorings to the Democratic Party. In a return to the pattern of earlier in his career, ideology rather than partisanship guided his endorsements. He praised the antiwar positions of Charles Goodell (R–New York), appointed to Robert Kennedy's seat following the senator's assassination, and championed Goodell's unsuccessful bid for reelection with the comment that "party considerations are only minor to the overwhelming issue of ending the utterly needless, immoral, and senseless war." In the Texas Senate race, meanwhile, he also backed a Republican, Representative George Bush, whom he had come to know because of their joint support for birth control. Gruening saw a vote for Bush as a way to rebuke Lloyd Bentsen, who had employed a "villainous smear campaign" to oust Ralph Yarborough in the Democratic primary.[31]

World events on the second anniversary of his departure from the Senate gave Gruening little ground for optimism. Age clearly was taking its toll; the Alaskan knew that he no longer could afford to wait for the electorate to embrace his viewpoint. More apt now to become frustrated, he swung wildly between proclaiming his faith in the American people and castigating them for their lack of idealism. Although Gruening still attacked the executive branch for concealing information, he could no longer excuse the public for going along. Perhaps in 1964 people did not know better, but now, the refusal to rally against Nixon's policies was to him "inexcusable." (He did take some satisfaction, however, in the fact that history had vindicated his earlier warnings, tweaking Harvard historian Oscar Handlin, who had criticized his position in 1965 and 1966, "wondering whether today—5 1/2 years later—you still hold the same views.") Political commentator Jules Witcover perceptively described him as a "prophet with very little proclaimed honor." Although Gruening remained "just as lucid as the day . . . when he became the first U.S. senator to call on his country to get out of Vietnam," the former senator's views, Witcover noted, "now travel only as far as the sound of his own voice." More extreme than ever in his public comments, Gruening began accusing the Kennedy, Johnson, and Nixon administrations of waging a "war of aggression" in Southeast Asia through tactics comparable to those of Hitler and Mussolini. The only difference, he claimed, was that "we do it in the name of liberation," thereby "adding hypocrisy to our sins." After joining the Citizens' Committee on U.S. War Crimes in Vietnam, he demanded a Nuremberg-style prosecution of those responsible for sending American soldiers to Vietnam.[32]

Then, as the jockeying for the 1972 presidential election began, Gruening had yet another change of heart. Perhaps the American people would again embrace traditional ideals after all, he thought, if only the Democrats presented an attractive presidential nominee: George McGovern. The Alaskan quickly dismissed the party's early front-runners, Edward Kennedy, whose "stability" he questioned and whose endorsement of Gravel he had not forgotten, and Edmund Muskie, whom he criticized for an insufficiently strong position against U.S. involvement in Vietnam. The campaign allowed the former senator to make his voice heard once again. On the hustings, this "uninhibited and indefatigable orator" emerged as "the darling of the McGovern speaker bureau," especially effective "in softening up the most politically activist wing of the Democratic party" in states such as Massachusetts, Oregon, and Wisconsin. Age may have contributed to his extreme views on national and international events, but it did not cramp his campaign style. Appearing in Wisconsin, the eighty-four-year-old expressed puzzlement when he saw that the time from 3:00 to 4:00 on his schedule had been allotted for rest. His liaison from the campaign informed him that McGovern liked to take a nap to break up a long day of campaigning. Gruening responded, "At my age you do not need as much rest. Let's schedule another stop." He regularly made ten or eleven appearances a day on McGovern's behalf, denouncing the president as a "crook" for having "kept us in a wholly unconstitutional, illegal, immoral war." Gruening also indulged in substantially more radical opinions, continuing to compare U.S. aggression to that of the Nazis. While such passion contributed to his sharing with Wayne Morse SANE's Eleanor Roosevelt Peace Medal in 1972, it did not help McGovern win any additional support from moderate Democrats.[33]

But in the political climate of 1972, backing from such constituencies did not seem necessary. The campaign gained momentum as the spring progressed, and, when McGovern bested Hubert Humphrey in the California primary, he clinched the nomination. For Gruening, however, the triumph was bittersweet. The former senator traveled to the Democratic national convention in Miami to see McGovern accept the nomination, but he fell ill and remained hospitalized throughout the gathering. Doctors diagnosed colon cancer. After receiving chemotherapy, Gruening responded well enough to make a limited number of campaign appearances for McGovern in the fall campaign.[34]

That effort got off to a rocky start and never recovered. Despite disheartening poll figures, Gruening continued to predict a McGovern victory up until Election Day, a judgment which seemed mostly determined by wishful thinking. Typically, he responded to Nixon's overwhelming victory by chastising the electorate. Confessing that he was "deeply depressed," Gruening could not "understand what really happened because never were the issues . . . so clear," the same words he had used in 1928 when Ralph Brewster fell to Frederick Hale. Perhaps, he mused, the H. L. Mencken aphorism—"ruled by shady men a nation itself becomes shady"—explained the result, since "we have been ruled by two shady men during the last eight years." Still, the former senator wondered if the American people had "lost their spirit"; clearly they had "deteriorated sadly." Convinced that four more years of Nixon would produce "a police state," Gruening promised to "keep plugging in my feeble way against these forces of darkness."[35]

By this point in his career, however, he harbored little hope of triumph in the fight. Throughout his life Gruening believed that as long as the people received the necessary information, they would act to uphold the country's honor, whether by demanding a withdrawal of U.S. forces from Haiti in the 1920s or by ending the war in Vietnam in the 1960s. McGovern's defeat shattered this conviction. The electorate had access to all of the facts, as people such as Gruening himself had ensured, and yet overwhelmingly repudiated American idealism by reelecting Nixon. Gruening never recovered from the result.

In combination with his declining health, this sense of depression produced an increasingly pessimistic view of national and international affairs after 1972. Still trying to influence public opinion, Gruening returned to Maine in early 1973, an excursion that did little to improve his frame of mind. In a contest described by the *New York Times* as one of the most bitter in the state's history, Pine Tree State voters went to the polls to decide a referendum question on whether to create a state power authority. The battle reminded Gruening of the Smith-Carlton campaign, when he and the *Evening News* had successfully resisted the Insull interests. Despite poor health and an alarmingly frail appearance, he made a whirlwind tour of the state, aiming, as usual, to influence the next generation's intellectual elite by visiting the state's four major college campuses—Bates, Bowdoin, Colby, and the University of Maine. An old friend, Jim Abramson, asked observers "to put

Ernest in his proper perspective." The former Bowdoin professor believed that Gruening could not help but to recall 1929, when "the situation was much more black and white—there were real 'good guys and bad guys.'" When the power authority measure overwhelmingly went down to defeat, Gruening "reluctantly" concluded that his "apparent achievements were eroded by the passage of time." Unfortunately, he said, "our beloved country is passing through a grim phase of determination which challenges those of us who cherish our historic legacy."[36]

In this context of philosophical depression and intellectual and physical decline, Gruening's autobiography finally appeared. Given these obstacles, it was impressive, easily his finest work since *Mexico and Its Heritage* over four decades before. One observer found reading the autobiography an "exercise in credulity," since one could not begin "to comprehend how one man could have had so many important jobs, traveled to so many distant places, written so many books, edited so many newspapers, and known so many persons who are the landmarks of the Twentieth Century." As Gruening's final political testament, the book served its purpose. The passage of time had vindicated the most controversial positions from Gruening's career: his opposition to U.S. interventionism in the Caribbean Basin, his revenue and developmental initiatives as Alaska's governor, his support for birth control, his critique of the Alliance for Progress, and his crusade against U.S. involvement in Vietnam. The sense that history would look upon him favorably gave Gruening the reassurance to tone down much of his extreme rhetoric. Any discussion of his failures, however, was another matter. Embarrassing episodes such as the collapse of his Puerto Rican agenda, his support for the Dominican intervention, or his write-in bid against Gravel simply were not mentioned; he likewise ignored the ambivalent aspects of his Alaskan record, ranging from his attempts to evade the gubernatorial appointment to his exploitation of the Cold War to boost federal assistance for the territory. Finally, he could not resist the temptation to strike back at the man who had sent him into retirement: he ended his discussion of the 1968 primary campaign by comparing Gravel's tactics to those of Joseph McCarthy. In the end, *Many Battles* captured Gruening's career and personality—in both its remarkable breadth and its occasional pettiness.[37]

The appearance of the autobiography coincided with one of the supreme honors of Gruening's public career. In March 1974, five members of the Senate—McGovern, Church, Nelson, Mark Hatfield, and James Abourezk (D–South Dakota)—nominated him for the Nobel Peace Prize, observing that "Gruening's leadership in the quest for peace spans many issues and several generations." Throughout all of these efforts, they continued, he embodied beliefs central to the American dissenting tradition: "that small lands as well as large have a right to settle their own affairs; that a policy of unilateral intervention can only degrade the international agencies created to resolve disputes; that even powerful nations confront the tides of nationalism at their own peril." The senators particularly praised Gruening's coupling of "his words of warning with ceaseless efforts both in Congress and around the country to win a reevaluation and a reversal of U.S. policy." In this "personal crusade" he had given all of his "indomitable spirit," even though his actions ultimately cost him his Senate seat.[38]

The Peace Prize nomination touched Gruening deeply, especially after he discovered the next month that his cancer had spread to his liver. The tumors were inoperable, and the former senator realized that he did not have long to live. He kept up his public appearances to the greatest extent possible. In March 1974 he testified before the House Judiciary Committee, urging amnesty for those who had resisted the draft. The next month he returned to Hotchkiss, nearly seventy years after attending the school, to speak on the decline of American idealism. But Gruening had come to understand that the United States would not adopt a foreign policy to his liking in the brief time that he had left. He confided to his son that he was living for the possibility of winning the Peace Prize and celebrating his sixtieth wedding anniversary with Dorothy in November. Nonetheless, he was philosophical about his impending death, writing Hunt that he had "already lived seventeen years beyond the life-span accorded by the psalmists (three score and ten), and have had except for our two tragedies, Sonny and Peter, a very happy life." In a telling comment, the editors of *The Nation* remarked that "the persona never engulfed the self with Ernest Gruening. The public citizen and the private person were one and the same; he was always of one piece." This connection gave him a greater sense of strength and consistency in his public life, fortifying his often lonely dissenting battles and inspiring a self-confidence that sometimes bordered on arrogance. At the same time, it transformed politics into an all-consuming passion, particularly at the expense of his family life. Gruening himself never harbored any illusions about the price demanded by the choices which he made, and, for the most part, he willingly paid it. Yet this, his final letter to his surviving son, contained a hint of regret that his obsession with his "many causes"—as he wanted to title his autobiography—had prevented him from knowing better the two sons taken prematurely from him.[39]

After Gruening's return to Washington from Hotchkiss, his condition declined sharply, and he was again hospitalized. Although gravely ill, he followed the impeachment hearings against Nixon from his hospital room, greeting one visitor "with an arm-waving, fist-shaking denunciation" of the president. Gruening hoped that Nixon would be not only impeached, convicted of high crimes and misdemeanors, and thrown out of office, but also prosecuted as a private citizen and imprisoned. Only such an outcome would reaffirm faith in the U.S. justice system. The issue consumed his attention; visitors found conversation with the former senator on any other topic all but impossible. Gruening, however, would not live to see Nixon's departure from office. He died on June 26.[40]

The following days featured widespread tributes, the most revealing of which came from outside the Senate. Linking Gruening's personal with his professional life, William O. Douglas recalled the former senator's "minorities" as "not only social and religious but . . . political and ideological as well." George Sundborg memorialized his mentor as a man who "inspired followers" with his broad vision, the product of a keen intellect "honed by an excellent education." Another admirer stated the sentiment more bluntly: Gruening was a "Renaissance man with guts." Jack Germond and Jules Witcover remembered him as both the "doctor of diversity" and a "20th century Thomas Jefferson," while the editors of *The Nation* hailed this "man of impeccable honor and integrity, indomitable spirit and extraordinary moral courage." Perhaps the most perceptive observation came from the *Washington Post.* It noted that the eulogies for the late senator unsurprisingly focused on his early and consistent opposition to the U.S. involvement in Vietnam. Yet Gruening's crusade against the war had represented "only the continuation of a career always remarkable for its versatility and for the fidelity it revealed to certain ideas."[41]

Notes
Bibliography
Index

Notes

Abbreviations

BJ	*Boston Journal*
BT	*Boston Traveler*
CR	*Congressional Record*
GD	Ernest Gruening Diaries, Elmer Rasmuson Library, University of Alaska, Fairbanks
GP	Ernest Gruening Papers, Rasmuson Library
GPSS	Ernest Gruening Papers, Post-senatorial Series, Rasmuson Library
GSP	Ernest Gruening Senatorial Papers, Rasmuson Library
Many Battles	Ernest Gruening, *Many Battles: The Autobiography of Ernest Gruening* (New York: Liveright, 1973)
PEN	*Portland Evening News*

1. The Progressive Impulse

1. *Many Battles*, pp. 3–4; Hunt Gruening interview, Seattle, Feb. 22, 1995; *New York Times*, May 31, 1914.

2. *Many Battles*, pp. 3–4.

3. Ibid., p. 4; *New York Times*, May 31, 1914.

4. Ernest Gruening 1899 diary, copy in possession of Hunt Gruening; *Many Battles*, pp. 4–5; Hunt Gruening interview.

5. *Many Battles*, pp. 5–7; Selma Berrol, "Education in New York City, 1900–1920," *Illinois Quarterly* 35 (1973), 20–30; Hunt Gruening interview. For more on the Sachs Institute, see Ronald Steel, *Walter Lippmann and the American Century* (New York: Vintage Books, 1980), pp. 9–11.

6. *Many Battles*, pp. 7–10, 14–18; Hunt Gruening interview; George Sundborg interview, Seattle, Nov. 10, 1994.

7. *Many Battles,* pp. 15–16; Gerald MacFarland, *Mugwumps, Morals, and Politics* (Amherst: University of Massachusetts Press, 1975), pp. 97–101; Martin Schiesl, *The Politics of Efficiency: Municipal Administration and Reform in America, 1880–1920* (Berkeley: University of California Press, 1977), pp. 48–51; Richard McCormick, *The Party Period and Public Policy* (New York: Oxford University Press), p. 298.

8. *Many Battles,* pp. 19–29; James McLachlan, *American Boarding Schools: A Historical Study* (New York: Charles Scribner's Sons, 1970), pp. 196–197; Lael Tucker Weternbaker and Maude Basserman, *The Hotchkiss School: A Portrait* (Lakeville, Conn.: Hotchkiss School, 1963).

9. Eliot's reforms did not fundamentally alter the social makeup of the average Harvard class, and on this front Gruening was typical in most ways. Only in his religious views did he stand out. Of the 312 members of the class who responded to a questionnaire, only one listed himself as a nonbeliever, and fewer than 5 percent were of Jewish heritage. *Harvard College, Class of 1907, Secretary's First Report* (Cambridge, Mass.: Crimson Printing Company, 1908), pp. 16–18.

10. *Many Battles,* pp. 24–29; Steel, *Walter Lippmann,* pp. 12–13; Samuel Eliot Morison, *Three Centuries of Harvard* (Cambridge, Mass.: Harvard University Press, 1936), pp. 434–437.

11. B. S. Hurlbut to Emil Gruening, April 3, 6, 1904; A. E. Ahlers to Hurlbut, June 1, 1904; Phebe Gruening to Hurlbut, May 28, 1904; all in "Gruening, Ernest, 1907" file, Harvard University Archives, Pusey Library, Harvard University.

12. "Ernest Gruening, 1907," March 20, 1905; B. S. Hurlbut to Gruening, April 8, 1905; Gruening to Hurlbut, April 2, 1906; Gruening grade report; all in "Gruening, Ernest, 1907" file; *Many Battles,* pp. 25–26.

13. *Many Battles,* pp. 25–27; Steel, *Walter Lippmann,* pp. 12–13; George Sundborg, "Senator Gruening's Last Campaign: What an Alaska Political Race Looked Like from the Inside," unpublished ms., copy in author's possession, p. 29.

14. *Many Battles,* pp. 26–36; Hunt Gruening interview; Jack Germond interview, Washington, D.C., June 19, 1995.

15. *Many Battles,* pp. 37–40.

16. Hunt Gruening interview.

17. *Many Battles,* pp. 39–40; Ernest Gruening statement, Aug. 12, 1918, "In the Matter of the Investigation into German Propaganda as Carried on in the United States by German Agents," Office of Attorney General, State of New York, copy in Box 340, President's Secretary's File [hereafter Truman PSF], Harry S Truman Presidential Library, Independence, Mo.; Hunt Gruening interview; Frank Moss interview, Salt Lake City, May 21, 1995; Jack Germond interview; *New York Times,* June 29, 1915.

18. [Gruening], "Roosevelt for Hughes," *BT,* June 27, 1916; [Gruening], "Their Fatal Mistake," *BT,* Jan. 17, 1916; *Many Battles,* pp. 40–43. For more on the campaign of 1912, see Norman Wilensky, *The Taft Republicans of 1912* (New Haven: Yale University Press, 1965); James Holt, *Congressional Insurgents and the Party System* (Cambridge, Mass.: Harvard University Press, 1967), pp. 44–67; David Thelen, *Robert La Follette and the Insurgent Spirit* (Boston: Little, Brown, 1976), pp. 53–65; John Milton Cooper, Jr., *The Warrior and the Priest: Woodrow Wilson and Theodore Roosevelt* (Cambridge, Mass.: Belknap Press of Harvard University Press, 1988), pp. 141–215; Thomas Knock, *To End All Wars: Woodrow Wilson and the Quest for a New World Order* (New York: Oxford University Press, 1992), pp. 31–46.

19. New York *World*, Jan. 31, 1910; Hunt Gruening interview; *New York Times*, Aug. 1, 1934; *Many Battles*, pp. 44–45; Robert O'Brien statement, in Report by Special Agent Patrick Rice, Nov. 14, 1950, Washington, D.C., "Re: ERNEST GRUENING, aka Ernest H. Gruening, Governor of Alaska—Appointee," Box 341, Truman PSF; David Levering Lewis, *W. E. B. Du Bois: Biography of a Race* (New York: Henry Holt and Company, 1993), p. 418.

20. *Many Battles*, pp. 37–46; *Boston Herald*, Nov. 20, 1914; Hunt Gruening interview; Maurine Neuberger interview, Portland, Ore., May 28, 1995; George Sundborg interview, Seattle, Feb. 23, 1995; *Class of 1907, Secretary's Fourth Report* (Norwood, Mass.: Plimpton Press, 1913), p. 162.

21. Robert O'Brien statement, in Report by Special Agent Patrick Rice, Nov. 14, 1950; "Statement of Ernest H. Gruening, taken at 15th & N Streets, N.W., April 16, 1918," in Report by Special Agent Patrick Rice, Dec. 1, 1950, Washington, D.C., "Re: ERNEST GRUENING, aka Ernest H. Gruening, Governor of Alaska—Appointee," both in Box 341, Truman PSF.

22. [Gruening], "Why Should the Public Pay for It?" *BT*, May 9, 1916; [Gruening], "A Test Case," *BT*, July 8, 1916; Gruening quoted in James Howard Means, "Doctors Afield: Ernest Gruening," *New England Journal of Medicine*, Nov. 4, 1954; *Many Battles*, pp. 47–57.

23. [Gruening], "The South Is Consistent," *BT*, June 19, 1915; [Gruening], "As Georgia Sows She Reaps," *BT*, Jan. 3, 1916; *Many Battles*, pp. 52, 56, 58.

24. [Gruening], "The Facts Concerning City Hall," *BT*, March 6, 1916; [Gruening], "Victims of the Press," *BT*, April 28, 1916; *Many Battles*, pp. 59–60. For more on Curley's politics and policies, see Jack Beatty, *The Rascal King: The Life and Times of James Michael Curley* (New York: Addison-Wesley, 1992).

25. Gruening, "The Preparation for Peace," *BJ*, Oct. 2, 1917; Knock, *To End All Wars*, pp. 89–99; Arthur Link, *Wilson: Campaigns for Progressivism and Peace* (Princeton: Princeton University Press, 1965). For Brandeis's background and philosophy, see Philippa Strum, *Brandeis: Beyond Progressivism* (Lawrence: University of Kansas Press, 1993), pp. 1–79; idem, *Louis D. Brandeis: A Justice for the People* (Cambridge, Mass.: Harvard University Press, 1984), pp. 139–215; and Melvin Urofsky, *A Mind of One Piece: Brandeis and American Reform* (New York: Charles Scribner's Sons, 1971), pp. 5–132. [Gruening], "President Wilson for Equal Suffrage," *BT*, Oct. 7, 1915; [Gruening], "New Jersey and Suffrage," *BT*, Oct. 22, 1915; *Many Battles*, pp. 46, 57. For a good summary of the anti-monopoly sentiment in the Progressive movement, see Daniel Rodgers, "In Search of Progressivism," *Reviews in American History* 10 (1982), 113–131.

26. [Gruening], "Bryan versus the Country," *BT*, Nov. 6, 1915; [Gruening], "De-Danielize the Cabinet," *BT*, Dec. 28, 1915; Robert O'Brien statement, in Report by Special Agent Patrick Rice, Nov. 14, 1950; "Statement of Ernest H. Gruening, taken at 15th & N Streets, N.W., April 16, 1918"; William Widenor, *Henry Cabot Lodge and the Search for an American Foreign Policy* (Berkeley: University of California Press, 1981).

27. *Many Battles*, pp. 59–60. For foreign policy and Wilson's appeal to left-wing progressives in the 1916 campaign, see Knock, *To End All Wars*, pp. 89–99.

28. *Many Battles*, pp. 60–64; Robert O'Brien statement, in Report by Special Agent Patrick Rice, Nov. 14, 1950.

29. [Green], "Wilson within the Three-Mile Limit," *BJ*, Jan. 31, 1917;

[Green], "Reason vs. Sentiment," *BJ*, Feb. 2, 1917; *The Crisis* (6 Feb. 1915); *Many Battles*, pp. 65–66, 70; Lewis, *W. E. B. Du Bois*, p. 538. For Massachusetts politics of the era, see Richard Abrams, *Conservatism in a Progressive Era: Massachusetts Politics, 1900–1912* (Cambridge, Mass.: Harvard University Press, 1964).

30. *Many Battles*, pp. 64–65.

31. Ibid., pp. 67–70; Michael Pearlman, *To Make Democracy Safe for America: Patricians and Preparedness in the Progressive Era* (Urbana: University of Illinois Press, 1984), pp. 58–81.

32. Woodrow Wilson, "An Address to a Joint Session of Congress," April 2, 1917, in *The Papers of Woodrow Wilson*, ed. Arthur Link, 68 vols. (Princeton: Princeton University Press, 1966–1993), 41:519–527; Knock, *To End All Wars*, pp. 100–115; Thomas Ryley, *A Little Group of Willful Men: A Study of Congressional-President Authority* (Port Washington, N.Y.: Kennikat Press, 1975); John M. Cooper, *The Vanity of Power: American Isolationism and the First World War* (Westport, Conn.: Greenwood Press, 1968), pp. 185–201; Gruening, "Why America Fights," *BJ*, June 15, 1917.

33. Gruening, "Censorship Must Not Be a Blindfold," *BJ*, April 21, 1917; Gruening, "Essence of Democracy," *BJ*, May 24, 1917; David Kennedy, *Over Here: The First World War and American Society* (New York: Oxford University Press, 1980), pp. 25–26; Morton Keller, *Regulating a New Society: Public Policy and Social Change in America, 1900–1933* (Cambridge, Mass.: Harvard University Press, 1994), p. 95.

34. "Statement of Ernest H. Gruening, taken at 15th & N Streets, N.W., April 16, 1918"; Gruening statement, Aug. 12, 1918, "In the Matter of the Investigation into German Propaganda"; Gruening, "On Hating," *BJ*, June 16, 1917.

35. *New York Tribune*, June 3, 1917; *New York Times*, June 3, 1917; Lewis *W. E. B. Du Bois*, pp. 538–540.

36. For civil liberties issues, see Gruening, "A Bad Time for Suppression," *BJ*, July 10, 1917; for Gruening on civil rights, see Gruening, "Strange Distinctions in an American Army," *BJ*, May 28, 1917.

37. Gruening, "America Must Arm," *BJ*, April 21, 1917; Gruening, "More Equitably," *BJ*, May 28, 1917; Gruening, "Signs of Life in Congress," *BJ*, June 12, 1917; Kennedy, *Over Here*, pp. 107–112.

38. Gruening, "Register the Food Kings," *BJ*, June 7, 1917; Gruening, "Words—and Laws," *BJ*, July 13, 1917; William Clinton Mullendore, *History of the United States Food Administration, 1917–1919* (Stanford: Stanford University Press, 1941), pp. 52–67.

39. Gruening, "The Preparation for Peace," *BJ*, Oct. 2, 1917; Gruening, "America's Six Months' Achievements in the War," *BJ*, Oct. 5, 1917.

40. Gruening statement, Aug. 12, 1918, "In the Matter of the Investigation into German Propaganda"; *Many Battles*, p. 72.

41. *Many Battles*, pp. 72–74; Nathaniel Benchley, *Robert Benchley: A Biography* (New York: McGraw-Hill, 1955), pp. 70, 119.

42. "Statement of Ernest H. Gruening, taken at 15th & N Streets, N.W., April 16, 1918."

43. *Many Battles*, pp. 75–76; Benchley, *Robert Benchley*, p. 123.

44. Neal Jones statement, 1918, enclosed in Report by Special Agent Vern Davis, Oct. 4, 1950, Portland, Ore., "Re: ERNEST GRUENING, aka Ernest H.

Gruening, Governor of Alaska—Appointee"; New York Superior Court, County of New York, "Ernest H. Gruening, Plaintiff, against the Tribune Association, Defendant, Defendant's Bill of Particulars"; both in Box 340, Truman PSF; *Many Battles*, pp. 77–79.

45. Harold Cross statement, enclosed in Report by Special Agent Arthur Hart, Oct. 20, 1950, New York City, "Re: ERNEST GRUENING, aka Ernest H. Gruening, Governor of Alaska—Appointee"; "Ernest H. Gruening, Plaintiff, against the Tribune Association"; both in Box 340, Truman PSF.

46. Neal Jones statement, 1918; *Many Battles*, pp. 79–81; Benchley, *Robert Benchley*, pp. 83, 123–127.

47. *Many Battles*, pp. 79–81; Benchley, *Robert Benchley*, pp. 83, 123–127; *New York Times*, July 13, 14, 1918; *New York Journal*, July 13, 15, 16, 18, 1918.

48. Garet Garrett statement; Denis Lynch statement; Kay Phelps statement; Jay Rausin statement; Harold Cross statement; all in Report by Special Agent Arthur Hart, Oct. 20, 1950; New York Superior Court, County of New York, "Ernest H. Gruening, Plaintiff, against the Tribune Association"; Robert O'Brien statement, enclosed in Report by Special Agent Patrick Rice, Nov. 14, 1950.

49. Kay Phelps statement, in Report by Special Agent Arthur Hart, Oct. 20, 1950; *Many Battles*, pp. 81–82; *New York Times*, Aug. 4, Oct. 13, 1918.

50. *Many Battles*, pp. 81–82. For Haitian policy, see David Healy, *Drive to Hegemony: The United States in the Caribbean, 1898–1917* (Madison: University of Wisconsin Press, 1989), pp. 164–202; Hans Schmidt, *The United States Occupation of Haiti, 1915–1934* (New Brunswick, N.J.: Rutgers University Press, 1971), pp. 42–107; John Blassingame, "The Press and American Interventions in Haiti and the Dominican Republic, 1904–1920," *Caribbean Studies* 9 (1969), 27–43.

51. *Many Battles*, p. 82.

52. Ibid., pp. 82–84.

53. Ibid., pp. 82–86; Ernest Gruening, *Experiencias y Comentarios sobre el México Post-revolucionario* (Mexico City: Instituto Nacional de Antropología y Historia, 1970), pp. 14–17.

54. Arthur Hart, "Results of Investigation," in Report by Special Agent Arthur Hart, Nov. 2, 1950, New York City, "Re: ERNEST GRUENING, aka Ernest H. Gruening, Governor of Alaska—Appointee," Box 340, Truman PSF; Robert O'Brien statement, in Report by Special Agent Patrick Rice, Nov. 14, 1950; Hunt Gruening interview.

55. Gruening to George Wickersham, March 27, 1928, Series 36, Box 12, GP. For the disputes between Wilson and the U.S. left over the treaty, see Robert David Johnson, "Article XI in the Debate on the United States' Rejection of the League of Nations," *International History Review* 15 (1993), 502–524.

56. James Kloppenberg, *Uncertain Victory: Social Democracy and Progressivism in European and American Thought, 1870–1920* (New York: Oxford University Press, 1986), p. 362; for the League fight, see Lloyd Ambrosius, *Woodrow Wilson and the American Diplomatic Tradition: The Treaty Fight in Historical Perspective* (New York: Cambridge University Press, 1987); Herbert Margulies, *The Mild Reservationists and the League of Nations Controversy in the Senate* (Columbia: University of Missouri Press, 1989); Ralph Stone, *The Irreconcilables: The Fight against the League of Nations* (Lexington: University Press of Kentucky, 1970).

57. Gruening to George Barr Baker, April 8, 1920, Box 27, Herbert Hoover

Pre-Commerce Papers, Herbert Hoover Presidential Library, West Branch, Iowa; Edward Eyre Hunt to George Akerson, Sept. 20, 1928, Box 30, Herbert Hoover Campaign and Transition Papers, Hoover Library; Gruening to Herbert Hoover, March 8, 1928, Series 36, Box 9, GP.

58. Michael Wreszin, *Oswald Garrison Villard: Pacifist at War* (Bloomington: Indiana University Press, 1965), pp. 15–113; Sara Alpern, *Freda Kirchwey: A Woman of the Nation* (Cambridge, Mass.: Harvard University Press, 1987), p. 33.

59. *Many Battles*, pp. 91–92.

60. Gruening to William Allen White, June 10, Oct. 6, 1921; both in Box C-56, William Allen White Papers, Library of Congress; Gruening to Oswald Garrison Villard, Sept. 2, 1921, File 1423, Oswald Garrison Villard Papers, Houghton Library, Harvard University; Hubert Herring to Carleton Beals, Oct. 27, 1926, Box 166, Carleton Beals Papers, Mugar Library, Boston University; Ernest Gruening, ed., *These United States*, 2 vols. (New York: Liveright, 1921–1923), 1:v–viii.

2. The Anti-imperialist Impulse

1. *Many Battles*, pp. 94–95.

2. U.S. Senate, Select Committee on Haiti and Santo Domingo, *Hearings, Inquiry into the Occupation and Administration of Haiti and Santo Domingo* [hereafter *Haiti and Santo Domingo Hearings*], 67th Congress, 1st and 2d sessions, pp. 1199–1200 (March 8, 1922); Herbert Seligman, "The Conquest of Haiti," *The Nation*, July 10, 1920.

3. *Boston Chronicle*, Jan. 22, 1921; *Boston Herald*, Jan. 24, 1921; both in Series C, Box 326, NAACP Papers, Library of Congress; Gruening to Georges Sylvain, Sept. 11, 1921, reproduced in Georges Sylvain, *Dix Années de lutte pour la liberté, 1915–1925*, 2 vols. (Port-au-Prince: Henri Deschamps, 1928), 1: 125–128; Hans Schmidt, *The United States Occupation of Haiti, 1915–1934* (New Brunswick, N.J.: Rutgers University Press, 1971), pp. 71–75; William Gibbs, "James Weldon Johnson: A Black Perspective on 'Big Stick' Diplomacy," *Diplomatic History* 8 (1984), 329–347.

4. *New York Call*, March 22, 1921; Gruening, "The Truth about Haiti," *The World Tomorrow* (4 June 1921).

5. Gruening to James Weldon Johnson, Oct. 31, 1921, Series C, Box 326, NAACP Papers.

6. Ibid.; *Haiti and Santo Domingo Hearings*, p. 1201; Schmidt, *The United States Occupation of Haiti*, p. 120.

7. Haitian press clippings, 1920s scrapbook, GP; Schmidt, *The U.S. Occupation of Haiti*, pp. 100–102; Gruening, *Many Battles*, pp. 96–99.

8. *Haiti and Santo Domingo Hearings*, pp. 1205–7, 1210; Gruening, "The Senators Visit Haiti and Santo Domingo," *The Nation*, Jan. 4, 1922; Gruening, "Haiti and Santo Domingo Today–II," *The Nation*, Feb. 15, 1922; Gruening, "Haiti under American Occupation," *Century*, no. 103 (April 1922).

9. Gruening to William Calder, July 11, 1922, 1920s Scrapbook, GP; *Haiti and Santo Domingo Hearings*, pp. 1202–4, 1219.

10. *Haiti and Santo Domingo Hearings*, pp. 1210–11, 1213–16; Gruening, "The Senators Visit Haiti and Santo Domingo."

11. Laurence Hauptman, "Utah Anti-imperialist: Senator William H. King

and Haiti, 1921–1934," *Utah Historical Quarterly* 41 (1973), 116–127; King quoted in Ernest Angell to Moorfield Storey, March 11, 1922, Box 4, Moorfield Storey Papers, Library of Congress.

12. Gruening to Moorfield Storey, March 1, April 7, 1922; both in Box 4, Storey Papers; Lewis Gannett to Francis Wheeler, Feb. 7, 1922; Arthur Capper to Gruening, June 24, 1922; both in 1920s scrapbook, GP; Gruening to William Borah, April 5, 1922, Box 114, William Borah Papers, Library of Congress; Joseph France to Gruening, June 28, 1922, "Imperialism, 1919–1941" box, GP; Bruce Calder, *The Impact of Intervention: The Dominican Republic during the U.S. Occupation of 1916–1924* (Austin: University of Texas Press, 1984), pp. 221–227.

13. William Borah to Gruening, June 20, 1922; William King to Gruening, July 22, 1922; Joseph France to Gruening, June 28, 1922; all in "Imperialism, 1919–1941" box, GP; Robert David Johnson, *The Peace Progressives and American Foreign Relations* (Cambridge, Mass.: Harvard University Press, 1995).

14. Gruening to Moorfield Storey, June 12, 1922, Box 4, Storey Papers; Gruening to William Borah, June 26, 1922, Box 114, Borah Papers; Gruening to Felix Frankfurter, March 21, 1933, Box 60, Felix Frankfurter Papers, Library of Congress; [Ernest Gruening], *The Seizure of Haiti by the United States: A Report on the Military Occupation of the Republic of Haiti and the History of the Treaty Forced upon Her* (New York: Foreign Policy Association, 1922); [idem], "Protesting Too Much," *The Nation*, June 21, 1922; *New York Times*, May 2, 3, 1922.

15. James Weldon Johnson to Charles Edward Russell, May 11, 1922; Johnson memorandum, Feb. 15, 1922; both in Series C, Box 327, NAACP Papers; Gruening to Oswald Garrison Villard, May 12, June 2, 1922; both in File 1423, Villard Papers; [Gruening], "The Republic of Brown Brothers," *The Nation*, June 7, 1922; Gibbs, "A Black Perspective on 'Big Stick' Diplomacy."

16. Oswald Garrison Villard to Gruening, March 24, Sept. 14, 1922; both in File 1423, Villard Papers.

17. Gruening to Oswald Garrison Villard, May 19, 1922, File 1423, Villard Papers; Gruening to Carleton Beals, Jan. 22, 1924, Box 165, Beals Papers; Hunt Gruening interview.

18. Friedrich Katz, *The Secret War in Mexico: Europe, the United States, and the Mexican Revolution* (Chicago: University of Chicago Press, 1981), pp. 1–83; John Womack, Jr., *Zapata and the Mexican Revolution* (Cambridge, Mass.: Harvard University Press, 1968); Lorenzo Meyer, *Mexico and the United States in the Oil Controversy* (Austin: University of Texas Press, 1976); Frederick Calhoun, *Power and Principle: Armed Intervention in Wilsonian Foreign Policy* (Kent, Ohio: Kent State University Press, 1986), pp. 34–68; Kendrick Clements, "Woodrow Wilson's Mexican Policy," *Diplomatic History* 4 (1982), 113–136.

19. Frank Tannenbaum to Louie, June 5, 1922, Box 5, Frank Tannenbaum Papers, Butler Library, Columbia University; John Britton, *Carleton Beals: A Radical Journalist in Latin America* (Albuquerque: University of New Mexico Press, 1987), pp. 35–36; idem, *Revolution and Ideology: Images of the Mexican Revolution in the United States* (Lexington: University Press of Kentucky, 1995), pp. 50–56; Robert Freeman Smith, *The United States and Revolutionary Nationalism in Mexico, 1916–1932* (Chicago: University of Chicago Press, 1972), pp. 210–227; George Bealan, "The Harding Administration and Mexico: Diplomacy by Economic Persuasion," *The Americas* 41 (1984), 179–193.

20. Gruening to Oswald Garrison Villard, Aug. 4, 1923, File 1423, Villard Papers; Hunt Gruening interview; S. Bolling Wright interview, in Report by Special Agent John Barrett, Feb. 28, 1951, New York City, "Re: ERNEST GRUENING, aka Ernest H. Gruening, Governor of Alaska—Appointee," Box 340, Truman PSF; Britton, *Carleton Beals*, p. 49.

21. William King to Oswald Garrison Villard, Dec. 19, 1922, File 1423, Villard Papers; *Many Battles*, pp. 108–110; Britton, *Revolution and Ideology*, pp. 55–57; Helen Delpar, *The Enormous Vogue of Things Mexican: Cultural Relations between the United States and Mexico, 1920–1935* (Tuscaloosa: University of Alabama Press, 1992), p. 26. For the efforts of Obregón and Calles to cultivate U.S. anti-imperialists, see John Britton, "Propaganda, Politics, and the Image of Stability: The Mexican Government and the U.S. Print Media, 1921–1929," *Annals of the Southeastern Council on Latin American Studies* 9 (1988), 5–28.

22. Gruening to Oswald Garrison Villard, April 12, 1923, File 1423, Villard Papers; Gruening to Carleton Beals, Jan. 22, 1924, Box 165, Beals Papers; *Many Battles*, pp. 108–110; Delpar, *Enormous Vogue of Things Mexican*, p. 26; Gilbert Joseph, *Revolution from Without: Yucatán, Mexico, and the United States* (New York: Cambridge University Press, 1982), pp. 185–287.

23. Gruening to Oswald Garrison Villard, April 26, 1923, File 1423, Villard Papers; Gruening, "Will Mexico Be Recognized?" *The Nation*, May 23, 1923; Gruening, "The Mexican Renaissance," *Century*, no. 108 (Feb. 1924); Britton, *Revolution and Ideology*, pp. 63–64.

24. Hunt Gruening interview; Carleton Beals, *The Great Circle: Further Advances in Free-lancing* (Philadelphia: J. B. Lippincott Company, 1940), pp. 326–327.

25. [Gruening], "Wall Street and Mexico," *The Nation*, June 28, 1922; Gruening, "Will Mexico Be Recognized?" *The Nation*, May 23, 1923; Carleton Beals to Herbert Croly, June 23, 1927, Box 167, Beals Papers; Gruening, *Experiencias y Comentarios*, pp. 17, 20.

26. Smith, *The United States and Revolutionary Nationalism in Mexico*, pp. 190–232; Joseph Tulchin, *The Aftermath of War: World War I and U.S. Policy toward Latin America* (New York: New York University Press, 1971), pp. 70–97; Bealan, "The Harding Administration and Mexico."

27. Gruening to Carleton Beals, Jan. 22, March 22, 1924; both in Box 165, Beals Papers; Gruening, "Felipe Carillo," *The Nation*, Jan. 16, 1924; Gruening, "The Assassination of Mexico's Ablest Statesman," *Current History* 20 (Feb. 1924).

28. Gruening to Roger Baldwin, Nov. 14, 1923, Series C, Box 327, NAACP Papers; William King to Lewis Gannett, Nov. 5, 1923, Series 36, Box 11, GP.

29. Oswald Garrison Villard to Walter White, Jan. 31, 1924, Series C, Box 327, NAACP Papers; Gruening to Moorfield Storey, Feb. 13, 1924, File 1423, Villard Papers.

30. Oswald Garrison Villard to Walter White, Jan. 31, 1924, Series C, Box 327, NAACP Papers; Gruening to Moorfield Storey, Feb. 13, 1924; Storey to Gruening, Feb. 14, 1924; both in File 1423, Villard Papers.

31. Paul Kellogg to Gruening, March 18, 1924; Samuel Guy Inman to Gruening, April 2, 1924; both in File 1423, Villard Papers.

32. Stephen Duggan to Gruening, March 22, 1924; Ernest Angell to Gruening, n.d. [April 1924]; both in File 1423, Villard Papers.

33. Gruening to Victor Klilbeck, Oct. 21, 1924, Series 32, Box 1, GP; Gruening, "Can Journalism Be a Profession?" *Century*, no. 109 (Sept. 1924).

34. Gruening to William Borah, July 1, 1922, Box 114, Borah Papers; Gruening to Borah, n.d. [late 1923], Series 36, Box 3, GP; LeRoy Ashby, *The Spearless Leader: Senator Borah and the Progressive Movement in the 1920s* (Urbana: University of Illinois Press, 1972), pp. 117–180; David Thelen, *Robert M. La Follette and the Insurgent Spirit* (Boston: Little, Brown, 1976), pp. 179–194; Kenneth McKay, *The Progressive Movement of 1924* (New York: Columbia University Press, 1947).

35. Oswald Garrison Villard to Robert La Follette, July 28, 1924, File 2158, Villard Papers; Gruening press release #1, Sept. 7, 1924, Box B-205, La Follette Family Papers, Library of Congress. Gruening's decision to join La Follette's campaign underscores how drastically World War I had altered his perspective; Gruening once had condemned La Follette's opposition to Wilsonian diplomacy, dismissing the Wisconsin senator as "an incurable egoist and visionary." Gruening, "La Follette," *Boston Journal*, Oct. 1, 1917.

36. Gruening's press releases can be found in Box B-205, La Follette Family Papers.

37. Louis Brandeis to Alfred Brandeis, Oct. 3, 1924, in Melvin Urofsky and David Levy, *Letters of Louis D. Brandeis*, vol. 5 *1921–1941: Elder Statesman* (Albany: State University of New York Press, 1978), p. 142; Philippa Strum, *Brandeis: Beyond Progressivism*, (Lawrence: University of Kansas Press, 1993), pp. 121–132; Michael Parrish, *Felix Frankfurter and His Times: The Reform Years* (New York: The Free Press, 1982).

38. Gruening to state managers, Sept. 23, 1924; Gruening to New York state manager, Oct. 3, 1924; both in Box B-205, La Follette Family Papers; Oswald Garrison Villard to Robert La Follette, Sept. 13, 1924, File 2158, Villard Papers; *New York Times*, Oct. 31, 1924.

39. Gruening to Robert La Follette, Jr., Nov. 1, 6, 1924; both in Box B-98, La Follette Family Papers; Gruening, "The Real Issue in the Campaign," *Century*, no. 109 (Oct. 1924).

40. Roberto Haberman interview, in Report by Special Agent Patrick Rice, April 12, 1951, Washington, D.C., "Re: ERNEST GRUENING, aka Ernest H. Gruening, Governor of Alaska—Appointee," Box 341, Truman PSF; *Many Battles*, pp. 91–92.

41. Hunt Gruening interview; Roberto Haberman interview, in Report by Special Agent Patrick Rice, April 12, 1951; William Flythe interview, in Report by Special Agent Patrick Rice, Nov. 14, 1950, Washington, D.C., "Re: ERNEST GRUENING, aka Ernest H. Gruening, Governor of Alaska—Appointee"; both in Box 341, Truman PSF; *Many Battles*, pp. 93–96; Britton, *Revolution and Ideology*, p. 242.

42. U.S. Senate, Committee on Foreign Relations, *Hearings, Foreign Loans*, 69th Congress, 1st session, pp. 45–61 (Feb. 25, 1925).

43. Gruening to Frank McLaughlin, March 4, 1926, Series 36, Box 13, GP; Hunt Gruening interview; Roberto Haberman interview and William Flythe interview; Erby Swift interview, in Report by Special Agents John Barrett and John Dodge, Jan. 24, 1951, San Antonio, Texas, "Re: ERNEST GRUENING, aka Ernest H. Gruening, Governor of Alaska—Appointee," Box 340, Truman PSF.

44. Hunt Gruening interview; *New York Times*, Aug. 1, 1926, Aug. 1, 1934. For Davis's work, see Arthur Lubow, *The Reporter Who Would Be King: A Biography of Richard Harding Davis* (New York: Charles Scribner's Sons, 1992).

45. Hunt Gruening interview.

46. Meyer, *Mexico and the United States in the Oil Controversy;* Smith, *The United States and Revolutionary Nationalism in Mexico*, pp. 229–258; James John Horn, "Diplomacy by Ultimatum: Ambassador Sheffield and Mexican-American Relations, 1924–1927" (Ph.D. diss., State University of New York, Buffalo, 1969).

47. Gruening to Walter Lippmann, Aug. 25, 1925, Box 12, Walter Lippmann Papers, Sterling Library, Yale University; Gruening, "Hands off Mexico," *PEN*, Oct. 31, 1927; James Sheffield to Frank Kellogg, July 1, 1926, Series 1, Box 5, James Sheffield Papers, Sterling Library, Yale University; Kellogg to Sheffield, Dec. 10, 1926, File 812.20211/44a, Record Group 59, National Archives, College Park, Md.; Sheffield to Kellogg, Dec. 11, 1926, File 812.20211/45, ibid.; Arthur Bliss Lane interview, in Report by Special Agent Patrick Rice, Nov. 14, 1950; *New York Times*, Feb. 8, 16, 1927.

48. Walter Lippmann to George Rublee, Feb. 1, 1927, Box 29, Lippmann Papers; Lippmann, "Vested Rights and Nationalism in Latin America," *Foreign Affairs* 5 (April 1927); Mary Flahaven to Nevin Sayre, May 9, 1929, Reel 41.50, NCPW Papers, Swarthmore College Peace Collection [hereafter SCPC]; Frederick Libby to Dudley Mackenzie, Jan. 21, 1927, Reel 41.11, NCPW Papers; *New York Times*, March 18, 1927; Charles Chatfield, *For Peace and Justice: Pacifism in America, 1919–1941* (Knoxville: University of Tennessee Press, 1971), p. 109; Ronald Steel, *Walter Lippmann and the American Century* (New York: Vintage Books, 1980), pp. 1–234, 326–328.

49. Gruening to José Padín, May 25, 1935, Series 36, Box 8, GP; Hubert Herring to Walter Lippmann, Oct. 25, 1926, Box 13, Lippmann Papers; CCRLA, "Proceedings of the Seminar of Relations with Mexico, 1–10 Jan. 1927," CCRLA file, Collective Documents Group A, SCPC. For the cultural anti-imperialists, see Robert David Johnson, "The Transformation of Pan-Americanism," in *On Cultural Ground: Essays in International History*, ed. Robert David Johnson (Chicago: Imprint Publications, 1994), pp. 156–169.

50. CCRLA, "Proceedings of the Seminar of Relations with Mexico," Frank Kellogg to William Hard, Aug. 17, 1927, Reel 27, Frank Kellogg Papers, Minnesota State Historical Society, St. Paul; James Sheffield to William Howard Taft, Feb. 9, 1927, Series 1, Box 5, Sheffield Papers.

51. James Sheffield to James Wadsworth, Nov. 3, 1927; Sheffield to Robert Olds, Dec. 22, 1927; both in Series 1, Box, 6, Sheffield Papers.

52. *Many Battles*, pp. 131–134; Tyler Abell, ed., *Drew Pearson: Diaries, 1949–1959* (New York: Holt, Rinehart, and Winston, 1974), entry for Sept. 25, 1950, p. 134. This event did not mark the first occasion on which Gruening took a major newspaper to court; in 1923 he sued the *Chicago Tribune* for labeling him a bolshevist, and settled out of court for $20,000. Carleton Beals to Bernard Postal, May 13, 1930, Box 170, Beals Papers.

53. Gruening to John Barry, Dec. 2, 1927, Series 3, Box 3, GP; Gruening to Oswald Garrison Villard, Aug. 3, Oct. 31, 1927; Villard to Gruening, July 29, 1927; all in File 1423, Villard Papers; Smith, *United States and Revolutionary Nationalism*, p. 244.

54. This and subsequent quotations are from Ernest Gruening, *Mexico and Its Heritage* (New York: The Century Company, 1928), pp. 63–68, 126–135, 217–222, 410–431, 506–515.

55. Gruening to Carleton Beals, Dec. 3, 1928, Box 168, Beals Papers.

56. George Ochs-Oakes to Gruening, Nov. 28, 1928, Series 22, Box 1, GP; Carleton Beals to Mark Van Doren, March 30, 1928, Box 167, Beals Papers; Josephus Daniels to Eduardo Hay, Oct. 6, 1936, Box 654, Josephus Daniels Papers, Library of Congress; Frank Tannenbaum review, *New Republic*, Dec. 12, 1928; *New York Times*, Oct. 7, 1928; Carleton Beals review, *The Nation*, Dec. 5, 1928; William Richardson interview, in Report by Special Agents John Barrett and John Dodge, Jan. 24, 1951, San Antonio, "Re: ERNEST GRUENING, aka Ernest H. Gruening, Governor of Alaska—Appointee," Box 340, Truman PSF. Negative comments did crop up, however; Wallace Thompson praised Gruening's research and writing style but asserted that "the book remains an apologia for the present government of Mexico," as, of course, it was (*Christian Science Monitor*, Oct. 24, 1928). For scholarly interpretations of Gruening's work, see Britton, *Revolution and Ideology*, pp. 69–73, 94–102; James William Park, *Latin American Underdevelopment: A History of Perspectives in the United States, 1870–1965* (Baton Rouge: Louisiana State University Press, 1995), pp. 125–126.

3. The Dilemmas of Progressivism

1. Gruening to Oswald Garrison Villard, Oct. 19, 31, 1927; both in File 1423, Villard Papers; *Many Battles*, pp. 135–136.

2. Duane Lockard, *New England State Politics* (Princeton: Princeton University Press, 1959), pp. 79–83; Elizabeth Ring, "The Progressive Movement of 1912 and Third Party Movement of 1924 in Maine," *University of Maine Studies*, 2d ser., no. 26 (1933), 20–25.

3. Gruening to Oswald Garrison Villard, Oct. 31, 1927, File 1423, Villard Papers; Gruening to Lincoln Colcard, Oct. 17, 1927, Series 3, Box 1, GP; Gruening to William Woodward, Dec. 12, 1927, Series 3, Box 3, GP.

4. Gruening to Oswald Garrison Villard, Oct. 19, 1927, File 1423, Villard Papers; Gruening, "The People and the Primary," *PEN*, Oct. 3, 1927; Gruening, "Primary Thoughts," *PEN*, Oct. 14, 1927.

5. Gruening to Edward Hunt, Oct. 22, 1927, Box 30, Hoover Campaign and Transition Papers, Hoover Library; Gruening to Oswald Garrison Villard, Oct. 31, 1927, File 1423, Villard Papers; Gruening, "Herbert Hoover," *PEN*, Oct. 24, 1927; Gruening, "Why Politicians Oppose Hoover," *PEN*, Nov. 7, 1927.

6. Gruening, "Labor Day," *PEN*, Sept. 1, 1928; Gruening, "The Greater City," *PEN*, Jan. 5, 1928; Gruening, "The Radio in Political Campaigns," *PEN*, July 6, 1928; Gruening, "The Mayor or the Manager," *PEN*, June 15, 1928.

7. Douglas Anderson, "State Regulation of Electric Utilities," in *The Politics of Regulation*, ed. James Q. Wilson (New York: Basic Books, 1980), pp. 11, 13; Morton Keller, "The Pluralist State," in *Regulation in Perspective: Historical Essays*, ed. Thomas McCraw (Cambridge, Mass.: Harvard University Press, 1981), pp. 85–86; Michael Parrish, *Securities Regulation and the New Deal* (New Haven: Yale University Press, 1970), pp. 128–145; Thomas McCraw, *TVA and the Power Fight, 1933–1939* (Philadelphia: J. B. Lippincott, 1971), pp. 1–25; David Nord, "The Experts

versus the Experts: Conflicting Philosophies of Municipal Utility Regulation in the Progressive Era," *Wisconsin Magazine of History* 58 (1975), 219–236; James Kloppenberg, *Uncertain Victory: Social Democracy and Progressivism in European and American Thought, 1870–1920* (New York: Oxford University Press, 1986), p. 385; Jay Lawrence Brigham, "Public Power and Progressivism in the 1920s" (Ph.D. diss., University of California, Riverside, 1992).

8. Hunt Gruening interview; Gruening, "Power: The Great Issue," *PEN*, Feb. 28, 1928.

9. Hunt Gruening interview.

10. Ibid.

11. Ibid.; *Many Battles*, pp. 146–148.

12. Gruening to George Norris, June 21, 1928, File 1424, Villard Papers; Gruening, "'I'll Stand on My Senatorial Record,'" *PEN*, June 5, 1928; Gruening, "The Records," *PEN*, June 14, 1928.

13. *Portland Press-Herald*, June 1, 4, 8, 9, 12, 1928.

14. Gruening to Oswald Garrison Villard, June 9, 1928; Gruening to George Norris, June 21, 1928; both in File 1424, Villard Papers.

15. Hoover Republican Club of Maine campaign brochure, Box 163, Hoover Campaign and Transition Papers; Gruening to Herbert Hoover, Sept. 17, 1928; Edward Eyre Hunt to George Akerson, Sept. 20, 1928; both in Box 30, Hoover Campaign and Transition Papers.

16. Gruening to Herbert Hoover, Oct. 5, 1928, Box 30, Hoover Campaign and Transition Papers.

17. Herbert Hoover address, San Francisco, June 18, 1928, Box 430, Hoover Commerce Papers, Hoover Library; Richard Lowitt, *George Norris: The Persistence of a Progressive, 1913–1933* (Urbana: University of Illinois Press, 1971), pp. 431–433.

18. Gruening to Oswald Garrison Villard, Sept. 28, 1928, File 1424, Villard Papers; Gruening, "Our Power Program," *PEN*, Oct. 12, 1928; Gruening, "More about a Power Program in Maine," *PEN*, Oct. 24, 1928.

19. Gruening to Herbert Hoover, Feb. 23, 1929, Box 82, Hoover Campaign and Transition Papers; Hoover quoted in entry for May 15, 1931, Henry Stimson Diaries, Sterling Library, Yale University.

20. Gruening to Carleton Beals, Aug. 23, 1932, Box 172, Beals Papers; Charles Chatfield, *For Peace and Justice: Pacifism in America, 1914–1941* (Knoxville: University of Tennessee Press, 1971), pp. 88–116.

21. Dwight Morrow to Gruening, April 30, 1929, Series 36, Box 15, GP; Gruening to Morrow, March 28, April 18, 1929; Morrow to Gruening, April 5, 1929; all in Series X, Reel 3, Dwight Morrow Papers; Amherst College Library; Robert Freeman Smith, *The United States and Revolutionary Nationalism in Mexico, 1916–1932* (Chicago: University of Chicago Press, 1972), pp. 244–265.

22. Gruening to Walter Lippmann, July 31, 1928, Box 12, Lippmann Papers; Gruening, "A New Era of Peaceful Relations with Mexico," *Current History* (30 March 1929); Gruening, "The Recurring Rebellion in Mexico," *New Republic*, March 27, 1929.

23. Gruening to Frederick Libby, Dec. 15, 1928, Series 22, Box 2, GP; Gruening to William Borah, Jan. 18, 1929, Series 36, Box 3, GP; Gruening, "President Coolidge and Naval Armament," *PEN*, Dec. 5, 1928; Gruening, "The Value of the

Kellogg Treaties," *PEN*, Jan. 10, 1929; Gruening, "An Open Letter to President Hoover," *PEN*, June 1, 1929.

24. Gruening to Lawrence Richey, June 1, 1929; Herbert Hoover, "Memo for Mr. Strother," June 4, 1929; Strother memo to Hoover, n.d.; all in Box 211, Hoover Presidential Papers.

25. Gruening, "How Much Tax Money Will the State Get If It Exports Power?" *PEN*, April 11, 1929; Gruening, "For Lower Power Rates Vote No," *PEN*, Sept. 4, 1929; Leonard Smith, *The Power Policy of Maine* (Berkeley: University of California Press, 1951), pp. 67–72.

26. Gruening to Oswald Garrison Villard, Dec. 6, 1929, File 1424, Villard Papers; Vincent Stillman interview, in Report by Special Agent Arthur Hart, Oct. 20, 1950, New York City, "Re: ERNEST GRUENING, aka Ernest H. Gruening, Governor of Alaska—Appointee," Box 340, Truman PSF; Silas Bent, "The Struggle for Portland," *New Republic*, March 20, 1929; Jim Abramson quoted in John Cole, "Ernest Gruening: The Mouse Who Keeps Roaring," *Maine Times*, Nov. 9, 1973.

27. George Norris to Gruening, March 28, 1928; Gerald Nye to Norris, Feb. 11, 1929; Norris to Robert Healy, Feb. 9, 1929; all in Box 235, George Norris Papers, Library of Congress; Bent, "The Struggle for Portland."

28. Gruening to George Norris, Feb. 7, 1929, Box 235, Norris Papers; Gruening, "Don't Be a 'Yes-Man,'" *PEN*, Sept. 5, 1929; Gruening, "It Is Maine's Power—Keep It in Maine," *PEN*, Sept. 7, 1929.

29. George McGovern interview, Washington, D.C., Dec. 8, 1994.

30. "One Way to Help Maine's Development," *Portland Press-Herald*, Sept. 2, 1929; "The Bogey Man," *Portland Press-Herald*, Sept. 3, 1929; "Political or Business Advice," *Portland Press-Herald*, Sept. 4, 1929; *Portland Press-Herald*, Sept. 7, 10, 1929.

31. Gruening to William Allen White, Oct. 1, 1929, Box C-152, White Papers; Gruening to Oswald Garrison Villard, July 5, 1930, File 1424, Villard Papers.

32. Charles Kindleberger, *The World in Depression, 1929–1939* (Berkeley: University of California Press, 1975), pp. 109–127.

33. Gruening, "Business as Usual," *PEN*, Nov. 21, 1929; Gruening, "Mr. Hoover Getting Results," *PEN*, Nov. 23, 1929; *Many Battles*, p. 147; Akira Iriye, *The Cambridge History of American Foreign Relations*, vol. 3, *The Globalizing of America, 1913–1945* (New York: Cambridge University Press, 1993), pp. 113–125; Alexander DeConde, *Herbert Hoover's Latin American Policy* (Stanford: Stanford University Press, 1951).

34. Gruening to Frederick Libby, Dec. 15, 1928, Series 22, Box 2, GP. The only other foreign policy–related organization in which Gruening served during his time in Portland was Hubert Herring's Committee on Cultural Relations with Latin America.

35. Gruening to Oswald Garrison Villard, March 6, 1930, File 1424, Villard Papers; Gruening to William Borah, March 8, 1930, Series 36, Box 3, GP; Gruening, "President Hoover's Great Achievement and His Further Opportunity," *PEN*, Feb. 2, 1931; Gruening, "Borah, Realist," *PEN*, Oct. 29, 1931.

36. Gruening to Walter Lippmann, Feb. 19, 1930; Walter Lippmann to Gruening, Feb. 20, 1930; both in Series 36, Box 12, GP.

37. Gruening to Oswald Garrison Villard, Oct. 6, 1929, File 1424, Villard Papers; Hans Schmidt, *The United States Occupation of Haiti, 1915–1934* (New

Brunswick, N.J.: Rutgers University Press, 1971), pp. 138–163; Robert Spector, *W. Cameron Forbes and the Hoover Commission to Haiti* (New York: University Press of America, 1985).

38. Oswald Garrison Villard to Gruening, Feb. 10, 1930; Gruening to Villard, Feb. 11, 1930; both in File 1477, Villard Papers; W. Cameron Forbes to Gordon Johnston, April 8, 1930, Box 15, W. Cameron Forbes Papers, Library of Congress; Gruening, "The Story of Haiti," *PEN*, Dec. 16, 1929–Jan. 7, 1930.

39. William Allen White to Gruening, Feb. 14, 1930, April 11, 1930; both in Box C-165, White Papers; Gruening to Oswald Garrison Villard, March 3, 1930; Gruening to Earl Biggers, Dec. 12, 1930; both in Series 3, Box 3, GP.

40. Gruening to Oswald Garrison Villard, March 6, 16, 1930; both in File 1424, Villard Papers; Gruening to Benjamin Shambrough, May 22, 1930, Series 3, Box 4, GP.

41. Gruening to Oswald Garrison Villard, May 14, 1931, File 1424, Villard Papers; Gruening, "Progress in Haiti," *PEN*, Oct. 2, 1931; Gruening, "What Has Become of the Federal Public Works Program?" *PEN*, Sept. 25, 1930; Gruening, "A Raid on the Treasury?" *PEN*, Dec. 11, 1930; Gruening, "Examining the Depression," *PEN*, June 1, 1931.

42. Gruening to William Chartland, Feb. 21, 1930, Series 3, Box 1, GP; Gruening, "A Constructive Plan for a Maine Water Power Policy," *PEN*, Sept. 5, 1930; Gruening, "Holding Company Charges," *PEN*, March 6, 1931; Gruening, *The Public Pays* (New York: Liveright, 1931), pp. 248–249; Lowitt, *George Norris*, pp. 444–450.

43. Gruening, "The New Colby," *PEN*, Aug. 15, 1930; Gruening, "Vote Monday!" *PEN*, Nov. 29, 1930; Gruening, "Maine's New Educational Survey," *PEN*, Dec. 8, 1930; Gruening, "Bowdoin's Victories," *PEN*, Nov. 16, 1931; Hunt Gruening interview.

44. Gruening to Hubert Herring, March 10, 1931, Series 36, Box 8, GP.

45. Gruening to Edward Lindeman, March 30, 1931, Series 3, Box 3, GP; Gruening, "Cuba under the Machado Regime," *Current History* (May 1931); Louis Pérez, Jr., *Cuba under the Platt Amendment, 1902–1934* (Pittsburgh: University of Pittsburgh Press, 1986), pp. 257–300.

46. Theodore Roosevelt, Jr., to John Finley, Oct. 24, 1930; Roosevelt to Joseph Cotton, Oct. 1, 1930; both in Box 16, Theodore Roosevelt, Jr., Papers, Library of Congress.

47. Gruening, "Hope for Porto Rico," *The Nation*, Sept. 30, 1931; Gruening, "Progress in Porto Rico," *PEN*, Sept. 16, 1931; Luis Muñoz Marín, "Porto Rico: The American Colony," in *These United States*, ed. Ernest Gruening, 2 vols. (New York: Liveright, 1921–1923), 2:373–393.

48. Gruening to Theodore Roosevelt, Jr., March 17, 26, April 25, Oct. 27, 1931; Roosevelt to Gruening, March 29, 31, Nov. 6, 1931; all in Box 16, Roosevelt Papers.

49. Gruening to Oswald Garrison Villard, Nov. 12, 1931, File 1424, Villard Papers; Gruening to Frederick Libby, Nov. 7, 1931, Series 3, Box 2, GP; Gruening, "What Will Japan Do?: A Matter of World-Wide Concern," *PEN*, Nov. 2, 1931; Gruening, "A Boycott against Japan?" *PEN*, Nov. 20, 1931; Gruening, "Preparing against the Next War," *PEN*, Oct. 14, 1931; Chatfield, *For Peace and Justice*, pp. 106–116; Michael Barnhart, *Japan Prepares for Total War: The Search for Eco-*

nomic Security, 1919–1941 (Ithaca, N.Y.: Cornell University Press, 1987), pp. 23–49; Christopher Thorne, *Limits of Foreign Policy: The West, the League, and the Far Eastern Crisis of 1931–1933* (London: Hamilton, 1972).

50. Gruening to Theodore Roosevelt, Jr., April 30, 1932, Box 17, Roosevelt Papers; Gruening, "A Great Note," *PEN*, Jan. 8, 1932; Gruening, "The Geneva Conference and the Far Eastern Crisis," *PEN*, Feb. 2, 1932; Iriye, *The Globalizing of America*, pp. 126–127; Barnhart, *Japan Prepares for Total War*, pp. 50–59.

51. Gruening to John Fahey, May 11, 1932, Series 3, Box 4, GP; Gruening, "Ready to Tackle Power Trusts," *PEN*, Feb. 27, 1931; Gruening, "Hands Off the Federal Trade Commission!" *PEN*, March 1, 1932.

52. Gruening to Lewis Gannett, July 8, 1931, File 1882, Gannett Family Papers, Houghton Library, Harvard University; Hunt Gruening interview; *Many Battles*, pp. 148–149.

53. Gruening to Oswald Garrison Villard, April 4, 1932, File 1424, Villard Papers; Gruening to William Bratton, Oct. 15, 1932, Box 62, Brown Boxes Series, GSP; Gruening to Carleton Beals, Dec. 2, 1932, Box 172, Beals Papers; Hunt Gruening interview.

54. Gruening to Theodore Roosevelt, Jr., April 30, 1932, Box 17, Roosevelt Papers; Theodore Roosevelt, Jr., to Walter White, May 17, 1932; Gruening to White, June 17, Aug. 17, 1932; all in Box C-329, NAACP Papers. For early evidence of Gruening's distrust of FDR over the Haitian issue, see Gruening to Freda Kirchwey, Dec. 8, 1928, Series 3, Box 3, GP.

55. Walter White to Francis White, June 29, 1932; Lawrence Richey to Walter White, Aug. 11, 1932; Theodore Roosevelt, Jr., to Richey, May 20, 1932; all in Box 989, Hoover Presidential Papers, Hoover Library.

56. Walter White to Ludwell Denny, Aug. 16, 1932; Gruening to William King, Sept. 28, 1932; Walter White to Herbert Lehman, Sept. 23, 1932; all in Box C-329, NAACP Papers; Gruening to Dantes Bellegarde, Sept. 10, 1932, "Imperialism, 1919–1941" box, GP; Gruening to Oswald Garrison Villard, Sept. 21, 1932, File 1424, Villard Papers.

57. Gruening to Theodore Roosevelt, Jr., Nov. 16, 1932, 23, Box 17, Roosevelt Papers.

58. Hunt Gruening interview; *Many Battles*, pp. 151–152, 156–158, 171–176; Michael Wreszin, *Oswald Garrison Villard: Pacifist at War* (Bloomington: Indiana University Press, 1965), pp. 221–224.

59. [Gruening], "Do We Need a Dictator?" *The Nation*, March 1, 1933; Ronald Steel, *Walter Lippmann and the American Century* (New York: Vintage Books, 1980), pp. 300–303.

60. [Gruening], "Destroy the Money Power!" *The Nation*, March 22, 1933; Lloyd Dawson Nelson, *Louis D. Brandeis, Felix Frankfurter, and the New Deal* (Hamden, Conn.: Anchor Books, 1982), pp. 30–48; Philippa Strum, *Brandeis: Beyond Progressivism* (Lawrence: University of Kansas Press, 1993), pp. 92–93; Ellis Hawley, *The New Deal and the Problem of Monopoly* (Princeton: Princeton University Press, 1966), pp. 284–302, 344.

61. Michael Parrish, *Felix Frankfurter and His Times: The Reform Years* (New York: The Free Press, 1982), pp. 211–230; Hawley, *The New Deal*, pp. 306–310; Frank Friedel, *Franklin D. Roosevelt: A Rendezvous with Destiny* (Boston: Little, Brown, 1990), pp. 94–142; William Leuchtenberg, *Franklin D. Roosevelt and the*

New Deal, 1932–1940 (New York: Harper & Row, 1963), pp. 32–36, 64–71; Donald Brand, *Corporatism and the Rule of Law: A Study of the National Recovery Administrations* (Ithaca, N.Y.: Cornell University Press, 1988), pp. 74–92; Thomas Ferguson, "From Normalcy to New Deal: Industrial Structure, Party Competition, and American Public Policy in the Great Depression," *International Organization* 38 (1984).

62. Gruening to Felix Frankfurter, June 20, 1933; Frankfurter to Gruening, June 21, 1933; both in Box 60, Frankfurter Papers; [Gruening], "Morgan's Friends Must Go," *The Nation*, June 7, 1933; [Gruening], "President Roosevelt's Appointments," *The Nation*, July 5, 1933; Parrish, *Felix Frankfurter*, pp. 220–221.

63. [Gruening], "The Bankers at Work," *The Nation*, Oct. 4, 1933; *New York Herald Tribune*, April 26, 1933.

64. [Gruening], "Hail, Exiled Scholars!" *The Nation*, Oct. 11, 1933; Arthur Hart, "Results of Investigation," Box 340, Truman PSF; *Many Battles*, pp. 172–179; for Gruening's work on behalf of his German relatives, see Box 6, GP. Gruening lectured widely in the early and mid-1930s on topics ranging from foreign policy issues to "The Problems of City Government" to "Editing the Nation's News"; Hart, "Results of Investigation," Box 340, Truman PSF.

65. Gruening to Felix Frankfurter, June 7, 1933, Series 36, Box 6, GP; Gruening to Florence Allen, Sept. 13, 1933, Series 36, Box 1, GP.

66. Gruening to Felix Frankfurter, March 21, 1933, Box 60, Frankfurter Papers; Felix Frankfurter, as recorded in talks with Harlan Phillips, *Felix Frankfurter Reminisces* (New York: Reynal & Co. 1960), pp. 241–242; Parrish, *Felix Frankfurter*, pp. 200–202; Nelson, *Louis D. Brandeis*, p. 8.

67. [Gruening], "President Roosevelt's Appointments," *The Nation*, July 5, 1933. For the early stages of the Good Neighbor Policy, see Bryce Wood, *The Making of the Good Neighbor Policy* (New York: Columbia University Press, 1961).

68. Gruening to Juan Lliteras, Feb. 21, 1933; Gruening address, March 30, 1933; both in Series 27, Box 6, GP; Gruening to Edward House, June 26, 1933, Box 53, Edward House Papers, Sterling Library, Yale University; [Gruening], "Wanted: A New Deal for Cuba," *The Nation*, April 19, 1933.

69. Felix Frankfurter to Gruening, June 21, 1933, Box 60, Frankfurter Papers; Gruening to Margaret Marsh, May 3, 1933, Series 27, Box 6, GP; [Gruening], "Mr. Welles' Opportunity," *The Nation*, May 3, 1933; [Gruening], "Cuba and the Future," *The Nation*, Aug. 23, 1933; Louis Pérez, Jr., *Cuba under the Platt Amendment, 1902–1934* (Pittsburgh: University of Pittsburgh Press, 1986), pp. 301–332; Irwin Gellman, *Roosevelt and Batista: Good Neighbor Diplomacy in Cuba, 1933–1945* (Albuquerque: University of New Mexico Press, 1973); Wood, *Making of the Good Neighbor Policy*, pp. 48–117.

70. Gruening to Juan Lliteras, July 24, 1933, Series 27, Box 6, GP; Gruening to Felix Frankfurter, June 20, 1933; Frankfurter to Gruening, June 21, 1933; both in Box 60, Frankfurter Papers.

71. Walter White to Gruening, June 13, 1933; Gruening to Felix Frankfurter, June 14, 1933; both in Box 60, Frankfurter Papers; Gruening to Edward House, June 26, 1933; House to Gruening, June 21, 1933; both in Box 53, House Papers; Gruening address, WEVD, June 21, 1933, Series 35, Box 2, GP; Gruening to Raymond Buell, Oct. 6, 1934 [1933], Series 27, Box 6, GP; Gruening to Dorothy Detzer, Nov. 10, 1933, Series C, Box 13, WILPF Papers, SCPC.

72. Gruening to Felix Frankfurter, Sept. 5, Oct. 27, 1933; both in Series 36, Box 6, GP.

73. Gruening to Felix Frankfurter, Oct. 27, 1933, Series 36, Box 6, GP; Dorothy Detzer to Hubert Herring, Nov. 1, 1933, Series C, Box 13, WILPF Papers.

74. Gruening to Freda Kirchwey, Dec. 26, 29, 1933; both in Box F11/186, Freda Kirchwey Papers, Schlesinger Library, Harvard University; "Oral Statement Handed to the Haitian Delegation to the Seventh International Conference of American States by a Member of the American Delegation," enclosed in Norman Armour to William Phillips, Dec. 14, 1933, *Papers Relating to the Foreign Relations of the United States* [hereafter *FRUS*], 1933, 5:776; Phillips to Armour, Jan. 9, 1934, *FRUS* 1934, 5:777; Gruening, "A New Deal for Latin America?," *Current History* (Dec. 1933); *Many Battles*, pp. 162–167.

75. Cordell Hull to Gruening, Dec. 26, 1933, Box 2, General Records, Records of the U.S. Delegation to the Seventh International Conference of American States, Records of International Conferences, Commissions, and Expositions, Record Group 43, National Archives; Gruening to Freda Kirchwey, Nov. 31, 1933, Box C-329, NAACP Papers; Gruening to Freda Kirchwey, Dec. 29, 1933, Box F11/186, Kirchwey Papers.

76. Cordell Hull to Gruening, Feb. 7, 1934, Reel 11, Cordell Hull Papers, Library of Congress; Wood, *Making of the Good Neighbor Policy*, pp. 118–125, 285–287.

77. Gruening to Cordell Hull, Jan. 29, 1934, Reel 10, Hull Papers; Gruening, "Our Era of Imperialism Nears Its End," *New York Times Magazine*, June 10, 1934; Gruening, "At Last We're Getting Out of Haiti," *The Nation*, June 20, 1934.

78. Edward Moran to Franklin Roosevelt, Jan. 6, 1934; Roosevelt to Moran, Jan. 13, 1934; both in Series 400A, Box 27, President's Official File [hereafter FDR POF], Franklin Delano Roosevelt Presidential Library, Hyde Park; *The Nation*, Jan. 4, 1934.

79. Gruening quoted in Walter White memorandum, Oct. 19, 1933; White to Gruening, Oct. 24, 1933; both in Box C-329, NAACP Papers; Gruening to White, Jan. 17, Sept. 6, 1935; both in Box C-330, NAACP Papers.

80. Gruening draft article, "Dictatorship and the Dominican Debt," Series 22, Box 1, GP; Gruening, "The Dictatorship in Santo Domingo: A 'Joint Concern,'" *The Nation*, May 22, 1934.

81. William Baldwin to Gruening, Feb. 2, 1934, Series 22, Box 2, GP; Frank Tannenbaum to Carleton Hayes, May 16, 1929, Box 3, Tannenbaum Papers; Gruening to Josephus Daniels, March 13, 1934, Box 658, Josephus Daniels Papers; *Many Battles*, pp. 127–134.

82. Gruening, "Can Mr. Roosevelt Distinguish between Friends and Foes?" *New York Post*, March 23, 1934; Gruening, "The Politicians against the People," *New York Post*, Feb. 21, 1934.

83. Hunt Gruening interview; J. David Stern interview, in Report by Special Agent Arthur Hart, Oct. 20, 1950, New York City, "Re: ERNEST GRUENING, aka Ernest H. Gruening, Governor of Alaska—Appointee," Box 340, Truman PSF; *Many Battles*, pp. 132–134.

84. Hunt Gruening interview.

85. Foreign Policy Association, *Problems of the New Cuba* (New York: Foreign Policy Association, 1935), pp. 439–441.

86. Carleton Beals to Gruening, Aug. 24, 1933; Gruening to Beals, Sept. 6, 1933; both in Box 173, Beals Papers; Beals, "Saving Cuba," *The Nation*, Feb. 13, 1935; John Britton, *Carleton Beals: A Radical Journalist in Latin America* (Albuquerque: University of New Mexico Press, 1987), pp. 108–121.

4. The Dilemmas of Anti-imperialism

1. Hubert Herring, "Rebellion in Puerto Rico," *The Nation*, Nov. 29, 1933.

2. George Dern to Lewis Douglas, April 23, 1934; Douglas to FDR, May 22, 1934; both in Series 400, Box 23, FDR POF; T. H. Watkins, *Righteous Pilgrim: The Life and Times of Harold L. Ickes, 1874–1952* (New York: Henry Holt and Co., 1990), p. 517; Rexford Tugwell, *The Stricken Land: The Story of Puerto Rico* (Garden City, N.Y.: Doubleday & Co., 1947), pp. 3–11; Theodore Roosevelt, Jr., "Puerto Rico: Our Link with Latin America," *Foreign Affairs* 13 (July 1934), 271–280.

3. FDR memo for Lewis Douglas, April 27, 1934; FDR to George Dern, May 28, 1934; both in Series 400, Box 23, FDR POF; Harold Ickes to FDR, Aug. 15, 1934, Series 6s, Box 18, FDR POF; *Many Battles*, p. 181.

4. Hubert Herring to Elizabeth Wallace, Sept. 6, 1934; Gruening to Elizabeth Wallace, Sept. 15, 1934; both in Box 2, Elizabeth Wallace Papers, Minnesota State Historical Society, St. Paul; Samuel Guy Inman to Gruening, Sept. 9, 1934, Series 36, Box 10, GP; *The Nation*, Aug. 29, 1934; *La Democracia*, Aug. 29, 1934; *Washington Post*, Sept. 17, 1934; both in 1934 Scrapbook, GP.

5. Oswald Garrison Villard to Gruening, Aug. 17, 1934, File 1424, Villard Papers; Villard, "Issues and Men," *The Nation*, Aug. 29, 1934.

6. Michael Vincent Namorato, *The Diary of Rexford G. Tugwell: The New Deal, 1932–1935* (Oxford: University of Mississippi Press, 1993), entries for March 8, 9, 1934, pp. 99–100; Gonzalo Córdova, *Resident Commissioner Santiago Iglesias and His Times* (San Juan: Editorial de la Universidad de Puerto Rico, 1993), p. 343.

7. Córdova, *Santiago Iglesias*, pp. 175–188; Henry Wells, *The Modernization of Puerto Rico: A Political Study of Changing Values and Institutions* (Cambridge, Mass.: Harvard University Press, 1968), pp. 107–108; Whitney Perkins, *Denial of Empire: The United States and Its Dependencies* (Leiden: A. W. Sythoff, 1962), pp. 114–115; Truman Clark, "The Imperial Perspective: Mainland Administrator's Views of the Puerto Rican Economy, 1898–1941," *Revista Interamericana* 4 (1975), 510; Ronald Fernandez, *The Disenchanted Island: Puerto Rico and the United States in the Twentieth Century* (New York: Praeger, 1992), p. 116.

8. Gruening to FDR, May 27, 1935, Series 400B, Box 27, FDR POF; Executive Order 7057, May 28, 1935; Executive Order 7180, Sept. 6, 1935; both in Series 3, Box 10, Record Group 323, Records of the Puerto Rican Reconstruction Administration, National Archives, New York City [hereafter RG 323]; Harold Ickes to FDR, July 12, 1935, Series 400, Box 23, FDR POF; Córdova, *Santiago Iglesias*, p. 359.

9. Gruening to FDR, Dec. 17, 1934, Series 400, Box 23, FDR POF; Gruening, "Background of the Puerto Rican Situation," 1935, Series 9-8-107, Record Group 126, Office of Territories, Classified Files, National Archives, Washington, D.C. [hereafter RG 126]; Gruening to James Bourne, Sept. 9, Oct. 11, 1935, both

in Series 1, Box 9, RG 323; Gruening to Blanton Winship, May 28, 1935, Series 9-8-98, Box 1043, RG 126; Clark, "The Imperial Perspective," p. 506.

10. Wells, *Modernization of Puerto Rico*, pp. 95–107; Córdova, *Santiago Iglesias*, pp. 193–252; Bolívar Pagan, *Historia de los Partidos Políticos Puertoriqueños* (San Juan: Lusrería Campos, 1959).

11. For the background to the relationship between Gruening and Muñoz Marín, see Luis Muñoz Marín, *Memorias: Autobiografía Pública, 1898–1940* (San Juan: Universidad Inter Americana de Puerto Rico, 1982), pp. 53–54, 58–62.

12. Wells, *Modernization of Puerto Rico*, pp. 108–115; Córdova, *Santiago Iglesias*, pp. 243–256; Fernandez, *The Disenchanted Island*, p. 114; Frank Otto Gatell, "Independence Rejected: Puerto Rico and the Tydings Bill of 1936," *Hispanic American Historical Review* 38 (1958), 27.

13. Luis Muñoz Marín to Gruening, March 22, 1935, Series 4, Box 2, GP; José Padín to Gruening, June 12, 1935, "Personnel—Chardón, Carlos" file, RG 126; Harwood Hull to Steve Early, July 20, 1935, Box 255, Harold Ickes Papers, Library of Congress; Gruening to FDR, Sept. 24, 1935, series 400, Box 23, FDR POF; Muñoz Marín, "Memorandum re Further Investment of Absentee Capital in Puerto Rico," Dec. 1934; Muñoz Marín to Gruening, Feb. 25, 1935, Series 4, Box 2, GP; Muñoz Marín, *Autobiografía*, pp. 127–131.

14. "Message of Blanton Winship," Feb. 12, 1935, Series 9-8-79, Box 938, RG 126; Winship to Marvin McIntyre, Nov. 19, 1935, Series 400, Box 23, FDR POF; Gatell, "Independence Rejected," p. 27; *New York Times*, Oct. 28, 1935; Thomas Mathews, *Puerto Rican Politics and the New Deal* (Gainesville: University of Florida Press, 1960), p. 204.

15. Gruening to Winship, June 29, July 16, 1935; both in Series 9-8-98, Box 1043, RG 126; Winship to Gruening, April 1, 3, 1935; Charles Fahy to Ickes, Aug. 22, 1935; all in Series 9-8-51, Box 794, RG 126; Gatell, "Independence Rejected," pp. 25–26.

16. Oscar Chapman interview, in Report by Special Agent Patrick Rice, Nov. 14, 1950, Washington, D.C., "Re: ERNEST GRUENING, aka Ernest H. Gruening, Governor of Alaska—Appointee," Box 340, PSF; *The Journals of David Lilienthal*, vol. 1, *The TVA Years, 1939–1945* (New York: Harper and Row, 1964), p. 564; [Gruening], "Secretary Ickes Cleans House," *The Nation*, May 31, 1933; Lloyd Dawson Nelson, *Louis D. Brandeis, Felix Frankfurter, and the New Deal* (Hamden, Conn.: Anchor Books, 1982), p. 49; Watkins, *Righteous Pilgrim;* p. 514; Harold Ickes, *The Secret Diary of Harold L. Ickes*, 3 vols. (New York: Simon and Schuster, 1953), entry for Jan. 13, 1936, 1:503–504.

17. *El Imparcial*, Feb. 7, 1935; *El País*, Feb. 14, 1935; both in 1935 Scrapbook, GP; Miranda, "Ernest Gruening Is a 'Case,'" *El Imparcial*, Nov. 13, 1936, Series 4, Box 2, GP.

18. Gruening to D. W. Bell, Feb. 24, April 23, 1936; both in Series 1, Box 2, RG 323; Gruening to Comptroller General, Aug. 8, 1936, Series 1, Box 26, RG 323.

19. FDR to Gruening, Nov. 26, 1934; Harold Ickes to FDR, July 19, 1935; FDR to Blanton Winship, July 19, 1935; FDR, "Memorandum for the Acting Attorney General," Aug. 31, 1935; Gruening to FDR, Oct. 28, 1935; all in Series 400, Box 23, FDR POF; Nathan Margold memorandum, May 7, 1936, Box 255, Ickes Papers; Sumner Welles memorandum, "Conversation," June 18, 1935; Welles

memorandum, "Conversation," July 18, 1935; both in Box 149, Sumner Welles Papers, FDR Library.

20. Gruening, "Memorandum for the Acting Director of the Budget," March 18, 1935; Gruening to Harold Ickes, July 17, 1935; both in Series 400, Box 23, FDR POF.

21. Gruening, "Memorandum for the Secretary," Jan. 2, 1935; Gruening, "Memorandum on the Puerto Rican Land Policy Situation," July 24, 1935; Gruening to Harold Ickes, Dec. 28, 1935; all in Series 9-8-77, Box 929, RG 126.

22. Puerto Rican Policy Commission, Report, Series 400, Box 23, FDR POF; Gruening, "Background of the Puerto Rican Situation," 1935, Series 9-8-107, Box 1073, RG 126.

23. Gruening to Carlos Chardón, May 4, 1936, Series 2, Box 2, RG 323; Gruening to Comptroller General, Aug. 8, 1936, Series 1, Box 26, RG 323; Gruening to Miles Fairbank, June 25, 1937, series 1, Box 42, RG 323.

24. Gruening to Rafael Fernández García, July 24, 1936; Fernández García to Gruening, Aug. 20, 1936; both in Series 4, Box 1, GP; Fernández García to Harold Ickes, Dec. 23, 1936, Box 255, Ickes Papers.

25. Ickes, *Secret Diary*, entry for Feb. 28, 1935, 1:304–305; Nelson, *Louis D. Brandeis*, p. 114; Anthony Badger, *The New Deal: The Depression Years, 1933–1940* (New York: Macmillan, 1989), pp. 94–101.

26. Michael Parrish, *Felix Frankfurter: The Reform Years* (New York: The Free Press, 1982), pp. 247–250; Ellis Hawley, *The New Deal and the Problem of Monopoly* (Princeton: Princeton University Press, 1966), pp. 327–334, 344–357; Frank Friedel, *Franklin D. Roosevelt: Rendezvous with Destiny* (Boston: Little, Brown, 1990), pp. 167–169.

27. Hawley, *The New Deal*, pp. 327–334.

28. Alan Brinkley, *The End of Reform: New Deal Liberalism in Recession and War* (New York: Knopf, 1995), pp. 50–55; U.S. House of Representatives, Committee on Rules, *Hearings, Investigation of Lobbying on Utility Holding Company Bills* [hereafter *Utility Hearings*], 74th Congress, 1st session, p. 17 (July 9, 1935).

29. *Utility Hearings*, pp. 2–4, 15–23, 63, 80–93 (July 9, 11, 1935).

30. *Time*, July 22, 1935; Parrish, *Felix Frankfurter*, p. 250; Hawley, *The New Deal*, p. 334.

31. Gruening to Blanton Winship, Jan. 18, 1935, Series 9-8-51, Box 794, RG 126; Gruening to Bishop Edwin Byrne, July 3, 1935, Series 9-8-116, Box 1137, RG 126; Gruening quoted in *El Imparcial*, Nov. 5, 1934, 1934 Scrapbook, GP; U.S. House of Representatives, Committee on Appropriations, *Hearings, Interior Department Appropriations Bill for 1938, Part 1*, 75th Congress, 1st session, p. 79 (March 15, 1937); Clark, "The Imperial Perspective," p. 513.

32. Gruening to Blanton Winship, March 15, 1935, Series 9-8-51, Box 794, RG 126; Gruening to Robert Cornelia, Feb. 19, 1937, Series 9-8-60, Box 840, RG 126; Gruening quoted in *El Imparcial*, Nov. 9, 1934, 1934 Scrapbook, GP. On the ideology of the Latin American Democratic Left, see Charles Ameringer, *The Democratic Left in Exile* (Coral Gables, Fla.: University of Miami Press, 1974).

33. Gruening to Herbert Priestly, Sept. 24, 1934; Gruening to Carlos Chardón, Nov. 17, 1934; both in Series 9-8-94, Box 1031, RG 126; Gruening to Blanton Winship, April 8, 1935, Series 9-8-51, Box 794, RG 126.

34. José Padín to Gruening, July 27, 1936, Series 3, Box 26, RG 323; Gruening

to Miles Fairbank, Dec. 18, 1936, Series 1, Box 60, RG 323; Gruening, "Memorandum for Mr. Banse," Feb. 2, 1937, Series 1, Box 2, RG 323; Ernest Gruening, *Mexico and Its Heritage* (New York: Century Company, 1928), pp. 520–528.

35. Gruening to Samuel Guy Inman, Feb. 23, 1936, Box 14, Inman Papers; *FRUS* 1935, 4:814–817; Bryce Wood, *The Making of the Good Neighbor Policy* (New York: Columbia University Press, 1961), pp. 142–145.

36. Hunt Gruening interview.

37. Arthur Hart, "Results of Investigation," Nov. 2, 1950, Box 340, Truman PSF.

38. U.S. Senate, Committee on Appropriations, *Hearings, District of Columbia Appropriations Bill, 1938*, 75th Congress, 1st session, pp. 325–332 (May 27, 1937); Hunt Gruening interview; George Sundborg interview, Feb. 23, 1995; Washington League of Women Shoppers pamphlet, enclosed in Report by Special Agent Patrick Rice, Nov. 14, 1950, Washington, D.C., "Re: ERNEST GRUENING, aka Ernest H. Gruening, Governor of Alaska—Appointee," Box 341, Truman PSF.

39. Gruening to Blanton Winship, March 9, 1936, Series 9-8-78, Box 933, RG 126; Gerald Johnson, "Puerto Rico: Imperial Headache," *Baltimore Sun*, June 16, 1937, 1937 Scrapbook, GP; Gatell, "Independence Rejected," pp. 41–42.

40. Gruening, "Memorandum for the Secretary," Jan. 21, 1937, Series 4, Box 1, GP; Gruening to Lewis Gannett, Aug. 25, 1936, File 1882, Gannett Family Papers; Johnson, "Puerto Rico: Imperial Headache."

41. Luis Muñoz Marín to Harold Ickes, quoted in Gruening, "Memorandum for the Secretary," Jan. 21, 1937, Series 4, Box 1, GP; Gruening to Talcott Powell, Oct. 31, 1936, Series 9-8-84, Box 954, RG 126; Mathews, *Puerto Rican Politics and the New Deal*, p. 255; Gatell, "Independence Rejected," p. 30.

42. Edward Angly in *New York Herald Tribune*, May 17, 1936, 1936 Scrapbook, GP; Murray Paddock, "Puerto Rico's Plight," *Current History* 44 (June 1936); *Washington Post*, Feb. 25, 1936; *New York Times*, May 14, 1936.

43. Millard Tydings quoted in *Washington Star*, 1936 Scrapbook, GP; GD, July 15, 1936.

44. Gruening to Harold Ickes, March 13, 1936, Box 255, Ickes Papers; Gruening to Millard Tydings, March 27, 1936, Series 9-8-68, Box 864, RG 126.

45. Harold Ickes to Gruening, March 19, 1936; Alexander Weddell to Cordell Hull, April 29, 1936; Gruening to Ralph Louisbury, May 7, 1936; all in Series 9-8-68, Box 864, RG 126; Gruening quoted in *Washington Star*, 1936 Scrapbook, GP; Tydings quoted in *New York Times*, April 24, 1936.

46. Gruening to Carlos Chardón, May 1, 1936, Series 4, Box 3, GP.

47. Ibid.

48. GD, June 2, 4, 7, 1936; *El Mundo*, April 26, 1936, 1936 Scrapbook, GP.

49. GD, June 2, 4, 1936.

50. William King to FDR, Oct. 19, 1936; Luis Muñoz Marín to FDR, April 19, 1937; both in Series 400, Box 24, FDR POF; Oswald Garrison Villard to Roger Baldwin, March 1, 1938, Box 114, Villard Papers; GD, Aug. 13, 1936, Oct. 19, 25, 31, 1936.

51. Gruening to Harold Ickes, March 13, 1936, Box 255, Ickes Papers; Gruening, "Memorandum Concerning Puerto Rico," Sept. 24, 1936, Series 4, Box 2, GP.

52. Gruening to Earl Hanson, July 27, 1936, Series 4, Box 1, GP; Gruening quoted in *La Correspondencia*, Sept. 28, 1936; Luis Muñoz Marín quoted in *El*

Mundo, Sept. 23, 1936; all in 1936 Scrapbook, GP; Muñoz Marín to Ruby Black, Sept. 25, 1936, quoted in Mathews, *Puerto Rican Politics and the New Deal*, p. 272.

53. Gatell, "Independence Rejected," pp. 36–39; Tugwell, *The Stricken Land*, p. 10.

54. Transcript of conversation between Gruening and coalition leaders, Sept. 5, 1935, Series 4, Box 4, GP; Gruening to Harry Hopkins, Dec. 28, 1935, Series 1, Box 33, RG 323; Gruening to Francis Shea, April 10, 1936, Series 4, Box 3, GP.

55. Gruening to Earl Hanson, July 27, 1936, Series 4, Box 1, GP; Gruening radiogram #821 to Carlos Chardón, July 25, 1936; Gruening radiogram #992 to Raúl Esteves, Sept. 25, 1936; both in Series 5, Box 4, RG 323; GD, Sept. 8–12, 1936; *La Correspondencia*, Sept. 23, 1936, 1936 Scrapbook, GP; Wells, *Modernization of Puerto Rico*, pp. 117–118.

56. Gruening, *Mexico and Its Heritage*, p. 293.

57. James Bourne to FDR, April 21, 1936; Eleanor Roosevelt, "Memorandum for the President," Feb. 12, 1936; both in Series 400, Box 24, FDR POF.

58. Luis Muñoz Marín to Ruby Black, Nov. 5, 1936, copy in Box 48, President's Secretary's File, FDR Library [hereafter FDR PSF]; *El Mundo*, Nov. 5, 6, 1936; Gatell, "Independence Rejected," pp. 42–44.

59. Gruening, "Memorandum for the Secretary," Jan. 21, 1937, Series 4, Box 1, GP; GD, Oct. 21, 1936.

60. Miles Fairbank to Fernando Luis Toro, Dec. 3, 1936; Gruening to Jaime Annexy, May 26, 1937; both in Series 10, Box 1, RG 323; Carlos Chardón to FDR, Nov. 11, 1936, Series 400B, Box 27, FDR POF; GD, Nov. 3, 6, 7, 1936; Luis Muñoz Marín quoted in Watkins, *Righteous Pilgrim*, p. 522.

61. Gruening to FDR, Sept. 14, 1936, Series 1, Box 45, RG 323; W. F. Banse to Gruening, April 17, 1937, Series 1, Box 2, RG 323; GD, June 7, Aug. 22, Oct. 16, 1936.

62. D. W. Bell, "Memorandum for the President," June 27, 1936; FDR, "Memorandum for the Acting Director of the Budget," Aug. 13, 1936; both in Series 400B, Box 27, FDR POF; FDR to Gruening, Oct. 28, 1936, Series 1, Box 44, RG 323; Gruening, "Memorandum for Mr. Burlew," Nov. 21, 1936; D. W. Bell to E. K. Burlew, Dec. 9, 1936; Burlew, "Memorandum for Administrator Gruening," Dec. 10, 1936; all in Series 1, Box 2, RG 323.

63. E. E. Glover to E. G. Royster, Dec. 10, 1936, Series 1, Box 17, RG 323; Leona Graham, "Preliminary Memorandum for the Secretary of the Interior," Dec. 28, 1936, Series 4, Box 1, GP; E. K. Burlew to Harold Ickes, April 21, 1937, Box 256, Ickes Papers.

64. Harold Ickes to FDR, June 10, 1937, Box 55, FDR PSF; Gruening, "Memorandum for the Secretary," July 12, 1937; Ickes to Gruening, Dec. 29, 1937; both in Series 36, Box 10, GP; Ickes, *Secret Diary*, entry for Feb. 6, 1937, 2:64.

65. Gruening to Lewis Gannett, April 3, 1937, File 1882, Gannett Family Papers; Gruening to Earle James, Aug. 21, 1937, Series 4, Box 2, GP.

66. Roger Baldwin to Gruening, March 7, 1936; Gruening to Harold Ickes, July 9, 1936; both in Series 9-8-78, Box 933, RG 126; Luis Muñoz Marín to Baldwin, Jan. 15, 1937, vol. 1064, p. 93, ACLU Papers, Mudd Library, Princeton University; Gruening to Baldwin, March 27, 1937, vol. 1064, p. 117, ACLU Papers; Ickes, *Secret Diary*, entry for Jan. 13, 1937, 2:47.

67. Gruening to Freda Kirchwey, April 30, 1936, File 1424, Villard Papers; "Hobson's Choice for Puerto Rico," *The Nation,* May 6, 1936.

68. Gruening to George Eliot, June 2, 1936; Eliot to Gruening, June 6, 1936; both in Box 10, George Eliot Papers, Hoover Institute on War, Revolution, and Peace, Palo Alto.

69. Miguel Guerra-Mondragón to Baldwin, April 5, 1937; Baldwin to Gruening, May 15, 1937; Gruening to Baldwin, March 30, 1937; Hays to Gruening, June 10, 1937; all in vol. 1062, ACLU Papers, pp. 177, 205, 174, 241.

70. Gruening to Michael Francis Doyle, April 19, 1937, Series 4, Box 2, GP; Gruening to Freda Kirchwey, June 5, 1937, Series 9-8-78, Box 933, RG 126; "The Puerto Rican Problem," *New Republic,* April 14, 1937; *Chicago Tribune,* July 1, 1937.

71. Oswald Garrison Villard to Mrs. Luis Muñoz Marín, April 27, 1937, File 2720; Villard to Arthur Garfield Hays, June 21, 1937, File 1594; Gruening to Villard, June 26, 1937, File 114; Villard to Gruening, April 2, 1937, File 1424; all in Villard Papers; Villard, "Liberty and Death in Puerto Rico," *The Nation,* April 3, 1937; Villard, "Reconstruction in Puerto Rico," *The Nation,* April 10, 1937.

72. Oswald Garrison Villard to Gruening, Nov. 28, 1936, File 1424, Villard Papers.

73. Gruening to Manuel Gamio, June 6, 1939, Series 22, Box 1, GP; Gruening to Robert Murray, Dec. 16, 1940, Box 3, Senate Miscellaneous Files, GP; Wood, *Making of the Good Neighbor Policy,* pp. 179–215.

74. Gruening to Ellis Briggs, Jan. 11, 1939, Series 9-8-78, Box 933, RG 126; GD, April 7, 8, May 3, 16, 1938.

75. GD, Sept. 17, 20, 23, 25, 1938.

76. GD, Oct. 12, Nov. 22, 1938.

77. GD, May 12, 18, 31, 1939.

5. The Alaskan Agenda

1. Oswald Garrison Villard to Roger Baldwin, May 29, 1939, Box 114, Villard Papers; Mike Gravel interview, Pebble Beach, Calif., April 22, 1995.

2. GD, Aug. 8, 1939; *Many Battles,* pp. 281–283.

3. Harold Ickes to FDR, Oct. 12, 1939; EMW, "Memorandum for the President," Feb. 12, 1940; both in Series 400, Box 2, FDR POF; Gruening to Freda Kirchwey, Oct. 13, 1939, Box F11, Folder 186, Kirchwey Papers; Harold Ickes, *The Secret Diary of Harold L. Ickes,* 3 vols. (New York: Simon and Schuster, 1953–1954), entry for May 20, 1939, 2:636; Hunt Gruening interview; *U.S. News & World Report,* April 22, 1949.

4. For Gruening's early perspective on Alaska, see GD, July 2, 8, 1936; U.S. House of Representatives, Committee on Appropriations, *Hearings, Interior Department Appropriation Bill for 1938, Part 1,* 75th Congress, 1st session, pp. 662–669 (March 15, 1937).

5. Claus Naske, *An Interpretive History of Alaskan Statehood* (Anchorage: Alaska Northwest Publishing Company, 1973), pp. 54–56, 86.

6. Claus Naske and Herman Slotnick, *Alaska: A History of the 49th State* (Grand Rapids, Mich.: William Eerdmans Publishing Company, 1979), pp. 94–109; Frederick Calhoun, "Power and Chaos: Marshaling Principles from Uses," in *On*

Cultural Ground: Essays in International History, ed. Robert David Johnson (Chicago: Imprint Publications, 1994), pp. 56–58; Claus Naske, "Some Attention, Little Action: Vacillating Federal Efforts to Provide Territorial Alaska with an Economic Base," *Western Historical Quarterly* 26 (1995), 31–68.

7. Gruening to Oscar Chapman, Nov. 29, 1940, Series 4, Box 2, GP; Gruening to Eric Thomsen, June 21, 1940, Series 230, Box 1, GP; Gruening to Richard Neuberger, Nov. 24, 1941, Box 37, Richard Neuberger Papers, University of Oregon Library, Eugene. For U.S. foreign policy and the altered international climate, see Waldo Heinrichs, *Threshold of War: Franklin D. Roosevelt and American Entry into World War II* (New York: Oxford University Press, 1988).

8. Harold Ickes to Bruce Bliven, May 19, 1942, Box 93, Ickes Papers; Gruening to Warren Magnuson, Oct. 24, 1940, Box 42, Warren Magnuson Papers, Allen Library, University of Washington.

9. For the transformation of liberalism, see Alan Brinkley, *The End of Reform: New Deal Liberalism in Recession and War* (New York: Knopf, 1995), pp. 62–170.

10. Gruening to Richard Neuberger, Aug. 4, 1941, Box 37, Neuberger Papers; Gruening to Oscar Chapman, Nov. 6, 1940, Box 20, Oscar Chapman Papers, Truman Library; Ernest Gruening, *A Message to the People of Alaska from Governor Ernest Gruening* (Juneau: Territory of Alaska, 1941), p. 2; "Message to the Thirty-First Annual Convention of the Alaska Native Brotherhood at Kake," Nov. 13, 1944, Series G 125, Box 2 of 3, Drew Pearson Papers, Lyndon Baines Johnson Presidential Library, Austin; George Sundborg interview, Feb. 23, 1995.

11. *Many Battles*, pp. 299–301; George Sundborg interview, Feb. 23, 1995; Steve McCutcheon interview, Anchorage, May 30, 1995.

12. Steve McCutcheon interview; "Memorandum, Re: Lobbying Activities; Territorial Legislature of Juneau, Alaska, January 1941," March 4, 1942, enclosed in J. Edgar Hoover to Gruening, March 5, 1942, copy in possession of Hunt Gruening.

13. Gruening to Anthony Dimond, July 7, 1941; Gruening to John Donaher, Dec. 3, 1941; both in Series 230, Box 1A, GP; Gruening to Thomas Dewey, Aug. 6, 1952, Series 230, Box 8, GP; Stewart Udall interview, Santa Fe, May 28, 1995; Steve McCutcheon interview.

14. Gruening, "Memorandum on Alaska's Military Situation," Feb. 14, 1942, Box 93, Ickes Papers; Gruening to Harold Ickes, Feb. 19, 1942, Series 9-1-96, Box 506, RG 126; H. M. Waite to Harold Smith, March 12, 1942, Series 400, Box 2, FDR POF.

15. Drew Pearson, "Notes on Alaska," 1943, Series G 125, Box 2 of 3, Pearson Papers; FDR, "Memorandum for General Marshall and Admiral King," Jan. 20, 1942; FDR, "Memorandum for the Director of the Budget," March 16, 1942; both in Series 400, Box 2, FDR POF; Dwight Eisenhower to John McCloy, May 18, 1942; Henry Stimson to Harold Smith, May 25, 1942; both in Box 1231, Records of the War Department, General and Special Staff, Record Group 165, National Archives II, College Park, Md.: T. H. Watkins, *Righteous Pilgrim: The Life and Times of Harold L. Ickes, 1874–1952* (New York: Henry Holt and Co., 1990), pp. 786–789; George Sundborg interview, Feb. 23, 1995.

16. Gruening to Harold Ickes, Sept. 25, 1942; Gruening to Byron Price, Dec. 19, 1942; both in Series 9-1-96, Box 506, RG 126; Price, "Memorandum for the President," Dec. 10, 1942, Series 400, Box 2, FDR POF; Ickes to Byron Price, Dec.

28, 1942, Box 93, Ickes Papers; U.S. Senate, Committee on the Judiciary, *Hearings, Amendment of First War Powers Act of 1941 by Extending Geographical Scope of Censorship of Military-Related Communications*, 76th Congress, 2d session, pp. 2, 7 (Nov. 30, 1942); U.S. Senate, Committee on the Judiciary, *Hearings, Office of Censorship Review*, 76th Congress, 2d session, p. 149 (Dec. 9, 1942); *New York Times*, Sept. 6, Dec. 10, 1942.

17. Gruening to Abe Fortas, Dec. 19, 1942, Series 9-1-24, Box 288, RG 126; Gruening to S. B. Buckner, Sept. 9, 1943; both in Series 9-1-96, Box 506, RG 126; Gruening to Harold Ickes, Sept. 21, 1942, Series 9-1-24, Box 288, RG 126; *New York Times*, Feb. 14, 1942.

18. Gruening to Richard Neuberger, April 13, 1942, Box 37, Neuberger Papers; George Sundborg interview, Feb. 23, 1995; Maurine Neuberger interview, Portland, Ore., June 1, 1995; Robert Atwood interview, Anchorage, May 29, 1995.

19. Gruening to Guy Swope, July 30, 1942, Series 230, Box 1A, GP; Gruening to Charles Bunnell, June 15, 1943; June 7, 1944; both in Series 230, Box 1B, GP; Harold Ickes to Gruening, Dec. 29, 1944, Box 93, Ickes Papers; Claus Naske, "Ernest Gruening and Alaskan Native Claims," *Pacific Northwest Quarterly* 82 (1991), 141–142; Terrence Cole, "Jim Crow in Alaska: The Passage of the Alaska Equal Rights Act of 1945," *Western Historical Quarterly* 23 (1992), 429–450.

20. Naske and Slotnick, *Alaska*, pp. 11–123; Naske, *Alaskan Statehood*, p. 59.

21. Gruening to Oscar Chapman, May 25, 1944, Box 20, Chapman Papers; Steve McCutcheon to Drew Pearson, May 3, 1965, Series G 284, Box 1 of 2, Pearson Papers; Robert Atwood interview; Steve McCutcheon interview; George Sundborg interview, Seattle, Nov. 10, 1994; Mike Gravel interview.

22. Gruening to Mrs. C. A. Wilder, Jan. 23, 1943, Series 230, Box 1B, GP; Gruening to Richard Neuberger, April 8, 1946, Box 37, Neuberger Papers; Oscar Chapman to Gruening, May 31, 1944, Box 20, Chapman Papers; *New York Times*, "Phantom Senator," July 1, 1958.

23. Gruening to Oscar Chapman, May 25, 1944, Series 230, Box 1D, GP; *Anchorage Daily Times*, Jan. 25, Feb. 14, 23, 1945; *Many Battles*, p. 333.

24. Gruening to Richard Neuberger, Aug. 24, 1944, Box 37, Neuberger Papers; George Sundborg interview, Feb. 23, 1995; Robert Atwood interview.

25. Robert Atwood interview; Steve McCutcheon interview; Hunt Gruening interview; "Phantom Senator"; George Sundborg, "Senator Gruening's Last Campaign: What an Alaska Political Race Looked Like from the Inside," unpublished ms., pp. 2–3.

26. George Sundborg interview, Nov. 10, 1994; Hunt Gruening interview; Hunt Gruening, "The Eaglerock Story," unpublished ms., copy in possession of author.

27. Hunt Gruening interview; Robert Atwood interview; George Sundborg interview, Feb. 23, 1995; Maurine Neuberger interview.

28. Hunt Gruening interview; George Sundborg interview, Feb. 23, 1995; Robert Atwood interview; Steve McCutcheon interview.

29. Gruening to Felix Frankfurter, n.d. [1950], Box 60, Frankfurter Papers; Hunt Gruening interview; George Sundborg interviews, Nov. 10, 1994, and Feb. 23, 1995; Maurine Neuberger interview.

30. Gruening to Henry Morgenthau, Sept. 30, 1944, Series 230, Box 1A, GP; Gruening to Francis Shea, May 25, 1945, Series 230, Box 1C, GP.

31. Joseph Lash, ed., *From the Diaries of Felix Frankfurter* (New York: W. W. Norton & Co., 1978), entry for Nov. 17, 1946, p. 300.

32. *Anchorage Daily Times*, Jan. 30, Feb. 14, 1947; *Jessen's Weekly*, Feb. 7, 21, 1947; *Many Battles*, p. 346.

33. Gruening to Oscar Chapman, March 26, 1946, Box 20, Chapman Papers; *Anchorage Daily Times*, Feb. 20, March 26, 1947; *Jessen's Weekly*, Feb. 21, 1947; George Sundborg interview, Nov. 10, 1994; Steven Levi, "Labor History and Alaska," *Labor History* 30 (1989), 585–607.

34. Gruening to Oscar Chapman, Aug. 19, 1947, Box 20, Chapman Papers; Gruening to Robert Allen, Sept. 10, 1948, Series G 125, Box 2 of 3, Pearson Papers; Robert Atwood interview; *Many Battles*, p. 337; Claus Naske, "Governor Ernest Gruening's Struggle for Territorial Status: Personal or Political?" *Journal of the West* 20 (1981), 34–36.

35. Brinkley, *The End of Reform;* Alonzo Hamby, *Beyond the New Deal: Harry S Truman and American Liberalism* (New York: Columbia University Press, 1973), pp. 299–301; Steven Gillon, *Politics and Vision: The ADA and American Liberalism, 1947–1985* (New York: Oxford University Press, 1987), pp. 62–64; Gale Peterson, *President Harry Truman and the Independent Regulatory Commissions, 1945–1952* (New York: Garland, 1985), pp. 306–309.

36. Robert S. Allen, "Next on a List of New Dealers to Be Dropped by Truman?" *Boston Globe*, Jan. 30, 1948.

37. Gruening to Oscar Chapman, June 30, Sept. 10, 1948; Gruening address, Ketchikan, enclosed in Katherine Alexander to Oscar Chapman, Jan. 22, 1948; all in Box 20, Chapman Papers; *Many Battles*, p. 352; Alonzo Hamby, *Man of the People: A Life of Harry S. Truman* (New York: Oxford University Press, 1995), pp. 452–466; David McCullough, *Truman* (New York: Simon and Schuster, 1992), pp. 590–717.

38. *Anchorage Daily Times*, Jan. 25, 1949; *Jessen's Weekly*, March 11, 1949.

39. Robert Atwood interview; *Anchorage Daily Times*, Jan. 28, Feb. 8, 1949; *Fairbanks Daily News-Miner*, Jan. 18, 26, 1949; *Jessen's Weekly*, April 1, 1949; *Many Battles*, pp. 352–354.

40. Naske, "Governor Ernest Gruening's Struggle," pp. 35–37.

41. U.S. Senate, Committee on Interior and Insular Affairs, *Hearings, Nomination of Dr. Ernest Gruening to Be Governor of Alaska* [hereafter *Gruening Hearings*], 81st Congress, 1st session, pp. 4–66 (April 1, 1949).

42. Ibid., pp. 6–86 (April 1, 1949); "Phantom Senator."

43. *Gruening Hearings*, pp. 70–84 (April 1, 1949).

44. Gruening to Julius Krug, Aug. 24, 1949, Series 9-1-87, Box 482, RG 126; Gruening to Oscar Chapman, Aug. 20, 1951, Box 46, Chapman Papers; George Sundborg interview, Feb. 23, 1995.

45. For the origins of national liberalism, see Hamby, *Beyond the New Deal*, pp. 56–213; Gillon, *Politics and Vision*, pp. 13–118; Brinkley, *The End of Reform*, pp. 175–272; Robert Dallek, *Lone Star Rising: Lyndon Johnson and His Times, 1908–1960* (New York: Oxford University Press, 1991), pp. 392–464. For U.S. foreign relations during the early stages of the Cold War, see McGeorge Bundy, *Danger and Survival: Choices about the Bomb in the First Fifty Years* (New York: Random House, 1988); John Lewis Gaddis, *The United States and the Origins of the Cold War, 1941–1947* (New York: Columbia University Press, 1972); Michael Hogan, *The Marshall Plan: America, Britain, and the Reconstruction of Western Europe, 1947–1952* (New

York: Cambridge University Press, 1987); Gabriel and Joyce Kolko, *The Limits of Power: The World and United States Foreign Policy, 1945–1954* (New York: Harper and Row, 1972); Melvyn Leffler, *A Preponderance of Power: National Security, the Truman Administration, and the Cold War* (Stanford: Stanford University Press, 1992); John Lewis Gaddis, "The Emerging Post-Revisionist Synthesis on the Origins of the Cold War," *Diplomatic History* 7 (1983), pp. 171–190; David Reynolds, "The Origins of the Cold War: The European Dimension, 1944–1951," *Historical Journal* 28 (1985), 497–515.

46. Drew Pearson to Gruening, Nov. 21, 1949, Series G 125, Box 2 of 3, Pearson Papers; Tyler Abell, ed., *Drew Pearson: Diaries, 1949–1959* (New York: Holt, Rinehart, and Winston, 1974), entry for April 5, 1949, p. 38. For other Gruening comments on this issue, see Gruening to Richard Peter, March 11, 1948, Series 230, Box 1D, GP; Gruening interview, "Alaska—Another Pearl Harbor?" *U.S. News & World Report*, Nov. 18, 1949; *Washington Post*, Jan. 13, 1950; Marquis Childs, "Alaska's Defenses," 1950 [no specific date]; all in Series 9-0-42, Box 149, RG 126.

47. For such comments, see *Anchorage Daily Times*, Feb. 14, March 18, 29, 1947.

48. Harry Truman memorandum for John Steelman, March 6, 1948; George Killion report, enclosed in Killion to Truman, March 1, 1948; both in Box 2, White House Confidential File, Truman Library; Gruening to Arthur Schlesinger, Jr., Oct. 25, 1949, Box P-15, Arthur Schlesinger, Jr., Papers, John F. Kennedy Presidential Library, Boston; U.S. House of Representatives, Committee on Appropriations, *Hearings, Department of Labor—Federal Security Agency Appropriations for 1951, Part 3*, 81st Congress, 2d session, p. 638 (Jan. 20, 1950).

49. Gruening to Claude Pepper, May 23, 1950, Jan. 12, 1951; both in Series 230, Box 1D, GP; Gruening to Herbert Lehman, Nov. 8, 1950, Special Correspondence File, Herbert Lehman Papers, Columbia University.

50. For a typical example of this tactic, see U.S. Senate, Committee on Public Works, *Hearings, Alaskan Public Works*, 81st Congress, 1st session, pp. 105–109 (Aug. 28, 1949).

51. Leffler, *A Preponderance of Power*, pp. 312–494; David Oshinsky, *A Conspiracy So Immense: The World of Joe McCarthy* (New York: Free Press, 1983); Gary Hess, *The United States' Emergence as a Southeast Asian Power, 1940–1950* (New York: Columbia University Press, 1987).

52. Gruening to Oscar Chapman, Nov. 14, 1949, Jan. 6, 1950; Gruening to Bob Atwood, Nov. 24, 1950; all in Series 230, Box 1D, GP; Gruening to Arthur Schlesinger, Jr., Oct. 25, 1949, Box P-15, Schlesinger Papers; U.S. Senate, Committee on Appropriations, *Hearings, Interior Department Appropriation Bill for 1949*, 80th Congress, 2d session, pp. 560–563 (June 3, 1948). For the development of foreign aid, see Leffler, *Preponderance of Power*, pp. 267, 309–311; Chester Pach, *Arming the Free World: The Origins of the United States Military Assistance Program, 1945–1950* (Chapel Hill: University of North Carolina Press, 1991).

53. Gruening to Oscar Chapman, Oct. 14, 1949, Box 46, Chapman Papers; Gruening to Harry Truman, Jan. 8, 1949, Box 1090, President's Office File, White House Central File, Truman Library [hereafter Truman POF]; U.S. House of Representatives, Committee on Merchant Marine, *Hearings, Alaskan Problems, Part 3*, 80th Congress, 1st session, pp. 451–454, 457–458 (Nov. 21, 1947); Alan Brinkley,

"The Decline of the Antimonopoly Idea: The Case of Thurman Arnold," *Journal of American History* 80 (1993), 557–579.

54. Gruening quoted in Oscar Chapman to Harry Truman, Aug. 14, 1950; Charles S. Murphy, "Memorandum for the President," April 21, 1951; both in Box 41, Truman POF; David Bell, "Memorandum for Mr. Elmer Staats," March 10, 1950, Box 1, David Stowe Files, White House Central Files, Truman Library; Robert Lovett to Truman, Nov. 16, 1950, Box 10, White House Confidential File, Truman Library.

55. Gruening to Nathan Twining, Sept. 3, 1952, Series 230, Box 8, GP; Marjorie Belcher, "Memorandum for Dr. Steelman," Jan. 18, 1952, Box 2, White House Confidential File, Truman Library; Naske and Slotnick, *Alaska*, pp. 124–130.

56. Gruening to Richard Neuberger, Aug. 27, 1952, Series 230, Box 8, GP; Felix Frankfurter to Gruening, June 25, 1950, Box 60, Frankfurter Papers; Drew Pearson to Gruening, Dec. 6, 1949, Series G 125, Box 2 of 3, Pearson Papers; George Sundborg interview, Feb. 23, 1995; Maurine Neuberger interview. For examples of Gruening's linking Cold War rhetoric with the statehood effort, see U.S. House of Representatives, Committee on Public Lands, *Hearings, Statehood for Alaska*, 80th Congress, 1st session, p. 405 (April 23, 1947); Gruening to Brooks Emery, Jan. 10, 1948, Series 230, Box 1D, GP; Gruening to Dwight Eisenhower, Aug. 4, 1949, Box 48, Name File, Pre-Presidential Papers, Dwight Eisenhower Presidential Library, Abilene, Kans.

57. Herbert Lehman to Gruening, March 15, 1950, Special Correspondence File, Lehman Papers; U.S. Senate, Committee on Interior and Insular Affairs, *Hearings, Alaska Statehood*, 81st Congress, 2d session, pp. 488, 491 (April 29, 1950).

58. U.S. Senate, Committee on Interior and Insular Affairs, *Hearings, Investigation of Charges by Senator Andrew F. Schoeppel*, 81st Congress, 2d session, pp. 148–157 (Sept. 11, 1950).

59. FBI Report, "In the Case of Dr. Ernest Gruening"; Robert Hoopes interview, Peter Gilmore interview, both in Report by Special Agent John Desmond, Oct. 31, 1950, Anchorage, "Re: ERNEST GRUENING, aka Ernest H. Gruening, Governor of Alaska—Appointee"; George Miskovich interview, in Report by Special Agent John Hannaker, Nov. 15, 1950, Anchorage, "Re: ERNEST GRUENING, aka Ernest H. Gruening, Governor of Alaska—Appointee"; all in Box 340, Truman PSF; "Message of the Governor of Alaska to the 25th session of the Alaska Territorial Legislature," Juneau, Jan. 25, 1951, copy in possession of Hunt Gruening.

60. John Steelman, "Memorandum for Mr. Dawson"; Oscar Chapman interview, in Report by Special Agent Patrick Rice, Nov. 14, 1950, Washington, D.C., "Re: ERNEST GRUENING, aka Ernest H. Gruening, Governor of Alaska—Appointee"; FBI Report, "In the Case of Dr. Ernest Gruening"; all in Box 340, Truman PSF; Richard Neuberger, "Ernest Gruening," *Collier's*, Dec. 23, 1944.

61. Gruening to Richard Neuberger, March 20, 1952, Series 230, Box 7, GP; Gruening to Herbert Lehman, Nov. 27, 1942, Special Correspondence File, Lehman Papers.

62. George Sundborg interview, Nov. 10, 1994.

63. Gruening to Blair Moody, July 29, 1952, Series 230, Box 8, GP; Gruening to Richard Neuberger, March 20, 1952, Series 230, Box 7, GP; Gruening to Richard Neuberger, n.d. [1952], Box 37, Neuberger Papers.

64. Gruening to William Loeb, Jr., Jan. 8, 1952, Series 230, Box 7, GP; Gruening to Felix Frankfurter, n.d. [1953], Box 60, Frankfurter Papers.

6. The Washington Agenda

1. Robert Atwood interview; Claus Naske, *An Interpretive History of Alaskan Statehood* (Anchorage: Alaska Northwest Publishing Company, 1973), pp. 54–56, 86; Claus Naske and Herman Slotnick, *Alaska: A History of the Forty-ninth State* (Grand Rapids, Mich.: William Eerdmans Publishing Company, 1979), pp. 149–152.

2. Gruening to Saxe Cummins, Feb. 23, April 17, 1954; Cummins to Gruening, Feb. 25, 1954; all in Catalogue Correspondence, Random House Papers, Butler Library, Columbia University; Ernest Gruening, *The State of Alaska* (New York: Random House, 1954).

3. Gruening to Felix Frankfurter, n.d., [1954]; Gruening, "Plan for Use of Fellowship"; both in Box 60, Frankfurter Papers.

4. *Many Battles*, pp. 398–399; Hunt Gruening interview.

5. Peter Gruening to William O. Douglas, Oct. 13, 1954, Box 334, William O. Douglas Papers, Library of Congress, Washington, D.C.; *Many Battles*, pp. 399–400.

6. Peter Gruening to "Folks," Sept. 2, 1949, copy in Box 46, Chapman Papers; *Many Battles*, pp. 400–402; Hunt Gruening interview; George Sundborg interview, Nov. 10, 1994.

7. Peter Gruening to William O. Douglas, Oct. 13, 1954; Nancy Monktan to William O. Douglas, Sept. 13, 1954; both in Box 334, William O. Douglas Papers; *Many Battles*, pp. 400–402; Hunt Gruening interview.

8. Robert Atwood interview.

9. William O. Douglas to H. B. Evatt, May 28, 1958; Dorothy Gruening to William O. Douglas, May 13, 1963; both in Box 334, William O. Douglas Papers; Hunt Gruening interview.

10. Gruening to Robert Atwood, March 18, 1955, Series 36, Box 1, GP; Gruening to Walter Lippmann, Jan. 16, 1956, Series III, Box 374, Lippmann Papers; *Many Battles*, p. 402.

11. Gruening to Robert Atwood, March 18, 1955, Series 36, Box 1, GP; Gruening address, "Let Us End American Colonialism," Fairbanks, Nov. 9, 1955, reproduced in Ernest Gruening, *The Battle for Alaska Statehood* (College: University of Alaska Press, 1967), pp. 72–91.

12. Gruening to Felix Frankfurter, July 26, 1956; Frankfurter to Gruening, July 30, 1956; both in Box 60, Frankfurter Papers; Gruening to Robert Atwood, July 20, 1956, Series 36, Box 1, GP; Naske, *Interpretive History of Alaskan Statehood*, pp. 121–157.

13. Robert Atwood interview; George Sundborg interview, Feb. 23, 1995.

14. Gruening to Bennett Orf, Jan. 20, 1958, Series 240, Box 1, GP; "Phantom Senator," *New York Times*, July 1, 1958; Claus Naske, *A Short History of Alaska Statehood* (New York: University Press of America, 1985), pp. 228, 243–244; Tyler Abell, ed., *Drew Pearson: Diaries, 1949–1959* (New York: Holt, Rinehart, and Winston, 1974), entry for Jan. 3, 1959, p. 497; Stewart Udall interview, Santa Fe, May 28, 1995; Steve McCutcheon interview.

15. Gruening to Hamilton Fish Armstrong, July 23, 1957, Series 240, Box 1, GP. For Eisenhower's Latin American policy, see Stephen Rabe, *Eisenhower and Latin America: The Foreign Policy of Anticommunism* (Chapel Hill: University of North Carolina Press, 1988), pp. 84–116; Charles Ameringer, *The Democratic Left in Exile: The Antidictatorial Struggle in the Caribbean, 1945–1959* (Coral Gables, Fla.: University of Miami Press, 1974), pp. 222–299.

16. Naske, *Interpretive History of Alaskan Statehood*, pp. 160–161; "Phantom Senator"; George Sundborg interview, Nov. 10, 1994; Hugh Gallagher interview, Bethesda, Md., Oct. 22, 1995.

17. Julius Edelstein, "Memorandum to Senator Lehman," July 28, 1958, Special Correspondence File, Lehman Papers; George Sundborg interview, Feb. 23, 1995; Naske, *Interpretive History of Alaskan Statehood*, pp. 160–161.

18. George Sundborg interview, Nov. 10, 1994; Steve McCutcheon interview; Robert Atwood interview; *Boston Globe*, Nov. 9, 1958; Donald Moberg, "The 1958 Election in Alaska," *Western Political Quarterly* 12 (1959), 259–265; Naske and Slotnick, *Alaska*, pp. 159–160; *Many Battles*, p. 404.

19. Paul Boller, *Congressional Anecdotes* (New York: Oxford University Press, 1991), p. 135.

20. Julius Edelstein, "Memorandum to Senator Lehman," July 28, 1958; Gruening to Herbert Lehman, Aug. 24, 1956; both in Special Correspondence File, Lehman Papers; Steve McCutcheon interview; Robert Atwood interview; George Sundborg interview, Feb. 23, 1995; Don Greeley interview, Fairfax, Va., Dec. 3, 1995; Moberg, "The 1958 Election in Alaska," pp. 259–265.

21. Thomas Corcoran to Gruening, April 26, 1949; Leon Hickman to Gruening, Oct. 1, 1958; both in Box 61, Thomas Corcoran Papers, Library of Congress; Julius Edelstein, "Memorandum to Senator Lehman," July 28, Aug. 15, 1958; both in Special Correspondence File, Lehman Papers; Gruening to James Howard Means, Sept. 19, 1958, copy in Secretary's Scrapbook 1907, Harvard University Archives, Pusey Library, Harvard University; Gruening to Lyndon Johnson, Nov. 6, 1958, Box 44, LBJ A Papers, Lyndon Baines Johnson Presidential Library, Austin; George Sundborg interview, Nov. 10, 1994; Mike Gravel interview.

22. William O. Douglas to Gruening, Nov. 29, 1958, Box 334, William O. Douglas Papers; George Sundborg interview, Nov. 10, 1994; Moberg, "The 1958 Election in Alaska," pp. 259–265; Naske and Slotnick, *Alaska*, pp. 159–160.

23. Robert Mann, *The Walls of Jericho: Lyndon Johnson, Hubert Humphrey, Richard Russell, and the Struggle for Civil Rights* (New York: Harcourt, Brace, 1996), pp. 135–146, 236–239, 290–291; Fred Harris, *Deadlock or Decision: The U.S. Senate and the Rise of National Politics* (New York: Oxford University Press, 1993), pp. 33–158; Nelson Polsby, *Congress and the President*, 4th ed. (Englewood Cliffs, N.J.: Prentice Hall, 1988), p. 89; Michael Foley, *The New Senate: Liberal Influence on a Conservative Institution, 1959–1972* (New Haven: Yale University Press, 1980), p. 251; Donald Matthews, *U.S. Senators and Their World* (Chapel Hill: University of North Carolina Press, 1960).

24. Jack Germond interview; Mike Gravel interview; Laura Olson interview, Beaverton, Ore., Oct. 18, 1995.

25. Gruening to Lyndon Johnson, Dec. 16, 1958, Box 366, LBJ Senate Papers, LBJ Library.

26. George Sundborg interview, Feb. 23, 1995; Hunt Gruening interview; Laura Olson interview; Ray Beaser interview, Philadelphia, Dec. 15, 1995; Gruening to Herbert Lehman, Aug. 24, 1956, Special Correspondence File, Lehman Papers; GD, Jan. 21, 1969.

27. George Sundborg interview, Feb. 23, 1995; Laura Olson interview.

28. Don Greeley interview; George Sundborg interview, Feb. 23, 1995.

29. George Sundborg interview, Feb. 23, 1995; Laura Olson interview; Don Greeley interview; Ray Beaser interview.

30. Gruening to Herbert Lehman, Oct. 4, 1949, Special Correspondence File, Lehman Papers; George Sundborg interview, Feb. 23, 1995; Hunt Gruening interview; Jack Germond interview; Abell, *Drew Pearson: Diaries*, entry for Jan. 3, 1959, p. 497.

31. George Sundborg interview, Feb. 23, 1995; Hunt Gruening interview; Jack Germond interview; Hugh Gallagher interview; Gaylord Nelson interview, Washington, D.C., Dec. 9, 1994; George McGovern interview, Washington, D.C., Dec. 8, 1994.

32. George Sundborg interview, Feb. 23, 1995; Jack Germond interview; Gaylord Nelson interview; George McGovern interview; Frank Moss interview, May 31, 1995; *The Journals of David Lilienthal*, vol. 4, *The Road to Change, 1955–1959* (New York: Harper and Row, 1969), entry for May 5, 1959, p. 344.

33. Hunt Gruening interview; Jack Germond interview.

34. Gruening to Joseph Josephson, Sept. 13, 1961, Box 17, GSP; Howard Shuman Oral History, p. 577, National Archives, Washington, D.C.; George Sundborg interviews, Nov. 10, 1994, Feb. 23, 1995; Mann, *The Walls of Jericho*, p. 239.

35. George Sundborg interviews, Nov. 10, 1994, Feb. 23, 1995; Laura Olson interview.

36. Gruening to J. William Fulbright, June 5, 1959; Fulbright to Gruening, June 2, 1959; both in Box BCN 140, Folder 48, 1943–1960 Series, J. William Fulbright Papers, Mullins Library, University of Arkansas; unsigned Foreign Relations Committee memorandum, [May?] 1959, copy in Box 80, Foreign Relations Committee series, Bourke Hickenlooper Papers, Herbert Hoover Presidential Library, West Branch, Iowa; U.S. Senate, Committee on Foreign Relations, *Hearings, Mutual Security Act of 1959*, 86th Congress, 1st session, pp. 942–945 (May 21, 1959); George Sundborg interview, Feb. 23, 1995.

37. Gruening draft speech, 1959, Box 42, GS 59–63, GSP; 105 *CR*, 86th Congress, 1st session, pp. 8448 (May 19, 1959), 13953 (July 22, 1959); Harris, *Deadlock or Decision*, p. 139.

38. U.S. Senate, Committee on Foreign Relations, *Hearings, Mutual Security Act of 1960*, 86th Congress, 2d session, pp. 624–626, 631–634 (April 5, 1960).

39. Frank Church to Jim Balderston, July 7, 1959; Church to A. L. Freese, June 2, 1959; both in Series 2.2, Box 8, Frank Church Papers, Albertson's Library, Boise State University; LeRoy Ashby and Rod Gramer, *Fighting the Odds: The Life of Senator Frank Church* (Pullman: Washington State University Press, 1994), pp. 1–98.

40. A. Robert Smith, *The Tiger in the Senate: A Biography of Wayne Morse* (New York: Doubleday, 1962); Mason Drukman, "Oregon's Most Famous Feud: Wayne Morse versus Richard Neuberger," *Oregon Historical Quarterly* 95 (1994), 300–367;

G. Q. Unruh, "Republican Apostate: Senator Wayne Morse and His Quest for Independent Liberalism," *Pacific Northwest Quarterly* 82 (1991), 83–89; Gaylord Nelson interview; William Proxmire oral history, LBJ Library.

41. 106 *CR*, 86th Congress, 2d session, pp. 14891 (June 29, 1960), 16845 (Aug. 19, 1960).

42. Ibid., pp. 7203 (April 4, 1960), 12810–11 (June 16, 1960), 15676–78 (July 2, 1960).

43. Jack Germond interview; Charles Fontenay, *Estes Kefauver: A Biography* (Knoxville: University of Tennessee Press, 1980), pp. 293–365; Paul Douglas, *In the Fullness of Time: The Memoirs of Paul H. Douglas* (New York: Harcourt Brace Jovanovich, 1971); Gruening to R. Holmes Johnson, Feb. 2, 1960, Box 25, GSP; Gruening to Chester Bowles, June 1, 1960, Box I-208, Chester Bowles Papers, Sterling Library, Yale University. For background, see Marc Allen Eisner, "Discovering Patterns in Regulatory History: Continuity, Change, and Regulatory Regimes," *Journal of Policy History* 6 (1994), 157–187; B. Dan Wood and James Anderson, "The Politics of U.S. Anti-trust Regulation," *American Journal of Political Science* 37 (1993), 1–39.

44. Gruening to LBJ, March 23, 1959, Box 366, LBJ Senate Papers; U.S. Senate, Committee on Public Works, *Hearings, Highways in Alaska*, 86th Congress, 2d session, pp. 7–12 (May 25, 1960); Frank Moss interview; Jack Germond interview; Laura Olson interview; Gruening to Abraham Ribicoff, March 21, 1961, Box 33, GSP; 106 *CR*, 86th Congress, 2d session, p. 2049 (Feb. 4, 1960). For the roads issue, see Claus Naske, "Alaska and the Federal-Aid Highway Acts," *Pacific Northwest Quarterly* 80 (1989), 133–139.

45. Frank Moss interview; Gruening to Gus Norwood, May 5, 1959, Box 82, GS 59–63, GSP; Gruening statement, "Alaska's Power Situation," 1960, Box 82, GSP; U.S. Senate, Committee on Interior and Insular Affairs, *Hearings, Eklutna Project, Alaska*, 86th Congress, 2d session, pp. 4–5 (May 11, 1960); U.S. Senate, Committee on Interior and Insular Affairs, *Hearings, Hydroelectric Requirements and Resources in Alaska*, 86th Congress, 2d session, pp. 1, 42–45 (Sept. 7, 1960); Naske and Slotnick, *Alaska*, pp. 197–198.

46. Gruening to LBJ, April 22, 1959, Box 366, LBJ Senate Papers; George Sundborg interview, Nov. 10, 1994; Frank Moss interview; Alex Radin, "Outlooks and Insights: A Great Human Being," *Public Power* 32 (July 1974).

47. Gruening to Christian Herter, Dec. 2, 1959, Box 45, GS 59–63, GP; George Sundborg interview, Nov. 10, 1994; Frank Moss interview; Radin, "Outlooks and Insights."

48. Gruening to LBJ, Nov. 11, 1960; LBJ to Gruening, Jan. 12, 1960; both in Box 372, LBJ Senate Papers; Oscar Chapman to Bob Bartlett, June 17, 1960, Box 91, LBJ Senate Political Files, LBJ Library; Vide Bartlett Oral History, LBJ Library; George Sundborg interview, Nov. 10, 1994; Mann, *The Walls of Jericho*, p. 141. On the campaign, see Theodore White, *The Making of the President—1960* (New York: Athenaeum, 1961).

49. Stewart Udall oral history, LBJ Library; Richard Reeves, *President Kennedy: Profile in Power* (New York: Simon and Schuster, 1993), pp. 10–19; James Giglio, *The Presidency of JFK* (Lawrence: University of Kansas Press, 1991), pp. 22–35; Arthur Schlesinger, Jr., *A Thousand Days: John F. Kennedy in the White House* (Bos-

ton: Houghton Mifflin, 1965); David Halberstam, *The Best and the Brightest* (New York: Random House, 1972).

50. U.S. Senate, Committee on Interior and Insular Affairs, *Hearings, Alaska Military Land Withdrawals*, 87th Congress, 1st session, p. 15 (May 10, 1961); Stephen Young to Joseph Baumgartner, March 2, 1964, Box 42, Stephen Young Papers, Western Reserve Historical Society, Cleveland; George McGovern interview; John Lewis Gaddis, *Strategies of Containment: A Critical Appraisal of Postwar American National Security Policy* (New York: Oxford University Press, 1982), pp. 198–236.

51. 107 *CR*, 87th Congress, 1st session, pp. 9727–30 (June 7, 1961); Hugh Gallagher interview; John Carver oral history, 8:101, JFK Presidential Library.

52. Gruening to Cole McFarland, March 29, 1961, Box 82, GSF 59–63, GSP; Mike Manatos to Lawrence O'Brien, Oct. 9, 1962, Name File—Gruening, JFK Presidential Library; O'Brien to Manatos, Aug. 19, 1963, Box 18, Lawrence O'Brien Files, Papers of the Congressional Liaison Office, JFK Presidential Library; GD, July 28, 1964; George Sundborg interview, Nov. 10, 1994; Stewart Udall interview; Stewart Udall oral history, LBJ Library; John Carver oral history, 8:101.

53. U.S. Senate, Committee on Public Works, *Hearings, Nomination of Aubrey J. Wagner to Be a Member of the Board of Directors of the Tennessee Valley Authority*, 87th Congress, 1st session, p. 11 (March 2, 1961); U.S. Senate, Committee on Commerce, *Hearings, Reorganization of Civil Aeronautics Board, Federal Trade Commission, and Federal Maritime Board*, 87th Congress, 1st session, p. 62 (July 19, 1961); Donald Ritchie, *James M. Landis: Dean of the Regulators* (Cambridge, Mass.: Harvard University Press, 1980), pp. 181–183; *Congressional Quarterly Almanac* 17 (1961), 352–356.

54. 108 *CR*, 87th Congress, 2d session, pp. 11286–11290 (June 21, 1962); Ray Beaser interview; *Many Battles*, p. 450; Walter McDougall, *The Heavens and the Earth: A Political History of the Space Age* (New York: Basic Books, 1985), pp. 351–356; Allen Matusow, *The Unraveling of America: A History of Liberalism in the 1960s* (New York: Harper and Row, 1984), pp. 33, 37–38; *Congressional Quarterly Almanac* 18 (1962), 546–553; *Congressional Quarterly Weekly Report*, Aug. 17, 1962, pp. 1361–67.

55. 108 *CR*, 87th Congress, 2d session, p. 18830 (Sept. 7, 1962); U.S. Senate, Committee on Public Works, *Hearings, Public Works Acceleration*, 87th Congress, 2d session, p. 40 (April 12, 1962); Joseph Barr to Claude DeSautels, n.d. [1962], President's Office File, Box 50, JFK Library [hereafter JFK POF]; Douglas quoted in *Memorial Addresses and Other Tributes in the Congress of the United States on the Life and Contributions of Ernest H. Gruening*, S. Doc. 93–118, 93d Congress, 2d session; James Sundquist, *Politics and Policy: The Eisenhower, Kennedy, and Johnson Years* (Washington, D.C.: Brookings Institution, 1968), pp. 43, 48.

56. Walt W. Rostow, *Eisenhower, Kennedy, and Foreign Aid* (Austin: University of Texas Press, 1985); idem, *Process of Economic Growth* (New York: Norton, 1952); Robert Packenham, *Liberal America and the Third World: Political Development Ideas in Foreign Aid and Social Science* (Princeton: Princeton University Press, 1973), pp. 69–75; *Congressional Quarterly Almanac* 17 (1961), 293–298.

57. J. William Fulbright to Albert Dowell, May 22, 1962, Series 48:16, Box 42,

Fulbright Papers; Fulbright address, University of Virginia, April 21, 1961, Series 72, Box 19, Fulbright Papers; Randall Bennett Woods, *Fulbright: A Biography* (New York: Cambridge University Press, 1995).

58. Pat Holt interview, Bethesda, Md., May 30, 1995; Jack Germond interview.

59. 107 *CR*, 87th Congress, 1st session, pp. 15978–79, 15983–86 (Aug. 16, 1961).

60. Gruening to Samuel Guy Inman, Jan. 16, 1962, Box 19, Samuel Guy Inman Papers, Library of Congress.

61. Garison Nelson with Clark Bensen, *Committees in the U.S. Congress, 1947–1992*, vol. 1, *Committee Jurisdictions and Member Rosters* (Washington, D.C.: Congressional Quarterly Press, 1993), p. 158.

62. William Wright, Jr., to Department of State, Feb. 21, 1963, Box 3154, Central Foreign Policy File, 1963, RG 59; George Sundborg interview, Nov. 10, 1994; Laura Olson interview; 108 *CR*, 87th Congress, 2d session, p. 11296 (June 21, 1962); William Burns, *Economic Aid and American Policy toward Egypt, 1955–1981* (Albany: State University of New York Press, 1985), pp. 121–133; Douglas Little, "A Fool's Errand: America and the Middle East, 1961–1969," in *The Diplomacy of the Crucial Decade: American Foreign Relations during the 1960s*, ed. Diane Kunz (New York: Columbia University Press, 1994), pp. 297–289.

63. Gruening to Chester Bowles, Jan. 24, 1963, Box I-279, Bowles Papers; Ernest Gruening, *Report of a Study of United States Foreign Aid in Ten Middle Eastern and African Countries*, 88th Congress, 1st session, CIS Doc. #S1375, pp. 2–12, 382, 436–442, 450, 462, 470; *Near East Report*, reprinted in 109 *CR*, 88th Congress, 1st session, p. 20855; Burns, *Economic Aid*, p. 144.

64. *Congressional Quarterly Weekly Report*, March 23, 1962, p. 477; Juan De Onís and Jerome Levinson, *The Alliance That Lost Its Way* (Chicago: Quadrangle Books, 1970); Stephen Rabe, "Controlling Revolutions: Latin America, the Alliance for Progress, and Cold War Anti-Communism," in *Kennedy's Quest for Victory: American Foreign Policy, 1961–1963*, ed. Thomas Paterson (New York: Oxford University Press, 1989); William Walker, "Mixing the Sweet with the Sour: Kennedy, Johnson, and Latin America," in Kunz, *The Diplomacy of the Crucial Decade*, pp. 42–56; Tony Smith, "The Alliance for Progress: The 1960s," in *Exporting Democracy: Themes and Issues*, ed. Abraham Lowenthal (Baltimore: Johns Hopkins University Press, 1991), pp. 71–89.

65. 107 *CR*, 87th Congress, 1st session, p. 15632 (Aug. 11, 1961).

66. Thomas Kuchel to Gruening, Nov. 8, 1963, Box 455, Thomas Kuchel Papers, Bancroft Library, University of California, Berkeley; Pat Holt interview; Frank Moss interview. For Gruening's pro-Mexican perspective, see Gruening to Mike Mansfield, Oct. 10, 1961; Gruening to Fernando Alatorre, June 27, 1961; Gruening to Antonio Carillo Flores, June 27, 1961; all in Box 46, GS 59–63, GSP; 107 *CR*, 87th Congress, 1st session, pp. 18969–72 (Sept. 11, 1961).

67. Gruening to Luis Muñoz Marín, July 11, 1961; Gruening to D. S. Belaxal, April 29, 1959; both in Box 102, GS 59–63, GSP; Jules Witcover, "Senator Ernest Gruening, Father of Alaska Statehood," *Washington Post*, June 27, 1974. On Muñoz Marín and the Democratic left, see Ameringer, *The Democratic Left in Exile*.

68. Gruening to Mike Mansfield, Oct. 10, 1961, Box 46, GS 59–63, GSP; Pat Holt interview; Arthur Schlesinger, Jr., "Memorandum for the President," Aug. 1, 1962, Box 123a, JFK POF; Gruening to C. H. Scherer, Nov. 19, 1962, Box 45,

GS 59–63, GSP; 108 *CR*, 87th Congress, 2d session, pp. 14107–9 (July 19, 1962); Walker, "Mixing the Sweet with the Sour," pp. 53–56; Packenham, *Liberal America*, pp. 71–73.

69. Ralph Dungan interview, St. John, Barbados, May 31, 1995.

70. Paul Douglas to Lenore Mark, Aug. 22, 1962, Box 594, Paul Douglas Papers, Chicago Historical Society, Chicago; NBC, "News in Depth," July 24, 1962, reproduced in 108 *CR*, 87th Congress, 2d session, p. 14667; *Anchorage Daily News*, Oct. 24, 1962.

71. Gruening to Leon Hickman, Sept. 11, 1962; Hickman to Gruening, Sept. 14, 1962; both in Box 243, Corcoran Papers; Ted Stevens form letter, June 11, 1962, copy in possession of Hunt Gruening; George Sundborg interviews, Nov. 10, 1994, and Feb. 23, 1995; Mike Gravel interview; Robert Atwood interview; *Anchorage Daily Times*, Sept. 10, Oct. 22, 1962.

72. George Sundborg interviews, Nov. 10, 1994, and Feb. 23, 1995; Steve McCutcheon interview; Robert Atwood interview.

7. The Dilemmas of Dissent

1. Jack Germond interview; Maurine Neuberger interview; Stewart Udall interview; George Sundborg interview, Nov. 10, 1994; Steve McCutcheon interview; Robert Atwood interview; GD, Sept. 1, 1964.

2. George Sundborg interviews, Nov. 10, 1994, Feb. 23, 1995; Mike Gravel interview; Don Greeley interview; Hugh Gallagher interview; Jack Germond interview; Maurine Neuberger interview; Stewart Udall interview; Vide Bartlett oral history; Claus Naske, *Edward Lewis Bob Bartlett of Alaska: A Life in Politics* (Fairbanks: University of Alaska Press, 1979), pp. 221–223.

3. U.S. Senate, Committee on Government Operations, Reorganization and International Organizations Subcommittee, *Hearings, Interagency Coordination in Drug Research and Legislation*, 88th Congress, 1st session, pp. 807–809 (March 20, 1963), 2221, 2225, 2277–79 (June 19, 1963), 2884–91, 2981, 2992 (June 26, 1963); 109 *CR*, 88th Congress, 1st session, p. 14555 (Aug. 8, 1963); *Many Battles*, pp. 450–452; Charles Fontenay, *Estes Kefauver: A Biography* (Knoxville: University of Tennessee Press, 1980), pp. 395–398.

4. Gruening to John Kennedy, May 21, 1963; Gruening to William Egan, June 27, 1963; both in Box 25, GS 59–63, GSP; 109 *CR*, 88th Congress, 1st session, pp. 9099–9103 (May 21, 1963); U.S. Senate, Committee on Commerce, *Hearings, Barrett Reappointment to Maritime Commission*, 88th Congress, 1st session, pp. 3–9 (July 12, 1963); Edward Mansfield, "Federal Maritime Commission," in *The Politics of Regulation*, ed. James Q. Wilson (New York: Basic Books, 1980), pp. 62–63.

5. Mike Manatos to Lawrence O'Brien, Aug. 5, 1963, Manatos File, Box 1, JFK Congressional Liaison Office Papers; 109 *CR*, 88th Congress, 1st session, pp. 12581–87 (July 15, 1963).

6. *Executive Sessions of the Senate Foreign Relations Committee* [hereafter *ESSFRC*], vol. 15, 88th Congress, 1st session, pp. 608–615, 619, 627–628 (Sept. 26, 1963).

7. Gruening to Mrs. E. H. Bell, Oct. 3, 1963, Box 30, GSP; 109 *CR*, 88th Congress, 1st session, pp. 18320–21, 18326–28 (Sept. 30, 1963); *Washington Post*, Sept. 30, 1963.

8. Drew Pearson to Gruening, Oct. 13, 1963, Series G 284, Box 1 of 2, Pearson Papers; Gruening to Wayne Morse, Sept. 30, 1963; Morse to Gruening, Oct. 1, 1963; both in Box B-58, Wayne Morse Papers, University of Oregon Library, Eugene; 109 *CR*, 88th Congress, 1st session, pp. 18327, 18368, 18369 (Sept. 30, 1963).

9. *ESSFRC*, vol. 15, 88th Congress, 1st session, pp. 662–665, 668–675, 686 (Oct. 3, 1963).

10. 109 *CR*, 88th Congress, 1st session, p. 18786 (Oct. 7, 1963); *Washington Post*, Oct. 6, 1963; Edwin Martin oral history, pp. 101, 111, JFK Presidential Library; Stephen Rabe, "Controlling Revolutions: Latin America, the Alliance for Progress, and Cold War Anti-Communism," in *Kennedy's Quest for Victory: American Foreign Policy, 1961–1963*, ed. Thomas Paterson (New York: Oxford University Press, 1989); William Walker, "Mixing the Sweet with the Sour: Kennedy, Johnson, and Latin America," in *The Diplomacy of the Crucial Decade: American Foreign Relations during the 1960s*, ed. Diane Kunz (New York: Columbia University Press, 1994), pp. 42–56; Robert Packenham, *Liberal America and the Third World: Political Development Ideas in Foreign Aid and Social Science* (Princeton: Princeton University Press, 1973), pp. 73–75.

11. Jack Germond interview; Edwin Martin oral history, pp. 107–110.

12. *U.S. News & World Report*, Nov. 25, 1963.

13. David Bell oral history, LBJ Library; Packenham, *Liberal America*, pp. 69–75.

14. David Bell oral history; *Congressional Quarterly Almanac* 19 (1963), 265, 279. For the administration's concern with the emerging Senate opposition, see Mike Manatos to Lawrence O'Brien, July 15, 1963, Box 53, JFK POF; Manatos to O'Brien, July 23, Aug. 27, 1963; both in Box 8, Office Files of Mike Manatos, White House Central File [hereafter WHCF], LBJ Library.

15. Gruening, "Dear Senator," June 26, 1963, Box 5, Legislative File, 88th Congress, GSP; Lawrence O'Brien, "Memorandum for the President," Oct. 7, 1963, Box 53, JFK POF; 109 *CR*, 88th Congress, 1st session, pp. 21840–42 (Nov. 14, 1963).

16. Gruening to Felix Putterman, Oct. 28, 1963, Box 32, GSP; J. William Fulbright to McGeorge Bundy, Nov. 12, 1963, Series 48:8, Box 29, Fulbright Papers; AID, "Significant Committee Amendments," n.d. [1963], Box 8, Office Files of Mike Manatos; Dean Rusk circular telegram, Nov. 9, 1963, Box 3308, State Department Central Files, 1963, RG 59; 109 *CR*, 88th Congress, 1st session, pp. 21357, 21365–70 (Nov. 7, 1963); William Burns, *Economic Aid and American Policy toward Egypt, 1955–1981* (Albany: State University of New York Press, 1985), pp. 135–140; Douglas Little, "A Fool's Errand: America and the Middle East, 1961–1969," in Kunz, *The Diplomacy of the Crucial Decade*, pp. 289–290.

17. Dean Rusk circular telegram, Nov. 14, 1963, Box 3308, State Department Central Files, 1963, RG 59; Burns, *Economic Aid*, pp. 145–146; *Congressional Quarterly Almanac* 19 (1963), 278, 280.

18. Gruening to Gordon Skrede, Sept. 4, 1963; Gruening to Ruth Davis, Oct. 22, 1963; both in Box 32, GS 63–65, GP; Morse to Chester Bowles, Aug. 19, 1963, Box I-334, Bowles Papers; Bourke Hickenlooper to Elaine Schramm, Oct. 31, 1963, Box 36, Hickenlooper Papers; Craig Raupe, "Memorandum for Hon. Jim Fry," Sept. 13, 1963, Box 1, Ralph Dungan Papers, JFK Presidential Library.

19. David Bell, "Memorandum for the President," Oct. 21, 1963; Lawrence O'Brien, "Memorandum for the President," Nov. 4, 1963; both in Box 53, JFK POF; Manatos, "Memorandum for the President," Nov. 21, 1963, Box 8, Office Files of Mike Manatos; David Bell, "Foreign Aid Program for FY 1965," Dec. 15, 1963, Box 46, White House Confidential File, LBJ Library; 109 *CR*, 88th Congress, 1st session, p. 20844 (Oct. 31, 1963); *Washington Post*, Nov. 8, 1963; *Congressional Quarterly Almanac* 19 (1963), 278.

20. Gary Hess, *The United States' Emergence as a Southeast Asian Power, 1940–1950* (New York: Columbia University Press, 1987); George Herring, *America's Longest War: The United States and Vietnam* (New York: Alfred A. Knopf, 1979), pp. 45–81; George Kahin, *Intervention: How America Became Involved in Vietnam* (New York: Alfred A. Knopf, 1986), pp. 131–141; Robert Schulzinger, "'It's Easy to Win a War on Paper': The United States and Vietnam, 1961–1968," in Kunz, *Diplomacy of the Crucial Decade*, pp. 185–187; John Newman, *JFK and Vietnam: Deception, Intrigue, and the Struggle for Power* (New York: Warner Books, 1992).

21. For the increasing intensity of Senate dissent concerning Vietnam, see U.S. Senate, Committee on Foreign Relations, *Hearings, International Development and Security*, 87th Congress, 1st session, p. 628 (June 14, 1961); *ESSFRC*, vol. 14, 87th Congress, 2d session, pp. 195, 200, 201 (Feb. 20, 1962), 232 (Feb. 27, 1962).

22. Gruening to Adlai Stevenson, Nov. 5, 1962, Series 36, Box 18, GP; Gruening to Guy Moyer, May 22, 1962, Box 43, GSP.

23. Kahin, *Intervention*, pp. 144–152; Schulzinger, "'It's Easy to Win a War on Paper,'" pp. 187–188.

24. Gruening to Gordon Skende, Sept. 4, 1963, Box 32, GSP; George McGovern oral history, LBJ Library; Kahin, *Intervention*, pp. 146–181; Newman, *JFK and Vietnam*, pp. 438–439; William Duiker, *U.S. Containment Policy and the Conflict in Indochina* (Stanford: Stanford University Press, 1994), pp. 284–309.

25. George Sundborg interview, Seattle, Jan. 15, 1996.

26. Ralph Dungan, "Memorandum for the President," April 16, 1964; Benjamin Read, "Memorandum for Mr. McGeorge Bundy," Sept. 2, 1964; both in Box 4, NSF File, NSAMs, LBJ Library; GD, Jan. 8, 1964, March 20, 1964; 109 *CR*, 88th Congress, 1st session, pp. 24867–69 (Dec. 16, 1963); William Walker, "Mixing the Sweet with the Sour," in Kunz, *The Diplomacy of the Crucial Decade*, pp. 61–62; H. W. Brands, Jr., *The Wages of Globalism: Lyndon Johnson and the Limits of American Power* (New York: Oxford University Press, 1995), pp. 44–49.

27. Gruening to Romulo Betancourt, June 15, 1964, Box 30, GSP.

28. American Consulate Cali to American Embassy Bogotá, Jan. 29, 1964; American Embassy Lima to Department of State, Dec. 24, 1964; both in Box 89, State Department Subject/Numeric File, 1964–1966, RG 59; Nicholas McCanstard to Ernest Siracusa, Nov. 17, 1964, Box 87, State Department Subject/Numeric File, 1964–1966, RG 59; John Carver oral history, 8:113.

29. 110 *CR*, 88th Congress, 2d session, pp. 4831–35 (March 10, 1964).

30. Jack Germond interview; William Bundy interview, Annapolis, June 22, 1995; *New York Times*, March 21, 1964. For the hard-line reaction to the speech, see 110 *CR*, 88th Congress, 2d session, pp. 4986–92 (March 11, 1964); Larry Berman, *Planning a Tragedy: The Americanization of the War in Vietnam* (New York: W. W. Norton, 1982), p. 32.

31. Dean Rusk, "The True Blessings of Peace," Salt Lake City, March 19,

1964, reproduced in 110 *CR*, 88th Congress, 2d session, pp. 5975–77; *Washington News*, March 20, 1964; *Washington Post*, March 23, 1964; Brian VanDeMark, *Into the Quagmire: Lyndon Johnson and the Escalation of the Vietnam War* (New York: Oxford University Press, 1991), pp. 10–11; Thomas Schoenbaum, *Waging Peace and War: Dean Rusk in the Truman, Kennedy, and Johnson Years* (New York: Simon and Schuster, 1988); *Congressional Quarterly Almanac* 19 (1963), 278, 280.

32. Hunt Gruening interview; 110 *CR*, 88th Congress, 2d session, pp. 5827–28 (March 20, 1964), 5977–78 (March 23, 1964).

33. 110 *CR*, 88th Congress, 2d session, 7690 (April 11, 1964), 10534 (May 11, 1964), 10820 (May 13, 1964), 11738 (May 22, 1964), 12142 (May 27, 1964), 12581 (June 3, 1964).

34. Gruening to J. William Fulbright, March 12, 17, 1964; both in Vietnam 1964 file, Brown Boxes Series, GSP; Fulbright memo to Pat Holt, March 14, 1964, Series 48:1, Box 6, Fulbright Papers; J. William Fulbright, "The Cold War in American Life," April 5, 1964, University of North Carolina, Series 72, Box 23, Fulbright Papers; 110 *CR*, 88th Congress, 2d session, pp. 6227–31, 6245–46 (March 25, 1964); William C. Gibbons, *The U.S. Government and the Vietnam War: Executive and Legislative Roles and Relationships*, 4 vols. (Princeton: Princeton University Press, 1986–), 2:225.

35. Frank Church to Ed Schlender, June 10, 1964, Series 2.2, Box 27, Church Papers; Gaylord Nelson, "Senator's Memo on Vietnam," March 1964; "Nelson's Comments on Vietnam Speech," n.d. [March 1964?]; both in Series 80, Box 97, Gaylord Nelson Papers, Wisconsin State Historical Society, Madison; *ESSFRC*, vol. 16, 88th Congress, 2d session, pp. 263 (June 30, 1964); Gibbons, *U.S. Government and the Vietnam War*, 2:249; *New York Times*, March 21, 1964.

36. George McGovern to Lella Smith, April 30, 1964; McGovern to Robert Driscoll, Aug. 4, 1964; both in Box 66A841/24, McGovern Papers; Hugh Gallagher interview; for U.S. reaction to de Gaulle's policies in Southeast Asia, see Fredrik Logevall, "De Gaulle, Neutralization, and American Involvement in Vietnam, 1963–1964," *Pacific Historical Review* 61 (1992), 69–102; H. W. Brands, Jr., "Johnson and De Gaulle: American Diplomacy *Sotto Voce*," *The Historian* 49 (1987), 482–485.

37. Gruening to Rhea Miller, April 21, 1964, Vietnam file, Brown Boxes Series, GSP.

38. GD, March 16, 1964; James Thomson to McGeorge Bundy, "More from Morse," April 29, 1964, Box 5, James Thomson Papers, JFK Presidential Library; Bundy, "Memorandum for the President," June 24, 1964, Box 2, Memos to the President, McGeorge Bundy series, National Security File, LBJ Presidential Library [hereafter Bundy NSF LBJ]. For Morse's comments against the war, see 110 *CR*, 88th Congress, 2d session, pp. 6796 (April 2, 1964), 9008–11 (April 24, 1964), 10826–27 (May 13, 1964).

39. Gruening to Walter Lippmann, May 28, 1964, Vietnam 1964 file, Brown Boxes Series, GSP; Walter Lippmann, "Today and Tomorrow . . . Our Commitment in Viet-Nam," *Washington Post*, May 28, 1964; Fredrik Logevall, "First among Critics: Walter Lippmann and the Vietnam War," *Journal of American-East Asian Relations* 4 (1995), 361–385; Ronald Steel, *Walter Lippmann and the American Century* (New York: Vintage Books, 1980), pp. 220–500.

40. GD, Aug. 21, 1965; George McGovern interview; George Sundborg interview, Feb. 23, 1995.

41. 110 *CR,* 88th Congress, 2d session, pp. 6245–46 (March 25, 1964), 10821 (May 13, 1964); Gibbons, *U.S. Government and the Vietnam War,* 2:277.

42. GD, April 7, 8, June 23, 1964; Hugh Gallagher interview; George Sundborg interview, Feb. 23, 1995; Ray Beaser interview; U.S. Senate, Committee on Appropriations, *Hearings, Interior Department and Related Agencies Appropriations for 1965,* 88th Congress, 2d session, pp. 1409–10 (Feb. 19, 1964); U.S. Senate, Committee on Interior and Insular Affairs, *Hearings, Alaska Reconstruction,* 88th Congress, 2d session, p. 20 (June 3, 1964).

43. Gruening to Waldo Coyle, May 12, 1964, Brown Boxes series, Rampart file, GSP; 110 *CR,* 88th Congress, 2d session, p. 16011 (July 6, 1964); Ernest Gruening, *The Public Pays . . . and Still Pays* (New York: Vanguard Press, 1964), p. xxiv; Alex Radin, "Outlook and Insight: A Great Human Being," *Public Power* 32 (July 1974).

44. Bureau of the Budget, "Memorandum for Mr. White," March 17, 1964, Box 21, NR 7-1/R Series, WHCF, LBJ Library; Stewart Udall oral history, LBJ Library; George Sundborg interview, Feb. 23, 1995; John Carver oral history, 3:12; 110 *CR,* 88th Congress, 2d session, p. 15975 (July 2, 1964).

45. Dorothy Gruening to Cathy Douglas, April 4, 1964, Box 334, William O. Douglas Papers; for an overview of the civil rights debate, see Hugh Davis Graham, *Civil Rights and the Presidency* (New York: Oxford University Press, 1992).

46. GD, March 14, 1964; Gruening quoted in Jules Witcover, "Ernest Gruening: Evolution of a War Critic," *Washington Post,* Feb. 8, 1971; Jack Germond interview; *Many Battles,* pp. 461–462.

47. GD, June 5, July 6, 30, Aug. 26, 1964.

48. Kahin, *Intervention,* pp. 219–227; Gibbons, *U.S. Government and the Vietnam War,* 2:280–342; Joseph Goulden, *Truth Is the First Casualty: The Gulf of Tonkin Affair, Illusion and Reality* (Chicago: Rand McNally, 1969), pp. 36, 138.

49. 110 *CR,* 88th Congress, 2d session, pp. 18413–14 (Aug. 6, 1964); Gruening to William Bauer, July 22, 1964, Vietnam 1964 file, Brown Boxes series, GSP; Gruening oral history, LBJ Library.

50. GD, Aug. 22, Sept. 5, 1964; George McGovern interview; Pat Holt oral history, pp. 195, 198; Carl Marcy oral history, pp. 152, 173; 110 *CR,* 88th Congress, 2d session, pp. 18402, 18406–9, 18413–16 (Aug. 6, 1964), 18442–50 (Aug. 7, 1964). Johnson quoted in Michael Beschloss, *Taking Charge: The Johnson White House Tapes, 1963–1964* (New York: Simon & Schuster, 1997), p. 508.

51. Stephen Young, "Straight from Washington," vol. 6, #33, Oct. 1964, Box 56, Young Papers; George McGovern interview; VanDeMark, *Into the Quagmire,* pp. 18–23.

52. For a sampling of their remarks, see "Interview: Senator Frank Church," *Ramparts* 3 (Jan.–Feb. 1965); 111 *CR,* 89th Congress, 1st session, pp. 784–786, 799 (Jan. 15, 1965), 979 (Jan. 19, 1965), 2869–81 (Feb. 17, 1965).

53. George McGovern oral history; GD, Jan. 15, Feb. 18, 1965.

54. For Gruening's public appearances, see GD, March 25, 27, April 1, 3, 5, May 11, 21, 22, 1965; *Miami News,* May 12, 1965; *Detroit Free Press,* May 14, 1965; *San Francisco Examiner,* May 18, 1965; all in 1965 Scrapbook, vol. 1, GP.

55. Wayne Crabtree to Gruening, Nov. 7, 1965, Alaska Con 1966–1968 file, Brown Boxes series, GSP; Gruening to Crabtree, Dec. 6, 1965, Alaska Con 1966–1967 file, Brown Boxes Series, GSP; George McGovern interview; *Congressional*

Quarterly Weekly Report, Nov. 12, 1965, p. 2309; Kahin, *Intervention*, pp. 270–311; VanDeMark, *Into the Quagmire*, pp. 69–97; Schulzinger, "'It's Easy to Win a War on Paper,'" pp. 192–196; David Barrett, *Uncertain Warriors: Lyndon Johnson and His Vietnam Advisors* (Lawrence: University of Kansas Press 1989), pp. 17–21.

56. William Bundy interview; *New York World Telegram*, April 23, 1995; *New York Herald Tribune*, April 23, 1965.

57. Hubert Herring to Gruening, April 22, 1965, Series 38, Box 8, GP; Gruening to Rick Goodfellow and Bruce Gazaway, Sept. 9, 1966, Vietnam 1966 file, Brown Boxes series, GSP; Freda Kirchwey, quoted in *The Nation*, Sept. 20, 1965; *New York World Telegram*, April 23, 1995.

58. Wayne Morse to Mrs. K. C. Tanner, March 5, 1965, Box B-53, Morse Papers; Gaylord Nelson to Fred Langhoff, Nov. 11, 1965, Series 74, Box 412, Nelson Papers; Gruening to John Satterlee, April 26, 1965, Vietnam 1965 file, Brown Boxes Series, GSP; Eisenhower and Byrd quoted in Charles DeBenedetti, with Charles Chatfield, *An American Ordeal: The Antiwar Movement of the Vietnam Era* (Syracuse, N.Y.: Syracuse University Press, 1990), pp. 110–111. For the backlash caused by the antiwar movement, see Adam Garfinkle, *Telltale Hearts: The Origins and Impact of the Vietnam Antiwar Movement* (New York: St. Martin's Press, 1995), pp. 44–65.

59. *Washington Star*, April 18, 1965; DeBenedetti, *American Ordeal*, pp. 111–112; Tom Wells, *The War Within: America's Battle over Vietnam* (Berkeley: University of California Press, 1994), p. 21.

60. DeBenedetti, *American Ordeal*, pp. 111–112; Wells, *The War Within*, pp. 24–25; Garfinkle, *Telltale Hearts*, pp. 44–51.

61. George McGovern interview; Gaylord Nelson interview; Frank Moss interview; *New York Post*, April 19, 1965.

62. William Bundy interview; George Sundborg interview, Feb. 23, 1995; Jack Germond interview; LBJ quoted in John McCone, "Memorandum for the Record," April 22, 1965, *FRUS, 1964–1968*, 2:599.

63. Jack Germond interview; George Sundborg interview, Feb. 23, 1995.

64. Frank Church to George McGovern, Box 70A2445/11, McGovern Papers.

65. George McGovern to Tom Taggart, April 9, 1965, Box 67A802/19, George McGovern Papers, Mudd Library, Princeton University; "Notes from Luncheon with Dick Dudman," Dec. 28, 1965, Box 70A2445/11, McGovern Papers; Frank Church to Eugene Chase, April 21, 1965, Series 2.2, Box 28, Church Papers; VanDeMark, *Into the Quagmire*, pp. 121–123; Melvin Small, *Johnson, Nixon, and the Doves* (New Brunswick, N.J.: Rutgers University Press, 1988), pp. 36–42; Herring, *America's Longest War*, pp. 134–135.

66. GD, April 7, 14, 1965; 111 *CR*, 89th Congress, 1st session, 9762–66 (May 6, 1965).

67. GD, June 9, 1965; 111 *CR*, 89th Congress, 1st session, pp. 12985–87 (June 9, 1965), 13606 (June 15, 1965); Tristin Coffin, *Senator Fulbright* (New York: E. P. Dutton and Co., 1966), p. 257.

68. Drew Pearson to Gruening, April 22, 1965, Series G 284, Box 1 of 2, Pearson Papers; GD, April 30, 1965; *Anchorage Daily Times*, April 30, 1965; *Fairbanks News-Miner*, May 1, 1965.

69. George Sundborg interviews, Nov. 10, 1994, Feb. 23, 1995; Mike Gravel

interview; Robert Atwood interview; Jack Germond interview; Hugh Gallagher interview.

70. 111 *CR*, 89th Congress, 1st session, pp. 9729–33 (May 6, 1965); Barrett, *Uncertain Warriors*, p. 49. For examples of Democratic skepticism toward Johnson's policies, see McGeorge Bundy, "Memorandum for the President," n.d., Box 3, Bundy NSF LBJ.

71. Brands, *Wages of Globalism*, pp. 50–55; Piero Gleijeses, *The Dominican Crisis: The 1965 Constitutionalist Revolt and American Intervention*, trans. Lawrence Lipson (Baltimore: Johns Hopkins University Press, 1978), pp. 25–64.

72. Gruening to F. Bradford Morse, May 11, 1965, Box 30, GSP; GD, April 29, May 4, 6, 7, 1965; Robert Atwood interview; 111 *CR*, 89th Congress, 1st session, pp. 9731–32 (May 6, 1965), 10338–40 (May 12, 1965).

73. GD, June 5, 1965; George Sundborg interview, Feb. 23, 1995; *Anchorage Daily Times*, May 14, 1965; *Fairbanks News-Miner*, May 7, 1965.

74. GD, June 5, Dec. 29, 30, 1965; *Anchorage Daily Times*, June 7, 1965; *Fairbanks News-Miner*, June 7, 1965; *Juneau Alaska Empire*, Jan. 7, 17, 1966; George Sundborg interview, Feb. 23, 1995.

75. Robert Allen to Jack Valenti, May 13, 1965, Box 321, Names Series, WHCF, LBJ Library; GD, May 21, June 1, Aug. 24, 1965; I. F. Stone, "The Forms of Democracy, But No Longer the Reality" (May 12, 1965), in *In a Time of Torment, 1961–1967* (Boston: Little, Brown, 1967), p. 234.

76. Gruening to Harry Guggenheim, Sept. 23, 1965; Gruening to Felix Benitez-Rexach, Jan. 20, 1966; both in Dominican Republic 1966–1968 file, Brown Boxes series, GSP; GD, Sept. 29, Oct. 15, 1965; Brands, *Wages of Globalism*, p. 56.

8. The Limits of Dissent

1. *Life* article reproduced in Gruening, "From the Nation's Capital," 1965, #26, Brown Boxes Series, GSP.

2. GD, Feb. 19, April 1, 1965; 111 *CR*, 89th Congress, 1st session, pp. 6642–48 (April 1, 1965); Linda Gordon, *Woman's Body, Woman's Right: A Social History of Birth Control in America* (New York: Grossman Publishers, 1976), pp. 340–402; *Congressional Quarterly Almanac* 21 (1965), 311–314.

3. Gruening to Orville Freeman, May 26, 1965, Box 2, Subcommittee on Foreign Aid Expenditures Papers [hereafter SFAE Papers], Records of the U.S. Senate, Record Group 46, National Archives, Washington, D.C. [hereafter RG 46]; Ed Hamilton to McGeorge Bundy, Jan. 30, 1966, Box 6, Bundy NSF LBJ; GD, Nov. 17, 1964, Jan. 12, 19, 1965, GP; Laura Olson interview.

4. Gruening to Eugene Black, Aug. 5, 1965, Box 3, Population Committee files, GP; Gruening to J. Edgar Hoover, June 25, 1965, Health and Welfare file, Brown Boxes Series, GSP; Pat Holt interview; U.S. Senate, Committee on Government Operations, Subcommittee on Foreign Aid Expenditures, *Hearings, Population Crisis*, 89th Congress, 1st session, pp. 636 (June 29, 1965), 1406–8 (Aug. 31, 1965).

5. Gruening to Jane Ewing, April 14, 1965, Box 1, Population Committee Files, GP; Jack Germond interview; Laura Olson interview; U.S. Senate, *Hearings*,

Population Crisis, pp. 1470 (Sept. 8, 1965), 1672 (Sept. 15, 1965); *Washington Post*, April 18, 1966.

6. Gruening to M. Hutchinson, Aug. 30, 1965, Box 3, Population Committee Files, GP; *Philadelphia Evening Bulletin*, May 23, 1966, clipping in 1966 Scrapbook, vol. 1, GP; *Christian Science Monitor*, Aug. 1, 1966; *Boston Globe*, Jan. 17, 1967.

7. GD, May 30, 1965; Laura Olson interview; 111 *CR*, 89th Congress, 1st session, pp. 233–234 (Jan. 6, 1965); U.S. Senate, Committee on Labor and Public Welfare, *Hearings, National Arts and Humanities Foundations*, 89th Congress, 1st session, pp. 585–590 (March 4, 1965).

8. GD, June 2, 1965, June 28, 1965; 111 *CR*, 89th Congress, 1st session, pp. 22028–30 (Aug. 26, 1965); U.S. Senate, Committee on Commerce, *Hearings, Clarifying Power Commission Jurisdiction over Nonprofit Cooperatives*, 89th Congress, 1st session, pp. 17–21 (April 22, 1965); Ernest Gruening, *The Public Pays . . . and Still Pays* (New York: Vanguard Press, 1964), pp. xiv–xix.

9. Gruening to Gaylord Nelson, Oct. 19, 1965; Brown Boxes Series, Rampart file, GSP; GD, Feb. 28, April 9, 1964; Gaylord Nelson interview; Stewart Udall interview; John Carver oral history, 8:104; Keith Muckleston, "Water Projects and Recreation Benefits," in *Congress and the Environment*, ed. Richard Cooley and Geoffrey Wandesforde-Smith (Seattle: University of Washington Press, 1970), pp. 113–121.

10. Gruening to Fulton Freeman, July 9, 1965; Gruening to Anita Brenner, June 2, 1965; both in Agency for International Development file, Brown Boxes Series, GSP; GD, Nov. 10, Dec. 2, 11, 1964; Pat Holt interview; Frank Moss interview.

11. Frank Church to Eugene Chase, July 27, 1965, Series 2.2, Box 29, Church Papers; Albert Gore to Church, Dec. 17, 1965, Series 2.2, Box 20, Church Papers; Church to Eli Oboler, July 28, 1965, Series 2.2, Box 8, Church Papers; Brian VanDeMark, *Into the Quagmire: Lyndon Johnson and the Escalation of the Vietnam War* (New York: Oxford University Press, 1991), pp. 190–211; David Barrett, *Uncertain Warriors: Lyndon Johnson and His Vietnam Advisors* (Lawrence: University of Kansas Press 1989), p. 31; Randall Bennett Woods, *Fulbright: A Biography* (New York: Cambridge University Press, 1995).

12. Gruening address, Harvard University, Dec. 9, 1965, copy in Box B-55, Morse Papers; Gruening to Gaylord Nelson, Dec. 15, 1965, Series 74, Box 412, Nelson Papers; Mike Manatos, "Memorandum for the President," Feb. 19, 1966, Box 342, Federal Government FG 431/F series, WHCF, LBJ Library; U.S. Senate, Committee on Foreign Relations, *Hearings, Vietnam Policy*, 89th Congress, 2d session; Melvin Small, *Johnson, Nixon, and the Doves* (New Brunswick, N.J.: Rutgers University Press, 1988), pp. 70–79; George Herring, *America's Longest War* (New York: Knopf, 1979), 144–167.

13. J. William Fulbright to Barbara Tuchman, Sept. 20, 1966, Series 48:18, Box 50, Fulbright Papers; Fulbright to Allen Gates, Feb. 21, 1966, Series 48:18, Box 48, Fulbright Papers; Fulbright to George McGovern, Feb. 3, 1966, Box 67A802/22, McGovern Papers; McGovern to Gruening, July 29, 1966, 1966 Scrapbook, vol. 2, GP; GD, Jan. 26, March 5, 1966; George McGovern interview.

14. Gruening to Editor, CONCERN, Feb. 8, 1966, Box 3, SFAE Papers; GD, Feb. 28, 1966; 112 *CR*, 89th Congress, pp. 1195 (Jan. 26, 1966), 2234 (Feb. 7, 1966).

15. Gruening to Robert McNamara, March 8, 1966, Box 2, SFAE Papers; Gruening to Sig Rosenblum, April 12, 1966, Box 3, SFAE Papers; 112 *CR*, 89th Congress, p. 3391 (Feb. 17, 1966); George McGovern interview; U.S. Senate, Committee on Government Operations, Subcommittee on Foreign Aid Expenditures, *Hearings, Disposal of Surplus and Excess Property Abroad*, 89th Congress, 2d session, pp. 2, 6, 79 (May 3, 1966); *New York Times*, May 4, 5, 1966.

16. Gruening to Paul Wagner, Feb. 9, 1966, Box 3, SFAE Papers; Gruening to Phil Kirby, Aug. 25, 1966, Vietnam 1966 file, Brown Boxes series, GSP; *Milton* (Pa.) *Standard*, May 9, 1966, 1966 Scrapbook, vol. 1, GP; Laura Olson interview.

17. GD, June 27, 1966; *Columbus Dispatch*, May 27, 1966; *Ohio State Lantern*, May 31, 1966; both in 1966 Scrapbook, vol. 1, GP; *New York Times*, Aug. 21, 1966.

18. Frank Church to Robert Farning, Jan. 12, 1966, Series 2.2, Box 9, Church Papers; Gruening to Robert Strother, Aug. 10, 1966, Foreign Aid 1966 file, Brown Boxes series, GSP; GD, Jan. 21, 26, 1966; 112 *CR*, 89th Congress, 2d session, p. 3402 (Feb. 17, 1966).

19. J. William Fulbright to Gruening, Feb. 25, 1967, Series 48:1, Box 8, Fulbright Papers; Fulbright to Henry Jackson, June 6, July 5, 1966; both in Box 74, Foreign Policy Defense Series, Henry Jackson Papers, Allen Library, University of Washington; "Staff Memorandum: Considerations Relating to Committee Organization," n.d., 1965 box, Carl Marcy Chronological Series, National Archives, Washington, D.C.; U.S. Senate, Committee on Rules, *Hearings, Executive Session*, 89th Congress, 2d session, p. 76 (Jan. 26, 1966); Pat Holt interview.

20. Gruening to Robert McNamara, April 26, 1966; Gruening to Paul Ignatius, June 6, 1966; both in Box 2, SFAE Papers; GD, Nov. 13, 17, 1965; H. W. Brands, Jr., *The Wages of Globalism: Lyndon Johnson and the Limits of American Power* (New York: Oxford University Press, 1995), pp. 89–105; Frank Costigliola, *The United States and France: The Cold Alliance since World War II* (New York: Twayne Publications, 1992), pp. 126–144; Thomas Alan Schwartz, "Victories and Defeats in the Long Twilight Struggle: The United States and Western Europe in the 1960s," in *The Diplomacy of the Crucial Decade: American Foreign Relations in the 1960s*, ed. Diane Kunz (New York: Columbia University Press, 1994), pp. 88–90.

21. Gruening, "Our Obsolete Concepts about NATO," Aug. 23, 1966, copy in Series 25, Box 3, GP; Gruening to Robert McNamara, June 15, 1966, Box 2, SFAE Papers.

22. GD, April 7, July 18, 1966; U.S. Senate, Committee on Government Operations, Subcommittee on Foreign Aid Expenditures, *Report, Disposal of United States Military Installations and Supplies in France*, 90th Congress, 1st session, CIS Document #S1597, pp. 1, 7, 12 (Jan. 30, 1967).

23. Herb Beaser to Dave Toyryla, 20 Oct. 1964, Box 31, GS 63–65, GSP; Laura Olson interview.

24. U.S. Senate, Committee on Government Operations, *Report, United States Foreign Aid in Action: A Case Study*, 89th Congress, 2d session, CIS Document #S0918, pp. vii–ix, 50, 76–77, 95–111, 114–124.

25. Gruening to John McClellan, June 28, 1966, Chile Foreign Aid file, Brown Boxes series, GSP; Robert Packenham, *Liberal America and the Third World: Political Development Ideas in Foreign Aid and Political Science* (Princeton: Princeton University Press, 1973), pp. 180–181.

26. Gruening to Simon Hanson, Aug. 1, 1966; Pamela de Groot, "Memoran-

dum to Senator Ernest Gruening," July 14, 1966; both in Chile Foreign Aid file, Brown Boxes series, GSP; Ralph Dungan interview; *Hanson's Latin American Newsletter*, July 30, Sept. 3, 1966; Wayne Morse press release, March 27, 1967, Box B-47, Morse Papers; *Washington Post*, July 11, 1966.

27. Gruening to Drew Pearson, Sept. 8, 1966, Foreign Aid 1966 file, Brown Boxes series, GSP; J. William Fulbright to J. W. Grisson, Aug. 9, 1966, Series 48:8, Box 30, Fulbright Papers; Mike Manatos, "Memorandum for the President," Sept. 26, 1966, Box 8, Office Files of Mike Manatos; LBJ Library; *ESSFRC*, vol. 18, 89th Congress, 2d session, p. 294 (Feb. 23, 1966).

28. David Bell oral history, LBJ Library; George Pavlik to Bourke Hickenlooper, Jan. 10, 1967, Box 37, Foreign Relations Committee series, Hickenlooper Papers; Frank Moss interview; 113 *CR*, 90th Congress, 1st session, pp. 3904–5 (Feb. 20, 1967).

29. 113 *CR*, 90th Congress, 1st session, pp. 7059–60 (March 16, 1967), 8325 (April 4, 1967).

30. U.S. Senate, Committee on Foreign Relations, *Hearings*, *Latin American Summit Conference*, 90th Congress, 1st session, pp. 89, 101, 102, 106–109, 112, 124, 127, 129, 134, 141 (March 21, 1967); George McGovern interview.

31. U.S. Senate, Committee on Foreign Relations, *Hearings*, *Latin American Summit Conference*, 90th Congress, 1st session, pp. 138–143, 149, 155 (March 21, 1967); W. W. Rostow, "Special Emissary to Discuss Latin American Arms Policy," Feb. 7, 1968, Box 48, White House Confidential File, LBJ Library; *Congressional Quarterly Almanac* 23 (1967), 337.

32. Frank Church, "The Role of Borah in American Foreign Policy," Moscow, Idaho, March 26, 1964, reproduced in 110 *CR*, 88th Congress, 2d session, pp. 6438–40; George McGovern, "Foreign Policy and the Crisis Mentality," *Atlantic Monthly*, no. 218 (Jan. 1967).

33. "The Seventh Mexico-U.S. Interparliamentary Conference," June 8, 1967, Box 10, White House Confidential Files, LBJ Library.

34. 113 *CR*, 90th Congress, 1st session, pp. 22965–72 (Aug. 17, 1967).

35. *New York Times*, Aug. 19, 1967; *Washington Post*, Aug. 18, 1967.

36. Gruening to James Kilpatrick, July 22, 1965, Box 2, Population Committee Files, GP; Harry McPherson to LBJ, Jan. 10, 1967, Box 164, Legislation LE/WE Series, WHCF, LBJ Library; George Sundborg interview, Feb. 23, 1995; J. Michael Sharp, ed., *The Directory of Congressional Voting Scores and Interest Group Ratings* (New York: Facts on File, 1988), 1:407.

37. GD, Aug. 16, 1966, July 9, 1967; Gruening quoted in *Tundra Times*, Aug. 26, 1966, clipping in 1966 Scrapbook, vol. 2, GP; Sharp, *Directory of Congressional Voting Scores*, 1:407.

38. George McGovern interview.

39. LBJ quoted in Joseph Califano, Jr., *The Triumph and Tragedy of Lyndon Johnson: The White House Years* (New York: Simon & Schuster, 1991), pp. 248–249; Terry Dietz, *Republicans and Vietnam, 1961–1968* (New York: Greenwood Press, 1986), pp. 117–127.

40. GD, May 4, 1967; Frank Church to Martin Grayson, Dec. 14, 1967, Series 2.2, Box 12, Church Papers; George McGovern to Jerome Anderson, Dec. 28, 1967, Box 68A3651/18, McGovern Papers; LeRoy Ashby and Rod Gramer, *Fighting the Odds: The Life of Senator Frank Church* (Pullman: Washington State University Press, 1994), pp. 226–227.

41. Gruening to Glen Becker, May 31, 1967, Soviet consular treaty file, Brown Boxes series, GSP; GD, May 16, 1967; 113 *CR*, 90th Congress, 1st session, pp. 13318–19 (May 19, 1967).

42. George McGovern to Gruening, May 18, 1967, Box 72A3053/11, McGovern Papers; Wayne Morse to Editor, LA WISP, June 8, 1967, Box B-56, Morse Papers; Small, *Johnson, Nixon, and the Doves*, pp. 94–95.

43. *Congressional Quarterly Almanac* 23 (1967), 307, 314; Robert Schulzinger, "'It's Easy to Win a War on Paper': The United States and Vietnam, 1961–1968," in Kunz, *Diplomacy of the Crucial Decade*, p. 205.

44. 113 *CR*, 90th Congress, 1st session, p. 23502 (Aug. 22, 1967); Fulbright quoted in Barrett, *Uncertain Warriors*, p. 66; Schulzinger, "'It's Easy to Win a War on Paper,'" p. 205.

45. GD, Jan. 20, June 12, 1966, Jan. 22, 1967; George Sundborg interview, Feb. 23, 1995; Edwin Webking, "The 1968 Gruening Write-In Campaign" (Ph.D. diss., University of California, Claremont, 1972), pp. 4–39; Claus Naske and Herman Slotnick, *Alaska: A History of the 49th State* (Grand Rapids, Mich.: William Eerdmans Publishing Company, 1979), pp. 215–222; Claus Naske, "Ernest Gruening and Alaskan Native Claims," *Pacific Northwest Quarterly* 82 (1991), 147–148.

46. GD, March 3, 1966, Jan. 22, April 3, June 27, July 9, 1967; *Anchorage Daily News*, June 9, 10, 1966; *Los Angeles Times*, Aug. 7, 1966; 110 *CR*, 89th Congress, 2d session, p. 4724 (March 2, 1966).

47. Don Greeley, "Note to File," April 5, 1967, gun control file, Brown Boxes series, GSP; Laura Olson, "Memo to Senator," Feb. 20, 1967, Soviet consular treaty file, Brown Boxes series, GSP; George Sundborg interview, Feb. 23, 1995; Don Greeley interview.

9. The Frustrations of Dissent

1. Gruening to Herbert Lehman, Aug. 24, 1956, Special Correspondence File, Lehman Papers; George Sundborg interviews, Nov. 10, 1994, Feb. 23, 1995; Don Greeley interview; *Anchorage Daily Times*, Nov. 3, 1965.

2. Gruening to Clifford Warren, March 5, 1968, Alaska Pro 1968 file, Brown Boxes series, GSP; William O. Douglas statement, Gruening testimonial banquet, Washington, D.C., March 22, 1967, Box 334, William O. Douglas Papers; Gruening to Thomas Corcoran, June 22, 1967, Box 243, Corcoran Papers; George Sundborg interviews, Nov. 10, 1994, Feb. 23, 1995; Sherwood Ross, *Gruening of Alaska* (New York: Liveright, 1968).

3. Al Haylor to *Anchorage Daily Times*, Aug. 1, 1966; William Ullom to Gruening, Sept. 15, 1967; Murleen Isaacs to Gruening, Nov. 10, 1967; all in Alaska Con 1966–1968 file, Brown Boxes series, GSP; GD, July 15, 1967; George Sundborg interview, Nov. 10, 1994; George Sundborg, "Senator Gruening's Last Campaign: What an Alaska Political Race Looked Like from the Inside," unpublished ms.

4. GD, Jan. 22, March 1, April 13, 1967; Frank Moss interview; Jack Germond interview; Robert Atwood interview; Steve McCutcheon interview; Sundborg, "Senator Gruening's Last Campaign."

5. Gruening to Dean Rusk, Jan. 27, 1968; Gruening to Editor, *Kodiak Mirror*, Feb. 2, 1968; both in Box 1, SFAE Papers; U.S. Senate, Committee on Government Operations, Subcommittee on Foreign Aid Expenditures, *Hearings, U.S. Economic*

Aid for Development of Foreign Fishing Industries in Competition with Domestic Industries, 90th Congress, 2d session, pp. 1, 5, 14 (Feb. 21, 1968).

6. Gruening to editor, *Valley Frontiersman*, Nov. 29, 1967, Alaska Con 1966–1967 file, Brown Boxes series, GSP; Albert Gore to Gruening, Feb. 6, 1968, "Senator—Personal" File, Albert Gore Papers, Gore Center, Middle Tennessee State University; Gruening to Drew Pearson, March 15, 1968, Series G 284, Box 1 of 2, Pearson Papers; George Sundborg interview, Feb. 23, 1995; Joseph Buttinger review, *New York Times Book Review*, March 10, 1968; *Choice* 26 (July 1968); *Library Journal* 93 (July 1968); Ernest Gruening and Herbert Beaser, *Vietnam Folly* (Washington, D.C.: National Press, 1968).

7. 114 *CR*, 90th Congress, 2d session, pp. 2064–66 (Feb. 5, 1968), 3812–13 (Feb. 21, 1968); *New York Times*, Feb. 29, 1968, March 7, 1968.

8. George Herring, *America's Longest War: The United States and Vietnam, 1950–1975* (New York: Knopf, 1979), pp. 186–192; Robert Schulzinger, "'It's Easy To Win a War on Paper': The United States and Vietnam, 1961–1968," in *Diplomacy of the Crucial Decade: American Foreign Relations during the 1960s*, ed. Diane Kunz (New York: Columbia University Press, 1994), pp. 205–209; Melvin Small, *Johnson, Nixon, and the Doves* (New Brunswick, N.J.: Rutgers University Press, 1988), p. 130.

9. George Sundborg interviews, Nov. 10, 1994, Feb. 23, 1995; Mike Gravel interview; *Anchorage Daily Times*, Aug. 24, 1968.

10. Don Greeley interview; John Cole, "Ernest Gruening: The Mouse Who Keeps Roaring," *Maine Times*, Nov. 9, 1973.

11. George Sundborg interview, Nov. 10, 1994; Mike Gravel interview; Hugh Gallagher interview; *New York Times*, April 28, 1968; Edwin Webking, Jr., "The 1968 Gruening Write-In Campaign" (Ph.D. diss., University of California, Claremont, 1972), pp. 38–63; C. Robert Zelnick, "A Dove's Struggle in Alaska," *The Progressive* 32 (Aug. 1968); Sundborg, "Senator Gruening's Last Campaign."

12. George Sundborg interview, Nov. 10, 1994; Robert Atwood interview; Mike Gravel interview; Gruening to Timothy Comfort, June 28, 1968, Brown Boxes series, military issues, GSP; 114 *CR*, 90th Congress, 2d session, p. 19625 (July 2, 1968); Webking, "The 1968 Gruening Write-In Campaign," pp. 38–63; Zelnick, "A Dove's Struggle"; *Anchorage Daily Times*, Aug. 24, 28, 29, 1968; *Fairbanks Daily News-Miner*, Aug. 24, 26, 29, 1968.

13. George Sundborg interview, Nov. 10, 1994; George McGovern interview; Laura Olson interview; *Anchorage Daily Times*, Aug. 28, 29, 1968.

14. George Sundborg interview, Feb. 23, 1995; Hunt Gruening interview; Mike Gravel interview.

15. Williams O. Douglas to Gruening, Sept. 9, 1968, Box 334, William O. Douglas Papers; *The Nation*, Sept. 9, 1968; "Ernie" memo, Sept. 10, 1968; Gruening to LBJ, Oct. 2, 1968; both in Box 321, Names File, WHCF, LBJ Library; GD, 22 Feb. 1969; *Congressional Quarterly Almanac* 24 (1968), 531. Gruening did not actually vote on the Fortas cloture motion; at the request of Church and Morse, both of whom supported the nomination but were away from Washington campaigning for reelection, the Alaska senator withheld his vote so as to provide both of them with a pair. He made sure, however, to announce his position publicly before the vote.

16. 114 *CR*, 90th Congress, 2d session, p. 29310 (Oct. 3, 1968).

17. Gruening to William O. Douglas, Sept. 10, 1968, Box 334, William O. Douglas Papers; George Sundborg interview, Feb. 23, 1995; Hunt Gruening interview; Steve McCutcheon interview.

18. *The Nation*, Oct. 21, 1968; *New York Times*, Nov. 27, 1968; Webking, "The 1968 Gruening Write-In Campaign," pp. 74, 99–145, 166–190; Sundborg quoted in *Acceptance of the Statue of Ernest Gruening*, S. Doc. 95–94, 95th Congress, 1st session (Oct. 5, 1977).

19. *New York Times*, Nov. 27, 1968; Webking, "The 1968 Gruening Write-In Campaign," pp. 166–190; Mike Gravel interview; Robert Atwood interview.

20. Gruening to Huntington Gruening, April 8, 1969, E-H Box, GPSS.

21. Gruening to Richard Carbray, Jan. 7, 1969, Box 13, Richard Carbray Papers, Allen Library, University of Washington; GD, Jan. 1, 2, 1969; Hunt Gruening interview.

22. Hugh Gallagher interview; GD, Jan. 6, 23, Feb. 6, 1969.

23. Harry Filmore to Gruening, Dec. 16, 1968, Box 334, William O. Douglas Papers; GD, Feb. 23, April 3, 1969.

24. Burton Wheeler to Gruening, Dec. 21, 1970, Series 36, Box 22, GP; Gruening to Al Hassler, May 29, 1969, E-H Box, GPSS; GD, Jan. 22, June 11, 1970.

25. Gruening address, "Two Ways to Get Out of Vietnam Right Now," Washington, D.C., April 21, 1969, reproduced in 113 *CR*, 91st Congress, 1st session, pp. 11320–21.

26. Gruening to J. William Fulbright, Oct. 13, 1969, Series 48:18, Box 56, Fulbright Papers; Gruening to Paul Findley, March 27, 1969; Gruening to Tom Ferrell, June 24, 1969; both in E-H Box, GPSS; GD, March 4, May 3, 1969, GP; *New York Times*, July 21, 1969.

27. Gruening to Carey McWilliams, May 2, 1969, misc. Box, GPSS; GD, June 14, 1967, May 26, Sept. 1, 17, 1969.

28. "Address of Senator Ernest Gruening: The Need for New Priorities," New York City, Feb. 17, 1970, reproduced in 114 *CR*, 91st Congress, 2d session, pp. 3993–94; Herring, *America's Longest War*, pp. 229–232.

29. Gruening to William O. Douglas, Sept. 22, 1971, Box 334, William O. Douglas Papers; GD, Feb. 18, March 2, 1970.

30. Gruening to Carey McWilliams, April 16, 1970, misc. Box, GPSS; Gruening letter to the editor, *Atlantic*, no. 224 (June 1970); Arthur Schlesinger, Jr., "The Lowering Hemisphere," ibid.

31. Gruening to Charles Goodell, Sept. 25, 1969, E–H Box, GPSS; Gruening to Kaye Northcott, July 22, 1970, A–D Box, GPSS; GD, March 10, April 8, May 7, June 8, 1970.

32. Gruening to Henry Schwarzchild, Oct. 27, 1971, A–D Box, GPSS; Gruening to Oscar Handlin, Sept. 14, 1971, E–H Box, GPSS; Gruening to Taylor Branch, Aug. 26, 1971, J–W Box, GPSS; Gruening quoted in *Los Angeles Times*, Feb. 8, 1971, copy in 1970 Scrapbook, GP; U.S. Senate, Committee on Foreign Relations, *Hearings, Legislative Proposals Relating to the War in Southeast Asia*, 92d Congress, 1st session, pp. 169–170 (May 27, 1971); Jules Witcover, "Ernest Gruening: Evolution of a War Critic," *Washington Post*, Feb. 8, 1971; *New York Times*, July 28, 1971.

33. Gruening to Edmund Muskie, Sept. 23, 1971, J–W Box, GPSS; McGovern to Gruening, June 15, 1972, Box 329–79–197/27, McGovern Papers; Gruening to

Stephen Schlesinger, March 8, 1972, A–D Box, GPSS; GD, Sept. 23, 1969; *Washington Evening Star*, Jan. 24, 1972, clipping in misc. Box, GPSS; *New York Times*, May 9, 1972; George McGovern interview.

34. Hunt Gruening interview.

35. Gruening to Morris Rubin, Nov. 10, 1972; Gruening to Arthur Schlesinger, Jr., Nov. 14, 1972; both in J–W Box, GPSS; George McGovern interview.

36. Gruening to William Douglas, Jan. 10, 1973, A–D Box, GPSS; Gruening to Martin Peretz, Feb. 26, 1973, J–W Box, GPSS; Abramson quoted in Cole, "Ernest Gruening"; *New York Times*, Oct. 20, 1973.

37. *Many Battles*; Cole, "Ernest Gruening."

38. Abourezk, Church, McGovern, Nelson, and Hatfield to Nobel Peace Prize Committee, March 7, 1974, reproduced in *Memorial Addresses and Other Tributes in the Congress of the United States on the Life and Contributions of Ernest H. Gruening*, S. Doc. 93–118, 93d Congress, 2d session, pp. 9–11.

39. Gruening to Hunt Gruening, April 13, 1974, copy in the possession of Hunt Gruening; "The (Ernest) Gruening of America," *Washington Star-News*, March 10, 1974, copy in Box 12, Carbray Papers; U.S. House of Representatives, Committee on the Judiciary, *Hearings*, *Amnesty*, 93d Congress, 2d session, pp. 217–218 (March 13, 1974); "Ernest Gruening," *The Nation*, July 20, 1974.

40. Jules Witcover, "Senator Ernest Gruening, Father of Alaska Statehood," *Washington Post*, June 27, 1974.

41. *Memorial Addresses*, pp. 41, 71; "Ernest Gruening," *The Nation*, July 20, 1974; Jack Germond and Jules Witcover, "Gruening, Doctor of Diversity," *Washington Star*, Oct. 10, 1977; A. Robert Smith, "Gruening of Alaska," *Argus Magazine*, Jan. 6, 1978; *Washington Post*, June 28, 1974.

Selected Bibliography

Manuscript and Archival Collections

Albertson's Library, Boise State University, Boise, Idaho
    Frank Church Papers
Allen Library, University of Washington, Seattle, Washington
    Richard Carbray Papers
    Henry Jackson Papers
    Warren Magnuson Papers
Amherst College Library, Amherst, Massachusetts
    Dwight Morrow Papers
Bancroft Library, University of California, Berkeley
    Thomas Kuchel Papers
Butler Library, Columbia University, New York, New York
    Random House Papers
    Frank Tannenbaum Papers
Chicago Historical Society, Chicago, Illinois
    Paul Douglas Papers
Dwight Eisenhower Presidential Library, Abilene, Kansas
    Frederick Seaton Papers
    Anne Whitman File
Gore Center, Middle Tennessee State University Library, Murfreesboro, Tennessee
    Albert Gore, Sr., Papers
Herbert Hoover Presidential Library, West Branch, Iowa
    Bourke Hickenlooper Papers
    Herbert Hoover Campaign and Transition Papers
    Herbert Hoover Commerce Papers
    Herbert Hoover Pre-Commerce Papers

Herbert Hoover Presidential Papers
Ray Lyman Wilbur Papers
Houghton Library, Harvard University, Cambridge, Massachusetts
Gannett Family Papers
Oswald Garrison Villard Papers
Lyndon Baines Johnson Presidential Library, Austin, Texas
McGeorge Bundy National Security File
Congressional Favors File
LBJ A Papers
Lyndon Johnson Senate Papers
Lyndon Johnson Senate Political Files
Drew Pearson Papers
White House Central File
White House Confidential File
John Fitzgerald Kennedy Presidential Library, Boston, Massachusetts
Congressional Liaison Office Papers
Ralph Dungan Papers
Name File
National Security File
President's Office File
Arthur Schlesinger, Jr., Papers
Library of Congress, Washington, D.C.
William Borah Papers
Thomas Corcoran Papers
Josephus Daniels Papers
William O. Douglas Papers
W. Cameron Forbes Papers
Felix Frankfurter Papers
Cordell Hull Papers
Harold Ickes Papers
Samuel Guy Inman Papers
La Follette Family Papers
National Association for the Advancement of Colored People (NAACP) Papers
George Norris Papers
Theodore Roosevelt, Jr., Papers
Elihu Root Papers
Moorfield Storey Papers
William Allen White Papers
Massachusetts Historical Society, Boston, Massachusetts
Henry Cabot Lodge Papers
Minnesota State Historical Society, St. Paul, Minnesota
Hubert Humphrey Papers
Frank Kellogg Papers
Eugene McCarthy Papers
Elizabeth Wallace Papers
Mudd Library, Princeton University, Princeton, New Jersey

American Civil Liberties Union (ACLU) Papers
George McGovern Papers
Mugar Library, Boston University, Boston, Massachusetts
Carleton Beals Papers
Mullins Library, University of Arkansas, Fayetteville
J. William Fulbright Papers
National Archives, College Park, Maryland
Record Group 43, Records of International Conferences, Commissions, and Expositions
Record Group 59, General Records of the Department of State
Record Group 126, Office of Territories, Classified Files
Record Group 165, Records of the War Department, General and Special Staff
National Archives, New York City
Record Group 323, Records of the Puerto Rican Reconstruction Administration
National Archives, Washington, D.C.
Record Group 46, Records of the United States Senate
Foreign Relations Committee Papers
Government Operations Committee Papers
Carl Marcy Chronological Series
Pennsylvania Historical Society, Philadelphia, Pennsylvania
Joseph Clark Papers
Pusey Library, Harvard University, Cambridge, Massachusetts
Ernest Gruening academic records
A. Lawrence Lowell Papers
Elmer Rasmuson Library, University of Alaska, Fairbanks
E. L. (Bob) Bartlett Papers
Ernest Gruening Papers
Franklin Delano Roosevelt Library, Hyde Park, New York
President's Official File
President's Personal File
President's Secretary's File
Sumner Welles Papers
Schlesinger Library, Harvard University, Cambridge, Massachusetts
Freda Kirchwey Papers
State University of New York Library, Stony Brook, New York
Jacob Javits Papers
Sterling Library, Yale University, New Haven, Connecticut
Chester Bowles Papers
Edward House Papers
Walter Lippmann Papers
James Sheffield Papers
Henry Stimson Diaries
Swarthmore College Peace Collection, Swarthmore, Pennsylvania
Collective Documents, Group A
Fellowship of Reconciliation Papers

National Council for the Prevention of War (NCPW) Papers
SANE Papers
Women's International League for Peace and Freedom (WILPF) Papers
Harry S Truman Presidential Library, Independence, Missouri
Oscar Chapman Papers
President's Office File
University of Maryland Library, College Park, Maryland
Millard Tydings Papers
University of Oregon Library, Eugene, Oregon
Wayne Morse Papers
Richard Neuberger Papers
Western Reserve Historical Society, Cleveland, Ohio
Stephen Young Papers
Wisconsin State Historical Society, Madison, Wisconsin
James Blaine Papers
Gaylord Nelson Papers

Publications by Ernest Gruening

Books

Experiencias y Comentarios sobre el México Post-revolucionario. Mexico City: Instituto Nacional de Antropología y Historia, 1970.
Many Battles: The Autobiography of Ernest Gruening. New York: Liveright, 1974.
Mexico and Its Heritage. New York: The Century Company, 1928.
The Public Pays. New York: Vanguard Press, 1931.
The Public Pays . . . and Still Pays. New York: Vanguard Press, 1964.
These United States (editor). New York: Liveright, 1921–1923.
The State of Alaska. New York: Random House, 1954.
Vietnam Folly (with Herb Beaser). Washington, D.C.: The National Press, 1968.

Articles

Gruening published over one hundred magazine and journal articles, most of which are indexed in the *Readers' Guide to Periodical Literature.*

Editorials

Gruening published over five thousand editorials during his career as a journalist. In addition to *The Nation*, available in bound form, microfilm copies of the newspapers for which he worked are available at the locations listed below.

Boston Herald (Boston Public Library)
Boston Journal (Boston Public Library)
Boston Traveler (Boston Public Library)
New York Tribune (New York Public Library)
New York Post (New York Public Library)
Portland Evening News (Portland Public Library)

Oral Histories and Interviews

Robert Atwood (interview with author)
Vide Bartlett (oral history, LBJ Library)
Larry Beaser (interview with author)
Ray Beaser (interview with author)
David Bell (oral history, LBJ Library)
William Bundy (interview with author)
John Carver (oral history, JFK Library)
Frank Church (oral history, LBJ Library)
Joseph Clark (oral history, JFK Library)
Ralph Dungan (interview with author)
Peter Edelman (oral history, JFK Library)
Allen Ellender (oral history, LBJ Library)
Hugh Gallagher (interview with author)
William Gaud (oral history, LBJ Library)
Jack Germond (interview with author)
Mike Gravel (interview with author)
Don Greeley (interview with author)
Ernest Gruening (oral history, LBJ Library)
Hunt Gruening (interview with author)
Pat Holt (interview with author; and oral history, National Archives)
William Macomber (oral history, LBJ Library)
Carl Marcy (oral history, National Archives)
Edwin Martin (oral history, JFK Library)
Steve McCutcheon (interview with author)
George McGovern (interview with author; and oral history, LBJ Library)
Frank Moss (interview with author)
Edwin Muskie (interview with author)
Gaylord Nelson (interview with author)
Maurine Neuberger (interview with author)
Laura Olson (interview with author)
Howard Shuman (oral history, National Archives)
George Sundborg (interviews with author)
Stewart Udall (interview with author; and oral history, LBJ Library)

Index